# Gendering Chinese Religion

# Gendering Chinese Religion

## *Subject, Identity, and Body*

Edited by

Jinhua Jia, Xiaofei Kang, and Ping Yao

SUNY PRESS

Published by State University of New York Press, Albany



Printed in the United States of America



For information, contact State University of New York Press, Albany, NY
www.sunypress.edu

Production by Diane Ganeles
Marketing by Michael Campochiaro

**Library of Congress Cataloging-in-Publication Data**

Gendering Chinese religion : subject, identity, and body / edited by Jinhua Jia, Xiaofei Kang, and Ping Yao.
pages cm
Includes bibliographical references and index.
ISBN 978-1-4384-5307-1 (hardcover : alk. paper)
ISBN 978-1-4384-5308-8 (pbk: alk. paper)
1. Taoist women—China—Congresses. I. Jia, Jinhua, editor of compilation.

BL1923.G46 2014
200.82'0951—dc23 2013044037

10 9 8 7 6 5 4 3 2 1

# Contents

# Tables and Figures

## Table



## Figures

# Acknowledgments

This volume has grown out of the first International Conference on Women and Gender in Chinese Religion, held at the University of Macau on June 17–20, 2011. The editors acknowledge the generous funding from the Faculty of Social Sciences and Humanities at the University of Macau and Macau Foundation that made the success of the conference possible. We also thank the contributors of this volume and other participants of the conference who contributed excellent papers and critical comments: Robert J. Antony, Rotislav Berezkin, Chen Jianhua, Paul R. Goldin, Maria Jaschok, Lai Chi Tim, Li Yu-Chen, Lin Mei-mei, Liu Xun, Qian Nanxiu, Julie Remoiville, Shui Jingjun, George C. X. Wei, Yi Jo-lan, and Zhu Tianshu.

In the process of revising the volume for publication, we benefited greatly from the expert advice of Beata Grant and Maria Jaschok. The two anonymous reviewers offered invaluable comments and suggestions for enhancing the volume. We are deeply indebted to Nancy Ellegate at State University of New York Press who chaperoned the book into completion with utmost enthusiasm and efficiency. We thank Phal Vaughter and Bruce Tindall for their professional work in copyediting, proofreading, and indexing at different stages of the production.

Our special gratitude also goes to the two secretaries of the Department of History and Department of Chinese and several undergraduate and graduate students at the University of Macau who worked hard and efficiently for the organization of the conference and the preparation of the volume: Bai Zhaojie, Chen Wenli, Laila Cheong, Huang Chenxi, Candy Kong, Reade Iao, Liu Gonghuang, Lei Xi, Wan Xianglan, Wang Qiuqiu, Wenny Wong, and Yu Chunli.

Last but by no means the least, we thank our families for their unfailing support: to Bingyu from Jinhua, to Alex and Wang Wei from Xiaofei, and to Patrick and Liz from Yao Ping.

# Introduction

*Jinhua Jia, Xiaofei Kang, Ping Yao*

There was once a young village girl from North China named Xi'er 喜兒 who was raped by a landlord with the encouragement of his mother, a "pious" Buddhist. Xi'er was finally able to escape into the mountains where she gave birth to a baby girl. Xi'er continued to hide away in the mountains, living in dark caves and surviving on the temple offerings made by local villagers who, because of her prematurely white hair, mistook her for a deity and called her the White-haired Goddess. Eventually, Xi'er was rescued and saved by a young Communist named Dachun 大春, who led her into the sunlight and offered her both love and a new life. Readers may recognize the storyline of the popular 1945 opera, *White-haired Girl* (*Baimaonü* 白毛女), arguably based on a real story, that played such a crucial role in the success of the Communist land reforms of 1946–1947 as well as in the creation of the cult of Mao during the Cultural Revolution of 1966 to 1976.

Despite having enjoyed such immense popularity since the 1940s, the opera's gender and religious implications have thus far rarely been recognized. In more than one way, the current understanding of *White-haired Girl*, or the lack thereof, reflects the common problem of "double blindness" in the study of gender and religion. It has been almost thirty years since the publication of Joan Scott's influential article proposing gender as a "useful category of historical analysis,"[1] and scholarship on women, gender, and religion has increasingly become much more inclusive, nuanced, and multidisciplinary. Nevertheless, in an article published in 2004 advocating the "gender-critical turn" in the study of religion, Ursula King defined a continuing blindness both on the side of gender studies and on the side of religious studies: "On one hand most contemporary gender studies, whether in the humanities, social sciences, or natural sciences, remain extraordinarily "religion-blind"; on the other hand many studies in religion continue to be profoundly "gender-blind."[2] In 2009, Susan Calef chose the title "Charting New Territory" for the introduction to her edited volume on women, gender, and religion; in that work, she spoke of the relative lack of gender lenses for "seeing, thinking, and working" religion.[3]

Many of the authors in this volume have chosen to utilize gender-critical perspectives on familiar sources. We will find that the story of the *White-haired Girl*, as well as the lack of awareness of its religious impact, embodies perfectly both the complexity and the compass of Chinese religious traditions: multiple practices and rituals competing, mingling, and evolving; religious roles and influences interacting with the changing faces of gender ideology, political power, moral order, and social strata. Moreover, by uncovering new sources and revisiting old ones, the authors in this volume show that women have been at the center of Chinese religions all along: their religious experiences duly accounted or misinterpreted; their religious role publically justified or manipulated; their gendered bodies and sexuality ardently exemplified or victimized. Such underrecognized complexity clearly attests to the urgency and importance of facilitating multidisciplinary and comparative dialogues, integrating the studies of women, gender, and religion in the China field and thoroughly investigating their scope, methodologies, sources, and perspectives.

## The Development of the Field

The study of women and gender in Chinese religions has been inspired by two separate trends within women's studies since the 1960s, one involving religious studies and one involving China studies. Scholars of religious studies, in what has been called a "paradigm shift from androcentric to androgynous models of humanity," have been aiming to discover women's experiences in major religious traditions not as a form of supplementary knowledge to male norms but as equally important, if often very different, human experiences.[4] Not surprisingly, at its beginning the study of women and gender in Chinese religions was focused on the three major traditions: Confucianism, Buddhism, and Daoism. Whereas the topic of women in Confucianism has become a major concern among social and cultural historians and anthropologists of China, the topics of women and gender in Buddhism and Daoism have often been left exclusively to China scholars belonging to departments of "Religion."

Within the China field, anthropological and historical studies have challenged the image of the "traditional Chinese woman" as passive victim as is characteristic of the May Fourth discourse on the Confucian "patriarchal" system.[5] Of course, in imperial China, and especially since the emergence of Neo-Confucian teachings in the Song dynasty (960–1279), women were expected to adhere to the principles of "Three Obediences and Four Virtues" (*sancong side* 三從四德), and elite women in particular were largely confined to their homes. Yet the degree to which the Confucian ideals of womanhood were actually striven for varied greatly according to age, class, family status, and location. There is much evidence that these ideals were often compromised, rejected, or manipulated by different social actors in different social, economic, political conditions. The most salient example is the late imperial cult of female chastity, which has been condemned since the late nineteenth century as one of the most heinous evils of Confucian patriarchy. However, recent historical studies have provided a far more nuanced and complicated picture of this cult, in which Confucian literati, state officials, imperial rulers, "faithful maidens," and "chaste wives" interacted, contested, and at times contradicted each other in order to promote their own social and moral agendas.[6]

The three major traditions of Confucianism, Buddhism, and Daoism developed in constant dialogue with each other, and whether intentionally or not, scholarship on the latter two has been framed largely in response to the changing perceptions of the Confucian woman in both scholarly and nonscholarly circles. Early works on women in Buddhism and Daoism tended to focus on whether or not these two religious traditions reflected different sets of gender perceptions or provided alternative paths for Chinese women. In the area of Buddhist tradition, since Diana Y. Paul's pioneering works on Buddhist women in Mahayana texts and Kathryn Ann Tsai's groundbreaking study of the sixth-century monk Baochang's 寶唱 *Biographies of Chinese Buddhist Nuns* (*Biqiuni zhuan* 比丘尼傳) in the early 1980s, studies on Chinese Buddhist women have appeared in great number.[7] During the 1990s, scholarship on Buddhist women largely focused on the nuns whose names appear in Buddhist texts, historical writings, and literature or in annotated translations of texts relevant to the topic.[8] While Buddhist nuns continued to be a popular topic during the first decade of the twenty-first century, scholars have broadened their research scope to explore the role of laywomen in spreading Buddhist teaching,[9] Buddhist women's agency and subjectivity,[10] women's contributions to the Chinese naturalization of Buddhism, as well as Buddhism's role in the configuration of gender ideology throughout Chinese history.[11] These studies clearly demonstrate the extent to which the study of gender in Chinese Buddhism has developed and matured over the last decade.

Similarly, studies on women and gender in Daoist tradition have also come a long way since the late 1960s and early 1970s when Ellen M. Chen's articles on the perceptions of femininity in Daoist classics first laid forth the claim that Daoism was more sexually egalitarian than Confucianism.[12] Although other scholars would continue to pursue this line of inquiry into Daoist "proto-feminism," beginning with Edward Schafer's works on divine and historical female figures of Daoism,[13] the academic focus gradually shifted to goddesses, immortals, priestesses, and sexuality in the Daoist tradition. One example of this is Suzanne Cahill's excellent study on the Queen Mother of the West.[14] Additionally, in their study of women in Daoism, Catherine Despeux and Livia Kohn traced various female roles portrayed in Daoist texts.[15] Recognizing the lack of social and historical contextualization of some of the earlier studies, recent scholarship has taken a more interdisciplinary approach to explore different dimensions. Scholars have demonstrated that Daoist priestesses have not only exemplified spiritual transcendence but also assumed multiple roles in society.[16] They have also investigated Daoist perceptions of the body, sexuality, ritual, meditation, and self-cultivation in terms of women and gender.[17] Many of their studies have combined methodologies of fieldwork, medicine, psychology, and sexology, as well as intertextual studies. In addition, they have produced excellent translations of Daoist texts that are particularly relevant to Daoist women.[18]

Studies of female deities, mythical figures, and gender-laden popular cults have begun to explore questions that lie outside traditional religious, cultural, and regional boundaries. They offer more nuanced analyses of the intermingling of religions, politics, gender institutions, and geography. Scholars have studied and compared erotic and magical goddesses and heroines of ancient cultures and discussed how changing political structures and, thus, changing perceptions of gender roles, dictated how myths were constructed and narrated.[19] The popular cults of Mazu 媽祖,[20] Goddess Taishan (Taishan niangniang 泰山娘娘), Lady Linshui (Linshui furen 臨水夫人),[21] and their relationship with local cultural traditions and the Daoist pantheon have been extensively studied. The worship of these and other major female deities is generally tied to beliefs about female pollution, and they embody countercultures to the established social norms and male hierarchy.[22] Vengeful ghosts and capricious spirits, such as the Wutong 五通 and foxes, also thrived on the margin of established religions, and their demonic characters were often associated with the dangerous power of female sexuality.[23]

The interdisciplinary nature of much recent research is also reflected in other studies. For example, the Bodhisattva Guanyin interweaves Buddhist scriptural traditions and popular religious practices; scholarship on Buddhist nuns' poetry contributes to the field of Chinese women's literature; and investigations of both premodern and modern Chinese Buddhist women and laywomen contribute to our understanding of such questions as the Sinification of Buddhism and, more generally, to the religious and ideological roles played by gender in Chinese culture, society, and politics.

Once scholars begin to shift attention to women's agency in religious practices, the limitation of conventional boundaries, whether of academic discipline or of religious traditions, becomes even clearer. Buddhist and Daoist texts, for example, often reinforced the male-centered cosmological order and fundamental Confucian values, such as filial piety, chastity, and obedience, even as monastic communities and religious spaces offered women the possibility of lives that went beyond narrowly defined political and moral norms. Furthermore, from ancient times to the present day, women, as "household ritualists, lay devotees of a deity, shamans, nuns, and sectarian leaders," have played a great variety of roles at home as well as within and beyond their local communities.[24] For example, the late imperial Confucian discourse confined women's religious practices to the domestic arena, and religious women who provided professional services under the derogatory label of "Three Aunties and Six Grannies" (*sangu liupo* 三姑六婆) were generally considered "dangerous."[25] At the same time, however, female healers and midwives were proving to be able competitors in the late imperial medical market.[26] Female masters and sectarian leaders attracted a large number of followers.[27] Despite official bans, women's visits to temples continued unabated and women's piety proved "irrepressible."[28]

The arrival of Islam and Christianity greatly enriched Chinese women's religious life and, most notably, brought to the fore the issue of women and religion in the larger scheme of Chinese modernity. In 1978, Barbara Pillsbury's pioneering work presented a study of ethnicity, gender, and identity of Taiwanese Muslim women.[29] Since the 1990s, a number of anthropologists, sociologists, and historians turned their critical attention to Chinese Muslim women.[30] Thanks to the groundbreaking works by Maria Jaschok and Jingjun Shui, we learn that from the mid-Ming dynasty (1368–1644) on, Chinese Islamic women had synthesized Muslim scriptural teachings and Confucian ethics and developed a distinct religious culture that included female-only mosques and women clerics.[31] In fact, the female clerical tradition in central China was so firmly established that many female mosques were able to stage a tenacious resistance against the Republican state's attempts at religious reform.[32]

While early encounters between Western Christian missionaries and Chinese women helped weaken traditional gender boundaries, women's active participation in family rituals, pilgrimages, temple festivals, and sectarian activities paved the way for women's use of the Christian church as a source of self-empowerment. This, in turn, allowed them to escape arranged marriages, fulfill vows of chastity, or exercise forms of leadership normally unavailable to them. In converting to Christianity, Chinese women also contributed to transforming Christianity into a "local" and Chinese religion.[33] From the late nineteenth to the twenty-first century, Chinese Christian women have played crucial roles in promoting women's education, gender equality, and women's roles in the public space. They have been an indispensable force in shaping the course of Chinese modernization.[34]

Scholars of contemporary China have also noted the ways in which the forces of modernity and, in particular, the market economy have unleashed tremendous social mechanisms for a post-Mao religious revival. Although middle-aged and elderly women with little or no education have been accused of being obstacles to modernization because of their attachment to outdated "superstitions," they have turned out to be a major force in transmitting religious knowledge and sustaining local religious and ritual practices in rural and urban settings all over China.[35] Some of these women engage in the officially condemned practice of spirit mediumship, while others develop gender- and age-specific rituals designed to establish or strengthen their own status and power.[36] In addition, a growing number of younger-generation women, whether following family traditions or impelled by current situations and choices, have joined churches and entered newly restored nunneries.[37] These women, many of whom are well or moderately educated, often assume positions of leadership in state-sponsored religious institutions as well as in officially banned underground churches and organizations. They have found that the Communist promotion of gender equality has its limits and that, with the destruction of the old Confucian hierarchy, many aspects of their religious lives are now dictated by the party-state.[38] Across the strait, highly educated nuns and wealthy and middle-class laywomen have been the primary participants of the Humanistic Buddhism movement in Taiwan since the 1980s. Led by the female charismatic leader Cheng Yen 證嚴, the "Mother Teresa of Asia," these nuns and laywomen have contributed significantly to the global success of Ciji gongdehui 慈濟功德會 (Buddhist Compassion Relief Foundation).[39] Through its many disaster relief efforts and charity work in the mainland in recent years, Ciji has inspired many burgeoning mainland religious communities in their ongoing struggle for an autonomous space between a weakened party-state and an increasingly commercialized society.

All of these different areas of scholarship reflect a shared aspiration for a comprehensive field of study that is comparative, multidisciplinary, multiperspective, and cross-cultural. Seizing the momentum, in 2008 Beata Grant edited a special two-issue volume of *Nan Nü: Men, Women and Gender in Early and Imperial China* that was dedicated to the theme of women, gender, and religion in premodern China. She grouped the eight articles thematically and chronologically rather than divide them conventionally by religious traditions, and in so doing she inspired the emergence of a subfield on the study of women, gender, and religion in China.

## Revisiting Women, Gender, and Religion in China

This volume has grown out of the first International Conference on Women and Gender in Chinese Religion held at the University of Macau in June of 2011. Following the example of Grant's pioneering efforts, the nine studies included in this volume further challenge "double blindness" in Chinese gender studies and Chinese religious studies. From various "gender-critical" perspectives this volume explores previously ignored gender patterns embedded in Chinese religious life. The studies are grouped thematically rather than being artificially divided by religious traditions and span a long historical period from medieval to the present day.

To overcome "double blindness," it is crucial to focus on the "gender-critical turn" in the study of Chinese religious traditions. Over the last decade, scholars studying questions of gender in the religious traditions have repeatedly emphasized the importance of gender as an analytical category.[40] However, gender and religion are themselves broad categories, each of which has been endlessly questioned and discussed, and the relationship between the two is even more complicated and problematic. What this volume attempts to do is to follow several major lines of inquiry that can shed light on certain deeply embedded gender patterns in Chinese religious traditions. These lines of inquiries are reflected in the three major parts of the book.

The editors of a recent collection of studies on women and Confucian cultures in premodern East Asia note in their introduction to the collection: "In focusing on gender, our goal is to return women to the center of historical analysis. In this sense 'gender' implies a focus on 'women.' Because of a long history of neglect, we have yet to command a full picture of even the rudimentary facts about women's locations in history and society."[41] We, too, fully recognize that because the study of women in Chinese religion and history is still very much in the beginning stages, women continue to be the focus of our gendering of religious studies, even though "gender is not a synonym for women."[42] Placing women at the center of our analysis of gender and religion requires, in turn, exploring the formation of the female subject of religiosity and women's agency in negotiation with religious and social norms.[43] One way of doing this is to recover new texts such as stele inscriptions written for women and previously ignored women's writings, as well as to reinterpret familiar texts, through a variety of disciplinary approaches, including the literary and historical, in addition to gender and religion. This approach is reflected in the first three chapters in this volume. The authors of these studies have recovered evidence that not only helps restore women to the religious landscape but also sheds light on women's religiosity and subjectivity and illumines their larger contributions to Chinese religious and cultural traditions.

Ping Yao's study explores an understudied dimension of Chinese filial relationships, that of mother and daughter, and discusses how this kind of female filiality found poignant expression in Tang-dynasty (618–907) funeral inscriptions that were composed for pious Buddhist women and couched in Buddhist terms. In so doing, she demonstrates the extent to which filiality was an essential element of Chinese Buddhism rather than merely a Buddhist form of Confucian filial piety. She also shows the important role played by women in defining, broadening, promoting, and manifesting this Buddhist filiality.

Beata Grant examines what may well have been the first extant autobiographical sermon, which is found in the collected discourse records of a woman Chan master, Jizong Xingche 繼總行徹 (b. 1606), an official dharma heir of the (male) Linji 臨濟 Chan Master Wanru Tongwei 萬如通微 (1594–1657). Through a close analysis of this self-narrative, Grant demonstrates that, although Jizong Xingche adhered closely to the by then conventional template established by her male counterparts, her sermon can also be read, and was perhaps also received, as a subtle reinscription of this template. It served to authenticate and legitimate her own spiritual experience and standing in the overwhelmingly male lineage of Linji Chan masters.

Zhange Ni also provides a close reading of a woman-authored text, although one produced much later in time. The focus of her attention is the autobiographical novel *Thorny Heart* (*Jixin* 棘心) written by Su Xuelin 蘇雪林 (1897–1999), a celebrated female novelist who was also a self-identified Catholic. Through a comparison of this 1929 novel and its 1957 reprint,

Ni argues that Su's Catholic identity was tightly interwoven into her engagement with nationalism, Communism, and the women's rights movement. Above all, however, this novel also reflects her intellectual commitment to the restructuring of traditional Chinese religion.

A second application of the gender-critical analytic framework is to analyze the gender lenses and discourses through which religious women have been commented upon and judged, and by doing so to identify some of the overlooked gender symbols and dilemmas of religious life that often get entangled with ideology and politics. In so doing, one can shed light on the nature and significance of religious women's activities in the public sphere and their dynamic interactions with men within the gender system.[44] These are the approaches highlighted by the next three chapters in this volume. From three different historical periods, each of the three chapters challenges conventional lenses and theories about religious women and gender symbols and seeks to recover and redefine women's identity, agency, and tradition from the Confucian, Christian, and Communist discourses.

Jinhua Jia in her study challenges the use of the term "courtesan," which so many scholars from the Song dynasty to the present day have indiscriminately applied to Daoist priestesses of the Tang dynasty. She examines three issues relating to how Daoist women negotiated their place within the cultural-religious and socioeconomic milieu of the Tang dynasty. First, the religious practice of sexuality and other gender patterns within the Daoist tradition legitimized the love experience of priestesses and helped shape new gender relations between them and their male counterparts. Second, the priestesses empowered themselves with their considerable education and by using the cult of erotic goddesses. Finally, their independent socioeconomic status separated them from courtesans. Jia demonstrates how and why the publicly active roles of "Tang Daoist priestesses" came to be constructed and the priestesses' identity generally recognized by Tang people.

Xiaofei Kang's study of the well-known story *White-haired Girl* examines the ways in which the Communist propaganda workers in the 1940s employed gendered language to repackage traditional religious symbols in the service of mass mobilization. The ghostly features of the White-haired Girl are made to symbolize the feminized and victimized peasant class as well as the Chinese nation as a whole. In this way, her lover, a young Communist soldier who brings her out from the shadows into the sunlight, comes to symbolize the cosmic yang force representing the CCP and Mao. This highly gendered symbolism served to entrench the notion of women as recipients of revolutionary largesse over their role as subjects of the revolution.

Has Christianity offered women only a patriarchal replacement of Chinese patriarchy? What role has Christianity played in the life difficulties of Chinese women in Hong Kong who have been heir to both Christianity and Chinese culture? Wai Ching Angela Wong's study reviews these questions in light of, first, Hong Kong as a unique crossroad of Chinese and Christian cultures and, second, the transition of Hong Kong from a colonial city to that of Chinese sovereignty governed under the dictum of "One Country Two Systems." Built on interviews with over forty Chinese Christian women from various age groups and different social and economic backgrounds, an in-depth examination of six cases shows how they would exercise concrete strategies of reinterpretation of tradition and manipulation of time and space in order to cope with their respective marital and life challenges. Despite the long traditions of conservative Christian and Chinese precepts that reinforce women's submission and the priority of familial integrity, women's everyday engagement in practice necessarily brings about the possibility of agency and change.

The third part of this volume makes use of yet another approach to the study of gender and religion, which involves the question of bodies and bodily differences, and embodiment and subjectivity. In the past thirty years, scholars have paid great attention to the roles played by religious discourses and practices in "ascribing meaning to bodies and bodily differences, such as those between male and female" as well as how "cultural discourses about the body and the differences between male and female bodies impact religious rituals and, for example, the roles that men and women may assume."[45] On the other hand, recent theorization of religious studies has also emphasized embodied subjectivity, demonstrating how experiences and beliefs are constituted and transformed through religious practices.[46] The three chapters in this third part all make use of this analytic perspective of body and religion and, in so doing, paint vivid pictures of how the body and bodily differences between male and female inscribed by religious texts and cultural discourses have influenced the formation of religious practices and rituals and contributed to the construction of gendered social values, family values, and religious subjects within Chinese religious traditions both past and present.

Through a close reading of medieval Daoist texts on embryology, Gil Raz's study explores how Daoists perceived differences between male and female bodies and what these differences can tell us about Daoist perceptions of women and "femaleness." Raz discusses the fact that texts aimed at male practitioners often describe the ultimate attainment as nurturing and then giving birth to a perfect self or a perfect embryo, which will ascend to the heavens upon the death of the gross physical body. In more complex meditative programs, the male practitioner is urged to meditate on the process of gestation and return to an embryonic stage—and then give birth to himself while avoiding the "embryonic knots" that are produced during birth by a woman and are the cause of death. Raz's discussion confirms what some other scholars have noted as well: despite the positive valuation of yin in Daoist texts, this valuation does not carry over to actual women. In fact, the idealized process of giving birth to a perfected self is presented as a negation of the type of birthing associated with women.

Elena Valussi examines various texts of *nüdan*, or female alchemy, written by male elite scholars of late imperial China. Female alchemy first emerged in the seventeenth century and developed in the nineteenth and twentieth centuries. This textual tradition can tell us a great deal about contemporary gender notions, the understanding of the female body, and the social tensions between men and women. It also points to the desire of women for their own specialized techniques and methods of spiritual refinement as well as men's need to continue to control these female practices. Valussi points out the final irony: while designed to teach women bodily practices for immortality, these texts by no means empower women but rather aim to contain the polluting power of the female body and the perceived danger of women in penetrating male-dominated social spaces.

The third chapter in this section, by Neky Tak-ching Cheung, examines the Jiezhu 接珠 (Receiving the Buddhist Prayer Beads) ritual that can be found today among the Hakka of southeast China. Cheung describes how rural elder Hakka women, influenced by cultural discourses about bodily differences, especially as they relate to female menopause, have created, performed, and transmitted a distinct female ritual tradition by integrating Confucian family values, popular beliefs about ritual purity, and Buddhist practices of mindful recitation. The Jiezhu ritual helps menopausal women to make critical transitions during the latter stage of their lives, to form their own social circles, and to assert status and power in their families. In particular, by both strengthening women's attachments to husbands and sons and by reinstating connections with their natal families as well as with their married daughters, the ritual celebrates and values all aspects of a woman's contributions as a wife, mother, and daughter.

Although the scholars represented in this volume all seek to find ways to apply gender-critical perspectives to the study of women, gender, and religion in China, they remain very conscious of the limitations of using Western concepts of religion. Thus, rather than treating Buddhism and Daoism as alternatives to Confucian norms, as has often been the case in the past, their studies probe how ideas and practices of the "three traditions" actually serve as "repertoires of resources," from which women in different times and circumstances selectively draw in order to construct their own traditions and identities, covering temporally from the medieval to contemporary times and spatially from metropolitan cities to rural areas.[47] Moreover, the range and scope of these nine studies illustrate the great value of multidisciplinary and comparative approaches to discovering and interpreting sources in the study of women, gender, and religion in China. The rich sources utilized by the authors of these studies are both extensive and varied, including Buddhist scriptures and sermons, Daoist medicinal and alchemical texts, historical records, stele inscriptions, anecdotal narratives, autobiographies, poetry, novels, Communist propaganda performance, and ethnographic reports. Together they suggest both the genuine urgency for and great possibilities of more in-depth conversations among scholars of history, anthropology, and literature as well as women and gender studies and religious studies.

In addition, although the chapters are purposefully not arranged according to the conventional divisions of religious traditions, in effect these studies touch upon questions of women and gender that spring from the various Chinese traditions of Buddhism, Daoism, popular religion, and Christianity. Moreover, though our emphasis has not been on the far-better-studied area of women, gender, and Confucianism, discussions of Confucian norms and influences can be found woven through many of the studies in this volume.

In sum, based on both sides of the Pacific and coming from a wide range of research fields, the contributors of this volume utilize interdisciplinary approaches and gender-critical perspectives to furnish new understandings of gendered subject, identity, and body in Chinese religions. Overall, the volume makes two compelling arguments. First, Chinese women have deployed specific religious ideas and rituals to empower themselves in different historical and social contexts. Second, the gendered perceptions and representations of Chinese religions have been indispensable in the historical and contemporary construction of social and political power. While each of the nine studies in the volume represents a distinct perspective on women, gender, and religion in China, together they form a coherent dialogue about the historical importance, intellectual possibilities, and methodological protocols of this subfield.

## Problems and Prospects

The present volume represents an initial attempt to open up what promises to be a field of immense possibilities. It also suggests some problems and prospects for future studies.

First and foremost, the "double blindness" referred to by Ursula King persists in the China field, especially when it comes to studies of women and gender in twentieth-century China.[48] In fact, this "double blindness" on the part of scholars of the twentieth century stands in stark contrast to the relatively active integration of women, gender, and religious studies in studies of traditional China on the one hand and contemporary China on the other. It is a well-known fact that the twentieth century witnessed the critical transformation and sometimes obliteration of Chinese religious traditions as secularism replaced religion as the chief identity marker of the modern citizen and the nation-state. It therefore becomes critical to ask: What happened during this period that would explain both the historical continuities as well as the creative transformations in the transmission of women's religious traditions as they exist in today's China? To what extent have the state's reorganizations of the five religions and the arbitrary bifurcation of "religion" and "superstition" reshaped female religiosity and women's constructions of religious identities in the post-Mao religious revival? How did women, especially religious women, act as agents of change to make religion relevant to China's goal of modernization? How does gender help us understand the destruction of traditional religions and the formation of the political religiosity reflected in the Chinese Communist Party and the cult of Mao?

Addressing this double blindness in regard to twentieth-century China will also help fill other important gaps in the study of women, gender, and religion. For example, while we know quite a lot about women's rituals and women's participation in all sorts of religious activities in Taiwan, Hong Kong, and southeast China, we know much less about their counterparts in other parts of the mainland. Similarly, while there is now excellent research on the religious history of north, northwest, and southwest China, respectively,[49] a fuller consideration of these histories in the context of women and gender should greatly enrich our understanding of them all.

Another area that needs to be addressed is the question of how to move beyond the recovery of women's voices, as essential as they are, to a more gendered perspective of religion as a whole. While studies on women (lay or monastic, masters or disciples), female deities, female rituals, and female practices have proliferated in recent years, we look forward to more theoretical, methodological, and historiographical efforts that will serve to firmly establish the subfield. In particular, we anticipate future research into the significance of the "gender-critical turn" in reshaping the structure of knowledge about Chinese religions. As some recent studies, including the chapters contained in this volume, already suggest, gender is not merely about women or about the relationship between men and women. Gender is everywhere. Its patterns are deeply embedded in all aspects of religion, and they render authority, power, and representations of self, other, age, class, and ethnicity in all religions. Gendering Chinese religions will compel us to ask new questions and perhaps even redefine what we mean by Chinese religions. If, as Campany and Hymes indicate, religion is a cultural repertoire from which human beings draw, then to what extent, in any given historical circumstance, do men and women draw from this cultural repertoire differently? Do men and women draw on it differently depending on their age, class, locale, or period? If so, to what extent are their different activities subject to gendered perceptions of social roles and religious power, and how in turn do they consolidate, challenge, or resist such power? If, as a growing number of recent studies have persuasively demonstrated, it has always been community cults and local ritual traditions (rather than institutions and doctrinal teachings) that have constituted the heart of Chinese religious life,[50] then it would follow that such cults and rituals were essential to the defense and the reproduction of gender roles, gender relations, and gendered religious authorities in local politics, both divine and lay. Indeed, as many scholars have shown, these sorts of village rituals and community-based religious pluralism permeated all aspects of Chinese life until the twentieth century, when they came to be relentlessly attacked as "superstition" by the Chinese state as well as the cultural elite. To what extent, then, have such attacks on traditional ritual life and communal religions, as well as popular resistance to these attacks, been a gendered social and political process? In what ways have the state reorganization and control of religious expression in modern China affected gendered representations of Chinese traditional religions in contrast to those of the modern West and by extension tradition versus modernity? What have the roles of Chinese women, elite and ordinary, urban and rural, been in preserving, reinventing, or developing Chinese religions? How have the movements of women's liberation and gender equality as well as nationalism, anti-imperialism, and Communism influenced women's perception and rejection of, and participation in, various religious practices? While it may be impossible to answer all of these questions fully, they nevertheless suggest how a gendered approach can greatly expand the possibilities of exploration and the potential for a deeper and more inclusive understanding of Chinese religion, history, and society.

Last but by no means least, in order to bring gender into the center of our inquiries, scholars must be trained to utilize a range of multidisciplinary and comparative methodologies. Because of the traditionally interdisciplinary nature of East Asian studies programs in North American and European institutions, China scholars are perhaps not faced with as much of an obstacle to the integration of religious studies with women's and gender studies as scholars in other areas and disciplines. Many of the authors represented in this volume, for example, work and teach across more than one department and discipline and therefore are more willing and able to engage in multidisciplinary studies. However, most universities are still divided by traditional disciplinary and academic boundaries, where women's and gender studies are represented by separate departments or programs rather than fully integrated into the various disciplines and where many religious studies faculty still feel the pressure to teach Chinese religions in terms of the traditions of "Buddhism," "Daoism," or "Confucianism," with perhaps a day or two devoted separately to the study of women and gender in these traditions.

Once scholars begin to look across disciplinary boundaries, they will have far greater chances of finding new source materials or, at the very least, discovering new topics with which to revisit familiar sources. For example, many scholars of women and gender in premodern Chinese religions have begun to look not only at the usual official documents and scriptural texts but also stele inscriptions, poetry, precious scrolls, anecdotal writings, and vernacular fiction. Although, as we can see from some of the studies in this volume, scholars of the modern period have also begun to look at religion in literary sources, efforts still must be made to bridge the period between traditional China and the modern and contemporary periods. Making the matter even more complex is that the high illiteracy rate among women in both traditional and modern rural China has greatly limited women's access to authoritative religious texts, as a result of which many laywomen past and present have transmitted (and sometimes modified and created) religious knowledge and assumed religious leadership through what they do and say/sing rather than what they read and write. An admirable model of the possibilities for addressing this is David Johnson's recent book in which he paints a rich and vivid historical picture of village ritual life in north China by weaving together ethnographic observations, early twentieth-century ritual manuals and opera scripts, and Ming-Qing gazetteers and stele inscriptions.[51] For this reason, it is especially important to corroborate ethnographic research and oral literature with historical sources in uncovering women and gender in the history of Chinese religions. In short, if we are to make the "gender-critical turn," we must embrace sources and disciplinary differences both "vertically" and "horizontally," so as to expand the scope and depth of our inquiries.

It is our hope that scholars of women, gender, religion, history, and literature may find the research exemplified by the chapters in this volume to be relevant to their own work and that some of the methodological protocols may be of use to their line of inquiry. Above all, we hope that this volume will contribute to the further development, growth, and maturation of the subfield of women, gender, and religion in China.

## Notes

1. Joan Scott, "Gender: A Useful Category of Historical Analysis," *The American Historical Review* 91.5 (1986): 1053–75.

2. Ursula King, "General Introduction: Gender-Critical Turns in the Study of Religion," in Ursula King and Tina Beattie, eds., *Gender, Religion and Diversity: Cross-Cultural Perspective* (New York: Continuum, 2004), 1–2.

3. Susan Calef, "Charting New Territory: Religion and 'the Gender-Critical Turn,'" *Journal of Religion and Society* 5 (2009): 1–2.

4. Rita M. Gross, "Studying Women and Religion: Conclusions Twenty-Five Years Later," in Arvind Sharma, ed., *Today's Women in World Religions* (Albany: State University of New York Press, 1994), 335.

5. Jinhua Emma Teng, "The Construction of the 'Traditional Chinese Woman' in the Western Academy: A Critical Review," *Signs* 22.1 (1996): 115–51. For the most representative works that contributed to these changes, see Margery Wolf, *Women and the Family in Rural Taiwan* (Stanford: Stanford University Press, 1972); Margery Wolf and Roxane Witke, eds., *Women in Chinese Society* (Stanford: Stanford University Press, 1975); Patricia B. Ebrey, *The Inner Quarters: Marriage and the Lives of Chinese Women in the Sung Period* (Stanford: Stanford University Press, 1993); Dorothy Ko, *Teachers of the Inner Chambers: Women and Culture in China, 1573–1722* (Stanford: Stanford University Press, 1994); and Susan Mann, *Precious Records: Women in China's Long Eighteenth Century* (Stanford: Stanford University Press, 1997).

6. While early works emphasized males' role in promoting widows' chastity (see, for example, T'ien Ju-k'ang, *Male Anxiety and Female Chastity: A Comparative Study of Chinese Ethical Values in Ming-Ch'ing Times*, vol. 14, *T'oung Pao Monographie* [Leiden: Brill, 1988]; and Katherine Carlitz, "Shrines, Governing-Class Identity, and the Cult of Widow Fidelity in Mid-Ming Jiangnan," *The Journal of Asian Studies* 56.3 [1997]: 612–40), recent scholarship has tended to examine the complexity of

women's agency in the cult of chastity. See, for example, Janet Theiss, *Disgraceful Matters: The Politics of Chastity in Eighteenth-Century China* (Berkeley: University of California Press, 2005); and Weijing Lu, *True to Her Words: The Faithful Maiden Cult in Late Imperial China* (Stanford: Stanford University Press, 2008).

7. Diana Y. Paul, *The Buddhist Feminine Ideal: Queen Srimala and the Tathagatagarbha* (Atlanta: Scholars Press, 1980); Paul, *Women in Buddhism: Images of the Feminine in Mahayana Tradition* (Berkeley: University of California Press, 1985); and Kathryn Ann Tsai, "The Chinese Buddhist Monastic Order for Women: The First Two Centuries," in Richard Guisso and Stanley Johannesen, eds., *Women in China: Current Directions in Historical Scholarship* (Youngstown, NY: Philo Press, 1981), 1–20.

8. See, for example, Miriam Levering, "Lin-chi (Rinzai) Ch'an and Gender: The Rhetoric of Equality and the Rhetoric of Heroism," in José Ignacio Cabezón, ed., *Buddhism, Sexuality, and Gender* (Albany: State University of New York Press, 1992), 137–56; Levering, "Dōgen's *Raihaitokuzui* and Women Teaching in Sung Ch'an," *Journal of the International Association of Buddhist Studies* 21.1 (1997): 77–110; Beata Grant, "Female Holder of the Lineage: Linji Chan Master Zhiyuan Xinggang (1597–1654)," *Late Imperial China* 17.2 (1996): 51–76; Ding-Hwa E. Hsieh, "Images of Women in Ch'an Buddhist Literature of the Sung Period," in Peter N. Gregory and Daniel A. Getz Jr., eds., *Buddhism in the Sung* (Honolulu: University of Hawaii Press, 1999), 148–87; and Shih Pao-ch'ang, *Lives of the Nuns: Biographies of Chinese Buddhist Nuns from the Fourth to Sixth Centuries: A Translation of the Pi-Ch'iu-Ni Chuan*, trans. Kathryn Ann Tsai (Honolulu: University of Hawaii Press, 1994).

9. See, for example, Mark Halperin, "Domesticity and the Dharma: Portraits of Buddhist Laywomen in Sung China," *T'oung Pao* 92.1–3 (2006): 50–100; and Ping Yao, "Good Karmic Connections: Buddhist Mothers in Tang China," *Nan Nü: Men, Women and Gender in Early and Imperial China* 10.1 (2008): 57–85.

10. See, for example, Beata Grant's series of articles and her two books, *Daughters of Emptiness: Poems of Chinese Buddhist Nuns* (Somerville, MA: Wisdom Publications, 2003) and *Eminent Nuns: Women Chan Masters of Seventeenth-Century China* (Honolulu: University of Hawaii Press, 2008); and Wendi Adamek, "The Literary Lives of Nuns: Poems Inscribed on a Memorial Niche for the Tang Nun Benxing," *T'ang Studies* 27.1 (2009): 40–65.

11. See, for example, Chün-fang Yü, *Kuan-yin: The Chinese Transformation of Avalokitesvara* (New York: Columbia University Press, 2001); Glen Dudbridge, *The Legend of Miaoshan* (Oxford: Oxford University Press, 2004); Yuet Keung Lo, "Recovering a Buddhist Voice on Daughters-in-law: *The Yuyenü jing*," *History of Religion* 44 (2005): 318–50; and Wilt L. Idema, *Personal Salvation and Filial Piety: Two Precious Scroll Narratives of Guanyin and Her Acolytes* (Honolulu: University of Hawaii Press, 2008).

12. See Ellen M. Chen, "Nothingness and the Mother Principle in Early Chinese Taoism," *International Philosophical Quarterly* 9.3 (1969): 391–405; and

Chen, "Tao as the Great Mother and the Influence of Motherly Love in the Shaping of Chinese Philosophy," *History of Religions* 14.1 (1974): 51–64.

13. See Edward H. Schafer, *The Divine Woman: Dragon Ladies and Rain Maidens in T'ang Literature* (Berkeley: University of California Press, 1973) and his series of articles.

14. Suzanne E. Cahill, *Transcendence and Divine Passion: The Queen Mother of the West in Medieval China* (Stanford: Stanford University Press, 1993).

15. Catherine Despeux and Livia Kohn, *Women in Taoism* (Boston: Three Pines Press, 2003).

16. See, for example, Russell Kirkland, "Huang Ling-wei: A Taoist Priestess in T'ang China," *Journal of Chinese Religions* 19 (1991): 47–73; Ping Yao, "Contested Virtue: The Daoist Investiture of Princesses Jinxian and Yuzhen and the Journey of Tang Imperial Daughters," *T'ang Studies* 22 (2007): 1–41; Shin-yi Chao, "Good Career Moves: Life Stories of Daoist Nuns of the Twelfth and Thirteenth Centuries," *Nan Nü: Men, Women and Gender in Early and Imperial China* 10.1 (2008): 121–51; and Jinhua Jia, "*Yaochi ji* and Three Daoist Priestess-Poets in Tang China," *Nan Nü: Men, Women and Gender in Early and Imperial China* 13.2 (2011): 205–43.

17. See R. H. van Gulik, *Sexual Life in Ancient China: A Preliminary Survey of Chinese Sex and Society from ca. 1500 B.C. till 1644 A.D.*, new introduction and bibliography by Paul R. Goldin (Leiden: Brill, 2003); Charlotte Furth, "Rethinking Van Gulik: Sexuality and Reproduction in Traditional Chinese Medicine," in Christina K. Gilmartin, Gail Hershatter, Lisa Rofel, and Tyrene White, eds., *Engendering China: Women, Culture, and the State* (Cambridge, MA: Harvard University Press, 1994), 125–46; Isabelle Robinet, "Sexualité et taoïsme," in Marcel Bernos, ed., *Sexualité et religion* (Paris: Les Éditions du Cerf, 1988), 51–71; Kristofer Schipper, *The Taoist Body*, trans. Karen C. Duval (Berkeley: University of California Press, 1993); Yan Shanzhao 嚴善炤, "Shoki dōkyō to kōaka konki bōchū jutsu" 初期道教と黄赤混氣房中術, *Tōhō shūkyō* 東方宗教 97 (2001): 1–10; Elena Valussi, "Female Alchemy and Paratext: How to Read *nüdan* in a Historical Context," *Asia Major* 21.2 (2008): 153–93; Robin Wang, "*Kundao*: A Lived Body in Female Daoism," *Journal of Chinese Philosophy* 36.2 (2009): 277–92; and Xun Liu, *Daoist Modern: Innovation, Lay Practice, and the Community of Inner Alchemy in Republican Shanghai* (Cambridge, MA: Harvard University Asia Center, 2009).

18. See, for example, Charles D. Benn, *The Cavern-Mystery Transmission: A Taoist Ordination Rite of A.D. 711* (Honolulu: University of Hawaii Press, 1991); and Suzanne E. Cahill, *Divine Traces of the Daoist Sisterhood* (Magdalena, NM: Three Pines Press, 2006).

19. See Miriam R. Dexter and Victor H. Mair, *Sacred Display: Divine and Magical Female Figures of Eurasia* (Amherst, NY: Cambria Press, 2010); and Anne Birrell, *Chinese Mythology: An Introduction* (Baltimore: Johns Hopkins University Press, 1999).

20. See James Watson, "Standardizing the Gods: The Promotion of T'ien Hou ('Empress of Heaven') along the South China Coast, 960–1960," in David Johnson et al., eds., *Popular Culture in Late Imperial China* (Berkeley: University of California Press, 1985), 292–324; Judith M. Boltz, "In Homage to T'ien-fei," *Journal of the*

*American Oriental Society* 106.1 (1986): 211–32; Mayfair Mei-hui Yang, "Goddess across Taiwan Strait: Matrifocal Ritual Space, Nation-State, and Satellite Television Footprints," *Public Culture* 16.2 (2004): 209–38; and Hsun Chang and Mei-rong Lin, *Culture, Narrative, and Community of the Cult of Mazu*, special issue, *Taiwan Journal of Anthropology* 6 (2008): 103–31.

21. See Kenneth Pomeranz, "Power, Gender, and Pluralism in the Cult of the Goddess of Taishan," in Theodore Huters, R. Wong, and Pauline Yu, eds., *Culture and State in Chinese History: Conventions, Accommodations, and Critiques* (Stanford: Stanford University Press, 1997), 182–204; and Brigitte Baptandier, *The Lady of Linshui: A Chinese Female Cult*, trans. Kristin Fryklund (Stanford: Stanford University Press, 2008).

22. Emily M. Ahern, "The Power and Pollution of Chinese Women," in Margery Wolf and Roxane Witke, eds., *Women in Chinese Society* (Stanford: Stanford University Press, 1975), 193–214; P. Steven Sangren, "Female Gender in Chinese Religious Symbols: Kuan Yin, Ma Tsu, and the 'Eternal Mother,'" *Signs* 9.1 (1983): 4–25; and Zheng Zhiming 鄭志明, *Wusheng laomu xinyang shuoyuan* 無生老母信仰溯源 (Taibei: Wenshizhe, 1985).

23. Richard von Glahn, "The Enchantment of Wealth: The God Wutong in the Social History of Jiangnan," *Harvard Journal of Asiatic Studies* 51.2 (1991): 651–714; Xiaofei Kang, *The Cult of the Fox: Power, Gender, and Popular Religion in Late Imperial and Modern China* (New York: Columbia University Press, 2006); and Judith T. Zeitlin, *The Phantom Heroine: Ghosts and Gender in Seventeenth-Century Chinese Literature* (Honolulu: University of Hawaii Press, 2007).

24. Daniel L. Overmyer, "Women in Chinese Religions: Submission, Struggle, Transcendence," in Koichi Shinohara and Gregory Schopen, eds., *From Benares to Beijing: Essays on Buddhism and Chinese Religions in Honour of Professor Jan Yün-hua* (Oakville, Ont.: Mosaic Press, 1991), 91–120; and Overmyer, ed., *Huaren zongjiao zhong de nüxing* 華人宗教中的女性 (Special Issue on Women in Chinese Religions), *Minsu quyi* 民俗曲藝 168 (2010).

25. Victoria B. Cass, *Dangerous Women: Warriors, Grannies, and Geishas of the Ming* (Lanham, MD: Rowman & Littlefield, 1999); and Yi Jo-lan 衣若蘭, *Sangu liupo: Mingdai funü yu shehui de tansuo* 三姑六婆: 明代婦女與社會的探索 (Taibei: Daxiang chubanshe, 2002).

26. Victoria B. Cass, "Female Healers in the Ming and the Lodge of Ritual and Ceremony," *Journal of the American Oriental Society* 106.1 (1986): 233–40; Charlotte Furth, *A Flourishing Yin: Gender in China's Medical History, 960–1665* (Berkeley: University of California Press, 1999); Angela Ki Che Leung, "Women Practicing Medicine in Premodern China," in Harriet T. Zurndorfer, ed., *Chinese Women in the Imperial Past: New Perspectives* (Leiden: Brill, 1999), 101–34.

27. Ann Waltner, "T'an-yang-tsu and Wang Shih-chen: Visionary and Bureaucrat in the Late Ming," *Late Imperial China* 8.1 (1987): 105–33; and Daniel L. Overmyer, "Values in Chinese Sectarian Literature: Ming and Ch'ing Pao-chuan," in David Johnson, Andrew J. Nathan, and Evelyn S. Rawski, eds., *Popular Culture in Late Imperial China* (Berkeley: University of California Press, 1985), 219–53.

28. Yiqun Zhou, "The Hearth and the Temple: Mapping Female Religiosity in Late Imperial China, 1550–1900," *Late Imperial China* 24.2 (2003): 109–55; and Vincent Goossaert, "Irrepressible Female Piety: Late Imperial Bans on Women Visiting Temples," *Nan Nü: Men, Women and Gender in Early and Imperial China* 10.2 (2008): 212–41.

29. Barbara Pillsbury, "Being Female in a Muslim Minority in China," in Lois Beck and Nikki Keddie, eds., *Women in the Muslim World* (Cambridge, MA: Harvard University Press, 1978), 671–87.

30. See, for example, Keng-Fong Pang, "Islamic 'Fundamentalism' and Female Empowerment among the Muslims of Hainan Island, People's Republic of China," in Judy Brink and Joan Mencher, eds., *Mixed Blessings: Gender and Religious Fundamentalism Cross Culturally* (New York: Routledge, 1997), 41–57; Elisabeth Allès, "Une organisation de l'islam au féminin: le personnel des mosquées féminines en Chine," *Lettre d'information*, Programme de Recherches Interdisciplinaires sur le Monde Musulman Périphérique 14 (1994): 1–12; Leila Cherif, "Ningxia, l'école au féminine," *Etudes Orientales* 13/14 (1994): 156–62; and Constance-Hélène Halfon, "Souvenirs de voyage dans la Chine islamique profonde: Être femme et musulmane à Lanzhou, au Gansu," *Etudes Orientales* 13/14 (1994): 151–55.

31. Maria Jaschok and Jingjun Shui, *The History of Women's Mosques in Chinese Islam: A Mosque of Their Own* (Richmond, Surrey: Curzon, 2000); and its revised Chinese-language version, Shui Jingjun 水鏡君 and Maria Jaschok 瑪利亞 雅紹克, *Zhongguo qingzhen nüsishi* 中國清真女寺史 (Beijing: Sanlian shudian, 2002).

32. Maria Jaschok and Jingjun Shui, *Women, Religion, and Space in China: Islamic Mosques and Daoist Temples, Catholic Convents and Chinese Virgins* (New York: Routledge, 2011).

33. Eugenio Menegon, *Ancestors, Virgins, and Friars: Christianity as a Local Religion in Late Imperial China* (Cambridge: Harvard University Asia Center, 2010); Robert Entenmann, "Christian Virgins in Eighteenth-Century Sichuan," in Daniel Bays, ed., *Christianity in China from the Eighteenth Century to the Present* (Stanford: Stanford University Press, 1996), 180–93.

34. Pui-lan Kwok, *Chinese Women and Christianity 1860–1927* (Atlanta, GA: Scholars Press, 1992); Wai Ching Angela Wong, *"The Poor Woman": A Critical Analysis of Asian Theology and Contemporary Chinese Women's Stories* (London: Peter Lang, 2002); Tao Feiya 陶飛亞, ed., *Xingbie yu lishi: jindai Zhongguo funü yu Jidujiao* 性別與歷史: 近代中國婦女與基督教 (Shanghai: Shanghai renmin chubanshe, 2006); Jessie G. Lutz, ed., *Pioneer Chinese Christian Women: Gender, Christianity, and Social Mobility* (Bethlehem: Lehigh University Press, 2010); and Wai Ching Angela Wong 黃慧貞 and Choi Po-king Dora 蔡寶瓊, eds., *Huaren funü yu Xianggang jidujiao: Koushu lishi* 華人婦女與香港基督教: 口述歷史 (Hong Kong: Oxford University Press, 2010).

35. See, for example, Pui-lam Law, "The Revival of Folk Religion and Gender Relationships in Rural China: A Preliminary Observation," *Asian Folklore Studies* 64.1 (2005): 89–109; and Xiaofei Kang, "Rural Women, Old Age, and Temple Work: A Case from Northwestern Sichuan," *China Perspectives* 4 (2009): 42–52.

36. Ellen Cline, "Female Spirit Mediums and Religious Authority in Contemporary Southeastern China," *Modern China* 36.5 (2010): 520–55; and Neky Tak-ching Cheung, *Women's Ritual in China: Jiezhu (Receiving Buddhist Prayer Beads) Performed by Menopausal Women in Ninghua, Western Fujian* (New York: Edwin Mellen Press, 2008).

37. Wenjie Qin, "The Buddhist Revival in Post-Mao China: Women Reconstruct Buddhism on Mt. Emei" (PhD diss., Harvard University, 2000).

38. Miriam Levering, "Women, the State, and Religion Today in the People's Republic of China," in Arvind Sharma, ed., *Today's Women in World Religions* (Albany: State University of New York Press, 1994), 171–224; and Beatrice Leung and Patricia Wittberg, "Catholic Religious Orders of Women in China: Adaptation and Power," *Journal for the Scientific Study of Religion* 43.1 (2004): 67–83.

39. Julia C.Y. Huang, *Charisma and Compassion: Cheng Yen and the Buddhist Tzu Chi Movement* (Cambridge, MA: Harvard University Press, 2009); Elise A. DeVido, *Taiwan's Buddhist Nuns* (Albany: State University of New York Press, 2010); and Chün-fang Yü, "Humanistic Buddhism and Buddhist Nuns in Taiwan," *Minsu quyi* 168 (2010): 191–224.

40. Randi R. Warne, "Making the Gender-Critical Turn," in Tim Jensen and Mikael Rothstein, eds., *Secular Theories on Religion: Current Perspectives* (Copenhagen: Museum Tusculanum Press, 2000), 249–60; and King, "General Introduction," in *Gender, Religion and Diversity*, 8.

41. Dorothy Ko, JaHyun Kim Haboush, and Joan R. Piggott, eds., *Women and Confucian Cultures in Premodern China, Korea, and Japan* (Berkeley: University of California Press, 2003), 2.

42. See Terrell Carver, *Gender Is Not a Synonym for Women* (Boulder, CO: Lynne Rienner Publishers, 1996).

43. About the emphasis of agency in feminist theorization, see, for example, Judith Butler, *Gender Trouble* (New York: Routledge, 1990), 145; and Lois McNay, *Gender and Agency: Reconfiguring the Subject in Feminist and Social Theory* (Cambridge: Polity Press, 2000), 1–30, 155–64.

44. Sue Morgan, "Rethinking Religion in Gender History: Historiographical and Methodological Reflections," in King and Beattie, eds., *Gender, Religion and Diversity*, 117; and Calef, "Charting New Territory," 3.

45. Calef, "Charting New Territory," 3.

46. See, for example, Amy Hollywood, "Performativity, Citationality, Ritualization," *History of Religions* 42 (2002): 93–115; and Hollywood, "Practice, Belief, and Feminist Philosophy of Religion," in Kevin Schibrack, ed., *Thinking through Rituals: Philosophical Perspectives* (New York: Routledge, 2004), 52–71.

47. On the powerful argument for treating religion as a "repertoire of resources" that emphasizes the power of human agency in making choices and negotiating for their lives in a given cultural context, see Robert P. Hymes, *Way and Byway: Taoism, Local Religion and Models of Divinity in Sung and Modern China* (Berkeley: University of California Press, 2002); Robert F. Campany, "On the Very Idea of Religions in the Modern West and Early Medieval China," *History of Religions* 42.4

(2003): 287–319; and Campany, *Making Transcendence: Ascetics and Social Memory in Early Medieval China* (Honolulu: University of Hawaii Press, 2009).

48. Two examples serve to illustrate this double blindness: in Gail Hershatter's exhaustive literature survey entitled *Women in China's Long Twentieth Century* (Berkeley: University of California Press, 2007), Confucianism and Christianity are briefly mentioned, but the whole subject of religion in relation to women and gender is absent. Vincent Goossaert and David A. Palmer's groundbreaking book, *The Religious Question in Modern China* (Chicago: University of Chicago Press, 2011), mentions gender and women occasionally, but the two topics appear to be altogether marginal to the Religious Question. In both cases, there is simply not much secondary literature available to the authors.

49. It is not possible to provide a complete list in this limited space. See, for example, on religion, Susan Naquin, *Peking: Temples and City Life, 1400–1900* (Berkeley: University of California Press, 2000); Vincent Goossaert, *The Taoist of Peking, 1800–1949: A Social History of Urban Clerics* (Cambridge, MA: Harvard Asia Center, 2007); Adam Chau, *Miraculous Response: Doing Popular Religion in Contemporary China* (Stanford: Stanford University Press, 2008); and Stephen Jones's various works, especially *In Search of the Folk Daoists of North China* (New York: Ashgate, 2010).

50. For representative studies, see, among others, Kenneth Dean, "Local Communal Religion in Contemporary China," and Paul Katz, "Religion and the State in Postwar Taiwan," both in Daniel Overmyer, ed., *Religion in China Today* (Cambridge: Cambridge University Press, 2003), 32–52, 89–106; Overmyer, *Local Religion in North China in the Twentieth Century: The Structure and Organization of Community Rituals and Beliefs* (Leiden: Brill, 2009); David Johnson, *Spectacle and Sacrifice: The Ritual Foundations of Village Life in North China* (Cambridge, MA: Harvard Asia Center, 2009); and Chau, *Miraculous Response.*

51. Johnson, *Spectacle and Sacrifice.*

# Part I

# Restoring Female Religiosity and Subjectivity

1

# Tang Women in the Transformation of Buddhist Filiality

*Ping Yao*

## Introduction

One dominant theme in the study of Chinese Buddhism is the Sinification of Buddhism through its endorsing the virtue of filial piety (*xiao* 孝), that is, that the inclusion of filial piety transformed Buddhism from a foreign religion into a Sinicized one. Scholars have argued that Buddhism flourished in China by promoting the idea that monastic life represented the ultimate form of the Confucian ideal of filial piety and thus was indispensable to the salvation of ancestors. They suggested that from very early on, Buddhist monks and scholars who translated Buddhist sutras often inserted Confucian concepts into their translations to make it seem as if Buddhism had all along advocated filial piety.[1] They also found that particular narratives—for instance, tales of a son's filial action in saving his mother's life and redeeming her sin—greatly accelerated the process of China's Buddhist transformation.[2]

This transformation theory, however, has been increasingly challenged by scholars of Indian Buddhism. As early as 1983, John Strong attested that early Indian popular Buddhist stories contain many tales of Buddhist monks performing filial deeds.[3] A more direct challenge to the theory is Gregory Schopen's study of Indian epigraphical texts from the first through fifth centuries.[4] Schopen finds that, among his data concerning donation of gifts for the purpose of benefiting parents, more than 60 percent of the donors were Buddhist monks, and many of them were the teachers and transmitters of "official" Buddhist literature. Thus, he argues that filial piety was an old, integral, and pervasive part of the practice of Indian Buddhism. Most recently, Guang Xing's 廣興 study of Pali Nikāyas and Vinaya and the Chinese translation of Āgamas and Vinayas further confirm that filial piety constituted an important aspect of early Buddhist ethical teachings.[5]

While acknowledging the originality of Indian Buddhist filiality, some scholars nevertheless stress that the perception of filiality in early Buddhist sutras is different from the perception of filial piety in the Confucian tradition[6] and that Indian Buddhist filiality was employed by Chinese Buddhists to advance the religion. Based on his reading of the Liang dynasty (502–557) monk Baochang's 寶唱 *Biographies of Chinese Buddhist Nuns* (*Biqiuni zhuan* 比丘尼傳) and Buddhist inscriptions and colophons from early medieval China, Bret Hinsch contends that Chinese Buddhists created images of filial Buddhist women to counter the attacks against Buddhism. In so doing, Buddhism became a tool of filial piety and filial piety justified Buddhism; the new gender ideal thus served to reconcile Confucianism with Buddhism and allowed the creation of Chinese Buddhism.[7] Indeed, it goes without saying that all early ethical systems had filial piety as a core component, as typified by the Ten Commandments in the Christian tradition. Most likely the Chinese Buddhists and scholars were aware of the discussion of filial piety in the Buddhist texts they translated and expressed the Buddhist ideal of filiality in specifically Chinese ways as they knew it, without a hidden agenda.[8]

This chapter takes the originality of Indian Buddhist filiality as a point of departure and focuses its inquiry on how such a borrowed tradition was manifested in medieval China, especially on the role women played in the making of a specifically Chinese Buddhist filiality. Epigraphical texts from the Tang dynasty (618–907), including votive inscriptions on Buddhist sculpture (*Fozaoxiang* 佛造像) and Buddhist pagodas (*futu* 浮圖) as well as funeral inscriptions on cremation stupas (*huishenta* 灰身塔) and epitaph stones (*muzhi* 墓誌), reveal that by the end of the Tang the Chinese had fully developed a broad and unique repertoire of expressions of Buddhist filiality that largely reflected Chinese cultural mores; they also reveal that Buddhist nuns and laywomen in medieval China played an extremely important role in the shaping, advancing, and expressing of Buddhist filiality. Moreover, these texts point to a close mother-daughter bond, which has been largely overlooked in the scholarship on the Chinese Buddhist tradition.

## The Manifestation of Buddhist Filiality in Medieval China

While it is now clear that filial piety had long been a core Buddhist tenet and that early Chinese Buddhists and devotees imitated Indian practices of Buddhist filiality, such as donating Buddhist gifts on parents' behalf or entering a Buddhist order to repay a parent for the favor and burden of one's upbringing, Chinese Buddhists engaged in a much broader range of filial activities than their Indian counterparts, eventually developing a unique repertoire of expressions of Buddhist filiality.

A key example of this is donations. The predominant gifts prior to the Tang dynasty were *Fozaoxiang* (Buddhist sculptures), which are amply evident at the Longmen 龍門, Yungang 雲崗, and Dunhuang 敦煌 Grottoes.[9] *Fozaoxiang* usually consisted of Buddhist statues or relief carvings that included inscriptions stating the purpose of the donation, the donor's name, and the beneficiary's name. Naming one's parents as the beneficiaries of the pious act of commissioning Buddhist sculpture was certainly more in line with the Indian tradition than with Chinese ancestor rituals, as such a practice was unheard of before the Han dynasty (202 BCE–220 CE).[10] Prior to the introduction of these Buddhist traditions, filial piety in China was chiefly manifested through ancestor-worship rituals and through everyday reverence of and obedience to living parents. Buddhist notions of "transference of merit" (*zhuifu* 追福), both in this life and in subsequent ones, were completely absent from the indigenous Chinese worldview. Donating gifts to a person or institution other than one's own parents and ancestors as an act of filial piety was nonexistent in early Chinese tradition. The large number of surviving Buddhist sculptures, however, proves that the Chinese quickly accepted the idea that such donations, though not being offered to the ancestors directly, would in fact greatly benefit those ancestors, as the merit from the generosity and devotion expressed by the donor was applied to the eternal well-being of the persons named by the donor.[11]

While the popularity of donating Buddhist sculptures (attesting to the success of Buddhism in early medieval China) was unprecedented, the overwhelming embrace of such expressions of Buddhist filiality by the Chinese is nevertheless understandable. If entering the monastic order might well appear to critics as an abandonment of filial duty,[12] donating gifts to benefit one's parents would not seem to be much of a departure from the ancestor-worship tradition. However, a close reading of the donation inscriptions shows that there is a difference between early India (first to fifth centuries CE) and early medieval China in terms of the individual donors:

Chinese women were more actively involved in such filial expressions than their Indian counterparts. Even though Buddhist women in early India were active donors,[13] and they held the same property rights as their male counterparts,[14] Buddhist monks far outnumbered nuns among the filial donors.[15] In contrast, Buddhist nuns in early medieval China clearly played a very dynamic role in *Fozaoxiang* donations: a large number of recorded donors in the Longmen Grottoes, Yungang Grottoes, and Dunhuang Grottoes were Buddhist nuns. In the case of the Longmen Grottoes, nuns outnumbered monks as the *Fozaoxiang* donors. Many empresses and palace ladies,[16] as well as elite and commoner laywomen, were enthusiastic *Fozaoxiang* donors as well. A recent study shows that laywomen, the majority of whom were commoners, accounted for a quarter of donors during the Sui (581–618) and Tang dynasties.[17] In addition, *Fozaoxiang* inscriptions indicate that parents outnumbered any other type of beneficiaries of the donations.[18]

During the Tang dynasty, while donating Buddhist sculptures continued to be a dominant form of transferring merit to ancestors, donating *xiejing* 寫經, or Buddhist sutra copies, on behalf of parents emerged and became increasingly popular.[19] Not surprisingly, Buddhist women constituted a sizeable percentage of *xiejing* donors, as among donors of *Fozaoxiang*.[20] In addition, the new practice of erecting Buddhist sutra steles (*zunsheng jingchuang* 尊勝經幢) took root, again with many steles intended to transfer merit to parents.[21] Yet another important development during this period was the practice of building funeral pagodas (*futu*) and cremation stupas (*huishenta*) for parents. These practices are clearly much more in line with Chinese ancestor worship than with the Indian practice of Buddhist filiality, as they do not seem to have a parallel to the Indian tradition of stupas serving as monumental reliquaries for relics of Buddhist "saints."[22] Since donations of Buddhist sutra copies and steles have been well documented and examined by scholars, this chapter will focus only on funeral inscriptions found on Buddhist pagodas (*futuming* 浮圖銘) and on cremation stupas (*huishentaming* 灰身塔銘, or *huishengtaji* 灰身塔記).

*Futuming* was usually carved on a stone pagoda. These pagodas often had Buddhist images and were built next to a deceased parent's tomb. It seems both men and women were enthusiastic participants in building pagodas and stupas for their parents, especially in the Chang'an and Luoyang regions.[23] However, existing data reveal that women were an important driving force behind the practice: the inscriptions dedicated to mothers by their daughters outnumber the ones that were dedicated to parents by their sons. Such a trend is best represented by one of the recent discoveries of *futu* donation for parents. The stone pagoda with an inscription entitled

"Inscriptions of Jiao Daniang Building Stone Pagoda" (Jiao Daniang zao futuming ji 焦大娘造浮圖銘記) was excavated in the summer of 2006 in Luoyang, Henan Province. The flat surface is 73 cm in height and 30 cm in width. It has one carved image of Buddha and two carved images of Bodhisattvas. Underneath is an eight-line inscription, which reads,

> Died on the nineteenth day of the fifth month, tenth year (722) of the Kaiyuan reign of the Great Tang. [The deceased] was commoner Liu Erniang of Linzhi Township, Luoyang District. The stone *futu* was built on the tomb site and recorded in inscription. [It was] Jiao Daniang who resolved to erect this for her mother. [It was] completed on the twenty-seventh day of the second month, the eleventh year (723) of the Kaiyuan reign.
>
> 大唐開元十年五月十九日．亡洛陽縣麟趾鄉百姓劉二娘造石浮圖在于墓所，銘記焦大娘爲母發心造．開元十一年二月廿七日成.[24]

While the language of this inscription is quite plain, or even colloquial, we do notice two very distinctive phrases in the text: *faxin* 發心 and *zao* 造. Both terms were prevalent in the inscription texts that record a Buddhist donation. *Faxin* implies an earnest intention to attain enlightenment for the sake of saving other sentient beings, as well as to give a donation. *Zao*, to build or to construct, usually indicates the result of such a *faxin*. "Inscriptions of Jiao Daniang Building Stone Pagoda" is thus an excellent example of how Buddhist filiality was expressed through such dedications and a testimony of a close mother-daughter bond within the medieval Chinese Buddhist tradition.

To this day, Tang cremation stupas have been found only at Bao shan 寶山, located near Anyang in Henan Province. A total of 155 stupas have been discovered, dating from the Sui dynasty to the Northern Song (960–1127), with a majority of them from the Tang period.[25] The cremation stupa inscriptions bear witness that during the Tang dynasty, building such stupas for the ashes of deceased parents was also utilized as an act of donation that would transfer merit to those parents. Among the six Baoshan *huishentai* inscriptions that were dedicated to a parent,[26] four of them used *zao* to identify the process,[27] and two used *qi* 起,[28] to raise. *Qi* is another commonly used word in Buddhist texts recording a donation. Even though the number of surviving Tang cremation stupas is very small, the texts do reflect the large trends that are evident in other genres discussed in this chapter. Among six *huishentaming* texts, three of them list daughters building cremation stupas for mothers,[29] one records sons and daughters erecting a stupa for their mother,[30] one details a daughter's effort to commemorate her father,[31] and one features male siblings' filial action toward their father.[32] Altogether, four such stupas were dedicated to mothers and two to fathers. Five such donations involved daughters, while two involved sons. Among the daughters, three were Buddhist nuns.[33]

The earliest Tang cremation stupa inscription was dated the eighth day of the second month, the nineteenth year (645) of the Zhenguan 貞觀 reign (627–649). Titled "Cremation Stupa Inscription for the *Upāsikā*, the Pure and Faithful Woman of Dashen" (Gu qingxinnü Dashen youpoyi huishentaji 故清信女大申優婆夷灰身塔記), it recounts that the stupa was "respectfully" (*jing* 敬) built by the *upāsikā*'s (*youpoyi* 優婆夷)[34] three daughters to commemorate their "loving mother" (*cimu* 慈母).[35] A more detailed *huishentaji* was dated a year later (646) and dedicated to Sun Baiyue 孫佰悅,[36] the magistrate of Hongdong 洪洞 District, Jin 晉 Prefecture, by his daughter, nun Zhijue 智覺 of the Shengdao 聖道 Convent. The inscription explicates that Sun Baiyue, an *upāsakā* (*youposai* 優婆塞),[37] died during the Sui dynasty and did not have a proper funeral. On the fifteenth day of the tenth month, the twentieth year (646) of the Zhenguan reign period, nun Zhijue had the cremation stupa constructed in Baoshan to express her gratitude to her father for his "kindness in giving [her] life" (*shengyu zhi en* 生育之恩) and to commemorate his "path toward enlightenment" (*jietuo zhi lu* 解脫之路).[38]

The aforementioned two types of funeral inscriptions demonstrate that the Buddhist ideal of filial piety clearly found an extremely receptive environment in Chinese society. However, such practices, along with other expressions of Buddhist filiality (such as donating Buddhist sculptures and Buddhist sutra copies on behalf of parents), eventually became fully developed by Chinese practitioners and constituted a unique system distinctive from the Confucian filial piety ethos and with a broader range of filial components than the original/Indian Buddhist tradition.[39] It is in this sense that I consider it appropriate to identify this repertory of expressions and practices as Chinese Buddhist filiality. In addition, as I have argued earlier and discuss further in the next two sections, unlike their counterparts in early India, Buddhist nuns and laywomen in medieval China played an extremely important role in the shaping of Buddhist filiality. Their active participation also generated a further unique aspect of Chinese Buddhist filiality when compared with either Confucian filial piety or Indian Buddhism: the emphasis on the mother-daughter bond both in lived religious practice and as the relationship that was imagined to embody the most perfect forms of ethical behavior.

## Filial Buddhist Daughters

Another new development of Buddhist filiality during the Tang was depicting Buddhist daughters as embodiments of filial piety. Filial daughters and daughters-in-law had all along been an element of Buddhist discourse on filiality. However, in early Chinese Buddhist literature, filial girls were often the product of parental admonition, or in some cases, the result of the Buddha's intervention.[40] During the sixth century, hagiographies of Buddhist nuns, notably Baochang's *Biqiuni zhuan*, began to celebrate Buddhist daughters' extraordinary filial actions.[41] By the Tang dynasty, a daughter's or daughter-in-law's filial acts in everyday life, though resembling the Confucian ideal for a young woman, were often viewed as manifestations of their inner Buddha nature. Taking an epitaph from the Tianbao 天寶 reign (742–756) as an example, the deceased Pei Fumin 裴夫民, a Buddhist laywoman, was said to be "extremely filial in nature" (*xing zhi xiao* 性至孝) as a young girl, and this was considered a sign of her Buddha nature. The epitaph recounts that, on one occasion, her paternal uncle remarked to relatives that Pei Fumin's appearance clearly resembled that of a Bodhisattva:

> This daughter has purple-blue hair and lotus eyes, delicate fingers and refined bearing. Her filial piety comes from the inner heart; her kindness resembles Buddha nature. Are these not the marks of a Bodhisattva? Are these not the virtues that were planted in her previous life?
>
> 此女紺髮蓮目, 柔指儀形, 孝出冥心, 慈稟佛性. 豈非菩薩相好, 宿殖德本歟?[42]

The phrases "purple-blue hair" (*ganfa* 紺髮) and "lotus eyes" (*lianmu* 蓮目) were traditionally used to describe the Buddha's appearance, and the term "mark" (*xianghao* 相好) originally indicated the primary and secondary marks of the Buddha's body but later was broadened to describe the excellent characteristics of an enlightened being. This passage, thus, clearly suggests that Pei Fumin's filial piety resulted from her Buddha nature.

In some cases, a daughter would enter a Buddhist order in the later stages of her life to repay the kindness of her parents or her mother- and father-in-law. A Tianbao era epitaph titled "Da Tang gu Hanshi Liufuren muzhiming bing xu" 大唐故韓氏劉夫人墓誌銘並序,[43] for example, tells of how the deceased Liu 劉[44] entered the Shengshan 聖善 Convent after her husband passed away and her two sons had reached adulthood. The epitaph also states that her determination was due to her desire to repay the virtue of her parents and her mother- and father-in-law.

Further examples of daughters-in-law demonstrating Buddhist filiality along the lines of Liu's actions are abundant. An eighth-century epitaph for a young wife reports that the deceased Lu Ying 陸英 was born into an official family that was known for having produced generations of Confucian scholars. Lu Ying nevertheless was said to be so bright and intuitive that from a young age she refused to eat meat or wear silk garments. Furthermore, during her girlhood, Lu Ying "stopped reading Ban Zhao's 班昭 (45–116) *Lessons for Women* (*Nüjie* 女誡) altogether and cultivated a deep interest in Buddhist sutras" (*chuojuan Nüjie shenhao Fojing* 輟卷女誡, 深好佛經).[45] Ban Zhao's *Lessons for Women* is of course the single most important Confucian didactic book for women in traditional China.[46] Because of her Buddhist faith and conduct, all her relatives looked up to her as a role model, and her compassionate traits were considered especially suited to her role in the household. Indeed, when her husband was appointed to a regional office, she insisted on staying home and fulfilling her duty as a "filial daughter-in-law" (*xiaofu* 孝婦). The epitaph thus proclaims that her "filial deeds were unmatched" (*xiaoxing nan qi* 孝行難齊) in all of Chinese history.

The most detailed story of a filial daughter-in-law was Lady Xue 薛, who passed away in 696 at the age of seventy. It recounts that Xue's mother-in-law was once critically ill and no medicine could cure her. Xue, with her pure faith, recited the *Lotus Sutra* (*Miaofa lianhuajing* 妙法蓮花經) ceaselessly. Her mother-in-law soon recovered completely, and all the relatives attributed this restoration of health to Xue's "ultimate filial piety" (*zhixiao* 至孝).[47]

The representations of Buddhist daughters in Tang epitaphs show that Tang society readily considered young women as embodiments of filial piety and that their actions were often perceived as being inspirational to others. One such exemplar was the daughter of Li Jin 李津 of the Dali 大曆 reign period (766–779). The epitaph, titled "Epitaph for the Late Mr. Li of the Great Tang" (Da Tang gu Ligong muzhiming bing xu 大唐故李公墓誌銘並序),[48] is dedicated to Li Jin, a failed civil service examination candidate. While the author, Li's brother-in-law, named Cui Yuanyang 崔元陽, dutifully recorded Li Jin's family background and his virtues, he nevertheless emphasized that his real purpose of writing this epitaph was to document the filial act of Li Jin's daughter, a Buddhist nun.[49] Li Jin apparently died in the Wu 吳 region and was temporarily buried in Linan 臨安. Even though it was a time of chaos, Li Jin's daughter was determined to escort his coffin back and have him properly buried in the family cemetery in Luoyang. Upon hearing this, her uncle, Li Jiang 李江, was moved to tears and eventually completed the task. It seems the story became widespread and that "public opinion" (*junzi yue* 君子曰) was very positive, rendering "the nun daughter utterly filial" (*nizi chunxiao ye* 尼子純孝也), so much so that her "love for her father even affected [her uncle] Jiang" (*ai qi fu shijiyu Jiang* 愛其父施及於江). In the eulogy section of the epitaph, the author exclaims: "I also wish to have a daughter" (*yi yuan sheng nü* 亦願生女).[50]

Why did Tang texts overwhelmingly portray Buddhist daughters as the embodiment of filial piety?[51] I assume this is due to the combination of three sociocultural factors. First, among eminent families, especially the so-called five grand last names (*wu daxing* 五大姓), who produced a great amount of epitaphs, more daughters than sons entered Buddhist orders, with the result that descriptions of filial Buddhist daughters numerically far exceed those of filial Buddhist sons.[52] Second, during the Tang, Buddhist daughters did in fact take on more filial responsibilities than Buddhist sons did. Chinese scholars have discovered ample evidence that among the Buddhist renunciants, nuns had a much closer tie with their secular families than monks did.[53] One obvious example of this is *zhujiani* 住家尼, stay-at-home nuns who carried on their familial duties. Existing Tang texts contain many cases of such stay-at-home nuns, but we have yet to find any evidence of a *zhujiaseng* 住家僧 (stay-at-home monk).[54] In addition, it seems that the families of Buddhist nuns were more likely than the families of Buddhist monks to write an epitaph for the deceased.[55] Third, praising a Buddhist daughter, rather than a Buddhist son, as an exemplar of filial piety might be a more acceptable proposition among the Confucian elite: it extolled Buddhist filiality without having to elucidate why a monk's leaving home (and not having an heir) should be celebrated as a filial action.

The key to such a trend is, nevertheless, Buddhist daughters' filial actions. In this sense, the writings about their filiality are more a record of their own agency than a reflection of the Tang male elite's prescription for womanly conduct.[56] It is also worth noting that scholars have linked the transformation of gender (from male to female) of Avalokiteśvara (Guanyin 觀音) to the popular legend of Princess Miaoshan 妙善, whose Buddhist faith and filiality were the salvation of her father.[57] I would venture to argue that the long history of the daughter as an embodiment of filial piety during the Tang era probably laid the groundwork both for Guanyin's transformation around the tenth century and for the popularity of the Miaoshan legend.

Tellingly, a Kaiyuan (713–741) era epitaph reveals that not only was Guanyin already readily accepted as a female during the Tang, but Tang people even entertained the image of a female Śākyamuni Buddha. The epitaph, authored by Tang official Yang Xiulie 楊休烈 (fl. 737), was titled "Epitaph for Buddhist Nun Huiyuan, the Dharma Master of the Jidu Convent" (Da Tang Jidusi gu Dade biqiuni Huiyuan heshang shenkong zhi ming 大唐濟度寺故大德比邱尼惠源和尚神空誌銘). It commemorates the life of the nun Huiyuan 惠源 (663–737), a great-granddaughter of the Xiaoming 孝明 Emperor of the Liang dynasty (502–557). Huiyuan was said to be known for her filial actions before she entered the Jidu 濟度 Convent at the age of twenty-two *sui*. Huiyuan's father died when she was nine and she lost her mother during her nunnery years. The epitaph reports that her filial piety, expressed through endless mourning, far exceeded that of the filial sons of ancient times (*gu zhi xiaozi wu zu dao zai* 古之孝子乌足道哉). In fact, throughout her life, she never forgot her filial feelings (*buwang xiao* 不忘孝).[58] The epitaph further purports that

> then there was a nun whose dharma name was Cihe [Benevolent Harmony], and the mundane did not know her true identity. She [had the ability of] auguring the unknown and channeling the divine and was not inhibited by the realm of forms and matter. Her contemporaries called her Bodhisattva Guanyin. Cihe once gazed at Master (Huiyuan) who was among many people and called out: The Sixteenth Monk. [The Sixteenth Monk] was in fact the Original Teacher in the *Lotus Sutra*; it was an old title name of Śākyamuni.
>
> 又有尼慈和者, 世莫之識, 知微通神, 見色無礙, 時人謂之觀音菩薩. 嘗於大眾中目大師曰: 十六沙彌. 即法華中本師, 釋迦牟尼之往號也.

Such overly apotheosized reaction to Nun Huiyuan's reputation as a filial daughter reflects the fact that the Tang dynasty was more than ready to credit women for their contribution in the formation of Buddhist filiality.

## The Mother's Role in Defining Buddhist Filiality

Epitaph writings also reveal that a Tang mother exerted a great influence in defining Buddhist filiality. Such agency is reflected foremost in a mother's role in her children's religious paths. Quite a few Tang epitaphs record that the children of Buddhist mothers eventually followed their mother's admonition and entered a Buddhist order. An epitaph from the early Tang period records that the deceased Lady Yang 楊 had long been interested in Buddhism and often immersed herself in reading sutras. Under her influence,

> her daughter[s] left home and entered a Buddhist order, while her son[s] cultivated himself [themselves] in the supreme way [of Buddha]. The entire household accumulated merits, and everyone was moral and upright.
>
> 夫人女則出家景福，男則恒修上道，合門積善，咸有直方.[59]

In another epitaph, Lady Moqi 万俟, who died in 740, is said to have been a devotee of Chan Buddhism; "following their mother's instructions and admonitions" (*sui mushi xunhui* 隨母師訓誨), all of her three children, two sons and a daughter, "determined to observe the precepts and regulations of the Buddha" (*zhi fawang jielü* 志法王戒律).[60] Additionally, many children were clearly pressured by their mothers to take the vow at a young age. Zhang Zhen 張軫 of the Kaiyuan period, for example, entered the monastery at the age of nine *sui* to fulfill "his mother's lifelong wish" (*mu suyuan* 母宿願).[61] In addition, a recently excavated epitaph reports that in the mid-seventh century, both a mother and a daughter from a Wang 王 household entered a Buddhist order. The "Epitaph for the Late Nun Zhihong of the Ningcha Convent, a Distant Aunt of the Emperor of the Great Tang" (Da Tang huang zaicongzugu gu Ningcha si biqiuni Zhihong muzhiming bing xu 大唐皇再從祖姑故寧刹寺比丘尼志弘墓誌銘並)[62] commemorates the life of Nun Zhihong 志弘, a great-granddaughter of Emperor Gaozong (r. 649–683). Zhihong had been married to Wang Liang 王諒, a high-ranking official and the author of the epitaph. The couple had five sons and three daughters. Long a Buddhist believer, Zhihong was ordained at the age of fifty-five *sui*, presumably when all eight children had reached adulthood. Her second daughter, whose dharma name was Wuzhen 悟真, followed suit. Having been married to an official named Li Bao 李保, Wuzhen also chose to leave home and become a Buddhist nun.

Some epitaphs purport that during the Tang, laywomen who sent their children to Buddhist monasteries were lauded as exemplars of ultimate filiality. In one such case, "Epitaph for Song, Wife of Mr. Wang, Assistant District Magistrate of the Ren District, Xing Prefecture" (Tang gu Xingzhou Renxianzhubu Wangjun furen Songshi zhi muzhiming bing xu 唐故邢州任縣主簿王君夫人宋氏之墓誌銘並序), Song was praised for saving her son by sending him to be a monk. In so doing, the epitaph claims, she extended her filial duty to several generations of ancestors. The mother, Song Nizi 宋尼子, was upheld as the paragon of a virtuous woman and characterized as being even more sage than the mother of Mencius (Mengmu 孟母). The epitaph discounts the canonical Confucian female paragon as someone whose only accomplishment was cutting the loom (*wei shi duanji* 唯事斷機). In comparison, the epitaph commends Song as one who "always remembered the kindness of those [ancestors] who have passed away" (*chang huai jiwang zhi qing* 長懷既往之情).[63]

Tang epitaphs for Buddhist mothers show that not only had Buddhist women become part of the discourse on Buddhist filiality, but they also used filial piety as a "token of reason" for their goal. In numerous cases, Buddhist mothers demanded that their children obey their dying wish as to what a filial child should do. Song Nizi certainly played such a role well. The epitaph for Song, who died of illness in 691, records such a deathbed scene:

> Before her death she instructed her sons: "My heart has followed Buddhism and my emotions are remote from the mundane world. Even though I did not leave the household, I have long wished to enter the order. You are all filial sons and should understand what I have reasoned. In ancient times, royal daughters and consorts did not follow the kings to wild fields;[64] even royal members and nobles barely had a burial. Returning the body to nature was the goal; joint burial, thus, differs from the ancient tradition. Since one should transform oneself along with the Dao, what purpose can a joint burial serve? I wish to have a coffin just big enough for my size and clothes just enough to cover my body. If you can fulfill my wish, then I will die without worry."
>
> 臨終之際, 謂諸子曰: 吾心依釋教, 情遠俗塵, 雖非出家, 恒希入道. 汝爲孝子, 思吾理言. 昔帝女賢妃, 尚不從於蒼野; 王孫達士, 猶靡隔于黃壚. 歸骸反真, 合葬非古. 與道而化, 同穴何爲? 棺周於身, 衣足以斂. 不奪其志, 死亦無憂.

In reiterating her Buddhist faith while affirming her sons as "filial" children, Song Nizi assumed not only that filial sons would follow Buddhist practices, but also that filial piety was implicitly a part of Buddhist teaching. In this sense, Song's life exemplifies how Tang society came to terms with Buddhist filiality. Such demands must have been quite common during the Tang, as some epitaphs show that in cases when a Buddhist mother did not leave instructions for her burial, her children would strive to make the arrangements that they considered would best reflect their mother's wishes in the name of filial piety.[65]

Scholars have noted that Tang Buddhism very much reflected a paternal model of discipline, both in family and in monastic life, where Buddhist filiality flourished. Meanwhile mothers have often been depicted as passively dependent, as being on the receiving end of a son's filial heroism.[66] Tang epitaphs, however, present to us a much more complex and richer narrative of Buddhist filiality. Buddhist mothers were not merely victims but active agents, heroines, and commanders. Tang mothers' Buddhist faith also greatly influenced their children's religious beliefs and behaviors as well as their life path. In contrast to this, in epitaphs for Buddhist laymen, fathers were rarely praised for their influence on their children and never for their filial piety. There are about a dozen published epitaphs for men that specify that the deceased were Buddhist believers; most of these did not mention their marriages. Of the two epitaphs that mentioned children, one does reveal that this Buddhist layman's daughter entered a Buddhist order;[67] the other, however, recounts that the deceased turned to Buddhism only after he instructed his adult son to seek an official career and get married.[68]

## Conclusion

This chapter examines the evolution of Chinese Buddhist filiality as well as women's roles in this process. Although Buddhist filiality was a borrowed tradition, from very early on its Chinese version developed a unique array of manifestations. Chinese Buddhist filiality matured into a much-affirmed ideal and practice during the Tang. While donating Buddhist sculptures reflected a practice of filial piety that came along with the importation of Buddhism, by the Tang era Chinese Buddhists had expanded the donation repertoire to include sutra copies and sutra stele. In addition, nuns and laywomen were evidently the driving force behind such elaborate efforts in honoring parents. Such endeavors were also apparent among funeral pagodas and cremation stupas constructed on behalf of deceased parents; both were new phenomena that probably were inspired by traditional practices of ancestor worship. More importantly, the unique social-cultural dynamics of the Tang—as revealed in the contents of elite epitaphs and in the fact that more daughters than sons of the elite entered monastic orders—resulted in Buddhist daughters' filial actions being glorified and Buddhist mothers' demands being duly obeyed. In addition, Tang epitaphs as well as funeral inscriptions reflect a close bond between mothers and daughters, a unique phenomenon that deserves a study of its own. All these point to the fact that Tang women were unequivocally recognized as paramount players in the transformation of Buddhist filiality in China.

## Notes

1. Kenneth K. S. Ch'en is the first scholar who suggested that filial piety occupied a special place in Chinese Buddhism and that such an emphasis was key for Buddhism to make inroads into Chinese society during the period when it was first introduced. See Ch'en, "Filial Piety in Chinese Buddhism," *Harvard Journal of Asiatic Studies* 28 (1968): 81–97; and Ch'en, *Chinese Transformation of Buddhism* (Princeton: Princeton University Press, 1973), especially 14–64. Another often-cited study is Jan Yün-hua's "The Role of Filial Piety in Chinese Buddhism: A Reassessment," in which Jan argues that filial piety was a minor merit in Buddhist ethics in India but became a supreme virtue in China; see Charles Wei-hsin Fu and Sandra A. Wawrytko, eds., *Buddhist Ethics and Modern Society* (New York: Greenwood Press, 1991), 27–39. See also Jan Yün-hua 冉雲華, "Zhongguo Fojiao dui xiaodao de shuorong ji houguo" 中國佛教對孝道的受容及後果, in Jan, *Cong Yindu Fojiao dao Zhongguo Fojiao* 從印度佛教到中國佛教 (Taibei: Dongda tushu, 1995), 42–55. In addition, in her study of the epitaph for the nun Wei Qiyi 韋契義, Cheng Ya-ju 鄭雅如 suggests that the epitaph reflects a Tang ideal of filial piety: in leaving home, Qiyi exemplified Buddhist filiality; by being buried in her clan cemetery, Qiyi returned home and would serve her parents in the afterlife. See Cheng, "Wei Qiyi muzhiming shidu jianlun Tangren de xiaodao yishi" 韋契義墓誌銘釋讀: 兼論唐人的孝道意識, *Zaoqi Zhongguo shi yanjiu* 早期中國史研究 1 (2009): 63–80.

2. Stephen Teiser, for example, finds that the ghost festival, centered on Mulian's heroic journey to save his mother from hell, was able to diffuse through the entire fabric of medieval Chinese society because it affirmed filial devotion, the motivating ideal of mainstream Chinese life. See Teiser, *The Ghost Festival in Medieval China* (Princeton: Princeton University Press, 1988). Alan Cole suggests that Buddhism was able to make such deep inroads into Chinese society and culture

because it utilized the emotional and uninstitutionalized bond between mothers and sons, as exemplified by the Mulian story. See Cole, *Mothers and Sons in Chinese Buddhism* (Stanford: Stanford University Press, 1998).

3. John Strong, "Filial Piety and Buddhism: The Indian Antecedents to a 'Chinese' Problem," in Peter Slater et al., eds., *Traditions in Contact and Change: Selected Proceedings of the XIVth Congress of the International Association for the History of Religions* (Waterloo, Ontario: Canadian Corporation for Studies in Religion, Wilfred Laurier University Press, 1983), 171–86.

4. Gregory Schopen, "Filial Piety and the Monks in the Practices of Indian Buddhism: A Question of Sinicization Viewed from the Other Side," *T'oung Pao* 70 (1984): 110–26.

5. Guang Xing, "Filial Piety in Early Buddhism," *Journal of Buddhist Ethics* 12 (2005): 82–106. See also Guang Xing 廣興, "Ru Fo xiaodaoguan de bijiao yanjiu" 儒佛孝道觀的比較研究, in Liu Xiaogan 劉笑敢 and Kawada Yoichi 川田洋一, eds., *Ru Shi Dao zhi zhexue duihua* 儒釋道之哲學對話 (Hong Kong: Shangwu yinshuguan, 2007), 121–53. A few Chinese scholars also pointed out that the teaching of filial piety existed in early Indian Buddhist texts, especially *The Syama Sutra* (*Shanzi jing* 睒子經), in which the filial son, Syama, would eventually be included in *Ershisixiao zhuan* 二十四孝傳 during the Song dynasty (960–1279). See Li Xiaorong 李小榮, "Lüelun Dunhuang bianwen zhong de xiaoqin sixiang" 略論敦煌變文中的孝親思想, *Yancheng shifan xueyuan xuebao* 鹽城師範學院學報 2 (2000): 19–22; and Xie Shengbao 謝生保, "Cong *Shanzi jing bian* kan Fojiao yishu zhong de xiaodao sixiang" 從睒子經變看佛教藝術中的孝道思想, *Dunhuang yanjiu* 敦煌研究 68 (2001): 42–50. Most recently, James Benn finds that Indian Buddhist stories were the source for some of the narratives of filial children appearing in *Ershisixiao zhuan*. See Benn, *Burning for Buddha: Self-Immolations in Chinese Buddhism*, Studies in East Asian Buddhism 19, Kuroda Institute (Honolulu: University of Hawaii Press, 2007), 138.

6. In a recent article, Chinese scholar Wu Fuxiu 吴福秀 briefly notes that even though filial piety was a core tenet of Buddhist teaching before it was introduced to China, Indian Buddhist filiality was notably different from filial piety in the Chinese tradition in that Indian Buddhism places filiality toward mother ahead of filiality toward father. See Wu, "Lun Fojing zhong de xiaoqinguan jiqi Zhongguohua" 論佛經中的孝親觀及其中國化, *Xiangfan xueyuan xuebao* 襄樊學院學報 29.4 (2008): 9–12. Such differences are also discussed in Guang Xing's 2007 essay, "Ru Fo xiaodaoguan," and Bret Hinsch's "Confucian Filial Piety and the Construction of the Ideal Chinese Buddhist Woman," *Journal of Chinese Religions* 30 (2002): 49–76. Most recently, Liu Shu-fen 劉淑芬 finds that Buddhist filiality serves a much broader range of beneficiaries, including seven generations of ancestors and Buddhist teachers. See Liu, "Tang Song shiqi de gongdesi yi: canhui yishi wei zhongxin de taolun" 唐宋時期的功德寺：以懺悔儀式為中心的討論, *Zhongyang yanjiu lishi yuyuan yanjiusuo jikan* 中央研究院歷史語言研究所集刊 82.2 (2011): 261–323.

7. Hinsch, "Confucian Filial Piety," 49–76.

8. In a recently published article, Victor H. Mair presented a lengthy discussion on the assertion that early Buddhist monks and scholars inserted Chinese concepts into their translations. Mair considers such interpretation misleading and distorted. See Mair, "What Is *Geyi*, After All?" in Alan K. L. Chan and Yuet-Keung Lo, eds., *Philosophy and Religion in Early Medieval China* (Albany: State University of New York Press, 2010), 227–64, especially 241–47.

9. For discussions on Buddhist sculptures from these periods, see Fong Chow, "Chinese Buddhist Sculpture," *The Metropolitan Museum of Art Bulletin*, New Series 23.9 Part 1 (1965): 301–24; Stanley Abe, "Art and Practice in a Fifth-Century Chinese Buddhist Cave Temple," *Ars Orientalis* 20 (1990): 1–31; Alexander C. Soper, "Imperial Cave-Chapels of the Northern Dynasties: Donors, Beneficiaries, Dates," *Artibus Asiae* 28.4 (1966): 241–70; and Eileen Hsiang-Ling Hsu, "Visualization Meditation and the Siwei Icon in Chinese Buddhist Sculpture," *Artibus Asiae* 62.1 (2002): 5–32. Soper's essay briefly mentions that some donations were made by members (both male and female) of royal families on behalf of their parents and that it was mostly a reflection of Confucian values of filial piety (258–61). Hsu's essay concurs with this argument (16). The most important work on *Fozaoxiang* is Amy McNair's *Donors of Longmen: Faith, Politics, and Patronage in Medieval Chinese Buddhist Sculpture* (Honolulu: University of Hawaii Press, 2007). It provides a detailed account of the history of the Longmen Grottoes between 493 and 730 as well as identities of the *Fozaoxiang* donors. In addition, Bret Hinsch's article "Confucian Filial Piety" (68–72) presents several important Longmen inscriptions recording female filial donors.

10. It is worth noting that while Gregory Schopen seems to imply a direct linkage between Indian donative practice and the Longmen Grottoes (Schopen, "Filial Piety," 110–26), John Brough contends that donatives in India and in China developed independently. See Brough, "A Kharosthi Inscription from China," *Bulletin of the School of Oriental and African Studies* 24 (1961): 517–30.

11. Robert Ford Campany suggests that behind such a readiness to accept the Buddhist ideal of transferring merit was the ancient Chinese view that "merit, guilt, and fortune were not only matters for individuals but were also collectively shared by the family, and not only its living but also some of its dead members." See Campany, *Making Transcendents: Ascetics and Social Memory in Early Medieval China* (Honolulu: University of Hawaii Press, 2009), 188.

12. For discussion of the early attacks on Buddhism, especially for its unfilial nature, see Chen Yifeng 陳一風, "Wei Jin Nan Bei chao shiqi Ru Fo de xiaodao zhi zheng" 魏晉南北朝時期儒佛的孝道之爭, *Nandu xuetan* 南都學壇 23.2 (2003): 23–27.

13. Vinay Kumar Rao's study of Buddhist monuments from the third century BCE to the third century CE shows that women were actively involved in donating money to propagate the Buddhist *dharma*. However, most of the donors opted to engrave the names, position, and social status of their children (especially sons) and their husbands. A few inscriptions mention parents or mothers- and fathers-in-law, but none of them indicates a filial expression. See Rao, "Women in Early Bud-

dhist Inscriptions," online documentation by Estonian Nyingma of Buddhism and Nordland conference, December 2010, http://budcon.com/index.php/2013-03-14-08-21-28/2013-03-15-11-40-47/articles/139-women-in-early-buddhist-inscriptions-by-vinay-kumar-rao (accessed August 7, 2011, and January 4, 2014).

14. Schopen's recent study shows that Buddhist nuns in early India enjoyed property rights equal to those of monks. See Schopen, "Separate but Equal: Property Rights and the Legal Independence of Buddhist Nuns and Monks in Early North India," *Journal of the American Oriental Society* 128.4 (2008): 625–40.

15. See Schopen, "Filial Piety," 110–26.

16. See McNair, "Sangha Donors," in McNair, *Donors of Longmen*, 56–59; and McNair, "Appendix: Chinese Texts of Longmen Inscriptions," in *Donors of Longmen*, 167–80.

17. See Li Xiaomin 李曉敏, "Zaoxiang ji: Sui Tang minzhong Fojiao xinyang chutan" 造像記: 隋唐民眾佛教信仰初探, *Zhengzhou daxue xuebao* 鄭州大學學報 (2007.1): 91–95. Among the 1,456 *Fozaoxiang* inscriptions in Li's data pool, 372 of them recorded female donors, while 234 inscriptions recorded that a woman was the sole donor.

18. See Li Xiaomin, "Zaoxiang ji," 94. Li's data indicates that 18.25 percent of the *Fozaoxiang* were dedicated to deceased parents. See also Bret Hinsch's discussion of female filial donors of Longmen Grottoes in his "Confucian Filial Piety," 49–76.

19. The most comprehensive collection of *xiejing* is Ikeda On's 池田溫 *Chūgoku kodai shahon shikigo shūroku* 中國古代寫本識語集錄 (Tokyo: Tokyo daigaku Tōyō bunka kenkyūjo, 1990), which contains 2,623 colophons dated from the Former Han (202 BCE–9 CE) to the eleventh century. The majority of the colophons are written on Buddhist sutras, documenting donors' names and intents. For studies of *xiejing* as a filial expression prior to the Tang, see Pan Zhonggui 潘重規, "Cong Dunhuang yishu kan Fojiao tichang xiaodao" 從敦煌遺書看佛教提倡孝道, Taiwan Zhongguo wenhua daxue 臺灣中國文化大學, *Huagang wenke xuebao* 華崗文科學报12 (1980): 197–268; and Liang Liling 梁麗玲, "Liuchao Dunhuang Fojiao xiejing de gongyang gongde guan" 六朝敦煌佛教寫經的供養功德觀, *Dunhuangxue* 敦煌學 22 (1999): 119–38. In addition, Hinsch's 2002 article provides an excellent translation of a colophon on *xiejing*, recording a Tang dynasty Buddhist nun donating a copy of the *Lotus Sutra* (*Fahuajing* 法華經) on behalf of her mother (Hinsch, "Confucian Filial Piety," 72).

20. Shi Xiaoying's 石小英 study of Tang copies of Buddhist sutras discovered in Dunhuang suggests that more nuns than monks made donations to their parents. See Shi, "Ba zhi shi shiji Dunhuang ni seng yu shisu jiating de guanxi" 八至十世紀敦煌尼僧與世俗家庭的關係, *Shijie zongjiao yanjiu* 世界宗教研究 1 (2009): 58–64.

21. In her comprehensive studies of Buddhist sutra steles, "Foding zunsheng tuoluonijing he Tangdai zunsheng jingchuang de jianli: jingchuang yanjiu zhiyi" 佛頂尊勝陀羅尼經和唐代尊勝經幢的建立: 經幢研究之一, *Zhongyang yanjiuyuan lishi yuyuan yanjiusuo jikan* 67.1 (1996): 145–93, and "Jingchuang de xingzhi, xingzhi he laiyuan: jingchuang yanjiu zhi er" 經幢的形制, 性質和來源: 經幢研

究之二, *Zhongyang yanjiuyuan lishi yuyuan yanjiu suo jikan* 68.3 (1997): 643–786, Liu Shu-fen confirms that sutra steles became popular during the mid-Tang period, and that many of these donations were related to transferring merits to parents, though she does not specify to what extent women participated in commissioning sutra steles.

22. Both Faxian 法顯 (ca. 337–422) and Xuanzang 玄奘 (602–664), the preeminent Chinese pilgrims to India, reported Indian Buddhist monks and nuns making offerings to cremation stupas of Buddhist saints in their respective works. See, for example, Guo Peng 郭鵬 et al., eds., *Foguo ji zhushi* 佛國記註釋 (Changchun: Changchun chubanshe, 1995), 54, 133–34; and Ji Xianlin 季羡林, ed., *Da Tang xiyu ji jiaozhu* 大唐西域記校註 (Beijing: Zhonghua shuju, 2000), 345, 368–69, especially 381–82.

23. In a recently published article, Zhang Naizhu 张乃翥 indicates that during the Tang dynasty, building funeral *futu* for parents was quite popular in the Zhongyuan 中原 region. See Zhang, "Luoyang xin ji shike suo jian Tangdai Zhongyuan zhi Fojiao" 洛陽新輯石刻所見唐代中原之佛教, *Zhongyuan wenwu* 中原文化 5 (2008): 81–93. Unfortunately, the article does not provide a detailed description of these funeral *futu*, nor does it give the total number or the locations of these inscriptions.

24. Zhang Naizhu, "Luoyang xin ji shike suo jian Tangdai Zhongyuan zhi Fojiao," 81–93.

25. For an overview of the site, see Henansheng gudai jianzhu baohu yanjiusuo 河南省古代建築保護研究所, ed., *Baoshan lingquansi* 寶山靈泉寺 (Zhengzhou: Henan renmin chubanshe, 1991); Ouchi Humio 大内文雄, "Hōzan Reisenji sekkutsu tomei no kenkyū: Zui-Tō jidai no Hōzan Reisenji" 宝山霊泉寺石窟塔銘の研究: 隋唐時代の宝山霊泉寺, *Tōhō gakuhō* 東方學報 69 (1997): 287–355; and Wang Zhongxu 王中旭, "Henan Anyang Lingquansi huishenta yanjiu" 河南安陽靈泉寺灰身塔研究 (master's thesis, China Central Academy of Fine Arts, 2006). In addition, Shu-fen Liu has studied the Baoshan burials extensively. See Liu, "Death and the Degeneration of Life: Exposure of the Corpse in Medieval Chinese Buddhism," *Journal of Chinese Religions* 28 (2000): 1–30; Liu, "Linzang: Zhonggu Fojiao lushizang yanjiu zhiyi" 林葬: 中古佛教露屍葬研究之一, *Dalu zazhi* 大陸雜誌 96.3 (1998): 22–136; and Liu, "Shishi cuoku: Zhonggu Fojiao lushizang yanjiu zhi'er" 石室瘞窟: 中古佛教露屍葬研究之二, *Dalu zazhi* 98.4 (1999): 49–152.

26. These six inscriptions are collected in Zhou Shaoliang 周紹良 and Zhao Chao 趙超, *Tangdai muzhi huibian* 唐代墓誌彙編 (Shanghai: Shanghai guji chubanshe, 1992), hereafter *HB*; and Zhou and Zhao, *Tangdai muzhi huibian xuji* 唐代墓誌彙編續集 (Shanghai: Shanghai guji chubanshe, 2002), hereafter *XJ*.

27. *HB*, Zhenguan 106; *XJ*, Zhenguan 070; *HB*, Xianqing 顯慶 061; *XJ*, Yonghui 永徽 031.

28. *HB*, Zhenguan 128; *XJ*, Linde 麟德 009.

29. *HB*, Zhenguan 106; *XJ*, Zhenguan 070; *XJ*, Xianqing 061.

30. *XJ*, Yonghui 031.

31. *HB*, Zhenguan 128.

32. *XJ*, Linde 009.

33. *XJ*, Zhenguan 070; *HB*, Zhenguan 128; *HB*, Xianqing 061. In *Tangdai taming yanjiu* 唐代塔銘研究 (master's thesis, Zhejiang University, 2010), Pan Gaofeng 潘高鳳 links nuns building cremation stupas to the close ties between Buddhist nuns and their families (44).

34. *Upāsikā*, or *youpoyi* 優婆夷 in Chinese transliteration, refers to a woman who took formal vows to observe the five precepts of Buddhism, refraining from killing, stealing, sexual misconduct, lying, and imbibing alcohol.

35. *HB*, Zhenguan 106; *HB*, Zhenguan 128; and *HB*, Xianqing 061.

36. Baiyue was Sun's courtesy name (*zi* 字).

37. *Upāsakā*, or *youposai* 優婆塞 in Chinese transliteration, refers to a man who took formal vows to observe the five precepts of Buddhism.

38. "Gu dayouposai Jinzhou Hongdongxianling Sun Baiyue huishentaiming" 故大優婆塞晉州洪洞縣令孫佰悅灰身塔銘, *HB*, Zhenguan 128.

39. Chinese scholars have pointed out another substantial transformation in Buddhist filiality during the Tang: filial piety became inseparable from Buddhist *sīla* or *jie* 戒 (behavioral discipline). Tang Buddhist masters Fazang 法藏 (643–712), Zongmi 宗密 (780–841), and Shenqing 神清 (d. 843), for example, all extensively discussed the relationship between *sīla* and filial piety. See Qiu Gaoxing 邱高興, "Xiao jie guanxi lun: Fojiao dui Zhongguo chuantong lunli guannian tiaohexing jieshi" 孝戒關係論: 佛教對中國傳統倫理觀念調和性解釋, *Shehui kexue zhanxian* 社會科學戰線 5 (2005): 24–29, especially 27–28. In addition, an important development during the Tang is the writing of the *Buddha Speaks the Sutra about the Deep Kindness of Parents and the Difficulty Repaying It* (*Fo shuo fumu en zhong nanbao jing* 佛說父母恩重難報經). The sutra had a profound influence in promoting Buddhist filiality; however, it was penned by Tang Buddhists and thus is not a translation of an original Buddhist sutra. For discussions on this sutra, see Li Chuanjun 李傳軍 and Jin Xia 金霞, "*Fumu en zhong jing* yu Tangdai xiaowenhua: jiantan Fojiao zhongguohua guocheng zhong de tongru yu jisu xianxiang" "父母恩重經" 與唐代孝文化: 兼談佛教中國化過程中的 "通儒" 與 "濟俗" 現象, *Kongzi yanjiu* 孔子研究 3 (2008): 90–96. Li and Jin argue that the creation of such a sutra reflects the Tang court's intention to uphold Confucian filial tradition and the Buddhists' willingness to accept Confucian dominance, and that Tang Buddhists welcomed Sinification since they were aware that Buddhism lacked filiality as one of its core values (93).

40. See Yuet-Keung Lo, "Filial Devotion for Women: A Buddhist Testimony from Third-Century China," in Alan Chan and Sor Hoon Tan, eds., *Filial Piety in Chinese Thought and History* (New York: RoutledgeCurzon, 2004), 71–90; and Lo, "Recovering a Buddhist Voice on Daughters-in-Law: The *Yuyenü Jing*," *History of Religions* 44 (2005): 318–50.

41. Hinsch, "Confucian Filial Piety," 49–76.

42. "Da Tang gu Sizhou cishi Langyewang qi Hedong Pei junjun Fumin muzhiming bing xu" 大唐故泗州刺史琅耶王妻河東裴郡君夫民墓誌銘並序, *HB*, Tianbao 078.

43. The epitaph was first published in Zhao Zhenhua 趙振華, "Luoyang xinchu biqiuni muzhi yu Tangdai Dongdu Shengshansi" 洛陽新出比丘尼墓誌與唐代東都聖善寺, *Luoyang shi zhi* 洛陽史誌 3 (2005): 13–20.

44. Liu's dharma name was Huiru 會如, and her title name Jingangshan 金剛山. In Zhao's essay, the deceased was misidentified as Jingang 金剛 (Zhao, "Luoyang xinchu biqiuni muzhi"). Shiying Pang was the first scholar who correctly identified her as Jingangshan 金剛山. See Pang, "Familial Identity and Buddhist Nuns in Tang China: A Study of Tomb Inscriptions" (master's thesis, University of Santa Barbara, 1999), 47n76.

45. "Tang Jinyunjun sima Jia Chongzhang furen Lushi muzhiming bing xu" 唐縉雲郡司馬賈崇璋夫人陸氏墓誌銘並序, *HB*, Tianbao 200.

46. For a study of Ban Zhao's life and a full-text translation of her *Lessons for Women*, see Nancy Lee Swann, *Pan Chao: Foremost Woman Scholar of China* (Ann Arbor: Center for Chinese Studies, University of Michigan, 2001).

47. "Yingzhou Wenanxianling Wangfujun Zhou gu furen Xueshi muzhiming bing xu 瀛州文安縣令王府君周故夫人薛氏墓誌銘並序," *HB*, Wansuitongtian 萬歲通天 014.

48. *HB*, Dali 018.

49. Unfortunately even though her Buddhist name was recorded, the epitaph was not in good condition when it was excavated. Only the first character of her name, Zhen 真, is recognizable.

50. *HB*, Dali 018.

51. It is worth noting that privileging the daughter as the embodiment of filial piety was not a uniquely Tang phenomenon. In her study of filial piety in Korea, JaHyun Kim Haboush presents a rather similar case: in Late Choson Korea, daughters instead of sons embodied the utmost filial piety toward their parents. See Haboush, "Filial Emotions and Filial Values: Changing Patterns in the Discourse of Filiality in Late Choson Korea," *Harvard Journal of Asiatic Studies* 55.1 (1995): 129–77. C. Julia Huang's recent study of the Buddhist Ciji 慈濟 movement in Taiwan suggests that part of the popularity of the movement and its founder, Cheng Yen, is based on her legendary actions as a filial daughter. See the chapter "From Filial Daughter to Embodied Bodhisattva," in Huang, *Charisma and Compassion: Cheng Yen and the Buddhist Tzu Chi Movement* (Cambridge, MA: Harvard University Press, 2009), 15–39. A detailed investigation of the extent and implication of the daughter as the ideal representation of filial piety would be well worth pursuing.

52. The number of epitaphs for Buddhist nuns collected in *HB*, *XJ*, and *Quan Tang wen* 全唐文(Dong Gao 董誥 [1740–1818] et al., comp., Shanghai: Shanghai guji chubanshe, 1995) represents an extremely high ratio (4.94%) among women described in the epitaphs. (The ratio of Buddhist monks among men recorded in epitaphs was 4.1%.) According to the *Xin Tangshu* 新唐書 (Ouyang Xiu 歐陽修 [1007–1072] et al., comp., Beijing: Zhonghua shuju, 1997), in a census conducted during the Kaiyuan reign (713–741) there were 50,576 registered Buddhist nuns and 75,524 registered monks, and the population in 732 was 45,431,265 (53.1365–75). Therefore, the ratio of Buddhist nuns among the female population

was 0.22 percent, lower than the ratio of monks among the male population, 0.33 percent, and much lower than the ratio represented in Tang epitaphs. The high ratio of Buddhist nuns recorded in epitaphs, as well as the discrepancy in the ratio between nuns and monks, probably indicates that a high percentage of Buddhist nuns were born to the five Tang eminent clans. Shiying Pang also suggests that, due to the fact that a sizable number of nuns were from the Tang eminent clans, affiliation with and service to the secular family (including showing piety to parents) became one of the virtues of the female renunciant. See Pang, "Familial Identity and Buddhist Nuns," 56–66.

53. See Shi Xiaoying, "Ba zhi shi shiji," 58–64; and Pang, "Familial Identity and Buddhist Nuns," 56–66.

54. For a detailed discussion of stay-at-home nuns in the Tang dynasty, see Pang, "Familial Identity and Buddhist Nuns," 46–56. Pang considers this practice a reflection of the strategies of adaptation in Chinese Buddhism: "Women from high social classes were inclined to bind themselves tightly to families due to the moral teachings they had received. They defended their action by saying that both monastic life and cremation are just forms: if their minds are unattached and formless, there is no difference in the place and format of Buddhist practice" (56).

55. Jinhua Chen is the first scholar to point out such a trend in the Tang. See Chen, "Family Ties and Buddhist Nuns in Tang China: Two Studies," *Asia Major* 15.2 (2002): 51–85, especially 81. Epitaphs for deceased monks were often authored by fellow renunciants.

56. In her book *The Making of a Savior Bodhisattva: Dizang in Medieval China* (Honolulu: University of Hawaii Press, 2007), Zhiru (Ng) uses Liang Su's 梁肅 (752–793) *Dizang pusa zan* 地藏菩薩贊 (Liang praising a daughter embroidering an image of Dizang on behalf of her deceased mother) as an example to argue that praising Tang Buddhist daughters' filial actions reflected "the male literati spelling out ways for elite court women to embrace a combination of Buddhist piety and Confucian social norms" (204).

57. See Chün-fang Yü, *Kuan-yin: The Chinese Transformation of Avalokiteśvara* (New York: Columbia University Press, 2001), 293–352. Recently, Wilt L. Idema also attributes the transformation of Guanyin's gender to Miaoshan, proposing that where Buddhism replaced local cults of goddesses, Guanyin became the logical replacement of the local female deity. See Idema, "Introduction," in Idema, *Personal Salvation and Filial Piety: Two Precious Scroll Narratives of Guanyin and Her Acolytes* (Honolulu: University of Hawaii Press, 2008), 8. Idema nevertheless considers the legend, especially as recorded in the sixteenth-century text *The Precious Scroll of Incense Mountain* (*Xiangshan baojuan* 香山寶卷), a reflection of the universal sexual tensions in the Chinese patriarchal family (42). Meanwhile, Sherin Wing argues that the legend of Miaoshan reflects male Buddhists' reauthorizing stereotypes of women in an effort to trump Buddhist values (and in the case of Miaoshan, Buddhist filial piety). See Wing, "Gendering Buddhism: The Miaoshan Legend Reconsidered," *Journal of Feminist Studies in Religion* 27.1 (2011): 5–31.

58. *HB*, Kaiyuan 459.

59. *HB*, Zhenguan 107.

60. *HB*, Tianbao 066.

61. *HB*, Zhenyuan 貞元 018.

62. The epitaph was excavated in 2004 in the Luoyang area and was first published in Zhang Naizhu's "Luoyang xin ji shike."

63. *HB*, Changshou 長壽 011.

64. This sentence implies that joint burial was not traditional.

65. For more examples of Buddhist mothers' funeral arrangements, see Ping Yao, "Good Karmic Connections: Buddhist Mothers in Tang China," *Nan Nü: Men, Women and Gender in Early and Imperial China* 10.1 (2008): 57–85.

66. See Alan Cole, "Homestyle Vinaya and Docile Boys in Chinese Buddhism," *Positions* 7.1 (Spring 1999): 38. Both *Mothers and Sons in Chinese Buddhism* by Cole and *The Ghost Festival in Medieval China* by Teiser center on the celebration of Mulian, who saved his mother from hell.

67. "Tang gu Fanyang Lufunjun muzhiming bing xu" 唐故范陽盧府君墓誌銘並序, *HB*, Xiantong 咸通 058. The epitaph reveals that the deceased Lu Gongbi 盧公弼 was born to an elite family. His father was a grantee of Grand Master for Closing Court (Chaosan dafu 朝散大夫); his mother was from the Boling Cui 博陵崔 clan. Lu nevertheless only held low-ranking administrative positions. He was drawn to Buddhism during his forties and died at the age of seventy-nine *sui*. Lu had three sons and two daughters. The older daughter had "early on obeyed [his] long-cherished wish" (*bing suyuan* 稟宿願) and entered a Buddhist convent.

68. "Tang gu yantie Heyinyuan xunguan shi zuowuwei bingcaocanjun Pengcheng Liufunjun muzhi bing xu" 唐故鹽鐵河陰院巡官試左武衛兵曹參軍彭城劉府君墓誌並序, *HB*, Xiantong 079.

2

# Writing Oneself into the Tradition

## The Autobiographical Sermon of Chan Master Jizong Xingche (b. 1606)

*Beata Grant*

### The Context: Women Monastics in the Seventeenth-Century Revival of Linji Chan

In his pioneering study of the autobiographical tradition in premodern China, Pei-yi Wu points out that, while Chinese Chan masters would seem to have all of the traits needed for writing about themselves, including "boldness, ebullience, exaltation of the individual, disdain for conventions and rules, and frequent contemplation of the self," it was not until the Song dynasty (960–1279) that they were able to "escape from the rigid canons of Chinese historiography and speak directly about their own inner religious experience."[1] The first Chan autobiographer, according to Wu, was the Linji 臨濟 Chan monk Zuqin Xueyan 祖欽雪巖 (1216–1287), a man he suggests "must have been a more than usually self-assured master, fully conscious of his place in the annals of Buddhism and confident that his line would be perpetuated."[2] Zuqin did not, however, "write" his autobiography; rather, he "narrated his life story while ostensibly delivering a sermon."[3] Zuqin's account established the model for many subsequent autobiographical sermonizers, so much so that the great Linji Chan master Zhongfeng Mingben 中峰明本 (1263–1323) felt obliged to "take a strong stand against self-revelation" in an effort to "shame and intimidate the contemporaries who falsely boasted of attainment of illumination or verification of such attainment, fraudulently claiming great wisdom in order to deceive the common people."[4] This, according to Wu, led to the demise of the autobiographical sermon. "My search in the vast collection of Buddhist sermons," Wu writes, "has not yielded any more digressions on the sermonizer's own spiritual experience beyond [Mingben's] time."[5]

There did appear, however, to have been a revival of just this sort of autobiographical sermon in the seventeenth century, most of which can be found in the discourse records of masters associated with the important, albeit ultimately short-lived, revival of Chan Buddhism. In fact, most of these sermons are associated with dharma successors of the primary figures behind the Linji side of this Chan revival: Miyun Yuanwu 密雲圓悟 (1566–1642) and his dharma brother Tianyin Yuanxiu 天隱圓修 (1575–1635).[6] That this should be so is perhaps not so surprising given that a major element in this Chan revival involved a return to the Chan literary forms popular in the Song dynasty, in particular the so-called encounter dialogues, with their representations of dramatic exchanges between master and disciple, accompanied by lively language and, at times, shouts and blows. While many participated and even delighted in such exchanges, others dismissed them as empty theater, a confirmation of the depths to which Chan had descended rather than a sign of its renewal. According to Wu, a major contributing factor behind the appearance of autobiographical sermons in the Song dynasty was the growing popularity of theater during this period.[7] He suggests that just as on the dramatic stage, "even the most humble and self-effacing have to make their appearances, each baring some of his or her private self," so the Chan master, while his performance was conducted on the platform rather than on the stage, might also have felt empowered to reveal more of himself than was customary. The performer on the stage, as Wu points out, "is nothing if he fails to project himself though his words." Unlike the historian or the biographer, he cannot hide behind "the convention of the selfless compiler, mute and invisible."[8] Whether or not the theatrical performances described in Song dynasty Chan literature corresponded to the actual practice of most Chan masters is arguable.[9] Even more arguable is whether the "private self" thus revealed was any less constructed than the self when it was purposely effaced or kept hidden.[10] Nevertheless, it may be that this renewed interest in performative Chan contributed to the relative proliferation of autobiographical sermons in the seventeenth century.

Another major element of Miyun Yuanwu's revival was a renewed emphasis on official verification of the enlightenment experience and direct master-to-disciple transmission, which resulted in a significant increase in the number of disciples officially designated as dharma successors. This, too, elicited considerable criticism and accusations of "indiscriminate transmission," especially, perhaps, since among those receiving dharma transmissions were a small but significant number of women. In the eyes of many, such women were living proof of "indiscriminate transmission," and those among them who went so far as to ascend the platform and "act like a Chan master" were even more despised. Qian Qianyi 錢謙益 (1582–1664), for example, bemoaned the audacity of some women who not only claimed dharma transmission from eminent masters but—and this is what offended him the most—they "stick out their heads and expose their faces almost as if they were acting in a play" (*chutou loumian, jicheng xishi* 出頭露面, 幾成戲事).[11]

There were those who greatly admired these women, however, and who went to considerable lengths to defend them, especially since a precedent had been set by the eminent Song dynasty Linji Chan master Dahui Zonggao 大慧宗杲 (1089–1163), who had conferred dharma transmission on at least three women, the most famous of whom were Chan masters Miaodao 妙道 and Miaozong 妙總 (1095–1170). There are extant sermons by both Miaodao and Miaozong, and the latter has also left a sizeable collection of religious poetry.[12] It is not until the seventeenth century, however, that we find an autobiographical sermon by a woman that fits the model established by Song dynasty masters such as Zuqin Xueyan. This sermon can be found in the official *yulu* 語錄 of Chan master Jizong Xingche 繼總行徹 (b. 1606), which were printed in 1656 and later preserved in the Jiaxing Buddhist canon.[13] Because there is so little detailed biographical material available about religious women from the premodern period, I have elsewhere used this sermon, along with other pertinent material, to piece together the general outlines of Jizong's life and teachings.[14] My primary aim here, however, is to show how this text may also be read as an autobiographical sermon, by means of which Jizong as a woman Chan master sought to write herself into what was almost exclusively a male tradition.

## Woman Chan Master Jizong Xingche and Her Autobiographical Sermon

Jizong Xingche, whose secular name was Liu, was born in 1606 to a highly educated and apparently quite wealthy family from Hunan. Indications of Buddhist devotion can be found on both her father's and her mother's sides: as a young girl, for example, she accompanied her maternal grandfather on a visit to the reliquary of the late Ming monk Hanshan Deqing 憨山德清 (1546–1623). Jizong was widowed at a young age, her husband having died while on an official posting in the Guangdong area. She subsequently devoted herself to religious practice and eventually took ordination in her early thirties under Linji Chan master Shanci Tongji 山茨通際 (1608–1645), who was then residing at the Lüluo 綠蘿 Monastery on Hengshan 衡山 (Mount Heng) in Hunan Province. After Shanci's untimely death, Jizong made her way to Jiangsu where she became the disciple—and, ultimately, dharma heir—of Wanru Tongwei, who, like Shanci, was a dharma successor of Tianyin Yuanxiu. It is worth noting that Wanru's discourse records, compiled and printed after his death, include an autobiographical sermon: whether or not Jizong was actually present when it was delivered is impossible to determine, but it is likely that she knew about it. In any case, as we shall see, she was definitely familiar with other such autobiographical Chan texts including the well-known letter by Gaofeng Yuanmiao 高峰原妙 written to his teacher, who was none other than our "first Chan autobiographer," Xueyan Zuqin.[15] Needless to say, we will not find either in Jizong's sermon or in similar sermons by her male counterparts the "baring of the inner self" that Pei-yi Wu observes in Zuqin's thirteenth-century sermon. For, by the seventeenth century at least, such sermons were, like European Christian conversion narratives of the same period, composed "within a framework of already prescribed experiences and emotions."[16] Moreover, as was the case with her seventeenth-century counterparts in the West, a religious woman like Jizong who dared speak in public, and with authority, would have had little choice but to "cast her story in the culturally compelling plots, ideals of characterization, and speaking postures associated with male or 'human' selfhood."[17] This does not mean, however, that we should dismiss Jizong's sermon as mere spiritual ventriloquism. I hope to show, in fact, that what Sidonie Smith says of Christian conversion narratives by seventeenth-century English women may also be said of autobiographical sermons by seventeenth-century Buddhist women such as Jizong, namely, that while they "constructed the subject through a strict narrative and linguistic conventions in order to create a conforming, if transcendent version of selfhood, for women they could also offer an alternative space, a place from which to contest their socially sanctioned position of silence and submission."[18] Jizong's sermon was delivered early in her religious career and before she had achieved the fame that would lead one admiring preface writer to comment that:

> The gentry officials all looked up to her with admiration; the four classes (monks, nuns, laymen, and laywomen) flocked to her in droves, and there were none who did not wish to extend her an invitation to preach the dharma. Her blows and shouts were delivered with the power and swiftness of lightning; her preaching of the dharma was of benefit to sentient beings, and among those who filled her quarters, there were many who achieved deep insight.
>
> 士紳仰慕, 四眾雲臻, 莫不延請弘揚法道. 棒喝交馳, 雷奔電掣, 說法利生,度籌盈室, 會下多有省發者.[19]

The emphasis thus is primarily on the religious training and spiritual development that led to her enlightenment experiences and, ultimately, to being named an official dharma heir of Wanru Tongwei. The narrative, which is about two thousand characters in length, can be divided into three major sections. In the first part Jizong briefly talks about her life before meeting her teacher, Shanci Tongji. In the second and longest section, which is also the heart of the narrative, she describes her determined practice of *huatou* 話頭 meditation under Shanci's guidance and her eventual spiritual breakthrough. In the final section, she recounts her departure from Hengshan and her journey to the Jiangsu-Zhejiang area, where she met with several other eminent Linji masters, including Wanru Tongwei, and where she ultimately assumed the rank of Chan master.

Jizong's narrative begins in much the same way as those of her seventeenth-century male counterparts, with a request to ascend the platform and speak of her life for the edification of the assembled congregation. As convention dictated, her initial response is to emphatically refuse (*guci* 固辭) a move that, however genuine it might have been, also serves to defuse possible accusations of self-promotion. It also defines the sermon as an autobiographical act, which Ken Plummer defines as an "[occasion] when people are coaxed or coerced into 'getting a life.'"[20] In Jizong's case, the request comes from two literati laymen, both surnamed Wang 王. Although the two Wangs present their request as being on behalf of an audience made up mostly of women, they may be regarded as representative of a larger male audience that Jizong knew might consider her public self-revelation to be particularly reprehensible. Thus, before embarking on her narrative, she makes sure that her listeners understand that the only rationale for this unusual focus on herself is to provide both example and inspiration for others on the path:

> The divine tortoise has no need to interpret omens; and when it has left behind its empty shell, it has no need to bore its way out; if the vermilion phoenix were to encircle the golden cage, it would be unable to soar up into the heavens. How much less someone like myself who has accomplished nothing to speak of? But if you do not know how to cultivate the Way, how then can you practice? [If you do not know] how to become a Buddha, then how can you become one? And if I do not relay information based on the facts, then how can I hope to be worthy of serving as a model?
>
> 靈龜無卦兆，空殼不勞鑽．丹鳳縈金網，翾霄恐不及．況我無狀，不知修道而無可修，成佛而無可成．不妨依實供通，要亦不堪取則.[21]

These sorts of self-deprecatory remarks can be found in the accounts of male monastics as well, reflecting in part the rhetorical Chan disinclination to speak of the ineffable, much less of the self that, supposedly, has been deconstructed and exposed as empty. Nevertheless, I would argue that while Jizong does not explicitly refer here to her gender, it is likely that this is what she means by "someone like myself." In other words, her self-deprecation is also designed to allay the fears of those who disapprove of women speaking publically. One is reminded of the medieval female mystic Julian of Norwich (1342–ca. 1416) who in her *Showings* compares her narrative to an "insignificant hazelnut" but then goes on to defend her efforts because they are for the benefit of a higher cause: "Because I am a woman, ought I therefore to believe that I should not tell you of the goodness of God!"[22] As Domna C. Stanton observes, the usurpation of traditionally male prerogatives and upsetting of gendered expectations "generated a particular self-consciousness about the fact of writing often manifested in a defensive or justificative posture."[23] It is also worth noting that, as a nun whose primary disciples were women, this "good news" was designed for them. Like Julian, Jizong is able to justify this inadequacy by the felt imperative to share the good news—that is, to show people how they might attain Buddhahood. Moreover, as a nun teaching women, the people for whom she wished to serve as a model were primarily women. Thus, in a sermon found elsewhere in her *yulu*, we find Jizong addressing her female disciples as follows:

> It is said again that: "In practicing Chan one must look for enlightenment; if there is no enlightenment, there will be no

way by which one may escape the great sea of birth and death." Nowadays [so-called] followers of the way mistakenly swindle by means of mouth and ear the denizens of the inner chambers when they tell them that they do not need to be enlightened in order to be liberated from life and death; glib and loquacious, they vilify the great wisdom of insight, and even go so far as to completely obscure its sacredness. This demonstrates a lack of gratitude toward the sages of the past. How can it not be lamented! Since you have taken refuge with me, then I hope you will seek the Great Way and urgently strive to distinguish between the different paths of clarity and blindness.

又云: 參禪須求玅悟, 若不玅悟, 無由出離生死大海. 今時道流, 謬以口耳哄弄閨閣, 不求玅悟而脫生死, 祗益滑稽, 謗大般若. 以致埋沒己靈, 辜負先聖, 可不哀邪. 汝既皈依山僧, 希求大道, 急將明昧兩岐, 與我一時坐斷.[24]

It is also worth noting Jizong's insistence that in telling her story, she is merely "relaying the facts." Although clearly central to all sorts of autobiographical writing, this "rhetoric of truthfulness" has been found by scholars to be especially pronounced in seventeenth-century English conversion narratives by women. The authors of *Her Own Life*, a study of these narratives, suggest that "the particularly female experience of vulnerability to persuasion leads to a defensive desire for accuracy of reputation—the commodity of truth—a desire heightened by the women's awareness of their own textuality."[25] In any case, although the self-deprecatory language of her opening remarks disappears completely in the sermon that follows, the justificatory impulse continues to shape Jizong's self-presentation, albeit in subtle ways. In true Chinese biographical mode, Jizong begins her personal life story by situating herself in a particular place and familial context: she was born in Hunan, she tells us, her father was surnamed Liu 劉, and her mother was surnamed Song 宋. But then she almost immediately switches to the hagiographic mode associated primarily with eminent monks:

One night, my father had a dream in which he agreed to the request of an old monk who came to him seeking lodging. After this, my mother found that she had conceived, and after carrying the child for twelve months, three cries were heard issuing from the womb, after which, on the night of the eighteenth day of the eighth month of the *bingwu* year of the Wanli reign period,

> she gave birth. At that time, a white glow that overpowered both the light of the lamps and of the moon filled the room, something noted by all in amazement.
>
> 一夕父夢老僧索住處, 許之. 母遂有赈, 懷十有二月. 既而胎鳴者三, 於萬曆丙午年八月十八日夜出生. 時有白光燭室, 燈月如蔽, 眾皆謂奇.

Descriptions of a semi-miraculous birth can, of course, be found in many hagiographical accounts; indeed, such a birth was regarded as proof of attributed eminence.[26] It is rather less common to find such descriptions in self-narrated accounts, although it is by no means unheard of: the seventeenth-century Linji Chan master Yuechuang Zheliao 月幢轍了, for example, in his autobiographical sermon tells his audience: "My mother dreamed that a monk gave her a peach and ordered her to eat it, after which she found she was pregnant."[27] By engaging in this sort of auto-hagiography, I would suggest that Jizong is claiming eminent status for herself, a claim that contrasts sharply with her profession of inadequacy earlier. One could even say that by claiming to be the reincarnation of a monk, Jizong is also claiming legitimacy as a woman Chan master. In other words, she had proven herself as a male monastic in a previous life and is thus entitled to perform as one in the present life.

Jizong's brief account of her childhood emphasizes, again quite formulaically, an early manifestation of religious tendencies, including a dislike for nonvegetarian food. She also tells her listeners:

> When I became a little older, I took pleasure in reading Confucian texts and Buddhist sutras. I felt distaste for the dust and confusion of the world and I thought deeply about the matters of life and death.
>
> 稍長好看儒佛經, 厭處塵繁, 痛念生死.

Of course, male literati had long been inspired by their reading to abandon the worldly life. In Jizong's case, however, this comment reflects the changed social and cultural climate of the seventeenth century, which saw the growing presence of highly educated women of the gentry class who no longer felt constrained to conceal their intellectual abilities and their passion for reading and writing. As we shall see, this love of reading (and writing) is a motif that runs throughout Jizong's account, even when it comes into direct conflict with her spiritual aspirations.

This brings us to Jizong's account of a particularly critical life juncture: marriage. Again, it is important to remember that, given the demands and expectations of filial duty, marriage posed a challenge for men as well. For example, Jizong's slightly older contemporary Linji Chan master Fushi Tongxian 浮石通賢 (1593–1667) relates in his autobiographical sermon how when he was nineteen his parents desperately wanted him to marry. However, "I sighed and said, 'If I don't go now, it will be difficult to leave later.' And so I abandoned my parents [and left]" 嘆曰: 此時不行, 他日難脫矣. 於是背親.[28] The main difference, of course, is that it was very difficult, if not impossible, for women to just leave home. Jizong's description of her predicament is made more poignant by its brevity:

> I begged permission from my father to sacrifice myself and leave home. He would not consent. And so I was married into the Chen family. Only a few years later, my husband Chen died in his official post far away from home.
>
> 懇父捨身出家, 父不允. 後許字陳氏, 不數年, 陳君遊宦沒.

The possible emotional drama behind this laconic account can only be surmised, although a clue is provided by the use of the word *ken* 懇, which implies not only a request for permission but entreaty and supplication. Equally suggestive is her use of the term *sheshen* 捨身, which literally means to sacrifice the body (in order to save others) but could be read here as "to shed the female body"—that is, to leave behind her gender, not to mention a woman's expected social and cultural roles. Although raised in a family with strong Buddhist leanings and allowed, perhaps even encouraged, to read religious and philosophical texts, in the end, the will of the father and, by extension, Confucian expectations of the proper female life course won the day. Normally, it would have also signaled the end of the story if fate, in the guise of the early death of her husband, had not intervened. Widowhood could, at least in the case of elite women with some financial and familial support, allow for a relatively greater freedom to pursue intellectual and religious interests, and this is precisely what Jizong did. What she did not tell her listeners, however, although later one of her prefacers would, was that after her husband's death, Jizong took it upon herself to write an official memorial to the throne in the attempt to clear his name—an indication that he had perhaps died as a result of factional infighting. Nor does she make any mention of children, although one later gazetteer writer makes mention of there having been several. Instead, she moves directly from a description of herself as daughter, wife, and widow to that of herself as dedicated and determined seeker of enlightenment. As noted earlier, the second part of Jizong's narrative constitutes its heart and justifies its being called a spiritual autobiography rather than just a *res gestae* or account of activities. It begins with an account of how Jizong built herself a small hermitage, presumably near or even within the family compound, where "from dawn to dusk, I would sit in quiet meditation." She describes her practice as being motivated not by despair over her husband's untimely death but by "a delight in observing the precepts and [religious] discipline." She soon finds, however, that quiet meditation is not getting her anywhere, and the spiritually ambitious Jizong decides to go in search of further religious instruction. It is possible, and even likely, that Jizong describes her early dissatisfaction through the lens of the seventeenth-century Linji Chan revivalists, who renewed emphasis on the strenuous practice leading to sudden enlightenment as opposed to quiet meditation or even the practice of *nianfo* 念佛 or Buddha recollection. Nevertheless, Jizong's decision to abandon the forms of religious cultivation considered appropriate to widows—namely, *nianfo* recitation carried out within the confines of the family home—speaks once again of her resolute rejection of expected female behavior.

Jizong's search for further spiritual guidance leads her to the Linji Chan master Shanci Tongji, who at the time was living at the Lüluo Monastery on nearby Hengshan. Shanci was a dharma successor of Tianyin Yuanxiu, Miyun Yuanwu's dharma brother, and thus an important player in the Linji Chan revival. In fact, he was drawn to Hengshan, also known as Nanyue, in part because of its association with Nanyue Huairang 南嶽懷讓 (677–744) and his famous student Mazu Daoyi 馬祖道一 (709–788), patriarchs of the Linji Chan lineage. Shanci even took it upon himself to gather together scattered accounts of eminent Chan monks in the Nanyue lineage, titled *Nanyue Chan denglu* 南嶽禪燈錄 (*Nanyue Chan [Lineage] Transmission of the Lamp*), which had been recently printed and put into circulation. It was this collection that fell into Jizong's hands just when she was looking for a teacher, and it was after reading it that she was moved to seek out its compiler—here again we see the literary foundation of the seventeenth-century Chan revival. Thus began several years of intensive religious practice under Shanci's guidance, first as a laywoman and finally as a nun.

As in Zuqin Xueyan's thirteenth-century sermon, Jizong also slows time down considerably when she records the successes and failures of her meditative practice. Pei-yi Wu, speaking of Zuqin's account, claims that it was precisely this "leisurely pace of narrative that made possible, perhaps for the first time in Chinese history, a baring of the inner self."[29] By the seventeenth century, as we noted earlier, this detailed description of religious practice had become largely conventional.

In general, the description of her religious practice adheres to the conventions associated with the practice of *huatou* investigation, also known as *kanhua Chan* 看話禪, to which Shanci introduced her as a replacement for her previous practice of *nianfo* recitation. This practice involved an intense investigation of a critical phrase (sometimes drawn from a well-known *koan* story or a public case, sometimes from other sources), a process designed to arouse an intense feeling of doubt, described sometimes as a ball of iron lodged in the throat. Ultimately, this almost unbearable doubt is shattered and dissolved, often by a seemingly insignificant event such as hearing the sound of a bell, leaving the practitioner forever transformed by a vision of nonduality.[30] In her account, Jizong describes two separate experiences: the first one rejected by Shanci as inauthentic, the second one pronounced to be a true experience of insight. In describing her practice, the first phase was conducted over a period of seven days and seven nights, while the second was over a longer period of forty-nine days. Jizong clearly draws on descriptions she has read about and thoroughly internalized. In describing what she thought was her first breakthrough, for example, Jizong notes that it was triggered by a passage in a collection of discourse records, "After one hundred years or thirty-six thousand days, coming and going, there is still this fellow" 百年三萬六千朝, 返覆元來是這漢.[31] It was these words, she tells us that "caused me to realize that the roots of karma are all illusory transformations and unreal, and the everyday and the ordinary are perfect as they are" 便知諸根行業, 皆幻化不實. 日用尋常, 了無他事. Although Jizong does not indicate the source of these lines, they are readily identifiable as being the last two lines of a self-eulogy composed by Wuzu Fayan 五祖法演 (1024–1104). Not coincidentally, it is these same two lines that Linji Chan master Gaofeng Yuanmiao, in the letter to his teacher Zuqin Xueyan referred to earlier, claims to have triggered one of his own early enlightenment experiences.[32] This account is found, among other places, in Yunqi Zhuhong's 雲棲株宏 (1535–1625) *Changuan cejin* (Strategic Advance through the Chan Gate), a collection of excerpts from earlier Chan masters designed as a handbook for practitioners, that Shanci had instructed her to study carefully. As mentioned earlier, Gaofeng Yuanmiao's autobiographical account may not just have provided the lines but also served as a template later when Jizong recalled her second enlightenment experience:

> Whether walking or sitting, I tirelessly investigated [the *huatou* I had been assigned] for forty-nine days and nights until suddenly I found myself in a state of consciousness lasting three or four hours in which I was not aware of having either a body or a

> mind. Then by chance I heard a peal of thunder, and with the speed of [a bird] released from his cage, at that moment my doubts vanished like a silver mountain and iron walls collapsing into smithereens.
>
> 行坐參究，四十九晝夜不倦．忽然呆去三四時，不見有身心(器界)．偶聞雷迅如，在網羅中跳出相似．當下不疑，銀山鐵壁，一時粉碎．

Jizong's description of her excruciating struggle with her *huatou* echoes the description Gaofeng gives of his first breakthrough: "All of a sudden I was no longer conscious of either my mind or my body, and I saw in front of my eyes nothing but a huge, solid substance, like a silver mountain or iron wall."[33] In short, Jizong's descriptions of her enlightenment experiences, however authentic and potentially inspiring to others, were by no means original. But then again, neither were those of most of her male monastic contemporaries. It is worth remarking, however, on the extent to which Jizong's intellectual prowess and literary ability are highlighted by her account, even when they appear to point to her religious failures.

Composing a poem that demonstrates one's insight had by the Song dynasty become an important component of Chan practice. So it is not unusual that Jizong would compose poems to show her teachers. In her autobiographical sermon, she includes not one but four such poems, each of which she cites in its entirety. More interestingly, she also quotes Shanci's responses to these poems. His response to her first attempt is decidedly ambivalent:

> Although the words of this *gatha* are beautiful, they are based on things remembered, studied and imitated. They are not words that reflect your personal witnessing, your personal enlightenment. If someone with enlightened eyes were to look at it, he wouldn't even think them worth a smile.
>
> 偈語雖佳，不離記憶揣摸，非親證親悟之言．明眼人見之，不值一笑．

While Jizong seems here to be recording a well-deserved admonishment, she manages also to lay claim to her intellectual powers and her talents as a writer: even Shanci declares her first poem to be beautiful, if ultimately spiritually shallow. We find a hint that this struggle between the writing self and religious self was a major issue in Jizong's life in a letter addressed to Jizong by her fellow student (and one of Shanci's dharma heirs) Mizhan Dazun 爾瞻達尊 (1609–1663):

> If you truly want to understand this great matter of life and death and [become] a good vessel of the dharma gate, then you must first cut off all empty words and apply yourself with greater diligence, strict until death without change; then your enlightenment will be like the turn of a palm, and who will be able to again cheat or beguile you? But if you [merely] utilize your broad learning and memory to engage in back-and-forth exchanges, it will be like cheating others and cheating yourself in order to live your life. Would that not be a case of forfeiting the true causes of leaving the household? I am afraid it will be hard to escape from this sin of slandering Buddhist wisdom.
>
> 實欲了生死大事，作法門良器，必要先斷虛詞，加之操履嚴密，至死不變，悟如翻掌，誰能欺惑汝哉？若只廣博記憶，應酬相似，欺人欺己，以當生平，不惟有失出家正因，謗般若罪恐難逃耳.[34]

We also see this underlying concern with the literary in Jizong's descriptions of her exchanges, both before and after her enlightenment, with her teacher Shanci. She presents these in the form of encounter dialogues such as those found in Chan Buddhist compilations from the Song and onward. Many scholars today would insist that these dialogues are for the most part literary creations and can tell us little or nothing about the actual lives and teachings of their protagonists. Mario Poceski cautions against going to this extreme, especially in the case of monks from the tenth century and later, since such accounts were based on stories "already in circulation while they were still alive or soon after their death."[35] Nevertheless, Poceski agrees that they should be viewed as "one-sided depictions of what in all likelihood were contrived performances that fitted into preexisting templates of behavior deemed apt for Chan teachers, even if in them there was some scope for individual expression and creativity."[36] There is no question that Jizong's descriptions of her encounters with Shanci adhere closely to such preexisting templates—templates that, as we have seen, were particularly popular among the seventeenth-century Linji Chan revivalists. However, given the "scope for individual expression" and the fact that what we have here is a woman describing her own encounters with her male master, these descriptions invite a closer examination. Perhaps the most important thing to note in this regard is that, after Shanci has acknowledged the authenticity of Jizong's enlightenment experience, the exchanges between them are described as being between equals rather than between master and disciple, who in this case were approximately the same age. We also see evidence yet again not only of the textual nature of the encounter but also of Jizong's own literary talent.

One such episode begins with Jizong presenting Shanci with a poem, again cited in its entirety. Shanci reads it but remains silent and does not say anything. Jizong then asks him the meaning of the lines "When the fragrant wind blows in from the south, the halls and pavilions become a bit cooler" 薰風自南來, 殿閣生微涼. These lines, again not coincidentally, are the ones spoken by the Song dynasty Linji master Yuanwu Keqin 圜悟克勤 (1063–1135) that are said to have triggered the initial insight of his famous disciple, Dahui Zonggao. This time, Shanci simply admonishes her that she should know better, "You should slap your cheeks with the palm of your hand." Undaunted, Jizong responds with yet another poem:

> The fragrant wind that blows in from the south—when will it end?
> The halls and pavilions are a bit chilly, only you yourself will know.
> In the fine weather, the butterflies flit about following the scent;
> At dawn the roosters herald the sun as it rises from east to west.
> From this moment I have penetrated the true meaning of things;
> And the myriad affairs and objects of the cosmos break into smile!
> 薰風南來有何極,
> 殿閣微涼祗自知.
> 晴蝶逐香翻上下,
> 辰雞閱日唱東西.
> 從今覷破真消息,
> 萬象森羅展笑眉.

Jizong's description of the dialogue that follows reflects a great spiritual self-confidence on her part, as well as a certain ambivalence on Shanci's part regarding her literary efforts:

> Master Shanci approvingly said: "Where is the place where you know yourself?" I said: "A sliver of moon hangs in the heavens;

> its glow shatters ten thousand mountains." Master Shanci said, "If the mountains are already shattered, where then will you be able to rest your feet?" I said: "I turn a somersault and vault into the heavens, and pull heaven along by the nose-ring." Master Shanci tossed the draft of the *gatha* back to me and I then left.
>
> 尚徵云: 如何是汝自知處? 某云: 空懸一片月, 爍破萬重山. 尚云: 山既破, 汝即今脚跟立在甚麼處? 某云: 翻身一擲騰霄漢, 管教鼻孔自撩天. 尚擲還頌稿, 某便出.

The final section of Jizong's sermon begins again in historical and biographical time as she tells her listeners how, when Shanci left his hermitage on Hengshan to take up residence at the Nanyuan 南元 Monastery in Changsha 長沙, she had planned to follow him. Here we are afforded a glimpse into the more personal emotional bond that appears to have been forged between master and disciple:

> After he left, feeling that it was too soon to be separated from my teacher, I also planned on leaving the mountain [to join him], but then he unexpectedly passed away at Nanyuan. [We] then made sure that his holy remains were returned back to the mountain. We also arranged for the painting of his posthumous portrait.
>
> 尚去後, 某覺離師太早, 亦欲出山. 適和尚示寂南元, 復請靈骨入山, 併追寫道儀.

What is worth remarking on here is the impression Jizong gives that it was she who not only was the one primarily responsible for overseeing the return of Shanci's remains to the mountain, but that she also took upon herself the duty of finding someone to paint his portrait. This seems hardly likely, since this responsibility would have fallen to Shanci's senior dharma heir, Mizhan Dazun, who had assumed the leadership of the Lüluo Monastery after Shanci left for Nanyuan.[37] It is not impossible, however, that Jizong was charged to take some of Shanci's personal effects to the Zhejiang/Jiangsu area, perhaps even some of the biographical materials that would go into the writing of his stupa inscription. As she tells her audience:

> After the stupa had been built, then on the eighth day of the sixth month of the year 1650, I bowed and took leave of my teacher's relic stupa and descended Hengshan. I then went to

> Wuchang. The place where I was lodging went up in flames, and all of the texts that the monk had left me were destroyed, as was all of my own baggage. However, the monastics and laity of Hankou invited me to stay at Puti Cloister.
>
> 建塔畢，乃於庚寅年六月初八日禮辭和尚骨塔，下衡山至武昌．遭寓處失火，和尚手澤俱焚，行李皆燼．漢口道俗請住菩提菴．

In the third and last sections of her sermon, Jizong recounts her visits to three Linji Chan masters, all of whom were dharma brothers of Shanci Tongji. Her travels take her first to Jinling 金陵 (present-day Nanjing 南京) and then to the Helin Monastery 鶴林寺 in Suzhou where she pays a call on Miyun Yuanwu's disciple, Muyun Tongmen 牧雲通門 (1599–1671). She then travels to Hangzhou where she visits Shanci's dharma brother Master Ruo'an Tongwen 箬庵同文 (1604–1655). In the stupa inscription he wrote for Shanci Tongji in 1652, Ruo'an notes that he was the man who knew Shanci the longest and the best. Jizong in fact stayed with Ruo'an for several months and even accompanied him when he left for two other monasteries: "I followed him to both so as to study with him from morning until night." Finally, Jizong returned to Yixing 宜興; here she went to the Longchi Monastery 龍池寺 outside of Yixing to pay respects to the stupa of Huanyou Zhengchuan 幻有正傳 (1549–1614), the teacher of both Miyun and Tianyin. There Jizong met with Wanru Tongwei, the monk from whom she ultimately received formal dharma transmission.

Jizong presents each visit in terms of an encounter dialogue, again a familiar convention in many Chan biographical accounts. Given its formulaically theatrical setting, then, what is worth noting is not so much what is said but rather the role played by the actors involved—in this case, three eminent male masters and a nun whose primary claim to fame is her association with these men's fellow monk, Shanci Tongji. Regarded in this way, what is striking is the way in which each encounter begins with the monk questioning Jizong's legitimacy and ends with the woman Chan master declaring, in no uncertain terms, her spiritual attainments. Here, for example, is how she describes her meeting with Ruo'an Tongwei:

> The monk [Ruo'an] asked: "Are you the Jizong who was the student of the Master of Nanyue [Shanci]?" I said: "Yes, I am." He said: "What do you mean by abandoning your home and wandering about aimlessly?" I said: "Leaping and vaulting through

> past and present, the brilliance is shattering both Heaven and Earth." He said: "You have indeed abandoned your home to wander aimlessly." I said, "I have leapt up and now stand on my own beyond the great void; from my nostrils emerge the upper lips of the stupa." He said, "I have thirty blows which have not yet touched you." I then shook out my sleeves and left the room.
>
> 尚問: 莫是拜南嶽和尚底季總麼? 某云: 是. 箬云: 抛家亂走作麼? 某云: 輝騰今古, 爍破乾坤. 箬云: 正是抛家亂走. 某云: 騰身獨立太虛外, 鼻孔從教塔上唇. 箬云: 我有三十棒, 未到你在. 某拂袖便出.

The five different encounters with Wanruo Tongwei, the master who was to give her dharma transmission, reflect the same self-confidence. This can be explained by the fact that she had already had her enlightenment experience confirmed by Shanci. Here, for example, is how she presents one of these encounters.

> The monk said: "What people have you been close to in the past?" "Master [Shanci] from Nanyue," I replied. The monk said: "So where is he now?" I said: "The disc of luminous clarity atop the solitary peak shatters Longchi's most all-encompassing purity." The monk then struck me saying: "That is nothing but idle talk." I said: "Lightly, lightly I drag my staff through Longchi, and in so doing cause the ponds to empty and cliffs to tumble." The monk struck me again. I said: "That is like offering a glass [of wine] after one is already drunk."
>
> 尚云: 曾親近甚麼人來? 某云: 南嶽茨和尚. 尚云: 他即今在甚麼處? 某云: 一輪皎潔孤峰頂, 爍破龍池徹底清. 尚打云: 閒言語. 某云: 輕輕曳杖龍池過, 惹得傾湫倒嶽來. 尚復打. 某云: 也是醉後添杯.

After a series of similarly triumphant encounters, Jizong appears to have decided that it was time to move on and also to bring an end to her sermon. This is how it ends:

> The next day I went to take leave of the monk. I was preparing to return home to Nanyue, but the monk said: "It is very difficult for people on the path to study the way. So put an end to your

> thoughts of returning to the mountains. When this old monk completes you, you will be able to liberate those on the path." He then presented me with the dharma transmission records and the flywhisk. I strongly resisted since I wanted to return home, but the monk said, "It is best if you live in Jiangnan, where you will benefit the flourishing of the lineage." When a master invited me to take up residence at the Pudu Convent, the monk ordered me to come live here.
>
> 次日辭尚, 欲歸南嶽. 尚云: 下路人學道甚難, 回山之念且止. 老僧完你底事, 可在下路度眾. 遂付某源流拂子, 某力辭欲歸. 尚云: 江南住住, 好適興化. 一師請住普度菴, 即命往焉.

## Concluding Remarks

As scholars of autobiography have noted, "autobiographical acts and texts are situated in a paratextual surround, what we might think of as the framing produced by their publication, reception, and circulation."[38] This framing "shapes and situates the narrative by constructing the audience and inviting a particular politics of reading."[39] In the case of Jizong's autobiographical sermon, the paratextual surround is comprised of the many other texts in her *yulu* collection, including letters, poems, and sermons, many of which, like the one quoted earlier, are addressed to women lay followers as well as disciples. The other important paratextual materials are the four prefaces attached to this *yulu*, several of which were composed by well-known literati figures. Prefaces are, of course, also written with preexisting templates in mind, and their often hyperbolic language must be taken with a grain of salt. Nevertheless, it is worth noting that, while Jizong makes every attempt in her autobiographical sermon to construct a picture of herself as a male Chan master, the authors of these prefaces—all of whom knew Jizong personally—emphasize the fact that she is a woman, albeit a most extraordinary one. The Ming-loyalist-turned-Buddhist-layman Yan Dacan 嚴大參 (1590–1671), for example, emphasizes the rarity of a woman Chan master like Jizong by comparing her to an Udambara flower, said to bloom only once every three thousand years. Yan was the person who, at Jizong's own request, saw to the publication of the *yulu* in 1656. He is also the most effusive when it comes to his praise of Jizong's writings and recorded sermons:

> Reading them left me feeling as refreshed and joyful [as if I'd] feasted on pears from the Ai family [orchard]; I felt as if I'd

entered into a shaded mountain path, unable to describe all of its beauty; like the bright sun shining and glowing in the middle of the sky such that it was impossible to look at it with the naked eye. I then had them carved and printed so that those with a discerning eye might witness the appearance of this Udambara flower, and those with some understanding might meet with a *kalyanamitra* (spiritual friend). I am very happy to write this preface.

讀之如食哀家梨，令人爽口快心. 又如入山陰道中，令人應接不暇. 又如杲日當空，光芒閃爍，令人不得正眼相覷. 余請付梓，使有目者共睹曇華出現，有識者咸欽知識相逢. 余興然作敘.[40]

One of the most well-known of Jizong's preface writers was the scholar-official and lay Buddhist Tan Zhenmo 譚貞默 (1590–1665).[41] Tan, whose religious name was Fuzheng 福徵, was a lifelong lay disciple of Hanshan Deqing and is known particularly for his *Commentary on the Chronological Autobiography of the Old Man Hanshan* (*Hanshan laoren nianpu zixu shilu shu* 憨山老人年譜自敘實錄疏), which was published in 1650, thirty-three years after Hanshan's death. According to Sung-peng Hsu, the reason that Tan took so long to complete his commentary is that he was busy "investigating the events recorded in the *Autobiography* by questioning [Deqing's] followers and government officials familiar with the imperial court. He was surprised to learn that all the events could be verified or substantiated."[42] Tan's preface to Jizong's *yulu* provides important biographical details about Jizong's family, in particular her grandfather's connections with his own teacher, Hanshan Deqing. Like Yan, Tan also emphasizes Jizong's exceptionality. He begins by quoting the remark attributed to Tang master Huangbo Xiyun 黃檗希運 (d. 850): "I do not say there is no Chan, only that there are no teachers."[43] He then goes on to note that while the great master Mazu had eighty-four students, in the end very few of these ever attained enlightenment, much less eminence. This, Tan says, is an example of "there being many but in the end only a few, and because of there being so few, these are to be valued." Tan then applies this rationale to women like Jizong, who because they are so rare are to be that much more valued. He then proceeds to situate her not in the direct male lineage of Wanru Tongwei but rather in a parallel female lineage of Miaozong and Miaodao, the most well-known of the three women dharma heirs of Song dynasty master Dahui Zonggao. He describes this parallel lineage as follows:

> Before Jingshan [Dahui] there was Foguo [Yuanwu Keqin]; before Longchi [Wanru] there was Tiantong [Miyun Yuanwu]. They were as close as bone and marrow, descendents of Linji. In the same way, Jizong's fine reputation is such that it most assuredly can compare with that of Wuzhuo [Miaozong] before and after; both are two great pillars of the Lineage Gate. In Master Jizong's advance to the top of the pole, in the great expanse of her preaching of the dharma, she harks back to Person of the Way Wuzhuo; truly, there have been few like her since.
>
> 徑山前有佛果, 龍池前有天童, 其為滴骨滴髓, 臨濟兒孫. 同是知繼總徽聲, 固足爭光無著為先後, 宗門兩大總持也. 迺繼總師之竿頭進步者, 在說法浩浩中, 還視無著道人, 實為得未曾有.

In other words, while in her autobiographical sermon Jizong makes every attempt to shed her gender and to situate herself squarely in the male lineage of Linji Chan master Shanci and his fellow male monastics, these prefaces make it impossible for her readers to completely forget or ignore her gendered status. In so doing, however, they encourage us to read her autobiographical sermon as having been composed by a woman, thus calling for more nuanced reading than similar sermons by male monastics. I would suggest then, that while Jizong's sermon clearly adheres closely to a preexisting (male) template, she exercised her agency by carefully selecting its elements and putting them together in a way that affirmed the authenticity of her experience, the strength of her resolve, and her eminent suitability as an exemplary Chan master. Indeed, she represents herself, whatever her inner insecurities may have been, much as Pei-yi Wu describes Zuqin—that is, as "a more than usually self-assured master, fully conscious of [her] place in the annals of Buddhism." She also appears to have felt confident of having met the expectations of her audience, and by extension, her later readers, as we can see from the closing lines of the written version of this sermon:

> After a long pause, she grasped her staff and raising it up high, said: "If you do not exert the strength that lifts tripods and uproots mountains, then it will be difficult to ride the ten-thousand-*li* black steed." The assembly was satisfied and delighted, and making their obeisances, they left [the hall].
>
> 良久, 拈拄杖卓一卓云: 若無舉鼎拔山力, 千里烏騅不易騎. 眾歡喜, 作禮而退.

## Notes

1. Pei-yi Wu, *The Confucian's Progress: Autobiographical Writings in Traditional China* (Princeton: Princeton University Press, 1990).

2. Wu, *The Confucian's Progress*, 76. Zuqin may not have actually been the first to do this: as Miriam Levering has pointed out, descriptions of personal inner experiences can also be found in the sermons of Zuqin's predecessor, Linji Chan master Dahui Zonggao 大慧宗杲 (1089–1163). See Levering, "Was There Religious Autobiography in China before the Thirteenth Century? The Ch'an Master Ta-hui Tsung-kao (1089–1163) as Autobiographer," *The Journal of Chinese Religions* 30 (2002): 97–122.

3. Wu, *The Confucian's Progress*, 76.

4. Wu, *The Confucian's Progress*, 91.

5. Wu, *The Confucian's Progress*, 91

6. There are, for example, autobiographical sermons by Miyun's dharma successor Fushi Tongxian 浮石通賢 (1593–1667) and Linye Tongqi 林野通奇 (1595–1652), as well as by Tianyin Yuanxiu's dharma successor Wanru Tongwei 萬如通微 (1594–1657) and Wanru's student Jie'an Wujin 介菴悟進 (1612–1673). Most of these sermons can be filed under the category of *xingshi* 行實, which like the related term *xingzhuang* 行狀, was originally used to refer to a person's moral conduct, but which later came to refer more generally to a record of a person's activities and was usually compiled after the death of a master by his disciples.

7. Wu, *The Confucian's Progress*, 84.

8. Wu, *The Confucian's Progress*, 85.

9. See Mario Poceski, "Chan Rituals of the Abbot's Ascending the Dharma Hall to Preach," in Steven Heine and Dale S. Wright, eds., *Zen Ritual: Studies of Zen Buddhist Theory in Practice* (Oxford: Oxford University Press, 2007), 83–112.

10. As Sidonie Smith reminds us, "every day, in disparate venues, in response to sundry occasions, in front of precise audiences (even if an audience of one), people assemble, if only temporarily, a 'life' to which they assign narrative coherence and meaning and through which they position themselves in historically specific identities. Whatever that occasion or that audience, the autobiographical speaker becomes a performative subject." Sidonie Smith, "Performativity, Autobiographical Practice, Resistance," in Sidonie Smith and Julia Watson, eds., *Women, Autobiography, Theory: A Reader* (Madison: University of Wisconsin Press, 1998), 108.

11. Qian Qianyi, "Zuotuo biqiuni Chaoyin taming" 坐脫比丘尼潮音塔銘, *Muzhai youxueji* 牧齋有學集 (*Xuxiu siku quanshu* 續修四庫全書 ed.), "Bu" 補, 29b–30b.

12. For more on these two women, see Miriam Levering's articles, "Miao-tao and Her Teacher Ta-hui," in Peter N. Gregory and Daniel A. Getz Jr., eds., *Buddhism in the Sung* (Honolulu: University of Hawaii Press, 1999), 188–219; "Dōgen's *Raihaitokusui* and Women Teaching in Sung Ch'an," *Journal of the International Association of Buddhist Studies* 21.1 (1997): 77–110; and "Women Ch'an Masters:

The Teacher Miao-tsung as Saint," in Arvind Sharma, ed., *Women Saints in World Religions* (Albany: State University of New York Press, 2000), 180–204.

13. We do not know how many other such sermons might have been in circulation, since most of the over thirty *yulu* of women Chan masters for which we have titles or references are no longer extant. But it is quite possible that they may have also contained similar autobiographical sermons.

14. As Grace Fong notes, late imperial women writers for the most part used poetry or self-prefaces to poetry collections to write autobiographically. A striking exception is Ji Xian 季嫺 (1614–1683), a Buddhist laywoman, author of an autobiographical account titled "Record of Past Karma," which Fong calls the "only example of an autobiographical essay written by a woman that focuses on her religious experience." See Ji, "Record of Past Karma," trans. Grace Fong, in Susan Mann and Yu-yin Cheng, eds., *Under Confucian Eyes: Writings on Gender in Chinese History* (Berkeley: University of California Press, 2001), 136.

15. For a complete translation of this letter, see Wu, *The Confucian's Progress*, 239–242 (Appendix A). A partial translation can also be found in J. C. Cleary's translation of the *Changuan cejin* 禪關策進. See J. C. Cleary, *Meditation with Koans* (Berkeley: Asian Humanities Press, 1992), 51–53.

16. Elspeth Graham, Hilary Hinds, Elaine Hobby, and Helen Wilcox, eds., *Her Own Life: Autobiographical Writings by Seventeenth-Century Englishwomen* (London and New York: Routledge, 1989), 4–5.

17. Sidonie Smith, *A Poetics of Women's Autobiography: Marginality and the Fictions of Self-Representation* (Bloomington: Indiana University Press, 1987), 52.

18. Smith, *A Poetics of Women's Autobiography*, 34.

19. Unless otherwise indicated, the primary texts quoted in this chapter are found in the Jiaxing Buddhist canon 嘉興大藏經. For ease of reference I here provide citations to the digital version of this important collection, which is available through the Chinese Buddhist Tripitaka Electronic Text Collection, Taipei Edition 台北版電子佛典集成, http://taipei.ddbc.edu.tw/jiaxingzang.php. Jizong's four-*juan yulu* collection—which I refer to in subsequent notes simply as *Jizong yulu*—is titled *Jizong Che Chanshi yulu* 季總徹禪師語錄, 28.B211, http://taipei.ddbc.edu.tw/sutra/JB211_001.php. The text cited here, from a preface by Ming-loyalist-turned-Buddhist-layman Yan Dacan 嚴大參 (1590–1671), can be found at J28nB211_p0442b10-12.

20. As Ken Plummer notes, an autobiographical act is constituted at its most basic by the interaction among three components or kinds of people: the coaxer, the producer, and the consumer. The coaxer, according to Plummer's scheme, is basically, "any person or institution or set of cultural imperatives that solicits or provokes people to tell their stories," as quoted in Smith and Watson, *Women, Autobiography, Theory: A Reader*, 64.

21. Jizong's autobiographical sermon (*xingshi* 行實) can be found in *juan* 2 of her *yulu* (see no. 17), J28nB211_p0453b01-p0454b08.

22. Quoted in Domna C. Stanton, "Autogynography: Is the Subject Different," in Smith and Watson, *Women, Autobiography, Theory: A Reader,* 139.

23. Stanton, "Autogynography: Is the Subject Different," 139.

24. "Shi Xiang Hanlin furen" 示項翰林夫人, J28nB211_p0452a23—p0452b04.

25. Graham et al., *Her Own Life*, 25.

26. See John Kieshnick, *The Eminent Monk: Buddhist Ideals in Medieval Chinese Hagiography* (Honolulu: University of Hawaii Press, 1997).

27. *Yuechuang Liao chanshi yulu* 月幢了禪師語錄, J29nB237_p0450b09J29nB237_p0450b10. Yuechuang Zheliao was a dharma heir of Linji master Zhangxue Tongzui 丈雪通醉 (1610–1695), who in turn was a student of Miyun's dharma heir Poshan Haiming 破山海明 *(1597–1666).*

28. *Fushi chanshi yulu* 浮石禪師語錄, J26nB185_p0616a04—05.

29. Pei-yi Wu, *The Confucian's Progress*, 83.

30. For more on *kanhua* investigation, see Robert E. Buswell, "The 'Short-cut' Approach of *K'an-hua* Meditation: The Evolution of a Practical Subitism in Chinese Zen Buddhism," in Peter N. Gregory, ed., *Sudden and Gradual: Approaches to Enlightenment in Chinese Thought*, Studies in East Asian Buddhism 5 (Honolulu: University of Hawaii Press, 1987), 321–77.

31. Gaofeng Yuanmiao's discourse records became extremely popular after they were reprinted by Yunqi Zhuhong 雲棲袾宏 (1535–1615) in 1599. It is interesting to note as well that Gaofeng Yuanmiao was the subject of one of the many vitriolic battles conducted by Miyun Yuanwu and his followers. As Jiang Wu notes, this particular debate, which was carried out between 1636 and 1638, was between Miyun Yuanwu and the eminent Caodong master Zhanran Yuancheng 湛然圓澄 (1561–1626) and his student, Ruibai Mingxue 瑞白明雪 (1588–1638). The contested matter was whether Gaofeng Yuanmiao's primary enlightenment (1266) was a single event or it was actually divided into two discrete events, the first leading gradually to the second. See Wu, *Enlightenment in Dispute*, 307.

32. See Pei-yi Wu, *The Confucian's Progress*, 240.

33. Pei-yi Wu, *The Confucian's Progress*, 240.

34. "Fu ni Jizong" 復尼繼總, in *Shishuang Erzhan chanshi yulu* 石霜爾瞻尊禪師語錄, J27nB200_p0580b03—p058b07.

35. Poceski, "Chan Rituals," 97.

36. Poceski, "Chan Rituals," 99.

37. Mizhan Dazun held this position until 1646, after which he became abbot of the famous Shishuang 石霜 Monastery outside of Changsha.

38. Smith and Watson, *Women, Autobiography, Theory: A Reader*, 99.

39. Smith and Watson, *Women, Autobiography, Theory: A Reader*, 100.

40. "Jizong Che chanshi yulu xu" 季總徹禪師語錄敘, J28nB211_p0442b16-p0442b19.

41. "Jizong chanshi yulu xu," J28nB211_p0441a01—p0442a11.

42. Sung-peng Hsu, *A Buddhist Leader in Ming China: The Life and Thought of Han-shan Te-ch'ing, 1546–1623* (University Park: Pennsylvania State University Press, 1979), 7.

43. See Thomas Cleary and J. C. Cleary, trans., *The Blue Cliff Record* (Boston: Shambhala, 1992), 73 (Eleventh Case, "Huang Po's Gobbler of Dregs").

3

# Making Religion, Making the New Woman

## Reading Su Xuelin's Autobiographical Novel *Jixin* (Thorny Heart)

*Zhange Ni*

### Introduction

The seventeenth-century female Chan master Jizong Xingche lived in a world far different from Su Xuelin 蘇雪林 (1897–1999), yet women's autobiographical writings continued to be a literary form for religious women to construct their religiosity and subjectivity in the twentieth century. However, autobiography, especially autobiographical fiction, cannot be treated as a passive depository where authors document their lived experiences or a transparent lens through which readers approach other people's lives. Autobiography is not a symbolic field where fiction and reality merely intersect or converge but a highly charged discursive space where the boundaries for each side are constantly problematized. These shifting boundaries duly direct our critical attention to the constructedness of categories such as "religion" and "woman."

I highlight at the outset that "religion" is not a transhistorical, cross-cultural sui generis experience; likewise, "woman" is a discursive practice rather than an ontological essence. In this light, to avoid an essentializing reading of the enactment of women characters' religious experience in Su Xuelin's autobiographical writing, I read the literary text as a dynamic process of exchanges, (mis)appropriations, and negotiations among various interest groups. This complex process encompasses the production, reception, and rewriting of the text over three decades and participates in the discursive formation of religion and the new woman in twentieth-century China.

When Su Xuelin published her debut novel *Jixin* 棘心 (Thorny Heart) in May 1929, this young woman, who had recently returned to Shanghai from France, immediately attracted the attention of both leftist intellectuals and Catholic clerics. The intersection of these two seemingly incompatible cohorts turned out to be most intriguing.[1] Based on the author's experience in France, *Thorny Heart* is a female Bildungsroman. Du Xingqiu 杜醒秋, the protagonist of this autobiographical novel and the author's doppelganger, is a rebellious woman who broke free from the confinements of Confucian ritual teachings to pursue a modern education. After having attended the Women's Normal College in Beijing, she traveled to France to study literature and the arts. Xingqiu was courted by Qin Feng 秦風, a fellow Chinese student and an aspiring art historian, but she rejected him for a lack of reciprocal feeling. Not in love with her fiancé Shujian 叔健 either, she attempted to break their engagement but eventually submitted to this arranged marriage. Quite unexpectedly, our protagonist was not a stone-hearted narcissist but a filial daughter. She sacrificed her right to free love and free marriage so as not to hurt her mother, who had already been victimized not only by Confucian patriarchy but also the "liberating" discourse of New Culture that flourished in the late 1910s and 1920s. When her mother's health deteriorated, Xingqiu abandoned her studies (and the better career opportunities they could lead to) and returned to China to get married at the deathbed of her mother.

Even more unexpectedly, she returned as a Catholic. During her sojourn in France, she was drawn to Catholicism because of her contact with Catholic nuns and laywomen, in whom she saw the virtue of self-sacrifice as practiced by her Confucian mother. Even though she was thousands of miles away from China, she fretted over every bit of news from her family, hometown, and motherland. She suffered with her people and envisioned a national salvation in the moral redemption of Catholic teachings, or, more precisely, the moral cultivation of her Catholic sisters and Confucian mother. Against the secularist tide of Chinese New Culture, our protagonist/author converted to Catholicism and endeavored to reconstruct her version of New Womanhood from the standpoint of religion. This reconstruction simultaneously constituted her attempt to reconfigure religion, another discourse under transformation, from a gender-specific perspective.

On June 28, 1929, the first review of *Thorny Heart* appeared in *Shenghuo zhoukan* 生活週刊 (Life Weekly) and was drafted by Zou Taofen 鄒韜奮 (1895–1944). The title of Zou's essay, "Jieshao yiben haoshu *Jixin*"

介紹一本好書 "棘心" (Recommending a Good Book, *Thorny Heart*), not to mention his praise for the novel's romantic mood and patriotic tone, spoke volumes and indeed helped to increase sales.[2] The three thousand copies of the first printing sold out in four months. In September, another three thousand hit the market. The third printing in 1930 and the fourth in 1931 brought the number up to ten thousand. Altogether, Beixin Press produced eight printings of *Thorny Heart* until the Second Sino-Japanese War broke out full-scale in 1937. Although the specific number of copies sold from printings five to eight is not available, the commercial success of the novel is undisputed.

The appeal of *Thorny Heart* to its readers in the late 1920s and 1930s was at least twofold. On the one hand, the themes of the woman question and romantic love, both crucial to the formation of the modern nation-state, or to the imagination of the revived national community, captured the enthusiasm of an entire generation of writers and readers. More specifically, the novel rode the wave of female writers' and domestic stories' rise in popularity in Republican Shanghai. On the other hand, the Catholic conversion narrative in Su Xuelin's novel, a rare phenomenon in modern Chinese literature, was eagerly celebrated by Chinese Catholics, who felt marginalized in their own native culture. However, as is demonstrated in what follows, although promoting women's liberation was crucial to Chinese nationalism and then the Proletarian revolution, the leftists misread the gendered reimagination of the nation as enacted by the novel and turned a blind eye to religion in *Thorny Heart*. Likewise, despite the resonance for Catholics of Su Xuelin's concern with the position of religion against the backdrop of the social-political upheavals in modern China, they ignored her refashioning of religion for Chinese women in particular and truncated her feminist visions within their rigid framework of Catholic morality.

What is the alternative imagination of womanhood and national revival explored as it was in Su Xuelin's novel? How did Chinese women experiment with religion in both subject formation and nation building? How was the modern Chinese iteration of religion shaped not only by women's everyday experience but also the discursive formation of the "new woman," and vice versa? To address these questions is the agenda of this chapter. In what follows, I first contextualize the novel by locating it within the history of modern Chinese literature and that of Chinese Catholicism. Particular attention is paid to the divergence of Su's text from, rather than its facile identification with, the prevailing nationalist literature and the indigenization project of Chinese Catholics. Next, through a comparative reading of the revised edition of *Jixin* (1957) and the 1929 original, I demonstrate that Su responded to her critics by further developing her alternative vision of the "new woman" and foregrounding her sensitivity toward the complexities that marked the translation of the modern, Western category of religion into the Chinese *zongjiao*. Together these two intricately intertwined discursive practices distanced Su from the literary mainstream and Catholic authority (or their simplified idealizations) and claimed her as a vivid encapsulation of the neglected messy contestations that have shaped our current conceptual framework.

## Mother-Daughter Love: "Feudal" Burden or Alternative Nationalism?

Thanks to the recommendation of Zou Taofen, leftist critics duly recognized Su Xuelin among the emerging women writers of the New Culture era. In the early 1930s, among the literary criticisms published about women writers,[3] Qian Xingcun's 錢杏邨 (1900–1977) monograph offered the most detailed reading of Su Xuelin's *Thorny Heart* and her prose writing. Qian labeled Su Xuelin a "boudoir writer" (*guixiu zuojia* 閨秀作家), the narrow scope and immature stance of whose writing, despite its aesthetic accomplishments, stood in stark contrast to ideal revolutionary literature. In his review essay, Zou Taofen gave due credit to the exquisite wording and genuine feeling of *Thorny Heart* and identified the love between mother and daughter as the central theme of the novel. However, in Qian Xingcun's reading, the exquisite wording lavished over the natural world in the novel amounted to an escape from harsh social realities, whereas the genuine feeling of the daughter toward her mother turned out to be a sign of conservativeness.

Su Xuelin (and her doppelganger Xingqiu), who placed her devotion to her mother above all and submitted to an arranged marriage, was a typical boudoir writer. "The female stance as demonstrated by Su Lüyi 蘇綠漪 [Su Xuelin] is not new, not the most progressive stance of the Bourgeoisie class during the May Fourth Movement,"[4] commented our proletarian (supposedly more progressive than the bourgeoisie) critic; "the stance unfolded under the pen of Su Lüyi is a female stance adopted by women recently liberated from feudal society, just beginning to acquire the sensibility of the Bourgeoisie class, and still exhibiting a sentimentalism dominated by feudal powers."[5] Qian Xingcun and other leftist critics posited an evolutionary scale by narrating the revolutionary progress that stretched from "feudal" society through a capitalist phase to the utopian world of socialism. They positioned women writers on this scale in light of the degree to which they were liberated from "feudal" ritual teachings and bourgeoisie moral propriety. Ding Ling 丁玲 (1904–1986) was their model feminist, whose amoral, if not immoral, depiction of sexual desires broke out of the confinement of feminine inner quarters and marked her entry into the world at large, a world where she was to be further awakened to the suffering of the proletariat.

As argued by scholars of modern Chinese literature, the emotional life of the individual was foundational to the relationship between the private (subject) and the public (political order). It is along the lines of heterosexual romance, supposedly free of social status and familial/communal tradition that writers and readers of Chinese New Literature tended to imagine the emerging national community. Moreover, the late 1920s and early 1930s witnessed the transition from the Enlightenment discourse of free love as the pursuit and exercise of a naturally given human right, as proclaimed during the May Fourth era, to the literary phenomenon of "revolution plus love." In this new trend of writing, heterosexual romance was reconfigured as a grand trope for the proletarian revolution, or in other words, appropriated by the discourse of the proletarian revolution, one that claimed to be more progressive than the bourgeois enlightenment, which was outdated and to be displaced.[6] In addition, popular writers such as the Mandarin-Ducks and Butterflies (Yuanyang hudie pai 鴛鴦蝴蝶派) produced their alternative "religion plus love" novels, prioritizing the importance of the "private realm" under the influence of late-Qing constitutional reformers such as Kang Youwei 康有為 (1858–1927) and Liang Qichao 梁啓超 (1873–1929).[7] The publication of *Thorny Heart* coincided with all those "revolution plus love" texts. Under the shadow of the latter, the failure of heterosexual romance, the submission to arranged marriage, and the emotional attachment between mother and daughter in *Thorny Heart* immediately distanced it from the literary mainstream of that time.

To invoke Zou Taofen again, although he stressed the intertwining of filial devotion and patriotic feelings in *Thorny Heart*, the overlapping images of mother and China (motherland) as well as the alternative national imagination along the lines of mother (nation) and daughter (citizen) were overlooked by leftist critics of the novel. They exiled this alternative vision, which was in potential competition with the imagination of the national order (and then the revolutionary cause) that consisted of free, heterosexual lovers, into the realm of femininity, aesthetic aloofness, and political conservativeness. Part and parcel of the "feudal powers" or "feminine sentimentalism," in the words of Qian Xingcun, was religion, another disruptive theme of the novel—but again, this was overlooked altogether by leftist critics. What I argue in this essay is that, the same way in which female solidarity challenged the hegemony of heterosexual love, religion in *Thorny Heart* occupied the position reserved for revolution, which was hailed to be formative and redemptive for the individual as well as the nation. Both (secular) revolution and (heterosexual) love were radically reconfigured in *Thorny Heart*, which fashioned itself as a narrative of "religion plus female homosociality."

As elaborated in my close reading of the novel, the struggles of our protagonist/author to embrace religion and her eventual self-sacrifice for her mother (nation) are portrayed as two sides of the same coin. In other words, the alternative gender configuration of the national imagination in *Thorny Heart* and the novel's dismantling of the secularism of both the bourgeoisie enlightenment and the proletarian revolution are mutually undergirding and reinforcing. When mother-daughter love, predicated upon the suppression/sacrifice of heterosexual love and free marriage, was subsumed under and sublimated into religion (that is, Catholicism and Confucianism, although neither in its orthodox sense) in Su Xuelin's novel, our author positioned herself as a conservative whose radicalism went beyond the receptive apparatus of the leftists and the Catholic clerics. On the one hand, leftist critics painted her as an elite woman happily caught up in her ivory tower. On the other hand, the Catholic clerics praised the moralism in her writing, but remained ignorant of, or chose to ignore, her efforts to transform Catholicism, Confucianism, and the generic category of religion from within.

## Whose Catholicism? Whose Confucianism? Whose Religion?

Immediately after the publication of *Thorny Heart*, Ma Xiangbo 馬相伯 (1848–1939), the renowned Catholic intellectual, educator, and indigenizer based in Shanghai, wrote to his fellow priest Xu Zongze 徐宗澤 (1886–1947)—a direct descendant of Xu Guangqi 徐光啓 (1562–1633), the Confucian scholar-official converted by Matteo Ricci—to request a casual meeting with the author.[8] It turned out that Xu Zongze, to whom Su Xuelin went for spiritual guidance when she arrived in Shanghai from France, was the very person who encouraged the writing of the novel, or, more precisely, a conversion narrative and spiritual biography. Ma Xiangbo and Xu Zongze invited Su Xuelin to contribute to the Catholic journal *Shengjiao zazhi* 聖教雜誌 (Sacred Teaching Magazine). In the next two decades, she published numerous articles in other Catholic journals as well, such as *Yishi zhoukan* 益世週刊 (Yishi Weekly) and *Xin beichen* 新北辰 (New North Star).

In the 1940s, Su Xuelin was acclaimed by European missionaries who endeavored to cultivate a Chinese Catholic literature.[9] For instance, Joseph Schyns (1899–1979), a Belgian missionary of Congregation Immaculati Cordis Mariae, headed the publication of *Commentaries on the Literary Art: Volume A* (*Wenyi yuedan jiaji* 文藝月旦甲集), first in French (*Romans a lire et romans a proscrire*, 1945) and then in Chinese (1947). In *Commentaries on the Literary Art: Volume A*, the fiction and prose of Su Xuelin was listed among the very few titles recommended for the free, that is, unguided, perusal of Catholic youth. In 1948, the sequel (Volume B) to the previous book was published, this timc in English, titled *1500 Modern Chinese Novels and Plays*. Su Xuelin was invited by Joseph Schyns to contribute her long survey essay "Present Day Fiction & Drama in China" (written in English) to the volume.[10]

The sustained popularity of *Thorny Heart* could be at least partly attributed to Su Xuelin's activity in and influence on the Catholic circle, although her readers from the New Literature camp must have contributed to its sales no less substantially. Needless to say, the Catholics read *Thorny Heart* first and foremost as a conversion narrative. Ma Xiangbo and Xu Zongze fully sympathized with the spiritual struggle of our protagonist/author over questions such as how to embrace Catholicism in the face of the assaults of the Enlightenment critique of religion and how to deal with the expansion of Protestant missions in China, as well as the Western hegemony that threatened to destroy Chinese tradition. The indigenization project of Chinese Catholics in the early decades of the twentieth century was plagued with and motivated by its own "thorny heart." It is in the project of national/ist imagination that the leftists, Catholics, and Su Xuelin all participated. However, in competition with the leftists (later Communists) who strived to monopolize nationalism, the Catholics (among whom we may count Su Xuelin) endeavored to diversify national imaginations, whereas Su Xuelin (in contrast to her Catholic readers/critics/collaborators, most of whom were male priests and missionaries) further called our attention to the possibility of appropriating Catholicism (and religion in general) for (Chinese) women.

Both Chinese indiginizers and European missionaries believed that the moral salvation of Catholicism was the much-needed cure for the rampant social ills of modern China. Hence Ma Xiangbo founded Aurora University for the education of Catholic youth, while Xu Zongze used his *Sacred Teaching Magazine* as a venue to reach toward, communicate with, and educate the Catholic community in Shanghai and nationwide.[11] In the rather exhaustive review of major and minor writers produced by Joseph Schyns and other missionaries, they critiqued the obsession with revolution among serious writers, on the one hand, and the further disintegration of proper moral and social order in popular literature, on the other. They extolled Su Xuelin as aesthetically accomplished yet morally upright and uptight, as the hope for Chinese Catholic literature. According to them, the impulse to destroy that was set loose by revolutionary discourse led Chinese youth away from performing their duties and obligations and situating themselves within family, society, and the national community. In contrast, both Catholicism and Confucianism emphasized the vital significance of keeping an ideal household infused with parental love and filial piety, with the household as the basic unit of social structure and national community. Hence national salvation depended on the proper maintenance of the worldly order starting from personal cultivation within the family and would ultimately elevate itself into spiritual aspiration toward the beyond.

Clearly, the story of Du Xingqiu in *Thorny Heart* illustrated the aforementioned vision. Su Xuelin the "conservative" was destined to be applauded by her fellow "conservatives." However, they either unwittingly missed or intentionally ignored something. They saw no women, neither the predicaments of individual women within the so-called ideal household nor the dynamic discursive practice of "woman" as one of the key terms in modern Chinese history. As a result, the Catholics let Su Xuelin's exploration into religion—another discursive practice, from the perspective of and for the sake of women, or, more precisely, her exploration into the symbiotic formation of modern religion and the new woman in late imperial and early Republican China—slip right through their fingers.

In 1949, the year of the Communist takeover, Su Xuelin left Mainland China for Hong Kong and worked for the Catholic Truth Society there. She revisited Europe in 1950 to make a pilgrimage to the Vatican, stayed in France for two years, and permanently settled in Taiwan in 1952. Five years later, unhappy with the two pirated versions of *Thorny Heart* that appeared in Hong Kong and Taiwan, she arranged for the publication of the revised and expanded edition of her 1929 novel by the Catholic Guangqi Press in Taizhong, Taiwan.[12] The original twelve thousand characters grew into eighteen thousand. On two topics, women and religion, six thousand more characters were lavished. As highlighted by the author herself in the preface to the 1957 edition:

> The agenda of this book is to introduce to the reader a young woman intellectual, who was born at the time of political turmoil, immersed in the new thoughts of the May Fourth era,

> and eventually converted to Catholicism. This book intends to encapsulate within her experience the entire epoch: fluctuations in familial, societal, national, and international affairs, predicaments and aspirations of intellectuals, and different approaches adopted by intellectuals in their engagement with love, self-formation, and salvation of their nation and the world.

Questioning the ideal (patriarchal) household upheld by Catholic clerics and other cultural conservatives, Su Xuelin defended the May Fourth movement out of her experience as a Chinese woman:

> Even now the May Fourth movement is criticized for having committed the brutality of crushing Chinese tradition. Up till now the delusion to turn back the wheel of time and revive pre–May Fourth culture has been persisting. For me, those people are either die-hard traditionalists or fortunate in two ways: first, having been born into a simple and harmonious household; second, born too late to experience the oppression of the old society. The former may be explained by referring to his personal inclination, whereas the latter means pure good luck. However, once the fate of a nation depends on personal idiosyncrasies and/or whimsical opportunities, who can say it is not extremely dangerous? Hence the author has always been defending the May Fourth movement.

In what sense was the May Fourth movement legitimate? Compared with the original novel, the 1957 edition was no longer just a portrait of the author as a young woman but a collective portrait of Xingqiu, Madam Du (Xingqiu's mother), Bailang 白朗 (a Catholic laywoman in France), and Masha 馬莎 (a Catholic nun in France). Madam Du, a woman who was born in the latter half of the nineteenth century and endured what most Chinese women had been suffering, was presented as both "a victim of Confucian family system and ritual teachings" and, more significantly, "a paragon of sagely virtue and filial piety." On the one hand, the brutality of the Confucian tradition toward women in the form of the patriarchal household was vividly portrayed in the new edition, in Madam Du's daily toil and little Xingqiu's fight for education. On the other hand, Madam Du was presented as ingeniously negotiating with her environment and manipulating the limited resources available to her, by no means a passive victim of the various liberation discourses that dismissed her as a woman left behind.

Catholic women in France were further developed as major characters in this revised novel as well. It is by these Catholic women that our protagonist/author was converted; she admired their freedom, no matter how restricted, in the public realm, and she felt more related to them than either God or the church. Hence it is perfectly understandable that, upon leaving France, Xingqiu visited the Cathedral of the Sacred Heart in Paris and prayed to Mary, Mother of God, for the well-being of her mother. Surrounded by and pierced with bitter thorns, the bleeding heart of the Mother of God was no different from the thorny hearts of human mothers who suffered labor, separation, and loss. Although the episode of Mary worship was already present in the 1929 novel, what is new in the 1957 edition is the deathbed conversion of Madam Du. *Thorny Heart* is not just a novel of mother-daughter love but the sanctification of female virtues and bondage.

In addition to women, religion—not Catholicism per se but the generic category of religion as well as its transformation in modern China—received a much more elaborate depiction in the 1957 edition. It is true that our narrator spilled more ink over diverse topics such as ancient cosmology, design argument, modern alienation, and religious revival in twentieth-century Europe; however, more than simply parroting the history of religious fluctuation in the West, *Thorny Heart* encapsulates the Chinese encounter with and remaking of the Western discourse of religion in the early decades of the twentieth century. The general consensus now is that religion as a modern, Western discourse has been deeply embedded within the historical developments of its Christian, or, more precisely, Protestant environment.[13] The modern Chinese term *zongjiao* 宗教 was a neologism borrowed from Japanese at the end of the nineteenth century to translate religion from the West. The translation of the Western model of religion into China had its sociopolitical consequences and to a considerable extent shaped the unfolding of modern Chinese history.[14] In this regard, the pretext of *Thorny Heart* is precisely the disintegration of the premodern Chinese system of religion (here the word is used retrospectively), the struggle of Chinese intellectuals to appropriate the alien category of religion, and the clash (or mutual shaping) of religion and the shifting manifestations of secularism. Even more valuable is that this novel wrestled with the modern, Chinese (re)making of religion within the relatively unexplored realm of women's experiences; furthermore, it shed light on the neglected field of religion in which Chinese women oriented and empowered themselves at the moment of social fermentation.

In the 1929 *Thorny Heart*, Xingqiu's conversion, although an immediate consequence of her personal contact with Catholic women in Lyon, was depicted as not unaffected by the religion debate in the late 1910s and the antireligion movement in the early 1920s, both of which were happening back in China. According to the record in Su Xuelin's diary (1957), a section was removed from the expanded 1957 version to avoid redundancy and published as a freestanding single article, "Wo youxiao shi de zongjiao huanjing" 我幼小時的宗教環境 (The Religious Environment of My Early Years).[15] In this article, she used the term *zongjiao* to designate Confucian ancestral worship and familial structure, Buddhist and Daoist practices, folk customs recently labeled superstitions, and the Christian religion, both Protestant and Catholic. It is worth noticing that Su Xuelin, instead of forcing non-Western traditions into the straitjacket of religion, was acutely sensitive toward the discrepancy between religion in the West and religion as practiced by ordinary Chinese people at the turn of the nineteenth and twentieth century. Although "The Religious Environment of My Early Years" failed to make its way into the 1957 *Thorny Heart*, Su Xuelin, safeguarded by the Taiwan Strait from the assaults of Communists, revisited the rivalry between religion and revolution, something overlooked by leftist critics back in the 1930s, and told the story of how in the late 1910s and early 1920s, the Communist Party and the Catholic Church competed for the body and soul of not only French youth but also Chinese laborers and students in France.[16] Xingqiu suffered setbacks in her spiritual quest and even struggled at the brink of apostasy after conversion, not only due to her post-enlightenment mentality (already prominent in the 1929 version), but also because (as fleshed out in the 1957 edition) her fellow students, bypassing the female community of Catholic sisters, viewed her conversion only within the framework of the Communism-Catholicism tug-of-war.

Having approached *Thorny Heart* via the mediation of its early reception among leftist critics and Catholic clerics, I proceed to read the 1957 edition, of course in close comparison with the 1929 original, in the next two sections. It is hard to imagine that Su Xuelin, a careful and incisive researcher working on contemporary literature, had never read reviews of her own novel. Each group of critics read into the text their respective agendas; in turn, they retrieved out of it their own concept of woman, religion, or the nation. Having lived through the collision and/or confluence of her vision with those of others, Su Xuelin returned to revise *Thorny Heart* and produced the 1957 edition. *Thorny Heart*, not only the text per se but also the production/reception/revision of it, presents a tale that encapsulates as well as envisions the intertwined making of religion and the new woman in early twentieth-century China.

## The "Woman Question" and the Dissenting Voice of Su Xuelin

In the 1930s, as evidenced by reviews from beyond the Communist and Catholic camps, *Thorny Heart* was read as a love story, no matter how unconventional, among Chinese students in the exotic West. The protagonist Xingqiu pined for love. She loved sentimental literature and movies, crying her heart out for star-crossed lovers. But she rejected Qin Feng, who had been abandoned by his former lover and was attracted to Xingqiu's talent in literature and the arts. More interestingly, she strenuously disciplined herself to love her fiancé Shujian, directing her sentiment that was aroused by the enchanting scent and sight of spring blossoms toward the man who was pursuing a PhD in America. However, Shujian seemed indifferent to their arranged marriage, making no effort to infuse it with romantic love as Xingqiu did, and corresponded with her out of mere formality. Hence Xingqiu had a fight with her father to cancel their engagement. She gave up out of consideration for her mother. Correspondingly, outside the fictional world, Su Xuelin (Xingqiu) married Zhang Baoling 張寶齡 (Shujian) in 1925 in Shanghai. Their marriage was listless at its best, but Su Xuelin published a collection of essays describing their idyllic family life and titled her book *Lütian* 綠天 (Green Sky), from which her penname Madam Lüyi 綠漪 was derived. "*Lütian* was a beautiful lie," Su Xuelin frankly admitted. She had to lie to herself, in order not to awaken from one of the biggest dreams of her day, romantic love and free marriage.

From the perspective of her contemporaries and even some readers of our time, Su Xuelin deserved her conservative reputation.[17] Although disillusionment with romantic love and free marriage was all too palpable in the writing of women authors, Su Xuelin's submission to and advocacy of the old system of arranged marriage made her a thorn in the side of those who would rather push their critique further by questioning the new:

> She [Xingqiu] contends love should be conditional: cultivation, personality, temperaments . . . are all cardinal conditions to be considered when choosing a spouse. Human temperaments are inconstant; even more so is the contingency of love. Without proper conditions, hollow love alone runs the danger of leading marriage astray.
>
> She used to think marriage could not be constrained. However, when divorce is too easy while getting together too romantic, problems arise too. Human temperaments are unpre-

> dictable. The more wanton, the less carefree; the more obsessed with perfection, the less unlikely to detect flaws. What is the point of flirting around, failing to secure one's heart, and suffering disappointment? Speaking of the two genders, men suffer less while women are the real victims. Once over thirty, they are no longer that fair and burdened with kids. Who is going to take care of her after divorce? Humanism seems not to allow her to pine away in eternal solitude either.
>
> Xingqiu did not dare to love Qin Feng out of her seriousness toward love. She has her reasons not to object to the marriage prearranged by her family too: First, she is not willing to hurt her mother; second, she is aware of the social status of Shujian, they make a good match; third, she fully understand the fickleness of human temperaments and does not mind letting the marriage arrangement restrict both Shujian and herself.[18]

This mini-lecture by Xingqiu critiqued the discourse of romantic love by opposing the order of social hierarchy to the inconstancy of human nature. It is natural that the leftist critics would read her as a remnant of the "feudal" world. However, they overlooked her attentiveness to gender inequality in the institution of modern marriage and misread her attachment to other women. When scholars showcased the transition from the literary masculinism produced by late imperial homosocial Confucian order to the heterosexual imagination of the modern nation in New Literature, they failed to pay enough attention to the homosocial ties between women. In typical New Literature texts, "New Women" were primarily and predominantly defined in their (no matter how troubled) sexual relation to men. We have read how Qian Xingcun dismissed Xingqiu's attachment to her mother as immature, whereas Su Xuelin's ideal "New Woman," embodied by Xingqiu, was generated by and in turn aspired to generate a homosocial order of women.

New women were not insensitive to other women—mothers, ex-wives, and maids—whom they left behind in their "liberation" through free love. However, Xingqiu stood alone in choosing her mother over freedom to love and building up a (seemingly) nonsexual network of female camaraderie. In the expanded edition, the original chapter 1, "Muqin de nanxuan" 母親的南旋 (Mother Returning South), grew to incorporate a detailed biography of the mother, portraying her *both* as a victim of the patriarchal household *and* a shrewd and resourceful "minister" with family affairs as her "state." Enjoying the same privilege as Xingqiu's mother, the Catholic nun Masha had her own biographical chapter, "Masha de jiating" 馬莎的家庭 (Masha's Family), chapter 11 of the 1957 *Thorny Heart*, while the 1929 original had already devoted a chapter to Bailang, the laywoman (and future nun) who initiated Xingqiu into Catholicism ("Bailang nüshi" 白朗女士, or Madam Bailang, chapter 11 of the 1929 edition, and chapter 9 of the 1957 version). Xingqiu saw her mother in Bailang, Masha, and other Catholic women who devoted themselves to education, nursing, and missionary work, not just with self-sacrificing virtue but also with the virtue of self-assertion through sacrifice.

Taking care of the elderly and sick, raising the next generation, overseeing ancestral rituals, and running the family business, her mother, to whose mind revolution was totally alien, negotiated with and within the patriarchal Confucian household, which was compared to a Confucian state blessed with a sagacious minister. Likewise, Catholic nuns, far from being cloistered, were portrayed as free women who remained active in the public realm and even traveled overseas (although only as assistants of priests). In early twentieth-century France, where Catholicism had already suffered through the secularizing revolutions of the nineteenth century and was severed from the public order, social work performed by Catholic women helped keep the church visible beyond its shrinking domain.[19] Given this mutual embrace of women and religion, it is no coincidence that Xingqiu was converted to Catholicism by women.

Catholicism in Xingqiu's world was a women's religion. Interestingly, when Catholicism was still foreign to her, she ridiculed the male clergy in the streets of Lyon as "white-necked crows to be washed away by the passage of time." Moreover, the only full-length prayer uttered by Xingqiu in the novel was addressed to Mary, Mother of God:

> Holy Mother . . . please listen to my prayer. Last time my mother was sick. I prayed to your Son; soon she recovered. Now she has fallen sick again and is in severe danger. I am so worried that I can only pray to you. Please pass my word to your Son and bless my mother with recovery. . . . You, Holy Mother, having given birth yourself, you deeply understand the love between a mother and her child. . . . When your Son was wearing a crown of thorns on his head, your heart was circled with a ring of roses. Roses have their thorns too, thorns of love. A heart pierced by love is incurable!
>
> The heart of my mother is pierced with sharp blades and surrounded by rose wreathes. Her sons either dead or sick, her

> beloved daughter far from home, all these misfortunes within the family were thrust at her heart like swords and thorns and made it bleed. I believe your heart is as pierced as hers. The line "Jixin yaoyao, mushi qulao" 棘心夭夭，母氏劬勞 (Fair and tender are thorny shrubs; toiled and moiled our mother), when read out of its original context, sounds like an implicit dedication to the thorny heart of mothers.[20]

In Xingqiu's prayer, our narrator explicates the meaning of "thorny heart," the central image within the novel. It is the bleeding heart of the mother, the guilt-ridden heart of the young girl, and the boundless compassion of the Holy Mother. When Xingqiu began to view Bailang and Masha as virtuous women in line with her mother, the barrier between her, a "New Woman" indoctrinated in May Fourth new thoughts, and Catholicism crumbled. It is this same emotional bond that kept her in the bosom of her mother and drew her into the Catholic/female community. It is this women's religion that provided a space for her to articulate her attachment to her mother (best exemplified in the preceding quotation), a space not available in the heterosexual "New Woman" discourse.

In the 1957 expansion, a whole new chapter titled "Zi guifang taru xuetang" 自閨房踏入學堂 (From Boudoir to School) was inserted between the biography of Xingqiu's mother (chapter 1) and Xingqiu's travel to France (chapter 3). A brief history of women's education was offered. Xingqiu was first educated at home because her illiterate grandmother needed girls to read Buddhist sutras to her. She was sent to a primary school for girls established by American missionaries since Chinese public schools were not open to women yet, and the few private girls' schools happened not to be located in her home province. When the Qing dynasty was finally replaced by the Republic of China, a modern nation-state, in 1912, women's education entered a new stage. Xingqiu rebelled against the marriage arrangement made by her family and succeeded in attending first the new girls' normal school in the provincial capital and then the prestigious women's normal college in Beijing. (Although the novel, either old or new, remained silent about it, it is worthy of mention that even before Su Xuelin left Beijing for France, she had already made her name as a promising as well as controversial columnist well known for her sharp tongue and fiery temper.)

This new chapter was added to flesh out Xingqiu, her mother, and their love. In the 1929 edition, our narrator told a moving story of Xingqiu and her mother, a story in which Xingqiu ignored her mother's enthusiasm for learning to read and write (with her help of course) and was beset with guilt when her half-literate mother, eager to communicate with her daughter in another country, on another continent, grabbed a teenage boy and dictated a letter to Xingqiu. When Xingqiu received the letter, she noticed it had been registered and sent by express post and realized her mother had paid extra money to compensate for the fact that she had not been able to write it herself. And, the ideal old age as dreamed of by Xingqiu's mother was to live with her daughter and other family members, while reading *Romance of the Three Kingdoms* (*Sanguo yanyi* 三國演義) and *tanci* 彈詞 fictions written by and for women.[21] This domestic "minister" was eager to have her adventure with the world of governance and warfare in imaginative literature. Moreover, when urging her daughter to teach her more characters, she said:

> "Don't laugh at me for 'learning to be a trumpet at the age of eighty.' If I were born blind, completely blind to all colors and shapes in the world, I would have nothing to complain about. But I have opened my eyes slightly and seen how the light shines. Do not fold my eyes, or my heart refuses to rest in peace. Isn't this mentality common to us ordinary people?"[22]

However, her daughter, who had to endure hardships to pursue education herself (the point of the new chapter), pushed her aside and was to suffer regrets. The new chapter "From Boudoir to School" highlighted Xingqiu's "*yaoqiu shangjin de tianxing*" 要求上進的天性 (nature to aspire and transcend) as what motivated her to pursue women's education and liberation. This "tianxing" 天性 (nature) was meant to resonate with her mother's restless heart. Xingqiu was willing to sacrifice love and marriage for her mother because in the first place they shared the same aspiration to transcend, although the specific contexts for these two generations differed. The existentialist tone of *Thorny Heart* is unmistakable. Since Su Xuelin spent two years in Paris from 1950 to 1952 (immediately in the wake of the publication of Simone de Beauvoir's *Le Deuxième Sexe* in 1949) and translated materials on the women's movement and feminist scholarship for the Catholic Truth Society in Hong Kong, it is safe to postulate she was under the influence of existential feminism. Moreover, the Chinese character *tian* in *tianxing* may be translated as either nature, (supernatural) heaven, or both. Moreover, it is not to be overlooked that the narrator even compared Xingqiu's determination to pursue education to Mohammed's founding of a religion. As mentioned earlier, at the end of the 1957 novel (again, not in the 1929 original), the mother on her deathbed was converted by her daughter and welcomed into the embrace of the Holy Mother in heaven. Existential feminism further evolved into religious feminism. Zou Taofen was incisive to celebrate mother-daughter love in *Thorny Heart*, but he would never expect mother and daughter to travel this far.

Despite the flourishing of women's studies in the China field, with much of the scholarship concentrated on the long twentieth century and emerging new interpretations of the imperial period, "[i]nterest in women and religion has generally lagged behind."[23] Identifying *nuxing* 女性 (women) as a repository of social experience, a productive misappropriation, and a historical catachresis, gender scholars forgot that *zongjiao* was neither an ontological entity nor a universal category. In this regard, the catachresis of religion (intertwined with that of women) and the messiness in the Chinese remaking of religion is what is to be investigated next. Having discussed how Su Xuelin not only reimagined the national community on the basis of female bondage but also infused this imagination with a religious sentiment, I now shift my attention to what she meant by the very term of *zongjiao* within and beyond the text of *Thorny Heart*.

## (Women) (Re)Making Religion in Modern China

When *Thorny Heart* was first published in 1929, the compound *zongjiao* had existed in modern Chinese for only three decades. Two years after the birth of Su Xuelin, in 1899, the late Qing reformer Liang Qichao popularized the neologism *zongjiao* with a Chinese audience and initiated the history of "religion" in modern China. Su Xuelin's protagonist Xingqiu grew up with the Chinese discourse of *zongjiao*, which, as to be argued in what follows, is not a passive reproduction of religion in the modern Western sense. In this light, when we read *Thorny Heart* as an autobiographical account of how a new woman wrestled with religion, we study the formation of *zongjiao* as encapsulated in the lives of Chinese women at the same time. Acknowledging religion (that is, both a sui generis experience and a generic category) as a modern, Western invention, myth-breakers in the field of religious studies have revealed how religion, when imposed onto the non-Western world, may be evidence-distorting and thought-limiting in our research and, in the sociopolitical realm, participated in and contributed to the domination of the West over the Rest. Under the impact of this ideological critique of religion, historians, anthropologists, and sociologists working on modern Chinese religions have duly studied how the imposition of the modern, Western, and, more specifically, Christian (Protestant) model of religion, at the hands of the state and its elites, forced an entire set of disparate practices, ideologies, and institutions into the alien shoes of religion to be trimmed or even annihilated. However, scholarly attention so far has been restricted to the religion-state interaction, while how the same transitional process has played out in the field of literature, culture, and nation-formation, especially in relation to the gender configuration of that field, still remains to be explored.[24]

As already pointed out, the ambition of the expanded 1957 edition was to illustrate the shifting configuration of the religious field from the crumbling of the imperial world up to the antireligion movement in the 1920s and to present the history of religion in modern China as intertwined with that in nineteenth- and twentieth-century Europe (France). First of all, Su Xuelin lived through the disintegration of the premodern Chinese system of religion, as captured in "The Religious Environment of My Early Years."[25] Her description of the Confucian clan organized around ancestral worship, the Buddhist devotion of her grandmother and mother, and "superstitious" practices such as divining local deities vividly illustrated the point made by historians of Chinese religion that although there was no exact equivalent of religion in premodern China, the Chinese people had been practicing their own form of religion and organized their own religious systems.

According to historians of Chinese religion, the premodern Chinese system of religion was internally diversified and contested; it consisted of individual spiritualities, communal practices, sectarian movements, and organized traditions such as Confucianism, Buddhism, and Daoism. This system evolved in close interaction with the imperial state and generated its usages and categories analogous to what we mean by religion. The Chinese character under the rubric of which a sophisticated system of knowledge was developed was *jiao* 教 (teachings). The Chinese discourse of *jiao* took Confucianism as its archetype and integrated teachings of other traditions into its universe as well. Moreover, the orthodox form of this *jiao* was appropriated by the imperial state as its ruling ideology.[26] What Su Xuelin reminded us of in her article, memoir, and novel is that this *jiao* was performed at the levels of the state as well as the household, with the latter serving as the very foundation for the former. Within the Confucian household, men and women practiced *jiao* and simultaneously received the discipline of *jiao*. Therefore, the encounter of religion and the Chinese *jiao* inevitably left its impact on the reconstitution of gender, family, and the national community.[27] This actually helps to explain the popularity of the "revolution plus love" trend and other domestic novels in early Republican China.

It is most remarkable that Su Xuelin wrote an essay surveying and analyzing the fascination with "religion" among late-Qing Confucian scholar-officials—to name a few, Kang Youwei, Liang Qichao, and Tan Sitong 譚嗣同 (1865–1898)—first in 1939 and at the same time expanding it when she revised *Thorny Heart*.[28] In "Qingmo zhishi jieji de zongjiao re" 清末智識階級的宗教熱 (Fascination with Religion among the Intellectual Class at the End of the Qing Dynasty), she reviewed how late-Qing reformers were attracted to Christianity, revived Buddhism, and attempted to reconstruct Confucianism in the model of Western religion. Echoing the conviction of those reformers, she contended that religion was crucial to the vitality of the nation:

> When the world was caught up in the whirlwind of changes, the life of the state and the nation was at the brink of extinction, the people lost their hearts and spirits; without promoting a vibrant faith as the center of ideas, it would be impossible to resuscitate anything. Among all the faiths, religious faith, most grandiose in its aspirations and endowed with the most fervent passion, was the greatest. The best example in history would be Saint Joan of Arc, who, a country girl by origin, was able to save France at the time of crisis.[29]

Religion itself was not a static entity, especially at the time of radical changes.

When Liang Qichao introduced the neologism *zongjiao* in China at the end of the nineteenth century, China was marked by the collapse of the imperial state and the formation of the modern nation-state. The modern state in its formation, beginning with the 1898 reforms, drew material and symbolic resources from the disintegrating field of *jiao*, by reinventing this field in the model of modern, Western, and, Christian religion. In this regard, current scholarship has highlighted a series of major events: (1) The imperial Qing government, seeking its modern transformation, ordered in 1898 and 1901 that Confucian academies as well as Buddhist, Daoist, and popular temples be converted into public schools; (2) In 1912, the new Republican state, in addition to further carrying out the converting-temple-to-school policy of the previous regime, decreed that religion be separated from the state, promised to grant religious liberty only to the officially recognized religions, and forced existing traditions to form church-like national associations to negotiate with the state in search of official recognition; (3) In the early years of the twentieth century, the crumbling Qing government launched its antisuperstitions campaigns, which were to be resumed by the Nationalist state established in Nanjing in 1927. What were targeted as superstitions to be destroyed turned out to be folk practices and sectarian movements. These phenomena constituted an integral part of the pre-encounter Chinese system but were excluded from the reconfigured religious field, which was modern, rational, and strictly regulated by the state.[30]

However, something is missing from this picture of state reinvention of religion, namely, the Chinese redefinition of religion as an integral part of the nation-building project, which may not be reduced to state formation. To take this even a step further, I highlight the Chinese discursive practice of religion as intertwined with that of modern womanhood and, most significant of all, not a monopoly of male intellectuals. First of all, little attention has been paid to the gap between 1912 and 1927 in terms of state formation. The Republic of China was founded in 1912; however, it was not until fifteen years later that the Nationalist government was established in Nanjing. What lies in between is what I mean by a "gap," that is, the virtual absence of a stably functioning central state, the power struggle among various political factions, the internal warfare of local warlords, and the incessant threats of Western colonization, all of which disturbed Xingqiu even though she was far away in France. Because of the frustration of state-building, the focus of nationalism shifted from state nationalism to cultural nationalism practiced by scholars and artists. The gap between 1912 and 1927 was actually filled by the May Fourth New Culture movement (in which Xingqiu proudly claimed to be an enthusiastic participant), the agenda of which was national enlightenment and salvation.

Our current scholarly focus on the state-religion interplay is to be complemented with attention paid to the rise of a national/ist culture (best exemplified by New Literature) shouldering the extra political weight of nation-formation. The rise of this national/ist culture was premised upon the Chinese redefinition of religion into *zongjiao* and intertwined with the appropriation of *zongjiao* by Chinese women in their self-fashioning. To substantiate my claim, I read the episode of the quarrel over *zongjiao*/religion between Xingqiu and Shujian in *Thorny Heart* through the lens of Liang Qichao's redefinition(s) of the term, which strongly resonated with Su Xuelin. Most interestingly, the first obstacle between Xingqiu and Shujian in their carefully cultivated relationship was their conflicting attitudes toward religion. Not yet finding her way into the community of her Catholic sisters, Xingqiu was a zealous antireligionist while Shujian defended religion on the grounds of individual freedom and human diversity. Xingqiu was disappointed at Shujian's detachment and indifference and viewed it as indeed a sign of his inability to love. However, it is Xingqiu the momentary New Culture secularist who converted to Catholicism eventually. The key to understanding this radical transformation lies in what Xingqiu (and Su

Xuelin), under the influence of intellectuals such as Liang Qichao, took *zongjiao* to be.[31]

When Liang Qichao first adopted *shukyo*, a term coined by the Japanese to translate religion, and read it in its Chinese pronunciation, *zongjiao*, this compound was a familiar stranger to his Chinese readers. On the one hand, *zongjiao* looked familiar to the Chinese because both characters could be easily identified in both Confucian classics and Buddhist scriptures. In Confucianism, although the compound *zongjiao* did not exist, *zong* signifies deities who were recipients of ritual sacrifice, while *jiao* signifies teachings established by sages. In Buddhism, *zong* referred to doctrines, texts, or schools, while *zongjiao* meant teachings of various schools.[32] On the other hand, *zongjiao*, as the Chinese translation for religion as interiorized belief in the supernatural and separated from the public and the political, was strange to the Chinese. Liang himself interpreted the term within the context of the Confucian *jiao*. He read *zong* (v.) *jiao* (n.) in a literal sense, that is, the teaching that one adopts in reverence, and further explained the neologism by giving a metaphor, the medicine that cultivates the brain of a nation (*zhuzao guomin naozhi zhi yaoliao* 鑄造國民腦質之藥料).[33]

In 1902, having absorbed Western theories of religion through Japanese mediation, Liang momentarily changed his definition of *zongjiao*. On the one hand, he dismissed religion (translated as *zongjiao*) as superstitious belief in the supernatural, stressed that religion should be separated from the state, and refused to recognize Confucianism as a religion. On the other hand, for him, *zongjiao* was still inseparable from *jiao* in the Chinese context. Liang never meant to discredit Confucianism as the foundation for the civilizational identity of China and conceptualized the Confucian discourse of *jiao* as internally diversified and dynamic, that is, inclusive of the social organizing and governing power of non-Christian traditions.[34]

The fissure between religion and *jiao* in *zongjiao* was mended when Liang articulated his mature theory of *zongjiao* in 1922. Between 1902 and 1922, the new Republic was founded; the new religious field was struggling into being as the result of the interaction between the state and religious institutions; the New Culture movement erupted when the state was severely weakened by restoration attempts and warlord conflicts; and the brutality of World War I brought forth disillusionment with Western modernity and progress. Liang visited Europe right after the war and began to question his uncritical embrace of Western ideas. Instead of defining the Chinese *zongjiao* as belief in the supernatural according to the narrow standard of religion in the West, he proclaimed that *zongjiao* was fervent emotions devoted to a whole range of natural, supernatural, and social objects and celebrated it as the vital energy for the individual and the nation. Among the examples he enumerated as *zongjiao*, the nation-building New Culture was particularly conspicuous. Moreover, he named the antireligion movement as *zongjiao* befitting his definition. In some sense, he abandoned his wavering position between religion and *jiao* in 1902 and returned to his 1899 original reading of the neologism as medicine for the nation.[35]

It is to the New Culture scholars and students, and during the Chinese religion debate that lasted from the late 1910s to the early 1920s and escalated into the anti-Christian movement in 1922, that Liang addressed his theory of *zongjiao*. The New Culture mainstream was agitated by an antireligion sentiment (picked up by Xingqiu in her reading of publications sent to France from China). However, the New Culture field was already diversified and heterogeneous. Liang was followed by many other intellectuals who problematized the Western construction of religion and developed *zongjiao* as a catachresis for Chinese modernity. In *Thorny Heart*, when Xingqiu was studying in France in early 1920s, she and her fellow students were duly tuned in to the antireligion (and anti-Christian) ferment of the Chinese New Culture movement.[36] Corresponding with her fiancé regularly, she sought the New Culture type of romantic love as well.

However, what initiated her disillusionment in romantic love was her break with Shujian's liberal attitude toward religion, that is, mere toleration of personal choice. Although using the same term *zongjiao*, Shujian embraced the modern, Western model of religion while Xingqiu had a Chinese understanding of *zongjiao*. Moreover, for her, *zongjiao* and love were coterminous, with *zongjiao* meaning "fervent emotions devoted to the nation," while love was to be sought between women themselves. It is in this light that we perceive her antireligious passion as a *zongjiao* defined by Liang Qichao and then understand her conversion as a natural outcome of her seemingly secularist sentiment earlier. Her conversion to Catholicism was her very effort to model herself after the virtuous life of her mother and Catholic sisters toward the end of national salvation. In her own words:

> I swear with my conscience, Catholicism is a good religion; the personality of its believers is truly admiring. I am afraid the rampant tradition of selfishness is to be blamed for the failure of China. Suppose we have ten thousand Chinese who are determined to sacrifice themselves just like Bailang and Masha, who are well educated and scholarly competent as well, we should set them up as paragons to serve our society and look forward to the empowerment of China. I am definitely sure that China will no longer be weak![37]

When *zongjiao* was redefined as "fervent emotions" and incorporated into the nation-building project, when the "religion plus love" theme in *Thorny Heart* challenged the literary trend of "revolution plus love," the convergence and competition of religion and revolution in modern China could no longer be swept aside. The 1957 *Thorny Heart* introduced a new character, Father Lai, the prototype of whom was the renowned Catholic missionary Vincent Lebbe (1877–1940). A sympathizer of the Boxer Rebellion and supporter of the indigenization of Catholicism in China, Lebbe was repositioned by the church back to France, where, in the post–World War I years, he offered financial aid to Chinese laborers and students (and converted some of them), who turned out to be the targets of the mobilizing project of the Comintern as well.[38] How the Communist Party and the Catholic Church imitated the discourses, policies, and institutions of one another in their competition over the youth on an international scale has already been subject to the investigation of scholars of European history. Su Xuelin's novel further demonstrates that the repercussion of this Communist-Catholic competition reached as far as China.

In *Thorny Heart*, Xingqiu's conversion was viewed as an act of betrayal by her fellow students, whose "fervent emotions" were devoted to the Altar of Nationalism and/or the Gospel of Communism. Her aversion to the detachment of Shujian paralleled her apology to her fellow students, who accused her of having taken money from the Catholic Church (although she was converted by Catholic women, not Father Lai) and thus having betrayed China:

> She did not hate her fellow students who despised her. Instead she admired them. . . . The brutal rule of warlords, the prevalence of corruption, and the recurring failures in politics were consequences of her fellow nationals' reluctance to make moral judgment. The Chinese were too numb, too cold, and too incapable of punishing for the sake of maintaining justice.
>
> Now her fellow students thought she had done something wrong and hated her fervently. Their fervent hatred attested to the heat in their blood and the abundance of their sense of justice. The heart of Chinese people was not dead yet. China still had a future. The more her fellow students despised her, the more she felt relieved for and assured of the future of China.[39]

Discerning the spirit of nation-saving *zongjiao* in these passionate youth, our protagonist/author stopped short of confronting the fervent devotion to the nation from the Communist side with her Catholic redemption of the nation. However, this confrontation was the lifetime enterprise of Su Xuelin. How did Christianity (both Catholicism and Protestantism) and Communism interact with each other in Republican China? Why did Su Xuelin attack Communism as an antireligious religion? These questions, beyond the limits of *Thorny Heart* and this chapter, await future research, the point of departure of which, as this chapter has endeavored to trace and stress, is the historical process through which religion was remade into *zongjiao* in modern China, by the hands of both men and women.

## Notes

1. Su Xuelin, *Jixin* (Shanghai: Beixin, 1929); and Chen Siguang 陳思廣, "Zai shengcheng yu ronghui zhizhong: 1929–2009 nian jixin de chuanbo yu jieshou yanjiu" 在生成與融匯之中: 1929–2009年 "棘心" 的傳播與接受研究, *Jianghan Luntan* 江漢論壇3 (2011): 127–31.

2. Zou Taofen, "Jieshao yiben haoshu *Jixin*," *Shenghuo zhoukan* (June 1929): 304–5.

3. He Yubo 賀玉波, *Zhongguo xiandai nüzuojia* 中國現代女作家 (Shanghai: Xiandai chubanshe, 1932); Cao Ye 草野, *Xiandai Zhongguo nüzuojia* 現代中國女作家 (Shanghai: Renwen shudian, 1932); and Qian Xingcun, *Dangdai Zhongguo nüzuojia lun* 當代中國女作家論 (Shanghai: Guanghua chubanshe, 1933).

4. Qian, *Dangdai Zhongguo nüzuojia lun*, 131.

5. Qian, *Dangdai Zhongguo nüzuojia lun*, 149.

6. Jianmei Liu, *Revolution plus Love: Literary History, Women's Bodies, and Thematic Repetition in Twentieth-Century Chinese Fiction* (Honolulu: University of Hawaii Press, 2003); David Der-wei Wang, *The Monster That Is History: History, Violence, and Fictional Writing in Twentieth-Century China* (Berkeley: University of California Press, 2004); Haiyan Lee, *Revolution of the Heart: A Genealogy of Love in China, 1900–1950* (Stanford: Stanford University Press, 2007).

7. For related discussion, see Nicole Huang, *Women, War, Domesticity: Shanghai Literature and Popular Culture in the 1940s* (Leiden, Boston: Brill, 2005).

8. Ma Xiangbo, "Ma Xiangbo zhi Xu Zongze xin" 馬相伯致徐宗澤信, in Zhu Weizheng 朱維錚, ed., *Ma Xiangbo ji* 馬相伯集 (Shanghai: Fudan University Press, 1996), 508.

9. Angel Pino and Isabelle Rabut, "Les Missionnaires Occidentaux Premiers Lecteurs de la littérature Chinoise Moderne," in Jean-Louis Bacqué-Grammont and Angel Pino, under the direction of Samaha Khoury, *D'un Orient l'autre, Actes des Troisièmes journées de l'Orient, Bordeaux, 2–4 octobre 2002* (Paris: Peeters, 2005), 465–93; Liu Lixia 劉麗霞, "Cong *Wenyi yuedan (jiaji)* kan Tianzhujiao chuanjiaoshi de zhongguo xiandai wenxue guan" 從 "文藝月旦 (甲集)" 看天主教傳教士的中國現代文學觀, *Guangxi shehui kexue* 廣西社會科學2 (2003): 111–12; and Liu,

"Jindai laihua shengmushengxin huishi dui zhongguo xiandai wenxue de pingjie" 近代來華聖母聖心會士對中國現代文學的評介, *Zhongguo xiandai wenxue yanjiu congkan* 中國現代文學研究叢刊 2 (2011): 171–82.

10. Joseph Schyns, *Romans a lire et romans a proscrire = Shuo pu chên p'ing* (Tianjin: Chihli Press, 1946); Joseph Schyns et al., *1500 Modern Chinese Novels & Plays* (Hong Kong: Lung Men Bookstore, 1966). For studies of Chinese New Literature in general and Su Xuelin in particular by other missionaries, see Henri van Boven, *Histoire de la Littérature Chinoise Moderne* (Beiping: Chihli Press, 1946); Jean Monsterleet, *Sommets de la littérature chinoise contemporaine* (Paris: Domat, 1953); Octave Brière, "Sou Mei [Su Mei] ou Lou I [Lu Yi], ses contes et sa critique," *Wanxiang* [Toutes choses], 4: 4.16 (1943): 920–33; Jean Monsterleet, "De l'amour d'une mère à l'amour de Dieu: Sou Siue-Lin [Su Xuelin] (Sou Mei [Su Mei]) témoin de son temps," *China Missionary Bulletin* 1 (1952): 8–15.

11. For an introduction to and discussion of Chinese Catholic figures, see Lei Libai 雷立柏 (Leopold Leeb), *Lun jidu zhi da yu xiao: 1900–1950 nian huaren zhishifenzi yanzhong de Jidujiao* 論基督之大與小: 1900–1950年華人知識份子眼中的基督教 (Beijing: shehui kexue wenxian chubanshe, 2000), 181–234; and Sigurd Bergmann, *God in Context: A Survey of Contextual Theology* (Aldershot, Burlington: Ashgate, 2003), 53–57.

12. Su, *Jixin* (Taizhong: Guangqi chubanshe, 1957), reprinted in Fu Yifeng 傅一峰, ed., *Jixin* 棘心 (*Jixin* and Other Writings) (Beijing: Yanshan chubanshe, 1998).

13. Wilfred Cantwell Smith, *The Meaning and End of Religion* (New York: Macmillan, 1963); Talal Asad, *Genealogies of Religion: Discipline and Reasons of Power in Christianity and Islam* (Baltimore and London: Johns Hopkins University Press, 1993); Timothy Fitzgerald, *The Ideology of Religious Studies* (New York and Oxford: Oxford University Press, 2000); and Fitzgerald, *Discourse on Civility and Barbarity: A Critical History of Religion and Related Categories* (Oxford: Oxford University Press, 2007).

14. Prasenjit Duara, *Rescuing History from the Nation: Questioning Narratives of Modern China* (Chicago: University of Chicago Press, 1995); Vincent Goossaert, "Le destin de la religion chinoise au 20e siècle," *Social Compass* 50.4 (2003): 429–40; Goossaert, "1898: The Beginning of the End for Chinese Religion?" *Journal of Asian Studies* 65.2 (2006): 307–36; Goossaert, "L'invention des 'religions' en Chine modern," in Anne Cheng, ed., *La pensée en Chine aujourd'hui* (Paris: Gallimard, 2007), 185–213; Mayfair Mei-hui Yang, ed., *Chinese Religiosities: Afflictions of Modernity and State Formation* (Berkeley: University of California Press, 2008); Yoshiko Ashiwa and David Wank, eds., *Making Religion, Making the State: The Politics of Religion in Modern China* (Stanford: Stanford University Press, 2009); Rebecca Nedostup, *Superstitious Regimes: Religion and the Politics of Chinese Modernity* (Cambridge: Harvard University Press, 2009); and Vincent Goossaert and David Palmer, *The Religious Question in Modern China* (Chicago and London: University of Chicago Press, 2011).

15. First published in *Ziyou Taipingyang yuekan* 自由太平洋月刊, included in her memoir *Wo de shenghuo* 我的生活 (Taibei: Wenxing shudian, 1967), and reprinted in Shen Wei 沈威, ed., *Su Xuelin wenji* 蘇雪林文集, volume 2 (Hefei: Anhui wenyi chubanshe, 1996), 35–44.

16. Susan B. Whitney, *Mobilizing Youth: Communists and Catholics in Interwar France* (Durham: Duke University Press, 2009); and Marilyn A. Levine and Chen San-Ching, "Communist-Leftist Control of the European Branch of the Guomindang, 1923–1927," *Modern China* 22.1 (1996): 62–92.

17. Other women writers of Su Xuelin's generation, such as Lu Yin 廬隱 (1898–1934), a classmate and then colleague of Su, tended to portray the break between a daughter and her mother and family as happening in the wake of a pursuit of romantic love. For translated texts, see Amy D. Dooling and Kristina M. Torgeson, *Writing Women in Modern China*, vol. 1 (New York: Columbia University Press, 1998). For more discussion, see Tani Barlow, ed., *Gender Politics in Modern China: Writing and Feminism* (Durham: Duke University Press, 1993); Wendy Larson, *Women and Writing in Modern China* (Stanford: Stanford University Press, 1998); Hu Ying, *Tales of Translation: Composing the New Woman in China, 1898–1918* (Stanford: Stanford University Press, 2000); Sally Taylor Lieberman, *The Mother and Narrative Politics in Modern China* (Charlottesville: University of Virginia Press, 1998); and Wang Lingzhen, *Modern and Contemporary Chinese Women's Autobiographical Writing* (PhD diss., Cornell University, 1998).

18. Su, *Jixin*, 89–90.

19. See the bibliography of women and religion in nineteenth-century France provided in *Mobilizing Youth*; for scholarship on Catholic nuns in France, see Jo Ann McNamara, *Sisters in Arms: Catholic Nuns through Two Millennia* (Cambridge: Harvard University Press, 1996); Sarah Ann Curtis, *Civilizing Habits: Women Missionaries and the Revival of French Empire* (Oxford, New York: Oxford University Press, 2010); Sioban Nelson, *Say Little, Do Much: Nurses, Nuns, and Hospitals in the Nineteenth Century* (Philadelphia: University of Pennsylvania Press, 2001); and Odile Sarti, *The Ligue patriotique des Françaises, 1902–1933: A Feminine Response to the Secularization of French Society* (New York: Garland, 1992).

20. Su, *Jixin*, 185–56.

21. Su, *Jixin*, 77.

22. Su, *Jixin*, 77.

23. Jessie G. Lutz, ed., *Pioneer Chinese Christian Women: Gender, Christianity, and Social Mobility* (Bethlehem: Lehigh University Press, 2010), introduction, 14. When surveying the "woman question" in relation to the grand project of nation formation in general, and, to late Qing nationalism, the May Fourth Enlightenment, and the Communist Revolution in the 1940s and 1950s in particular, Tani Barlow paid little attention to religion. See Tani E. Barlow, *The Question of Women in Chinese Feminism* (Durham: Duke University Press, 2004). For research related to the secular, secularism, and secularization, see Angela Zito, "Secularizing the Pain of Footbinding in China: Missionary and Medical Stagings of the Universal Body," *Journal of the American Academy of Religion* 75.1 (Spring 2007): 1–14; and

Joan Judge, *The Precious Raft of History: The Past, the West, and the Woman Question in China* (Stanford: Stanford University Press, 2008). Even when religion has been taken into account, such as in Patricia B. Ebrey's research on family rituals, Dorothy Ko's study of footbinding, or Jessie G. Lutz's edited volume *Pioneer Chinese Christian Women*, religion stays coterminous with Confucianism, Christianity, or other traditions. See Patricia B. Ebrey, *Confucianism and Family Rituals in Imperial China: A Social History of Writing about Rites* (Princeton: Princeton University Press, 1991); Dorothy Ko, *Cinderella's Sisters: A Revisionist History of Footbinding* (Berkeley: University of California Press, 2005); Jessie G. Lutz, ed., *Pioneer Chinese Christian Women: Gender, Christianity, and Social Mobility* (Bethlehem: Lehigh University Press, 2010).

24. Historical sociologist John Hutchinson contends that we need to distinguish between state-oriented political nationalism and the nation-building cultural nationalism that is aimed at a moral regeneration of the community through the work of scholars and artists. The activities of these two types of nationalism, both concerned with the autonomy and welfare of the nation, are complementary and alternating. See John Hutchinson, *The Dynamics of Cultural Nationalism* (London: Allen and Unwin, 1987).

25. Su, "The Religious Environment of My Early Years," in Shen Wei, ed., *Su Xuelin wenji*, 2:35–37.

26. In the words of Thomas David DuBois, the construction of religion in East and Southeast Asia "was not simply a function of naked European power, nor was it necessarily intentional. . . . [because] both before and after the period of European imperialism, states used religion to engineer social ethics and legitimate rule, scholars elaborated and enforced state theologies, and the missionary faithfully voiced the need for and nature of religious conversion." See DuBois's "Hegemony, Imperialism, and the Construction of Religion," *History and Theory*, Theme Issue 44 (December 2005): 116. If I read him correctly, the word "scholars" refers to the Confucian scholar-officials of precolonial Asia. However, his discussion of scholarship was devoted to the Euro-American academies, saving, graciously if not grudgingly, only the limited space of two footnotes for scholars of China and Japan (124, 126). He seemed to have deviated from his original topic, that is, the non-Western scholarly concerns that were channeled into the construction of religion and to have confused the construction of religion in East and Southeast Asia with the Western academic study of religion in East and Southeast Asia. What DuBois meant by religion, according to Chen Xiyuan 陳熙遠, is the discourse of *jiao* that took Confucianism as its archetype the same way that Christianity was the center of the solar system of religion—in other words, the Chinese counterpart, although not the exact equivalent, of religion. See Chen Xiyuan, *Confucianism Encounters Religion: The Formation of Religious Discourse and the Confucian Movement in Modern China* (PhD diss., Harvard University, 1999). However, exclusive focus on Confucian orthodoxy, the reign of which was only a prescribed ideal rather than social actuality, would run the danger of distracting us from an exploration of the full scope and complication of Chinese encounters with religion. In this regard, Anthony

C. Yu, through research into Chinese classics, identified the original appearance of the compound *zongjiao* (not to be confused with its modern usage though) with medieval Buddhism. In this light, Robert Campany's work on Chinese Buddhism in the medieval period is not irrelevant to our study of the modern translation of religion. He demonstrated that early medieval China (non-Western as well as premodern), "with its situation of new religious imports and plurality, generated analogous usages" that correspond roughly to the Western vocabulary of religion (319). See Anthony Yu, *State and Religion in China* (Chicago: Open Court, 2005); and Robert Campany, "On the Very Idea of Religions (in the Modern West and Early Medieval China)," *History of Religions* 42 (May 2003): 287–319. The legacy of these usages, or the influence of Buddhism, may be identified in the work of Japanese scholars who chose to retrieve the very term *zongjiao*, as well as in that of their Chinese colleagues who decided to take the term back home.

27. In this regard, the insight of Su Xuelin resonates with that of Joan Judge, a gender historian who viewed women's liberation in late imperial China as in close association with the secularization process marked by the breakdown of Confucian ritual teachings. See Judge, *The Precious Raft of History*. However, in contrast to Judge's uncritical usage of the rather problematic term "secularization," Su Xuelin turned out to be a postsecular religionist (by today's standards) and was cautious enough to talk about religious change instead of secularization half a century earlier than Judge.

28. Su Xuelin, "Qingmo zhishi jieji de zongjiao re," in *Xinnanxing* 新南星 5.11: 229–30. Reprinted in *Tulong ji* 屠龍集 (Beijing: Shangwu, 1941), 113–30.

29. Su Xuelin, "Qingmo zhishi jieji de zongjiao re," 114.

30. Yang, *Chinese Religiosities*; Ashiwa and Wank, ed., *Making Religion, Making the State*; Nedostup, *Superstitious Regimes*; and Goossaert and Palmer, *The Religious Question in Modern China.*

31. Basidi 巴斯蒂 (M. Bastid-Bruguiere), "Liang Qichao yu zongjiao wenti" 梁啓超與宗教問題, in Hazama Naoki, ed., *Liang Qichao, Mingzhi Riben, xifang* 梁啓超, 明治日本, 西方 (Beijing: Shehui kexue wenxian chubanshe, 2001), 400–57; Vincent Goossaert, "Le concept de religion en Chine et l'Occident," *Diogène* 205 (2004): 11–21; and Chen Xiyuan, "Zongjiao: yige Zhongguo jindai wenhuashi shang de guanjianci" 宗教: 一個中國近代文化史上的關鍵詞, *Xinshixue* 新史學 13.4 (2002): 37–54.

32. More specifically, *zong* refers to: (1) a specific doctrine or an interpretation of it; (2) the theme or theory of a text, or an exegetical tradition of it; (3) a group or tradition that traces its origin back to a founder and shares some common doctrines and practices among its lineal successors. See Tang Yongtong 湯用彤, "Lun Zhongguo fojiao wushizong" 論中國佛教無十宗, *Zhexue yanjiu* 哲學研究 3 (1962), 47–54; "Zhongguo fojiao zongpai wenti bulun" 中國佛教宗派問題補論, *Beijing daxue xuebao* 北京大學學報 5 (1963): 1–18; and Stanley Weinstein, "Schools of Buddhism: Chinese Buddhism," in Mircea Eliade, ed., *Encyclopedia of Religion* (New York: Macmillan, 1987), vol. 2, 482–87. On this basis, the meaning of *zongjiao* is broader than teachings of particular schools.

33. Liang Qichao, "*Lun Zhina zongjiao gaige*" 論支那宗教改革, in *Liang Qichao quanji* 梁啓超全集 (Beijing: Beijing chubanshe, 1999; hearafter *Quanji*), 262.

34. Liang, "Baojiao fei suoyi zun Kong lun" 保教非所以尊孔論, *Quanji*, 465; "Lun zongjiaojia yu zhexuejia zhi changduan deshi" 論宗教家與哲學家之長短得失, *Quanji*, 762.

35. Liang, "Ping feizongjiao tongmeng" 評非宗教同盟, *Quanji*, 3968.

36. Scholarship on the antireligion/Christian movement includes Ka-che Yip, *Religion, Nationalism and Chinese Students: The Anti-Christian Movement of 1922–1927* (Bellingham: Center for East Asian Studies, Western Washington University, 1980); Jessie Gregory Lutz, *Chinese Politics and Christian Missions: The Anti-Christian Movements of 1920–28* (Notre Dame: Cross Cultural Publications, Cross Roads Books, 1988); Yang Tianhong 楊天宏, *Jidujiao yu minguo zhishi fenzi: 1922–27 nian Zhongguo fei Jidujiao yundong yanjiu* 基督教與民國知識份子: 1922–27年中國非基督教運動研究 (Beijing: Renmin chubanshe, 2005); and Duan Qi 段綺, *Zhongguo Jidujiao bensehua shigao* 中國基督教本色化史稿 (Taibei: Yuzhouguang chubanshe, 2005).

37. Su, *Jixin*, 113

38. Jean-Paul Wiest, "The Legacy of Vincent Lebbe," *International Bulletin of Missionary Research* (January 1999): 33–37; and Yvon Tranvouez, "Mission et communisme: la question du progressisme chrétien (1943–1957)," *Le Mouvement social*, "Utopie Missionnaire, Militantisme Catholique" 177 (October–December 1996): 49–69.

39. Su, *Jixin*, 171–72.

# Part II

# Redefining Identity and Tradition

4

# The Identity of Tang Daoist Priestesses

*Jinhua Jia*

## Introduction

Daoist priestesses had a remarkable presence in the Tang dynasty (618–907), the "golden age" of Daoist tradition. Historical records show that about one-third of Tang Daoist abbeys were convents,[1] and women from all social strata could be ordained as priestesses, ranging from imperial princesses to daughters of the poorest families. Although the majority of the priestesses assumed the roles of religious leaders, teachers, preachers, and practitioners, a number of priestesses also took on the "unconventional" roles of poets, musicians, artists, or even politicians. Among the three most famous women poets of the Tang, two were Daoist priestesses, Li Jilan 李季蘭 (d. 784) and Yu Xuanji 魚玄機 (ca. 843–868),[2] both of whom excelled in writing love poems. Through their negotiation with the sociocultural context, both types of roles demonstrated the priestesses' strong agency in religious, social, artistic, or literary activities, and their achievements and identity as Daoist priestess were generally admired and recognized by contemporary people.[3]

Since the Song dynasty, however, many traditional and modern scholars have redefined those Tang priestesses who assumed the roles of poet, musician, and artist as "courtesans" or "semi-courtesans."[4] It is true that even traditional critics praised the literary talents and achievements of actual courtesan-poets. However, since the redefinition of Tang priestesses as courtesans has often been accompanied by the moral judgment that condemns them as "licentious" (*yindang* 淫蕩) and the literary criticism that their "poetic style is lustful and weak" (*shiti yi miruo* 詩體亦靡弱),[5] this kind of redefinition is obviously biased. Although this biased redefinition has been mainly directed against those "unconventional" priestess-poets who wrote many love poems, other priestesses who assume the "conventional" religious roles have also been criticized for their public activities. There seems to be mainly two reasons for the biased criticism. First, some scholars followed the traditional rites that forbade women to be active in the public sphere and to pursue and express their own love and desire. For example, Chen Zhensun said in his synopsis to Yu Xuanji's poetic collection, "I once said that because the government did not forbid women to enter Buddhist and Daoist orders, they seriously wrecked the rites and destroyed the social customs."[6] Second, perhaps because the post-Tang ethical demands on women, including Daoist and Buddhist nuns, became more and more strict, some scholars failed to notice the particular cultural-religious context of the Tang dynasty that provided a relatively free and "legal" environment for the gender relations between Daoist priestesses and their male counterparts, which are discussed in the following sections of this chapter. For example, a modern scholar commented that the "lowest members" of the female Tang priesthood "were frivolous and disobeyed the rites," and they "always associated with the literati licentiously, little different from courtesans."[7] Another modern scholar said, "They did not observe the pure regulations and blasphemed the religious communities, which was really a shame."[8]

Although the institutional structure of traditional society in general marginalized women, in certain historical conditions the sociocultural context could facilitate the discursive production of women's agency.[9] This is especially true in the case of religion, as religious faith and practice often served as a source of encouragement and empowerment for women in particular historical and cultural contexts.[10] The notion of gender identity as constitutive of culture, society, and discourse also means that there are possibilities for emancipatory remodeling of identity, and that "agency begins where sovereignty wanes."[11]

In this study, I attempt to examine three issues relating to how those Daoist priestesses who assumed the roles of poets, musicians, and artists negotiated their place within the cultural-religious and socioeconomic milieu of the Tang dynasty. First, the religious practice of sexuality and other gender patterns within the Daoist tradition legitimized the emotional and sexual experiences of priestesses and helped shape new gender relations between them and their male counterparts. Second, the priestesses empowered themselves by using the cult of erotic goddesses and their considerable education. Finally, their independent socioeconomic status separated them from courtesans. Through examinations of these issues, this chapter seeks to demonstrate how the "unconventional" roles of Tang Daoist priestesses were constructed through both the sociocultural context and their own agency and to reveal their true identity free of the lenses of post-Tang discourse and ideology.

## Sexual Practice in Daoist Tradition and the Changing of Gender Relations

Based on the cosmological doctrine of the universal unity and balance of yin and yang, sexuality, either in a physical or spiritual way, had been one of the religious practices used to attain longevity and immortality in early Daoist tradition. During the Tang dynasty, such practice was still followed by Daoists, while the rule of celibacy was not strictly observed and marriage was allowed in certain circumstances. These conditions legitimized the sexual and emotional experiences of priestesses and helped shape new gender relations between them and priests or scholar-officials.

Scholars have long noted the initiation rite called "Rite of Passage" (Guodu yi 過度儀) and its aspects of sexual practice called "conjoining *qi*" (*heqi* 合氣) in the movement of Celestial Masters from about the second to the sixth centuries.[12] The Daoist texts that discussed this kind of ritual and practice were called "yellow books" (*huangshu* 黄書), which were possibly formulated or reformulated in about the fourth century. Two of the "yellow books" are preserved in the *Daoist Canon*, namely, the *Yellow Book of the Dongzhen Canon* (*Dongzhen huangsh*u 洞真黄書) and *Rite of Passage of the Yellow Book of the Highest Clarity Canon* (*Shangqing huangshu guodu yi* 上清黄書過度儀).[13] Fragmental citations and records are also seen in many other Daoist texts.[14]

Early Celestial Masters absorbed the ancient "art of the bedchamber" (*fangzhong shu* 房中術), involving longevity and sexual techniques, and transformed it into religious ritual and practice. Since the contents of the two major extant "yellow books," as well as citations and criticisms of them in other texts, are obscure and contradictory, scholars have had different views on major issues concerning the interpretation of the initiation ritual, such as its goal, procedures, doctrinal framework, and the relationship between participants. Generally speaking, scholars have agreed that the ritual was performed by male and female initiates under the instruction of a senior master, and the whole procedure involved visualization, breathing exercises, praying, incantation, elaborate choreography, and ritualized sexual intercourse, which was modeled after the magic square and the network of the stars. While a few scholars insist that the sexual intercourse during the process was merely ritual and symbolic,[15] most scholars believe it involved physical intercourse.[16]

From the fourth century, about the same time the Rite of Passage was recorded, amplified, or even reformulated, many harsh criticisms toward it were raised not only by Buddhists but also by Daoists. The sexual ritual and practice were deprecated and described as "man and women mingled indiscriminately, with no difference from animals" (*nannü hunman, buyi qinshou* 男女溷漫, 不異禽獸);[17] "Husbands were instructed to exchange their wives to enjoy new faces. Their fathers and elder brothers stand before them, yet they know no shame" (*jiaofu yifu, weise weichu; fuxiong liqian, buzhi xiuci* 教夫易婦, 唯色為初. 父兄立前, 不知羞恥).[18] Within the Daoist traditions, the Northern Celestial Master Kou Qianzhi 寇謙之 (365–448), the southern Highest Clarity Master Tao Hongjing 陶弘景 (456–536), and others launched reforms, and a common target of their reforms was to remove the Rite of Passage.[19] By the Tang dynasty, this ritual did not appear in Daoist texts concerning rites, which indicates that it had possibly been removed from the Daoist ritual system.

However, it should be noted that the target of Daoist reformers of various lineages from the fifth to sixth centuries was to remove the Rite of Passage, not the age-honored sexual practice. After his serious criticism of the rite, which had already become licentious, Kou Qianzhi still advised his followers to exercise regulated sexual practice:

> The art of the bedchamber is the root of living, and there are more than one hundred methods in scriptures. Therefore, it is not on the list of prohibition. If a married couple enjoys the methods, they should earnestly consult a pure and upright master, follow his instructions to practice, and select one of the methods according to their interest. This should be sufficient.
>
> 然房中求生之本, 經契故有百餘法, 不在斷禁之列. 若夫妻樂法, 但勤進問清正之師, 按而行之, 任意所好, 傳一法, 亦可足矣.[20]

Although the Highest Clarity tradition started to advocate celibacy under the influence of Buddhism, it also carried on the sexual practice of early Celestial Masters under new disguises.[21] First, instead of the husband-wife relationship or man-woman partnership, Highest Clarity masters created a motif of divine marriage: goddesses descended from heaven to have encounters with Highest Clarity masters. They composed poems to express their affections toward the chosen ones, offered to marry them, revealed sacred texts to them, instructed them to go through various practices, and finally took them by the hand to ascend to heaven.[22] This kind of divine marriage was termed "copulating radiances" (*oujing* 偶景) in Highest Clarity scriptures.

Second, in the Highest Clarity practice of visualization, one of the objects is the goddess. The practitioner visualized a specific goddess and imagined having various kinds of intimate contact with her. For example, the *Instructions for the Scripture of Xuanzhen in the Mingtang* (*Shangqing mingtang xuanzhen jingjue* 上清明堂元真經訣) describes the visualization of a Jade Maiden named Xuanzhen 玄真 within the sun and the moon:[23]

> You visualize a maiden as present within the sun or the moon. . . . You command that the Jade Maiden's mouth press a kiss upon your own mouth, causing the liquor of the *qi* to come down into the mouth. . . . After practicing for five years, the Jade Maiden of Greatest Mystery will descend to you, and lie down to take her ease with you.
>
> 又存日月中有女子. . . . 令玉女之口歃我口上, 使氣液來下入於口中. . . . 行之五年, 太玄玉女將下降於子, 與之寢息.[24]

Third, superficially, both the copulating radiances and goddess visualization were described spiritually and symbolically: "Although they are named husband and wife, they do not have the sign of husband and wife."[25] "The sign of husband and wife" refers to sexual intercourse. However, in the Highest Clarity texts, including Tao Hongjing's *Zhengao*, descriptions of the spiritual practice contain strong erotic elements and hints of intimacy evident to all the senses, such as the kiss and sleeping together in the preceding quotation. As Edward Schafer pointed out, it may be inadequate to translate the word *cun* 存 as "to visualize"—it may be closer in meaning to "to make sensibly present," "to give existence to," or even "to materialize."[26] Li Fengmao also believes that the divine marriage was not purely spiritual but possibly presented a kind of illusory and psychic entrancement of sexual intercourse.[27]

All these physical, spiritual, and illusory ways of sexual practice were introduced into the Tang dynasty. During the Tang, along with the establishment of monasticism as the key form of organized and state-sponsored Daoist practice, various Daoist traditions were loosely integrated into an ordination hierarchy known as Three Caverns (Sangdong 三洞). The most lucid record of this hierarchy system is a short text titled *Sangdong xiudao yi* 三洞修道儀 (Rite for the Practice of the Dao of the Three Caverns) transmitted by the priest Liu Ruozhuo 劉若拙 (fl. 882–972) and compiled by the scholar-official Sun Yizhong 孫夷中 in 943, around the mid-Five Dynasties.[28] With some minor variations, this text is basically in accordance with two late Southern dynasty to early Tang Daoist texts, the *Dongxuan Lingbao Sandong fengdao kejie yingshi* 洞玄靈寶三洞奉道科戒營始 (Rules and Precepts for Daoist Practice in Accordance with the Scriptures of the Three Caverns, a Dongxuan Lingbao Canon), compiled by Jinming qizhen 金明七真 probably in the sixth to seventh century,[29] and the *Chuanshou Sandong jingjie falu lüeshuo* 傳授三洞經戒法籙略說 (Short Exposition on the Transmission of the Scriptures, Rules, and Registers of the Three Caverns), compiled by Zhang Wanfu 張萬福 in 713, along with Zhang's *Sandong fafu kejie wen* 三洞法服科戒文 (Treatise on the Code of Ritual Vestments of the Three Caverns).[30]

The *Sandong xiudao yi* summarizes that in the Tang, all the Daoist traditions, scriptures, rules, registers, and precepts were loosely integrated as Three Caverns with seven ranks of ordination.[31] The seven ranks described in the three texts are roughly the same with some differences: Zhengyi 正一 (Orthodox Unity) or Chu rudao 初入道 (Novice), Gaoxuan 高玄 (High Mystery), Dongshen 洞神 (Cavern Numinous), Dongxuan 洞玄 (Cavern Mystery), Dongzhen 洞真 (Cavern Perfection), Dadong 大洞 (Great Cavern), and Sandong 三洞 (Three Caverns).[32]

Among these seven ranks, Daoists at the rank of novices or Orthodox Unity were allowed to maintain their marital status or get married. More remarkably, they were instructed to conduct sexual practice:

> For those who have already become husbands and wives, men are called Disciple of Pure Perfection, and women are called Disciple of Pure Faith. They should always follow the rules, purgation, and precepts, and at the same time practice the way of yellow-red intercourse. . . . For those who are husbands and wives, order them to select time and date, harmonize with yin and yang, and conduct intercourse. In this way, the boys and girls they produce will be protected from perverting and foul *qi*. Also order them to cherish their bodies and semen, not to be indulgent in immoderate sexual activities. . . . Female Officials of Allied Dignity of Orthodox Unity: the so-called three and five of red heaven means that the movement of the sun and the moon follow the two courses of yellow and red, which

> are called Two Radiances. The Perfected Persons are in charge of matters of the yellow-red course, in order to adjust yin and yang, so they use the palaces of the sun, the moon, and stars as administrative places.
>
> 如已成夫婦者, 男稱清真弟子, 女稱清信弟子, 常依科齋戒, 兼行黃赤交接之道. . . . 其有夫婦者, 令選時日, 順陰陽, 行交接. 即所育男女, 免感悖戾淫濁之氣. 亦欲令其保身愛精, 不妄貪淫. . . . 正一盟威女官: 所謂赤天三五者, 大凡日月運行, 皆依黃赤二道, 號曰二景. 凡真人掌黃赤道事, 以正陰陽, 用日月星宮為治所也.[33]

In many fourth- to seventh-century texts, "the way of yellow and red" refers to the Rite of Passage, conjoining *qi*, or sexual practice. The production of children undoubtedly indicates the physical intercourse of sexuality. In the last passage, it is unclear whether the perfected person's management of the yellow-red way means a kind of sexual ritual. However, it is clear that during the Tang and Five Dynasties, male and female Daoists in the rank of Orthodox Unity were allowed to get married and were instructed to conduct regulated sexual practice.

According to the *Sandong xiudao yi*, from the second rank of Cavern Numinous onward, Daoists were required to be celibate, and those who had married should separate.[34] However, this did not seem to be observed strictly and also did not mean that Daoists other than Orthodox Unity were not allowed to conduct sexual practice. For example, Princesses Jinxian 金仙 (689–732) and Yuzhen 玉真 (d. 761) were ordained as Daoist priestesses in 706 and received the Cavern Mystery ordination in 711 and the Great Cavern ordination in 712.[35] According to the epitaph of Princess Yuzhen's daughter-in-law, the princess had at least two sons. Her second son's wife, who was the daughter of a Tang princess as well, was born in 730 and married to Yuzhen's son Zhang Ti 張倜 in 744 when she was fifteen *sui*. When Zhang Ti died in about 760–761, he was still in his "vigorous years" (*maonian* 茂年).[36] Thus, Zhang Ti was likely about the same age as his wife and therefore was likely born after Yuzhen was ordained to the rank of Great Cavern in 712. In addition, there is a famous story that Emperor Xuanzong, Yuzhen's elder brother, once intended to marry her to the Daoist priest Zhang Guo 張果.[37]

The Tang *Regulations for Daoist Priests and Buddhist Monks* (Daoseng ge 道僧格), issued during the Zhenguan reign period (627–649), prohibited women from staying overnight in priests' rooms and men staying overnight in priestesses' rooms.[38] According to Moroto Tatsuo's 諸戶立雄 study, however, only regulations that involved violation of secular codes were actually implemented, while for those that went beyond the secular domain, the Tang government usually left Daoist or Buddhist monasteries to discipline themselves.[39]

Looking at Daoist texts of precepts of various ordination ranks compiled in the Tang dynasty we find that these precepts often only emphasize the prohibition of adultery and unrestrained sexual activities, and advocate the control and retention of semen. This indicates that, in addition to Daoists in the rank of Orthodox Unity, Daoists of other Daoist ranks also carried on regulated sexual practice. For example, the second of the "Ten Precepts of Cavern Mystery" (Dongxuan shijie 洞玄十戒) admonishes: "Do not commit adultery with others' women" (*bu yinfan ren funü* 不婬犯人婦女).[40] The third of the "Ten Good Precepts of Cavern Mystery" (Dongxuan shishan jie 洞玄十善戒) admonishes: "Do not commit adultery with others' wives" (*bude yinfan taqi* 不得婬犯他妻).[41] The first of the "Thirteen Prohibitive Precepts" (Shisan jinjie 十三禁戒) of Cavern Numinous admonishes: "Do not excessively conduct sexual activities and ejaculate semen: this will make your body and life die early" (*wu yinyu shixie, ling shenming yaomo* 勿淫欲施泄, 令身命夭歿);[42] or in a clearer phrasing: "Do not ejaculate semen: this will lead you to die early" (*wu shijing, ming yaomo* 無施精, 命夭歿).[43] The control and retention of semen in sexual intercourse first appeared in early texts on the "art of the bedchamber" and was later adopted and developed into Daoist sexual practice.[44]

Under the heading of "Fangzhong buyi" 房中補益 (Health Benefits of the Bedchamber) in his *Beiji qianjin yaofang* 備急千金要方 (Essential Priceless Prescriptions for All Urgent Ills), for example, the Tang Daoist physician Sun Simiao 孫思邈 (d. 682) discusses sexual practice extensively:[45]

> When a man reaches forty, he needs the art of the bedchamber. The Way of the bedchamber art is within easy reach, yet none is able to practice it. To have intercourse with ten women but to remain securely locked oneself: this is the sum of the art of the bedchamber. . . . Those who are able to make contact a hundred times without ejaculating will gain long life. By mounting many women one can absorb their *qi*. . . . Man must not be without woman, and woman must not be without man. Without woman, a man's mind will be disturbed, the spirit is wearied. When the spirit is weary, one's life is shortened.

年至四十, 須諸房中之術. 夫房中之術者, 其道甚近, 而人莫能行其法. 一夕御十人, 閉固為謹, 此房中之術畢矣. . . . 能百接而不施瀉者長生矣. 若御女多者, 可采氣. . . . 男不可無女, 女不可無男. 無女則意動, 意動則神勞, 神勞則損壽.[46]

Sun Simiao advises that men who have reached the age of forty should conduct sexual practice, and he emphasizes ejaculation control and absorbing a partner's *qi* as keys to this; it will lead to good health, prolong life, and help one attain immortality, though by means of sexual vampirism.

Even Du Guangting, who followed the masters of the Maoshan 茅山 lineage such as Sima Chengzhen 司馬承禎 (647–735) and Wu Yun 吳筠 (d. 778) and further advocated serene meditation and pure cultivation,[47] did not prohibit sexual practice. He only deprecated sexual practice as a minor concern and indicated that the practice was very risky if one did not do it in a correct manner.[48]

From the previous discussion, we see that in the Tang Daoist tradition, sexual practice continued to be conducted as a way to attain longevity and immortality, celibacy was not strictly observed, and marital status could be maintained in certain circumstances. These conditions legitimized the sexual, emotional experiences of the priestesses and helped shape new gender relations between them and priests or scholar-officials. The early Tang poet Luo Binwang 駱賓王 (ca. 627–ca. 684), for example, wrote a long poem celebrating the love story between the priestess Wang Lingfei 王靈妃 (fl. 656–683) and the priest Li Rong 李榮 (fl. 656–683).[49] Li Rong was one of the most important thinkers in Daoist history, who annotated the *Daode jing* 道德經, *Zhuangzi* 莊子, and *Xisheng jing* 西昇經 (Scripture of Western Ascension), and was twice summoned to the capital by Emperor Gaozong (r. 649–683). The mid-Tang poet Bai Juyi's 白居易 (772–846) poem titled "To Refined Master Wei" (Zeng Wei lianshi 贈韋鍊師) reads:

If the female immortal from Heaven does not have any desire,
Why are we attracted to each other and reluctant to part?
We both suspect that in our previous life
We were husband and wife of a certain family.
上界女仙無嗜欲, 何因相顧兩裵回.
共疑過去人間世, 曾作誰家夫婦來.[50]

"Female immortal from Heaven" refers to priestess Wei. They are attracted to and have feelings for each other. The conjecture of "husband and wife" in their previous life hints at an intimate relationship between the two.

The late Tang poet Cui Zhiyuan 崔致遠 (857–ca. 928) was originally from Silla. In 874, he passed the civil examination and then served as a low-ranking official in south China. In 885, he had permission from Emperor Xizong (r. 873–888) to return to Silla. Before leaving, he wrote a poem titled "Poem Left to a Daoist Priestess at Parting" (Liubie nüdaoshi 留別女道士):

> I always resent my bad fortune in my official career,
> But delightfully I have been acquainted with Magu for many years.
> Before parting, I confide to you my true heart:
> Like the sea, how can it run dry?
> 每恨塵中厄宦塗，數年深喜識麻姑.
> 臨行與為真心說，海水何時得盡枯?[51]

"Bad fortune" refers to his long-term service as a local official in the south. Magu is a famous goddess, here referring to the priestess. In his unhappy official career of more than ten years, the love between him and the priestess had been a great comfort to him. He swears that like the sea his love for her will never run dry.

We should keep in mind that in the Tang dynasty, poetic writing was never a private matter. Poems were often composed in a communal way at public occasions such as gatherings at court, local offices, and other social occasions, adopting the form of the same titles or rhyme groups. Moreover, poems were always broadly circulated among all kinds of readers. For example, it is well known that Bai Juyi's poems were inscribed and copied everywhere—walls of pavilions, hotels, and wine shops, and were recited even by children and old women. Therefore, the gender relations between Daoist priestesses and priests or scholar-officials described in these poems should not have been regarded as irregular, abnormal, or a violation of Daoist precepts. In 783, after reading the priestess Li Jilan's works, which contained many love poems, Emperor Dezong (r. 779–805) summoned her to court to serve at the palace convent Yuchen 玉晨, which was a great honor to a priestess.[52] Obviously, the emperor did not regard Li Jilan's poetry or lifestyle as improper.

The spiritual, illusory, or psychic sexual practice of divine marriage and visualization of the goddess developed by the early Highest Clarity tradition inspired the imagination and passion of both Daoists and literati in the Tang, which, for the convenience of structure, is discussed in next section.

## The Cult of Erotic Goddesses and the Self-Empowerment of Daoist Priestesses

In ancient Chinese myths and popular legends, many goddesses are associated with fertility, divine matchmaking, the shaman-deity connection, irresistible sensual appeal, and erotic desire. In their encounter with human kings or common men, they always take the sexual initiative and play the role of a seductive maiden.[53] The most famous one is the erotic legend between the Goddess of Mount Shaman and the King of Chu: the goddess enters the dream of the king, makes love with him, and describes herself as "drifting clouds at dawn and showers of rain at evening."[54] This legend later became a motif in numerous popular stories and literary works that describe goddess-man encounters.[55]

While in the Han dynasty (206 BCE–220 CE) the ancient "art of the bedchamber" was developed and manuals of sexuality flourished, the erotic goddesses now became experts of sexual arts and central personae of sex manuals, such as the Mystery Maiden in the *Classic of Mystery Maiden* (*Xuannü jing* 玄女經), the Plain Maiden in the *Classic of Plain Maiden* (*Sunü jing* 素女經), the Colorful Maiden (Cainü 采女) in the *Classic of Pengzu* (*Pengzu jing* 彭祖經), and the Queen Mother of the West (Xiwangmu 西王母) in *Secret Instructions of the Jade Bedchamber* (*Yufang mijue* 玉房秘訣). They served as sex advisers and teachers to the Yellow Emperor and other sovereigns, teaching them to attain longevity and immortality through sexual techniques.[56]

Daoist tradition incorporated all the age-honored goddesses into their pantheon. In addition, as discussed earlier, from the fourth to sixth century, the Highest Clarity tradition created a new motif of divine marriage and a meditation skill of visualizing goddesses. Beautiful, forever-young goddesses descended from Heaven to introduce themselves or to be introduced by other accompanying goddesses to selected Highest Clarity masters: E Lühua 愕綠華 descended to Yang Quan's 羊權 home, presented a poem to express her love for him and offered to marry him; An Yupin 安郁嬪 descended with a divine company to Yang Xi's 楊羲 home and by her own presentation of a love poem and the matchmaking of several honorable goddesses, she was married to Yang; Wang Meilan 王媚蘭 came down along with other goddesses several times to Xu Mi's 許謐 home, and her marriage with Xu succeeded only after the goddesses repeatedly seduced and pursued Xu with their poems and revelations.[57]

In these divine marriages, all the characteristics and expertise of the old goddesses were incorporated: matchmaker, seductive maiden, irresistible sensual appeal, desirable lover, divine passion, sex teacher (though in an illusory or psychic manner), and instructor for the attainment of immortality. Moreover, two more fields of expertise were added to the Highest Clarity goddesses, namely, the revelation of secret scriptures and the composing of poetry.

Tang literati were fascinated by all these goddesses. They composed numerous verses dedicated to them to express their "wish for transcendence and desire for perfect love,"[58] including the Queen Mother, the Goddess of Mount Shaman, the water goddesses of the Xiang River and the Luo River, the two immortal wives of Liu Chen 劉晨 and Ruan Zhao 阮肇, the Highest Clarity master's divine bride E Lühua, the Weaving Maiden (Zhinü 織女), Chang E 嫦娥 or the goddess of the moon, and so forth.[59]

This cult of erotic goddesses was extended to include Daoist priestesses. They were seen as "semi-goddesses" and became popular personae in the poetry of the literati as well. Some music and song-lyric tunes were designed specifically for them, such as "Nüguan zi" 女冠子 (Female Cap/Daoist Priestess) and "Tianxian zi" 天仙子 (Heavenly Immortal). In these song-lyrics, poets describe the priestesses in both general and imaginary terms: they were analogized as immortals and intermediaries between humans and divinities, their beautiful appearance and costumes were erotically admired, and they were portrayed as emotional lovers often taking the initiative in courtship.[60]

The priestess-poets were fully aware of this cult of the goddess. They consciously modeled themselves on the personae of erotic goddesses as a way of self-empowerment. For example, in a poem entitled "Attending Xiao Shuzi to Listen to Someone Playing the Zither: Assigned with the Topic 'Song of the Flowing Streams of the Three Gorges'" (Cong Xiao Shuzi ting tanqin fude Sanxia liuquan ge 從蕭叔子聽彈琴賦得三峽流泉歌), Li Jilan starts with these lines:

> Once I had a home
> in mists of Mount Shaman,
> Where I always listened to
> flowing streams—
> Playing a jade zither
> echoing far,
> As I have heard
> in past dreams.
> 妾家本住巫山雲, 巫山流泉常自聞.
> 玉琴彈出轉寥敻, 直是當時夢裏聽.[61]

The "Song of the Flowing Streams of the Three Gorges" was a melody of the zither, which was attributed to Ruan Xian 阮咸 of the Western Jin dynasty

(265–316).[62] The "mists of Mount Shaman" and "past dreams" in Li's verses refer to the erotic legend of the Goddess of Mount Shaman and the King of Chu. The poet obviously analogizes herself to the goddess. In another poem entitled "Stirred by Emotions" (Ganxing 感興), Li again laments:

Morning clouds and evening rain,
I will always follow you;
Swans go and people come,
when will you be back?
朝雲暮雨鎮相隨, 去雁來人有返期.[63]

Here "morning clouds" and "evening rain" also refer to the Goddess of Mount Shaman and her erotic legend. Li Jilan deliberately and repeatedly acts out the role of the ancient erotic goddess in her poems, which seem to inspire her agency in her active pursuit of love. In her three poems, "Late Spring Sketch" (Muchun jishi 暮春即事), "I Heard Censor Li Had Returned from Angling and Send This Poem to Him" (Wen Li duangong chuidiao hui jizeng 聞李端公垂釣回寄贈),[64] and "Following the Rhyme Words of My New Western Neighbor's Poem and also Begging for Wine from Him" (Ciyun xilin xinju jian qijiu 次韻西鄰新居兼乞酒),[65] Yu Xuanji alludes to the legend of Ruan Zhao's 阮肇 encounter with his immortal wife, the goddesses of the Xiao and Xiang rivers, and the Weaving Maiden of the Milky Way, and analogizes herself as a loving goddess.[66] Another priestess-poet, Cui Zhongrong 崔仲容 (fl. eighth century), even directly describes herself as one of the female immortals under the command of the Queen Mother of the West, as seen in her poem titled "Xi zeng" 戲贈 (Playfully Presented):

I've just arrived at Mount Kunlun,
no way back;
Young Ruan, why do you teach me
to do what's not right?
I am wearing the registration
of the Highest Clarity now;
Please don't let the falling flowers
soil my feather dress.
暫到昆侖未得歸, 阮郎何事教人非.
如今身佩上清籙, 莫遣落花沾羽衣.[67]

In the legend, the Queen Mother of the West dwells in Mount Kunlun. "Feather dress" refers to the clothing of both immortals and Daoists in Tang poetry. The poet's announcement of her arrival at Mount Kunlun with both the registration of the Highest Clarity and the feathered dress clearly indicates that she has received a high-level ordination. Young Ruan also alludes to the legend of Ruan Zhao's encounter with his immortal wife. The "what's not right" the young man teaches her must refer to a love affair. Although the priestess-poet says "no" superficially, the playful tone and the use of the legend of Ruan Zhao and his immortal wife hint that she is in fact willing to accept his flirting.[68]

Empowered by the erotic goddesses, Tang priestesses sometimes even took the initiative in their pursuit of love and desire. Wang Lingfei actively sought her true love:

> Understanding human feeling
> we seek for each other,
> Eventually we share one heart
> with deep affections.
> One heart, one feeling,
> until endless;
> Like glue, like lacquer,
> we are inseparable.
> 想知人意自相尋, 果得深心共一心.
> 一心一意無窮已, 投漆投膠非足擬.[69]

Yu Xuanji proudly announced their strong agency:

> Eyes take in Song Yu as you wish,
> Why resent Wang Chang?
> 自能窺宋玉, 何必恨王昌![70]

## Educational Level and Socioeconomic Status of Tang Daoist Priestesses

Another means by which Tang Daoist priestesses empowered themselves was through education. In general the priestesses had a good or considerable education. The literary and artistic talents of priestesses of an aristocratic background were well cultivated by their families before they entered Daoist convents. For example, the priestess Zhang Rongcheng 張容成 was from an official family, and she "recited Confucian classics and understood their ideas and meanings, and she also had good command in various arts and talents."[71] Princess Yuzhen was a good calligrapher. One of the epitaphic inscriptions of her sister, Princess Jinxian, was copied by Yuzhen, and it is still extant today.[72] The late Tang poet Li Yuan 李遠 (*jinshi* 831) once wrote a poem titled "Observing the Funeral of the Perfected Woman Lian" (Guan Lian nüzhen zang 觀廉女真葬).[73] "Perfected Woman" was another name for a Daoist priestess. According to the preface to the poem, the priestess Lian was an excellent calligrapher and was summoned to court to serve as a female palace scholar before she became a priestess. According to the epitaph written for the priestess Zhang, the granddaughter of Emperor Ruizong and also the daughter-in-law of Princess Yuzhen, Zhang was well educated and loved reading. She knew all the popular tunes and was especially well versed in playing the *zheng* 箏.[74]

Priestesses from commoner families also had the opportunity to gain an education. For example, Yu Xuanji, the daughter of a commoner family in the capital city Chang'an, was well educated, with a high level of literacy:

> Her beautiful appearance could overthrow a state, and her thought reached the marvelous realm. She loved reading and writing. She was especially focused on poetic composition. . . . Her excellent verses admiring the moon and winds have spread among the literati.
>
> 色既傾國，思乃入神. 喜讀書屬文，尤致意於一吟一詠. . . . 而風月賞玩之佳句, 往往播于士林.[75]

Moreover, the Tang codes stipulated that Daoist priests and priestesses must have received the transmission of the *Daode jing* or more scriptures before they were allotted lands (see further on). Tang Daoist tradition also emphasized the transmission and learning of scriptures. In each rank of investiture, Daoists were required to receive and study a correspondent corpus of scriptures.[76] These indicate a considerably high educational level and degree of self-learning among priestesses, even those from more obscure families. As a matter of fact, a number of priestesses managed to reach the highest ranks of scripture transmission, the Great Cavern and Three Caverns (see discussions later). In addition, literary and artistic accomplishments, such as music, poetry, chess, calligraphy, and painting, were parts of Daoist ritual and cloistered life, as many male priests were also versed in these aspects.[77] In the *Beimeng suoyan* 北夢瑣言 (Trifling Talks from the North of the Yunmeng Marsh), Sun Guangxian recounts an interesting story about a priestess Wang 王. She was the daughter of the military commissioner Wang Baoyi 王保義 (fl. 924–948) and was once a priestess.[78] She was very bright and excelled in playing the *pipa* 琵琶. In her dreams, she encountered some Daoists and laymen who taught her more than two hundred musical tunes. She asked her brother to inscribe these tunes on stones. At the end of the story, Sun Guangxian states that his daughter-in-law was a nephew of Wang and still remembered a few of the tunes.[79] Thus, the story about the priestess seems to be true at least to a certain extent. If we uncover the mask of the mysterious dreams, Wang may be seen as first studying with some Daoists and artists in the convent and then composing all the tunes by herself.

Tang courtesans were trained in a variety of entertainment skills, including singing, dancing, playing musical instruments, drinking, offering companionship, and reciting and even composing poetry. These skills were professional qualifications, and the women were usually trained strictly and even cruelly from youth for the profession. They applied and performed these skills solely for the purpose of entertaining their clients.[80] Therefore, their educational background and literary accomplishments were very different from those of Daoist priestesses. A comparison between the poems of Tang courtesans and Daoist priestesses shows that courtesans' works usually focus on social occasions and currying favor with their clients, while priestesses' works often express their own emotions, display an independent personality, and change the image of woman from a "desired object" to a "desiring subject."[81]

Due to the particular sociopolitical milieu of the Tang dynasty, Daoist priestesses also sustained a relatively independent status in the economy and society. As is well known, during the process of the establishment of the Tang dynasty, Daoists helped the future rulers cement their authority and orthodoxy with religious and divine revelations. The Tang royal house then adopted Laozi, the alleged founder of Daoism, as their first ancestor and therefore greatly favored the religion.[82] Many members of the royal house and aristocratic families were attracted to the belief and practice of Daoism. Throughout the dynasty, seventeen imperial princesses and many palace ladies as well as other aristocratic women were ordained as Daoist priestesses, with a great number of nun-maids attending them in the Daoist convents. Once in a while, the imperial court also released retired or unneeded palace ladies, entertainers, and maids to Daoist convents to become priestesses.[83] As a result, Daoist convents in the two capital cities of Chang'an and Luoyang and on some of the great mountains were filled with priestesses of aristocratic background, who of course had strong economic support from the court and their families.[84]

Although there were also many priestesses from more obscure families, as the Daoist abbeys were supported by the state, they were in general economically independent. The Tang government implemented the policy of land allotment (*juntian* 均田). Common women were not included in the policy, but Daoist priestesses and Buddhist nuns were exceptions. The Tang code declared: "Regarding all Daoist priests and priestesses who have received the transmission of the *Daode jing* or more scriptures: a priest is allotted with thirty *mu*, and a priestess is allotted with twenty *mu*."[85] Although the establishment of the "law of two taxes" (*liangshui fa* 兩稅法) in 780 abolished the land allotment, many Daoist monasteries had already acquired a lot of land through government allotment and bestowal, private offering, buying and selling, merging, and management.[86] Many Daoist monasteries and priests were very rich. For example, the Xianyi 咸宜 Convent, where the priestess-poet Yu Xuanji was registered and lived, was comprised of grand buildings donated by the princess-priestess Xianyi when she was ordained in 762. When female members of official families in Chang'an were ordained, they usually entered this convent.[87] Yu Xuanji was the official Li Yi's 李億 concubine before she became a priestess, so she was able to enter this aristocratic convent and had her own chamber and courtyard within the monastery complex.[88]

One of the major attributes of Tang courtesans was that they provided professional service, that is, their service was their livelihood, and most of the income went to the "madams" of brothels who owned and controlled them. Therefore, they were physically and economically dependent.[89] As Daoist priestesses were economically independent, the love affairs between them and literati were more likely the result of pursuing personal desires and emotions as expressed in their own poems, not of fulfilling professional services and providing for financial needs. Therefore, they were substantially differentiated from courtesans.

Tang courtesans were closely associated with scholar-officials and sometimes even had love affairs with them.[90] However, courtesans did not have any freedom of choice and had to wait to be called upon by men. They often found themselves in the position of a humble servant; maltreatment was quite common and many courtesans had tragic encounters.[91] The official courtesans (*guanji* 官妓 or *yingji* 營妓) were often summoned to public parties, in which they were simply entertainers, and their status was unequal to that of other participants. For example, the official courtesan and famous poet-calligrapher Xue Tao 薛濤 (ca. 770–832), who was active in social occasions and exchanged poems with many male poets, was banished to Songzhou 松州 (present-day Songpan in Sichuan Province) in 789 because she offended Commissioner Wei Gao 韋皋 (745–805). From there she presented a ten-piece series titled "Poems on Ten Separations" (Shili shi 十離詩) to Wei Gao, asking for forgiveness.[92] The series uses ten metaphors—the dog separated from its master, the pen separated from its owner's hand, the horse separated from its stable, the parrot separated from its cage, the swallow separated from its nest, the pearl separated from the palm of its owner, the fish separated from its pool, the hawk separated from its owner's gauntlet, the bamboo separated from the pavilion, and the mirror separated from its stand—to beg her "master"/patron's forgiveness of her minor faults. These poems typically show the courtesan's dependency, helplessness, and submissive social status and feelings. After Xue Tao passed away in 832, Commissioner Li Deyu 李德裕 (787–850) wrote a poem titled "Lament on [the Death of] a Peacock and Xue Tao" (Shang kongque ji Xue Tao 傷孔雀及薛濤), and the poet Liu Yuxi 劉禹錫 (772–542) wrote a poem entitled "Lament on [the Death of] a Peacock and Xue Tao: Response to the Poem by Minister Li of Xichuan" (He Xichuan Li shangshu shang kongque ji Xue Tao zhishi 和西川李尚書傷孔雀及薛濤之什).[93] These poems also typically reveal Tang scholar-officials' general attitude toward courtesans: even though Xue was talented and famous, they still viewed her as an object owned by them, just like the peacock.[94]

As discussed earlier, Daoist priestesses enjoyed a certain freedom of choice in their active pursuit of love. In addition, after accepting an official ordination, they were issued a certificate, with which they had the freedom to travel through the country.[95] They participated in social events with men of all kinds of professions, especially scholar-officials, with a certain degree of equality. They were respected for their Daoist accomplishments and sometimes became teachers to literati, officials, and even emperors. The high-Tang priestess Jiao 焦, for example, was respected and extolled by several poets, including the great poet Li Bai 李白 (701–762), who swore to become her disciple if she would be interested in transmitting her longevity techniques.[96] Both mid-Tang priestesses Han Ziming 韩自明 (764–831) and Tian Yuansu 田元素 (d. 829) carried the title "Great Cavern and Three Radiances of Highest Clarity" (Shangqing Dadong Sanjing fashi 上清大洞三景法師), indicating that they received the transmission of Great Cavern and Three Radiances, the highest rank in Tang Daoist ordination hierarchy. Both were summoned to the palace, where they served as mentors to emperors and imperial ladies and were highly respected.[97] Another mid-Tang priestess, Wang 王, was associated with three famous poets, Meng Jiao 孟郊 (751–814), Li Yi 李益 (748–ca. 827), and Cui Fang 崔放, in the capital. Later, Wang returned to the Lou 樓 Abbey and planned to build mountain residences for the three scholar-officials. Before parting, the four had a party, during which each of the poets wrote a poem admiring the priestess's accomplishments.[98] As for the princess-priestesses, to become a Daoist priestess may have brought them freedom, independence, political power, economic wealth, and a virtuous reputation, in addition to practicing their belief and attaining transcendence.[99]

## Concluding Remarks

During the Tang dynasty, the particular cultural-religious and socioeconomic environment and the Daoist priestesses' negotiation with it facilitated their agency and "unconventional" roles as poets, musicians, and artists. Within the Daoist tradition, sexual practice, both physical and spiritual, was conducted as an effective way to attain longevity and immortality. Celibacy was not strictly observed, and marital status could be maintained in certain circumstances. These conditions legitimized the sexual, emotional experiences of priestesses and helped shape new gender relations between them and priests or scholar-officials. In the larger social scope, the age-honored erotic and sensual goddesses, as well as the motif of divine marriage and the practice of visualizing goddesses created by the Highest Clarity tradition, fascinated both Daoists and scholar-officials. Numerous literary works were composed to extol the beauty and sentiments of the goddesses and to express the authors' desire for transcendence and love. The priestesses consciously modeled themselves on the personae of erotic goddesses as a way of self-empowerment that enacted their desiring subject. The aristocratic background and Daoist monastic culture also provided opportunities of education and self-empowerment for the priestesses and fostered their literary and artistic talents. Unlike courtesans who maintained their livelihoods by their service, Daoist priestesses in general were economically independent. The love affairs between priestesses and scholar-officials were more likely the result of personal desires and emotions, not of professional services and financial needs.

The roles of poet, musician, and artist assumed by some Daoist priestesses did not go beyond the general expectations of their contemporaries. As mentioned earlier, after reading Li Jilan's poetry, which included many love poems, Emperor Dezong summoned her to serve as a palace priestess. In the ninth century, the scholar Cai Xingfeng 蔡省風 compiled an anthology of poetry solely by Tang female poets and titled it *Yaochi xinyong ji* 瑤池

新詠集 (Collection of New Songs from the Turquoise Pond). The works of three Daoist priestess-poets, Li Jilan, Yuan Chun 元淳 (d. ca. 779), and Cui Zhongrong, were placed at the beginning of the collection.[100] In the *Youxuan ji* 又玄集 (Mystery upon Mystery: An Anthology) and *Caidiao ji* 才調集 (Anthology of Talented Tones), two anthologies of poetry compiled respectively in the late Tang and Five Dynasties, Wei Zhuang 韋莊 (ca. 836–910) and Wei Hu 韋穀 selected some works of Tang female poets and enhanced their names with the titles "Lady" (Furen 夫人), "Young Lady" (Nülang 女郎), "Daoist Priestess" (Nüdaoshi 女道士), "Courtesan" (Changji 娼妓), and so on. Li Jilan, Yuan Chun, and Yu Xuanji are given the title "Daoist Priestess" in both anthologies.[101] From the recognition by their contemporaries, we can see that the Tang people understood and accepted the basic identity of the priestess-poets as Daoist priestesses.

By dispelling the faulty identity of "courtesan" as constructed by the discourses of later ages, this chapter restores Daoist priestesses to the religious landscape of the Tang dynasty, demonstrates their agency enacted by the interplay of the sociocultural environment and their negotiation with it, and verifies their true identity as Daoist priestesses.

## Notes

1. According to the *Tang liudian* 唐六典, during the Kaiyuan reign period (713–741), there were 1,687 Daoist abbeys, among which 550 were convents. In the *Xin Tangshu* 新唐書, the recorded number of convents is as high as 988. See Li Linfu 李林甫 (683–752) et al., *Tang liudian* (Beijing: Zhonghua shuju, 1992), 4.125; and Ouyang Xiu 歐陽修 (1007–1072), *Xin Tangshu* (Beijing: Zhonghua shuju, 1975), 48.1252.

2. Li Jilan's name is Li Ye 李冶, and Jilan is her courtesy name.

3. Concerning the life experience of Tang Daoist priestesses, there are three major groups of sources. First, among the transmitted and unearthed epitaphic inscriptions of Tang, more than thirty were written for Daoist priestesses, most of which record their religious experience as abbesses, teachers, or practitioners (I have a forthcoming paper studying these epitaphs). Second, in works by Tang literati and the priestess-poets' own works, their images as poets and artists are fully presented; see Jia Jinhua 賈晉華, "Tangshi zhong youguan nüdaoshi de lianqingshi kaobian" 唐詩中有關女道士的戀情詩考辨 *Daojia wenhua yanjiu* 道家文化研究 24 (2009): 126–14; and Jia, "The *Yaochi ji* and Three Daoist Priestess-Poets in Tang China," *Nan Nü: Men, Women and Gender in Early and Imperial China* 13.2 (2011): 205–43. Third, the *Yongcheng jixian lu* 墉城集仙錄, compiled by Du Guangting 杜光庭 (850–933), has at least eighteen hagiographies of Tang Daoist women extant. In these hagiographies, Du greatly modified and even rewrote origi-

nal sources and idealized the protagonists. As a result, these hagiographies should not be directly used to study the actual life experience of Tang Daoist priestesses. See Jia, "Du Guangting and the Hagiographies of Tang Female Daoists," *Taiwan Journal of Religious Studies* 1 (2011): 81–121.

4. Sun Guangxian 孫光憲 (d. 968) was the first to make such a criticism; see his *Beimeng suoyan* 北夢瑣言 (Shanghai: Shanghai guji chubanshe, 1981), 9.71–72. He has been followed by many critics even up to the present day. For example, Chen Zhensun 陳振孫 (d. ca. 1261), *Zhizhai shulu jieti* 直齋書錄解題 (Wuyingdian juzhen edition 武英殿聚珍本), 19.29b; Hu Zhenheng 胡震亨 (1569–1645), *Tangyin guiqian* 唐音癸籤 (Shanghai: Shanghai guji, 1981), 8.83; Qian Qianyi 錢謙益 (1582–1664), *Jiangyunlou shumu* 絳雲樓書目 (*Congshu jicheng chubian* ed.), 75; Zhang Caitian 張采田 (1862–1945), *Yuxi sheng nianpu huijian* 玉谿生年譜會箋 (Shanghai: Shanghai guji, 1983), 1.27, 4.206; Xie Wuliang 謝無量 (1884–1964), *Zhongguo funü wenxueshi* 中國婦女文學史 (1926; reprint, Shanghai: Shanghai shudian, 1990), 27; Gao Shiyu 高世瑜, *Tangdai funü* 唐代婦女 (Xi'an: Sanqin chubanshe, 1988), 94; Huang Shizhong 黃世中, "Lun *Quan Tangshi* zhong suo fanying de nüguan 'banchang shi' lianqing" 論全唐詩中所反映的女冠半娼式戀情, *Xuchang shizhuan xuebao* 許昌師專學報 15.2 (1996): 39–43; and Hu Wei 胡蔚, "Daojiao de qingxiuguan yu wenren de bairimeng" 道教的清修觀與文人的白日夢, *Journal of Sichuan University* 四川大學學報 5 (2006): 112–17.

5. Hu Zhenheng, *Tangyin guiqian*, 83.

6. Chen Zhensun, *Zhizhai shulu jieti*, 19.29b.

7. Xie Wuliang, *History of Chinese Women's Literature*, 2.27.

8. Gao Shiyu, *Tangdai funü*, 94.

9. In his theorization of agency, Paul Smith situates human agency in the interplay of social and cultural forces and personal desire, interest, and intentionality; see his *Discerning the Subject* (Minneapolis: University of Minnesota Press, 1988), xxxv. Drawing on this theory, Wimal Dissanayake and the essays included in his edited volume focus on how historical and cultural conditions in Asia facilitated the discursive production of agency. See his introduction to *Narratives of Agency: Self-Making in China, India, and Japan* (Minneapolis: University of Minnesota Press, 1996), ix.

10. Susan Calef, "Charting New Territory: Religion and 'the Gender-Critical Turn,'" *Journal of Religion and Society* 5 (2009): 2. Of course we should also keep in mind the dark side of religious traditions concerning women, as Calef also indicates.

11. Michel Foucault, "An Aesthetics of Existence," in Lawrence D. Kritzman, ed., *Politics, Philosophy, Culture: Interviews and Other Writings, 1977–1984* (New York: Routledge, 1988), 50; and Judith Butler, *Excitable Speech: A Politics of the Performative* (New York: Routledge, 1997), 16.

12. Scholars took note of this Daoist practice from quite early on; see, for example, Henri Maspero (1882–1945), *Taoism and Chinese Religion*, trans. Frank Kierman (Amherst: University of Massachusetts Press, 1981), 445–554; Chen Guofu 陳國符, "Nanbeichao Tianshidao kao changbian: Fangzhong diba" 南北朝天師道考長編: 房中第八 (1945), in *Daozang yuanliu kao* 道藏源流考 (Beijing: Zhonghua

shuju, 1963), 365–69; Yang Liansheng 楊聯陞, "Laojun yinsong jiejing jiaoshi" 老君音誦誡經校釋, *Lishi yuyan yanjiusuo jikan* 歷史語言研究所集刊 28.1 (1956): 17–54; R. H. van Gulik (1910–1967), *Sexual Life in Ancient China: A Preliminary Survey of Chinese Sex and Society from ca. 1500 B.C. till 1644 A.D* (Leiden: Brill, 2003), 72–90; Rolf A. Stein (1911–1999), "Remarques sur les mouvements du taoïsme politico-religieux au IIe siècle ap. J.-C," *T'oung-pao* 50 (1963): 1–78; and Kristofer M. Schipper, "The Taoist Body," *History of Religions* 17 (1978): 355–86.

13. *Daozang* 道藏 (Beijing, Shanghai, and Tianjin: Beijing wenwu chubanshe, Shanghai guji chubanshe, and Tianjin guji chubanshe, 1988; hereafter *DZ*), no. 1343, vol. 33; no. 1294, vol. 32; here citing the numbers as assigned by Kristofer Schipper and Franciscus Verellen in *The Taoist Canon: A Historical Companion to the Daozang* (Chicago and London: University of Chicago Press, 2004). For studies on the "yellow books," see mainly Michel Strickmann, *Le Taoïsme du Mao Chan: chronique d'une révélation* (Paris: Collège de France, Institut des hautes études chinoises, 1981), 36, 69; Kobayashi Masayoshi 小林正美, *Rikuchō Dōkyō shi kenkyū* 六朝道教史研究 (Tōkyō: Sōbunsha, 1990), 357–66; Wang Ka 王卡, "Huangshu kaoyuan" 黃書考源, *Shijie zongjiao yanjiu* 世界宗教研究 2 (1997): 65–73; and Zhu Yueli 朱越利, "Huangshu kao" 黃書考, *Zhongguo zhexue* 中國哲學 19 (1998): 167–88; and Schipper and Verellen, *The Taoist Canon*, 129–30.

14. Lin Fu-shih 林富士, "Lüelun zaoqi Daojiao yu fangzhongshu de guanxi" 略論早期道教與房中術的關係, *Lishi yuyan yanjiusuo jikan* 歷史語言研究所集刊 72.2 (2001): 241–48.

15. Stephen R. Bokenkamp, "Tianshidao hunyin yishi 'heqi' zai Shangqing Lingbao xuepai de yanbian" 天師道婚姻儀式"合氣"在上清靈寶學派的演變, *Daojia wenhua yanjiu* 道家文化研究 16 (1999): 241–48; and Gil Raz, "The Way of the Yellow and the Red: Re-examining the Sexual Initiation Rite of Celestial Master Daoism," *Nan Nü: Men, Women and Gender in Early and Imperial China* 10.1 (2008): 86–120.

16. See, for example, Kristofer Schipper, *The Taoist Body*, trans. Karen C. Duval (Berkeley: University of California Press, 1992), 150–52; Marc Kalinowski, "La transmission du dispositive des Neuf Palais sous les Six dynasties," in Michel Strickmann, ed., *Tantric and Taoist Studies* (Brussels: Institut Belge des Hauters Etudes Chinoises, 1985), 3: 773–811; Li Ling 李零, "Donghan Wei Jin Nanbeichao fangzhong jingdian liupai kao" 東漢魏晉南北朝房中經典流派考, *Zhongguo wenhua* 中國文化 15–16 (1997): 141–58; Ge Zhaoguang 葛兆光, "Huangshu heqi yu qita: Daojiao guodu yi de sixiangshi yanjiu" 黃書合氣與其他: 道教過度儀的思想史研究, *Gujin lunheng* 古今論衡 2 (1999): 62–76; Yan Shanzhao 嚴善炤, "Shoki dōkyō to kōaka konki bōchū jutsu" 初期道教と黃赤混氣房中術, *Tōhō shūkyō* 東方宗教 97 (2001): 1–10; and Catherine Despeux, "Women in Daoism," in Livia Kohn, ed., *Daoism Handbook* (Leiden: Brill, 2004), 404–5.

17. Dao'an 道安 (312–385), *Erjiao lun* 二教論, in Sengyou 僧祐 (445–518), ed., *Hongming ji* 弘明集 (*Sibu congkan*), 8.3a.

18. Zhen Luan 甄鸞 (535–566), *Xiaodao lun* 笑道論, in Daoxuan 道宣 (596–667), ed., *Guang hongmingji* 廣弘明集 (*Sibu congkan*), 9.31a; translation

adapted from Livia Kohn, *Laughing at the Dao* (Princeton: Princeton University Press, 1995), 149.

19. Kou Qianzhi, *Laojun yinsong jiejing* 老君音誦戒經, *DZ* 785, 18: 211–16; Wei Shou 魏收 (506–572), *Weishu* 魏書 (Beijing: Zhonghua shuju, 1974), 114.3051; and Tao Hongjing, *Zhengao* 真誥, *DZ* 1016, 20: 516–26, 497.

20. Kou Qianzhi, *Laojun yinsong jiejing*, 17–19.

21. Both Zhong Laiyin 鐘來因 and Zhu Yueli 朱越利 believe that Highest Clarity masters used the term "secret books" (*yinshu* 隱書) to refer to texts of sexual practice. They assert that the tradition advocated this kind of practice in a more discreet way. See Zhong, *Changsheng busi de tanqiu: Daojing Zhengao zhimi* 長生不死的探求：道經真誥之謎 (Shanghai: Wenhui chubanshe, 1992), 67–79; and Zhu, "Liuchao Shangqing jing de yinshu zhidao" 六朝上清經的隱書之道, *Zongjiaoxue yanjiu* 宗教學研究 2 (2001): 1–12.

22. See mainly Michel Strickmann, "A Taoist Confirmation of Liang Wu-ti's Suppression of Taoism," *Journal of the American Oriental Society* 98.4 (1978): 471; Isabelle Robinet, *La Révélation du Shangqing dans l'histoire du taoïsme* (Paris: Ecole française d'Extrême-Orient, 1984); Robinet, "Sexualité et taoïsme," in *Sexualité et religion*, ed. Marcel Bernos (Paris: Cerf, 1988), 51–71; Zhong Laiyin, *Changsheng busi de tanqiu*, 80–103; and Li Fengmao 李豐楙, "Wei Jin shennü chuanshuo yu Daojiao shennü jiangzhen chuanshuo" 魏晉神女傳說與道教神女降真傳說, and "Xiwangmu wunü chuanshuo de xingcheng jiqi yanbian" 西王母五女傳說的形成其演變, both in Li Fengmao, *Wuru yu zhejiang: Liuchao Sui Tang Daojiao wenxue lunji* 誤入與謫降：六朝隋唐道教文學論集 (Taibei: Xuesheng shuju, 1996), 143–87, 215–45.

23. The Song rulers fabricated a supreme god named Zhao Xuanlang 趙玄朗 as their divine ancestor, and as a result the character *xuan* 玄 was changed into *yuan* 元 in order to avoid the name taboo in many Daoist texts printed or reprinted in the Song. Later, during the Qing dynasty, because Emperor Kangxi 康熙 (r. 1661–1722) was named Xuanyue 玄燁, *xuan* was again changed into *yuan* in many texts produced or reprinted in the Qing.

24. *Shangqing mingtang xuanzhen jingjue*, *DZ* 424, 6: 639a–c. Translation adapted from Edward H. Schafer, "The Jade Woman of Greatest Mystery," *History of Religions* 17 (1978): 387–97.

25. Tao Hongjing, *Zhengao* 真誥, *DZ* 1016, 20: 2.497b–c.

26. Schafer, "The Jade Woman of Greatest Mystery," 387.

27. Li Fengmao, "Wei Jin shennü chuanshuo yu Daojiao shennü jiangzhen chuanshuo," 173–80.

28. *DZ* 1237. The preface to the text relates that in the year of *guimao* 癸卯, the Daoist priest Liu Ruozhuo visited Sun Yizhong, the author with the title name Baoguangzi 葆光子 in Jingzhou 荊州 (in present-day Hubei Province) where he served as an official, and transmitted the Daoist rites to Sun (32: 166a–c). The year *guimao* has been identified by scholars as 1003. However, according to historical records, Liu Ruozhuo served as Daoist Registrar in the capital from 967 to 972, and in 972 he was already over ninety years old. See Li Tao 李燾 (1115–1184),

*Xu Zizhi tongjian changbian* 續資治通鑒長編 (Beijing: Zhonghua shuju, 1979), 13.290; and Li You 李攸 (fl. 1111–1134), *Songchao shishi* 宋朝事實 (*Congshu jicheng chubian* ed.), 7.107. Therefore, *guimao* should refer to 943, sixty years earlier than the proposed date of 1003. In addition, the literatus Sun Guangxian, who also had the title name Baoguangzi, was an official in Jingzhou from 926 to 963. Thus, Sun Guangxian and Sun Yizhong had the same surname and title name and served at the same place in the same period. All these coincidences suggest that most likely Sun Yizhong and Sun Guangxian were one and the same person and that Yizhong is likely his Daoist name. The *Chongwen zongmu* 崇文總目 records a Daoist text titled *Taixuan jinque sandong bajing yinyang xianban chaohui tu* 太元金闕三洞八景陰陽仙班朝會圖 but omits the author's name; while the *Tongzhi* 通志 records the same text and attributes it to Sun Guangxian. This supports the possibility of Sun's interest in Daoism. See Wang Yaochen 王堯臣 et al., *Chongwen zongmu*, 4.36b (*Yueyatang congshu* 粵雅堂叢書 ed.); Zheng Qiao 鄭樵 (1104–1162), *Tongzhi ershilü* 通志二十略 (Beijing: Zhonghua shuju, 1995), 1625. For Sun Guangxian's life, see Jia Jinhua 賈晉華 and Fu Xuancong 傅璇琮, *Tang Wudai wenxue biannian shi: Wudai juan* 唐五代文學編年史: 五代卷 (Shenyang: Liaohai chubanshe, 1999), 60, 126, 539, 555.

29. *DZ* 1125. This text is incomplete, and some fragments have been discovered in Dunhuang manuscripts. For a summary of discussions on its textual history and date, see Florian C. Reiter and Ursula-Angelika Cedzich, "Dongxuan lingbao sandong fengdao kejie yingshi," in Schipper and Verellen, *The Taoist Canon*, 451–53. For a complete translation and research, see Livia Koln, *The Daoist Monastic Manual: A Translation of the Fengdao Kejie* (Oxford: Oxford University Press, 2004).

30. *DZ* 1241, 788.

31. *Sandong xiudao yi*, 32: 166b.

32. *Fengdao kejie*, 24: 757a–62a; *Jingjie falu*, 32: 185b–190c; *Fafu kejie*, 18: 229b–c; and *Sandong xiudao yi*, 166b–69b. The *Fengdao kejie* and *Sandong xiudaoyi* also record some other kinds of Daoists who seem not to be a part of the Daoist ordination hierarchy nor even of Daoist monasteries. Charles D. Benn, Catherine Despeux, and Livia Kohn have analyzed the hierarchy described in the *Fengdao kejie*; see Charles Benn, *The Cavern-Mystery Transmission: A Taoist Ordination of A.D. 711* (Honolulu: University of Hawaii Press, 1991), 72–95; Benn, "Daoist Ordination and Zhai Rituals," in *Daoism Handbook*, 311–22; and Despeux and Kohn, *Women in Daoism* (Cambridge: Three Pines, 2003), 119–20. My list is somewhat different from theirs.

33. *Sandong xiudao yi*, 32: 166c–167b, 168c.

34. *Sandong xiudao yi*, 32: 167b.

35. About the 711 and 712 ordinations, see Zhang Wanfu, *Chuanshou Sandong jingjie falu lüeshuo*, 32: 196c–197c; and Charles Benn, *The Cavern-Mystery Transmission*, 5–20. There are two extant epitaphic inscriptions for Jinxian (one incomplete). The first states that she was ordained as a priestess in the year *bingwu* 丙午 (706); the second records that she "entered Dao" at eighteen *sui* and received the transmission of Daoist scriptures at twenty-three *sui*. If she was eighteen in 706,

then she would be twenty-three in 711. Yuzhen possibly became a priestess in 706 too. See Xu Qiao 徐嶠, "Jianxian zhanggongzhu shendao beiming bingxu" 金仙長公主神道碑銘並序, in Dong Gao 董誥 (1740–1818) et al., eds., *Quan Tangwen* 全唐文 (Beijing: Zhonghua shuju, 1983), 267.9b–11a; and "Datang gu Jinxian zhanggongzhu zhishiming bingxu" 大唐故金仙長公主誌石銘並序, in Zhou Shaoliang 周紹良 and Zhao Chao 趙超, eds., *Tangdai muzhi huibian xuji* 唐代墓誌彙編續集 (Shanghai: Shanghai guji chubanshe, 2001), 552.

36. Zhang Jiong 張冏, "Tang gu Jiuhua shu [one character missing] shi cangxing ji" 唐故九華書□師藏形記, in *Tangdai muzhi huibian xuji*, 795.

37. Liu Xu 劉昫 (888–947) et al., *Jiu Tangshu* 舊唐書 (Beijing: Zhonghua shuju, 1975), 191.5107.

38. Zheng Xianwen 鄭顯文, "Tangdai *Daoseng ge* yanjiu" 唐代道僧格研究, *Lishi yanjiu* 歷史研究 4 (2004): 50.

39. Moroto Tatsuo, *Chūgoku Bukkyō seidoshi no kenkyū* 中國佛教制度史の研究 (Tokyo: Hirakawa, 1990), 180–213.

40. *Dongxuan siwei dingzhi jing* 洞玄思微定志經, incorporated in *Wushang biyao* 無上秘要, *DZ* 1138, 25: 162b.

41. *Dongxuan zhihui jing* 洞玄智慧經, incorporated in *Wushang biyao*, *DZ* 1138, 25: 162c.

42. *Wushang biyao*, 25: 175c.

43. Zhang Wanfu, *Sandong zhongjie wen* 三洞眾戒文, *DZ* 178, 3: 400b. See also *Dongshen badi miaojing jing* 洞神八帝妙精經, *DZ* 640, 11: 389b.

44. See Li Ling, *Zhongguo fangshu zhengkao* 中國方術正考 (Beijing: Zhonghua shuju, 2006), 330–39.

45. Although there is no early record of his ordination, according to his alchemical experiments and other hints in his works, some scholars assume that Sun Simiao was an ordained Daoist of the Celestial Masters level. See Livia Kohn, *The Daoist Monastic Manual: A Translation of the Fengdao kejie* (New York: Oxford University Press, 2004), 16.

46. Sun Simiao, *Beiji qianjin yaofang*, *DZ* 1163, 26: 544c–546a. Translation adapted from Douglas Wile, *Art of the Bedchamber: The Chinese Sexual Yoga Classics Including Women's Solo Meditation Texts* (Albany: State University of New York Press, 1992), 113–19. For discussions of Sun Simiao's idea on sexual practice, see R. H. van Gulik, *Sexual Life in Ancient China*, 193–97; Catherine Despeux, *Prescriptions d'acuponcture valant mille onces d'or: traité d'acuponcture de Sun Simiao du VIIe siècle* (Paris: Trédaniel, 1987); and Paul U. Unschuld, "Der chinesische 'Arzneikönig' Sun Simiao: Geschichte–Legende–Ikonographie," *Monumenta Serica* 42 (1994): 217–57.

47. For discussions of the Daoist thought and practice of Sima Chengzhen and other Maoshan masters, see, for example, Russell Kirkland, "Taoists of the High T'ang" (PhD diss., Indiana University, 1986), 43–71, 220–97; Kirkland, "Ssu-ma Ch'eng-chen and the Role of Taoism in the Medieval Chinese Policy," *Journal of Asian History* 31.2 (1997): 105–38; Livia Kohn, *Seven Steps to the Tao: Sima Chengzhen's Zuowang lun* (St. Augustin: Steyler Verlag, 1987); Qing Xitai 卿希泰, ed., *Zhongguo daojiao shi* 中國道教史 (Chengdu: Sichuan renmin chubanshe, 1992),

2: 217–53; and Ren Jiyu 任繼愈, ed., *Zhongguo daojiao shi* 中國道教史 (Beijing: Zhongguo shehui kexue chubanshe, 2001), 345–62.

48. Du Guangting, *Yongcheng jixian lu*, *DZ* 783, 18: 197c–99a.

49. Luo Binwang, "Dai nüdaoshi Wang Lingfei zeng daoshi Li Rong" 代女道士王靈妃贈道士李榮, in Peng Dingqiu 彭定求 (1645–1719) et al., eds., *Quan Tangshi* 全唐詩 (Beijing: Zhonghua shuju, 1960), 77.838–39. For a detailed analysis of this poem, see Jia, "Tangshi zhong youguan nüdaoshi de lianqingshi kaobian," 128–32.

50. *Quan Tangshi*, 440.4900.

51. Chen Shangjun 陳尚君, ed., *Quan Tangshi bubian* 全唐詩補編, 3 vols. (Beijing: Zhonghua shuju, 1992), 1: 19.313.

52. For a detailed discussion of Li Jilan, see Jia, "The *Yaochi ji*," 216–33.

53. See, for example, Wen Yiduo 聞一多, *Shenhua yanjiu* 神話研究 (Chengdu: Ba Shu shushe, 2002), 1–39; and Alan K. L. Chan, "Goddesses in Chinese Religion," in Larry W. Hurtado, ed., *Goddesses in Religions and Modern Debate* (Atlanta: Scholars Press, 1990), 9–25.

54. Song Yu 宋玉 (fl. fourth century BCE), "Gaotang fu" 高唐賦, in Xiao Tong 蕭統 (501–531), comp., *Wenxuan* 文選 (Beijing: Zhonghua shuju, 1977), 19.1b–6b.

55. See, for example, Li Dingguang 李定廣 and Xu Kechao 徐可超, "Lun Zhongguo wenren de Wushan shennü qingjie" 論中國文人的巫山神女情結, *Fudan xuebao* 復旦學報 5 (2002): 112–17.

56. See mainly van Gulik, *Sexual Life in Ancient China*, 73–90; Li Ling, *Zhongguo fangshu xukao* 中國方術續考 (Beijing: Zhonghua shuju, 2006), 267–80; and Paul R. Goldin, "The Cultural and Religious Background of Sexual Vampirism in Ancient China," *Theology and Sexuality* 12.3 (2006): 285–308. Fragments of these Han dynasty sex manuals, along with some other texts, are preserved in the *Ishinpō* 醫心方 compiled by the Japanese physician Tamba Yasuyori 丹波康賴 (912–995) in 982. They are collected in Li Ling's *Zhongguo fangshu zhengkao*, 396–416; translated in Douglas Wile, *Art of the Bedchamber*, 83–113.

57. Tao Hongjing, *Zhengao*, 20: 491a–515c.

58. Suzanne Cahill, *Transcendence and Divine Passion: The Queen Mother of the West in Medieval China* (Stanford: Stanford University Press, 1993), 190–212.

59. For discussions of these goddesses, see mainly Edward H. Schafer, *The Divine Women: Dragon Ladies and Rain Maidens in Tang Literature* (Berkeley: University of California Press, 1973); Schafer, "Three Divine Women of South China," *Chinese Literature: Essays, Articles, Reviews* 1 (1979): 31–42; Schafer, "Cantos on 'One Bit of Cloud at Shamanka Mountain,'" *Asiatische Studien* 36 (1983): 102–24; Suzanne Cahill, "Sex and the Supernatural in Medieval China: Cantos on the Transcendent Who Presides over the River," *Journal of the American Oriental Society* 105.2 (1985): 197–220; and Cahill, *Transcendence and Divine Passion*, 108–89.

60. See Schafer, "The Capeline Cantos: Verses on the Divine Loves of Taoist Priestesses," *Asiatische Studien* 32 (1978): 5–65.

61. *Quan Tangshi*, 805.9058.

62. See Guo Maoqian 郭茂倩 (fl. 1084), *Yuefu shiji* 樂府詩集 (Beijing: Zhonghua shuju, 1979), 60.876.

63. *Quan Tangshi*, 805.9058.

64. *Quan Tangshi*, 804.9051, 9053.

65. *Quan Tangshi*, 804.9050.

66. Liu Yiqing 劉義慶 (403–444), *Youming lu* 幽明錄 (Beijing: Wenhua yishu chubanshe, 1988), 1.1–2.

67. *Quan Tangshi*, 801.9011.

68. For a detailed study of Cui Zhongrong, see Jinhua Jia, "The *Yaochi ji*," 238–41.

69. *Quan Tangshi*, 77.838–39.

70. *Quan Tangshi*, 804.9047. Song Yu, the fourth-century BCE poet cited previously, was said to be very handsome. In a *fu* (rhapsody) attributed to Song, a girl who was his neighbor on the east side often climbed up the wall to peek at him; see Song Yu, "Dengtu zi haose fu" 登徒子好色賦, in Xiao Tong, comp., *Wen xuan*, 19.9b–11b. Wang Chang was a famously handsome man during the Wei-Jin period and later became the persona of a desirable husband for young girls in songs of the Southern dynasties; see Wu Zhaoyi 吳兆宜 (fl. 1672) and Cheng Yan 程琰, ed., *Yutai xinyong jianzhu* 玉台新詠箋注 (Beijing: Zhonghua shuju, 1985), 9.387; and Guo Maoqian, *Yuefu shiji*, 85.1204.

71. Anonymous, "Qinghe Zhangshi nüshang muzhiming" 清河張氏女殤墓誌銘, in Chen Yuan 陳垣, Chen Zhichao 陳智超, and Zeng Qingying 曾慶瑛, eds., *Daoijia jinshi lüe* 道家金石略 (Beijing: Wenwu, 1988), 169–70.

72. Zhou and Zhao, *Tangdai muzhi huibian xuji*, 552–53.

73. *Quan Tangshi*, 519.5930–31.

74. Zhou and Zhao, *Tangdai muzhi huibian xuji*, 795.

75. Huangfu Mei 皇甫枚, *Sanshui xiaodu* 三水小牘 (Lesser Documents from the Three Rivers), incorporated in Li Fang 李昉 (925–96) et al., eds., *Taiping guangji* 太平廣記, 10 vols. (Beijing: Zhonghua shuju, 1961), 130.922–23.

76. *Fengdao kejie*, 24: 757a–762a; *Jingjie falu*, 32: 185b–190c; and *Sandong xiudao yi*, 166b–169b. See Charles Benn, *The Cavern-Mystery Transmission*, 3; and Ren Jiyu, *Zhongguo Daojiao shi*, 363–409.

77. See Edward H. Schafer, "Wu Yün's 'Cantos on Pacing the Void,' " *Harvard Journal of Asiatic Studies* 41 (1981): 377–415; Schafer, "Wu Yün's Stanzas on 'Saunters in Sylphdom,' " *Monumenta Serica* 35 (1983): 1–37; Paul Kroll, "Notes on Three Taoist Figures of the T'ang Dynasty," *Society for the Study of Chinese Religions Bulletin* 9 (1981): 19–41; Kroll, "In the Halls of the Azure Lad," *Journal of the American Oriental Society* 105 (1986): 75–94; Sun Changwu 孫昌武, *Daojiao yu Tangdai wenxue* 道教與唐代文學 (Beijing: Renmin wenxue chubanshe, 2001), 344–47; and Kenneth Dean, "Daoist Ritual Today," in *Daoism Handbook*, 659–82.

78. Wang Baoyi's biography is included in Wu Renchen 吳任臣 (fl. 1679), *Shiguo chunqiu* 十國春秋 (Beijing: Zhonghua shuju, 1983), 1459.

79. Incorporated in *Taiping guangji*, 205.1568–69.

80. Sun Qi 孫棨 (fl. 884), *Beili zhi* 北里志 (Shanghai: Gudian wenxue chubanshe, 1957), 25; and Victor Xiong, "Ji-Entertainers in Tang Chang'an," in Sherry J. Mou, ed., *Presence and Presentation: Women in the Chinese Literati Tradition* (New York: St. Martin's Press, 1999), 150, 153–57.

81. See Liu Ning 劉寧, "Shixi Tangdai changji shi yu nüguan shi de chayi" 試析唐代娼妓詩與女冠詩的差異," *Zhongguo dianji yu wenhua* 中國典籍與文化 4 (2003): 49–57; and Jia, "The *Yaochi ji*," 233, 241.

82. See mainly Stephen R. Bokenkamp, "Time after Time: Taoist Apocalyptic History and the Founding of the T'ang Dynasty," *Asia Major* 3.7 (1994): 59–88; and T. H. Barrett, *Taoism under the T'ang* (London: Wellsweep Press, 1996).

83. See, for example, Li Fengmao, "Tangdai gongzhu rudao yu 'Song gongren rudao shi' " 唐代公主入道與送宮人入道詩, in *You yu you: Liuchao Sui Tang xiandao wenxue* 憂與遊: 六朝隋唐仙道文學 (1996; reprint, Beijing: Zhonghua shuju, 2010), 169–202.

84. For a detailed discussion of religious establishments in Tang Chang'an, see Victor Cunrui Xiong, *Sui-Tang Chang'an: A Study in the Urban History of Medieval China* (Ann Arbor: University of Michigan Press, 2000), 237–76.

85. *Tang liudian*, 3.74; *Bai Kong liutie* 白孔六帖 (*SKQS* ed.), 89.10a; and Tianyige bowuguan 天一閣博物館 and Zhongguo shehui kexueyuan lishi yanjiusuo Tianshengling zhengli ketizu 中國社會科學院歷史研究所天聖令整理課題組, eds., *Tianyige cang Ming chaoben Tianshengling jiaozheng, fu Tangling fuyuan yanjiu* 天一閣明鈔本天聖令校證, 附唐令復原研究 (Beijing: Zhonghua shuju, 2006), 38. During the Zhenguan reign period (627–649), at first the required scripture of transmission was the *Sanhuang jing* 三皇經, but this scripture was prohibited and replaced by the *Daode jing* in 648. See Daoxuan 道宣 (596–667), *Ji gujin Fodao lunheng* 集古今佛道論衡 (*Taishō shinshū daizōkyō* 大正新修大藏經 ed.), 52: 3.386a; Moroto Tatsuo, *Chūgoku Bukkyō seidoshi no kenkyū*, 368–70; Niida Noboru 仁井田陞 and Ikeda On 池田溫, *Tōrei shūi ho: tsuketari Tō-Nichi ryōrei taishō ichiran* 唐令拾遺補: 附唐日兩令對照一覽 (Tokyo: Tōkyō Daigaku Shuppankai, 1997), 194–96; and Dai Jianguo 戴建國, "Tang 'Kaiyuan ershiwu nian ling tianling' yanjiu" 唐 "開元二十五年令田令" 研究, *Lishi yanjiu* 歷史研究 2 (2000): 36–50.

86. See, for example, Han Guopan 韓國磐, *Beichao Sui Tang de Juntian zhidu* 北朝隋唐的均田制度 (Shanghai: Shanghai renmin chubanshe, 1984), 128–247; and Wang Yongping 王永平, *Daojiao yu Tangdai shehui* 道教與唐代社會 (Beijing: Shoudu shifan daxue chubanshe, 2002), 203–17.

87. Qian Yi 錢易 (968–1026), *Nanbu xinshu* 南部新書 (Shanghai: Zhonghua shuju, 1958), 50; and Xu Song 徐松 (1781–1848), *Tang liangjing chengfang kao* 唐兩京城坊考 (Beijing: Zhonghua shuju, 1985), 3.60.

88. See Huangfu Mei, *Sanshui xiaodu*, incorporated in *Taiping guangji*, 130.922–23.

89. For detailed discussions, see Robert des Rotours, *Courtisanes chinoises à la fin des T'ang, entre circa 789 et le 8 Janvier 881: Pei-Li Tche (Anecdotes du quartier du nord)* (Paris: Presses Universitaires de France, 1968); and Xiong, "Ji-Entertainers,"

149–69. There were different types of official and private *ji* 妓 in the Tang; for detailed discussions of the classifications of Tang courtesans, see Gao Shiyu, *Tangdai funü*, 56–80; Zheng Zhimin 鄭志敏, *Xishuo Tangji* 戲說唐妓 (Taibei: Wenjin chuban gongsi, 1997), 27–32. Translations for the term *ji* vary among scholars, including "courtesan," "prostitute," "whore," "geisha," and "entertainer." For a summary of different translations, see Ping Yao, "The Status of Pleasure: Courtesan and Literati Connections in T'ang China (618–907)," *Journal of Women's History* 14.2 (2002): 44–45. Since *ji* is not the main concern of this chapter, I simply use "courtesan" to name them generally.

90. See Ping Yao, "The Status of Pleasure," 37–43.

91. *Beili zhi*, 26; and Xiong, "Ji-Entertainers," 154, 157–59.

92. See Chen Wenhua 陳文華, *Tang nüshiren ji sanzhong* 唐女詩人集三種 (Shanghai: Shanghai guji, 1984), 74–76; Wu Qiming 吴企明, "Xue Tao," in Fu Xuancong 傅璇琮, ed., *Tang caizizhuan jiaojian* 唐才子傳校箋, 5 vols. (Beijing: Zhonghua shuju, 1990), vol. 3, 6.102–13; and Wilt Idema and Beata Grant, *The Red Brush: Writing Women in Imperial China* (Cambridge: Harvard University Asia Center, 2004), 182–89. There are different sayings about the author and context of the series, but according to Xue Tao's poem entitled "Fa fubian youhuai shang Wei linggong ershou" 罰赴邊有懷上韋令公二首 (*Tang nüshiren ji*, 30), a record by He Guangyuan 何光遠 (fl. 938–964; *Jianjie lu* 鑒戒錄, *SKQS*, 10.12b), and a piece from the series attributed to Xue Tao in the late-Tang anthology *Youxuan ji* 又玄集 (in Fu Xuancong 傅璇琮, ed., *Tangren xuan Tangshi xinbian* 唐人選唐詩新編 [Xi'an: Shaanxi renmin jiaoyu, 1996], 680), the series should have been written by Xue when she was banished to Songzhou by Wei Gao. See Zhang Pengzhou 張蓬舟, *Xue Tao shijian* 薛濤詩箋 (Beijing: Renmin wenxue chubanshe, 1983), 14–18.

93. Li Deyu's poem is no longer extant; Liu Yuxi's poem is included in the *Quan Tangshi*, 365.4121.

94. Liu Ning has noted this point; see her "Shixi Tangdai changji shi yu nüguan shi de chayi," 52–53.

95. Catherine Despeux, "L'ordination des femmes taoïste sous les Tang," *Etudes chinoises* 5 (1986): 53–100; and Despeux and Kohn, *Women in Daoism*, 119.

96. Li Bai, "Zeng Songshan Jiao lianshi" 贈嵩山焦煉師, *Quan Tangshi*, 168.1739–40.

97. Zhao Chengliang 趙承亮, "Tang gu nei Yuchenguan Shangqing Dadong Sanjing fashi cizi dade xiangongming bingxu" 唐故內玉晨觀上清大洞三景法師賜紫大德仙宮銘並序, *Tangdai muzhi huibian xuji*, 906; and Song Ruoxian 宋若憲 (d. 835), "Tang Daminggong Yuchenguan gu Shangqing Taidong Sanjing dizi Dongyue qingdi zhenren Tian fashi xuanshiming bingxu" 唐大明宮玉晨觀故上清太洞三景弟子東嶽青帝真人田法師玄室銘并序, in *Tangdai muzhi huibian xuji*, 892–93.

98. Meng Jiao, "Tong Li Yi, Cui Fang song Wang lianshi huan Louguan jianwei qungong xianying shanju" 同李益崔放送王錬師還樓觀兼為羣公先營山居, *Quan Tangshi*, 379.4250.

99. See Jowen R. Tung, *Fables for the Patriarchs: Gender Politics in Tang Discourse* (New York: Rowman & Littlefield, 2000), 49–50; Despeux and Kohn, *Women in Daoism*, 118–28; and Ping Yao, "Contested Virtue: The Daoist Investiture of Princesses Jinxian and Yuzhen and the Journey of Tang Imperial Daughters," *T'ang Studies* 22 (2004): 1–41.

100. The *Yaochi ji* has long been lost, but some fragments have been rediscovered from the Dunhuang manuscripts included in the Russian collections in St. Petersburg. For a detailed discussion of this text, see Jinhua Jia, "The *Yaochi ji*," 205–16.

101. *Tangren xuan Tangshi xinbian*, 672–82, 946–63.

5

# Revisiting *White-haired Girl*

## Women, Gender, and Religion in Communist Revolutionary Propaganda

*Xiaofei Kang*

### Introduction

Gender and religion are both important categories in the discourse of twentieth-century Communist revolution in China, yet the interactions between the two remain largely unexplored. This chapter is an initial attempt to address this gap in our knowledge and to further our understanding of women and gender in the construction/destruction of Chinese religions under Communism. It examines the evolution of the *White-haired Girl* (*Baimaonü* 白毛女) and analyzes how traditional religion is represented and reappropriated to serve changing political agendas in this classic of Chinese Communist literature and art. Presumably based on a true story from northern Hebei during the anti-Japanese war (1937–1945), *White-haired Girl* was collectively created as an opera by Yan'an Communist writers and artists in 1945. Since its inception, the opera has undergone many different textual, cinematic, and theatrical editions and enjoyed immense popularity among several generations of rural and urban Chinese who have lived through Communist rule.

Scholars of modern Chinese literature generally recognize the 1945 opera *White-haired Girl* as an enthusiastic response to Mao Zedong's famous "Talks at the Yan'an Conference on Literature and Art" in 1942.[1] Voluminous studies have been dedicated to the many different aspects of *White-haired Girl*, especially gender, and to the political significance of the opera.

As some literary critics have rightly pointed out, the narrative device of the opera, which features the suffering of a young peasant girl at the hands of a cruel landlord and her ultimate salvation by the Communist force, is intensely symbolic. It suppresses the sexual conflict and gender confrontations of the protagonists and replaces them with a new ideological discourse of class struggle. The opera represents Yan'an intellectuals' efforts to use gender imageries to create a new national myth. And it has succeeded only because it efficiently incorporates the political messages alongside the traditional themes of romance, revenge, and justice that cater to both peasant entertainment and urban culture consumption.[2]

This chapter builds on previous research by literary scholars but engages the issues of women and gender in a different dimension, as part of the twentieth-century reconstruction of Chinese religions in relation to revolution and nation-state building. Drawing on the Western experience of modernization, the twentieth-century Chinese state and the educated elite committed themselves to a secularization process that aimed to separate religion from Chinese social, economic, and political life and to replace religion with nationalism. Religion was redefined as personal beliefs and philosophical pursuits, whereas Buddhism, Daoism, and Confucianism were uprooted from local life and reinvented as church-like religious institutions. Intrinsic elements of Chinese religious practices and rituals, such as incense burning, paper offerings, communal worship, ghost pacification, demon exorcism, fortune-telling, and spirit possessions, were all denounced as "superstition" and hence hindrances to modernity.[3]

Coming out of the May Fourth era, most of the early Communist leaders and intellectuals were committed to the cause of gender equality, adopted the doctrine of atheism, and fervently advocated science, evolutionism, and nationalism. In the later shift of their revolutionary base to rural areas, however, the CCP's policies about women and religion had both changed in the face of the expedient needs of wartime survival and expansion. Women's liberation was reduced to making women into a productive labor force, and gender equality had to give way to winning the support of young male peasants in the army.[4] Moreover, as Tina Mai Chen has recently argued, the Maoist ideology postulates an intrinsic link between women and peasants, both as remnants of the "feudal past" and agents of transformation in the revolutionary present and future. The gendered construction of "the peasants" established legitimacy for Mao's leadership in the political campaigns for the sake of revolutionary progress, whereas "alternative projects for class and gender liberation are themselves denied historical relevance."[5]

CCP leaders also realized that traditional religions, or "superstitions," had been deeply rooted in Chinese peasant life. It was a daunting task to eradicate them, and sometimes it was even necessary to use them in the service of the Communist cause.[6] David Holm, for example, demonstrates how the Yan'an art workers transformed *Yangge* 秧歌, a northern China song-and-dance performance closely tied to local religious culture, into a propaganda genre loaded with political messages.[7] Ralph Thaxton finds that peasants themselves interpreted the war in religious terms, calling the Communists their Bodhisattva saviors and the Japanese demons.[8] More generally, Barend ter Haar shows that a "demonological messianic paradigm," which centers on the arrival of a savior prince and his celestial armies to fight off demons and to save people from imminent apocalyptic disasters, has characterized Chinese popular religious culture throughout history. It exerted a great impact on Communist political campaigns, especially the Cultural Revolution (1966–1976).[9] A number of scholars further argue that at the height of the Cultural Revolution, when almost all religions were banned and religious infrastructures destroyed, traditional religious languages and imageries persisted in shaping the political religiosity dedicated to the Cult of Mao.[10]

This chapter follows the path of the aforementioned scholarship and explores the gendered representations of both traditional Chinese religions and the CCP's power in the 1945 opera *White-haired Girl* and its film version in 1950. The different ways in which the female body, age, and sexuality are depicted in the opera epitomize the Communist propaganda workers' intentional efforts to disassociate traditional religion and Confucian morality from peasant life and to establish a new national myth of liberation under the leadership of the CCP. The success of the opera, however, did not necessarily lead to the alleged goals of anti-superstition and secularization, nor did it aim to promote gender equality. On the contrary, I argue, the opera relies on the same languages and gender imageries embedded in traditional Chinese religions to construct a new kind of political religiosity. The ghostly features of the White-haired Girl symbolized the feminized and victimized peasant class and the Chinese nation. Her salvation depended upon her lover, a young Communist soldier, who brought her back to a new life under the sun—the cosmic yang force representing the CCP and Mao. As the CCP emerged as the "liberator" of the Chinese nation in the late 1940s, the highly gendered symbolism in the opera served to establish the CCP's legitimacy as a new embodiment of heavenly order and justice, replacing the old gods and goddesses and mobilizing both the rural and urban populations to join the revolutionary force. Such gendering only further perpetuated the old gender relations: it moved attention away from women's issues in real-life situations, deprived peasant women of their revolutionary agency, and reduced them to being mere recipients of the CCP's benevolent salvation. Religion, therefore, was by no means absent from the Communist revolution. It remained useful for constructing the power of the CCP and later directly contributed to the Cult of Mao.

## A Brief History of *White-haired Girl*

The story of *White-haired Girl* was believed to have been widely circulated in the Communist-occupied areas of northern Hebei, Shanxi, and Shaanxi in the late 1930s and early 1940s. Later reconstructions of the story mention two possible origins of the story: (1) A village girl in western Hebei was forced to become a concubine of a landlord, who expected a son from her. After giving birth to a baby girl, she was driven out of the house. She and her daughter lived in the wilderness and survived on temple offerings, until they were saved by the Communist Eighth Route Army. She joined the Communist force afterward; (2) In a village in Fuping County of Hebei Province, a landlord father and son were both infatuated with a young girl. In an argument over her, the son accidently killed the father. He and his mother framed the girl as the murderer, which led to a similar exile story. In either case, the story was about young peasant women's sufferings from the abusive power of village landlords and from the traditional bias that favored boys over girls. The arrival of the Communist force ended these women's sufferings.[11]

When the story reached the Communist headquarters in Yan'an in 1943, it had already gone through many versions of recreation by grassroots propaganda workers.[12] In 1944, under the order of Zhou Yang 周揚 (1908–1989), then the head of Yan'an Lu Xun Academy of Art (Yan'an Lu Xun yishu xueyuan 延安魯迅藝術學院, commonly known as Luyi 魯藝), He Jingzhi 賀敬之 (1924–) organized a group of Luyi writers and composers to create the opera *White-haired Girl*.[13] The opera debuted in Yan'an in 1945 as a tribute to the Seventh Congress of the Communist Party and became an instant success. It was highly praised by top-level Communist leaders and soon spread throughout the Communist areas in northern China.

The 1945 opera has a simple plot: Xi'er 喜兒 is a seventeen-year-old village girl. The cruel landlord Huang Shiren 黃世仁 forces Xi'er's father,

Yang Bailao 楊白勞, to sell her to Huang in order to pay off his debt. Overwhelmed by guilt, Yang commits suicide on the eve of the Chinese New Year. Over her father's dead body Xi'er is taken to the Huang house, where she suffers daily abuse from Huang's Buddhist mother and eventually is raped by Huang. When mother and son later plan to sell the pregnant Xi'er to a human trafficker, Xi'er flees into the mountains and gives birth to a baby. In the wilderness, her clothing turns ragged and her disheveled hair and whole body turn "white." When she steals food offerings from a temple, she is taken to be a "White-haired Goddess" and attracts worshippers. She is later rescued by Dachun 大春, her fiancé, who has joined the Communist army and now returns to lead the village land reform. Huang is denounced in mass meetings, and his land is redistributed to poor peasants. Xi'er and Dachun are happily married.[14]

From 1945 to the 1970s, *White-haired Girl* went through many different editions. The opera was performed by many propaganda troupes in Yan'an and other Communist areas. In 1950, it was made into a film. When the film was released in the movie theaters of twelve major cities, the first-day ticket sales exceeded six million.[15] In 1951, the film won an international film award in what was then Czechoslovakia. In 1964, the Shanghai Ballet Academy transformed the story into a ballet opera. During the Cultural Revolution, the ballet opera was further revised under the direct leadership of Mao's wife Jiang Qing 江青 (1915–1991). As one of the eight "Model Operas" (*yangbanxi* 樣板戲), the ballet opera was made into a new color film. Many of its episodes were emulated in mass performances, and almost everyone, young and old, could sing at least one or two songs from the film. The White-haired Girl became a cultural icon of the oppressed in the old society and Huang Shiren a synonym for the condemned landlord class.[16]

## From Anti-Superstition to National Myth

Despite numerous studies of *White-haired Girl*, the representations of religion in the 1945 opera and the 1950 film still warrant further examination. What He Jingzhi heard in Yan'an, according to his recollection in 1946, was an anti-superstition story focusing on a "White-haired Goddess" (*Baimao xiangu* 白毛仙姑):[17]

> In a village by the mountain, the Eighth Route Army found it difficult to initiate any activities there after it was liberated, because the villagers and the village cadres were all deeply super-

> stitious. They said that indeed the village had a "White-haired Goddess." It was said that her whole body was white, she often appeared in the night, and she resided in the Nainai temple (*Nainaimiao* 奶奶廟) at the village entrance. She once ordered the villagers to make offerings to her on the first and fifteenth of each month. The villagers had obeyed her orders for a long time, and they indeed saw that the offerings they made the previous night would disappear the next morning. When sometimes the villagers neglected her and failed to make offerings to her, they would hear a strange shrieking voice coming from behind the dark altar: "You . . . do not worship the Goddess. Be warned of [upcoming] disasters and catastrophes."[18]

Disembodied spirits, extraordinary immortal maidens or ghosts, and the worship of goddesses have always been favorite topics in the long tradition of Chinese oral storytelling, ritual opera performance, and literati anecdotal writing. This story seems to belong to this long tradition. It was the mysterious white body, her nightly appearances, and her disembodied voice in the Nainai temple that captured the villagers' as well as the audience's attention. In most parts of China, white is the color of death and mourning: people wear and use white cloth in death rituals, which in general are called *baishi* 白事, white affairs. White is also the color of the yin force and therefore associated with ghosts and ghostly appearances.

The Nainai temples were widespread in northern China. Many female deities in northern Chinese religious life can be interchangeably called Nainai, Niangniang 娘娘, or Xiangu 仙姑. A village Nainai temple would be mostly likely dedicated to Taishan Niangniang 泰山娘娘 (Lady Taishan or Mother Taishan) or Bixia Yuanjun 碧霞元君 (the Perfected of the Azure Cloud), but it could also house any of several of popular female deities such as Bodhisattva Guanyin 觀音, the Eternal Mother (Wusheng Laomu 無生老母), the Goddesses of Three Heavens (Sanxiao Niangniang 三霄娘娘), and/or the Queen Mother of the West (Xiwangmu 西王母), and so on. It was also common for a temple to include side shrines for lesser and sometimes demonic spirits, or for some female deities who embodied both divine and demonic features and originated from vengeful ghosts of women who died young or a wrongful death.[19] Thus the notion that a white and nocturnal female creature had taken up residence in the Nainai temple drew on popular lore and popular worship of female deities and female ghosts in northern China.

The next part of the story inevitably delivers a Communist message of liberation, but it also contains key elements of folk religion. When the upper-level Communist cadres arrived at the village, the story continues, nobody came to the mass mobilization meeting, because all the villagers went to worship the White-haired Goddess. The cadres staged a midnight ambush at the Nainai temple and chased a "white thing" out of the temple, all the way into a dark cave deep in the mountain. There they found that the White-haired Goddess was in fact a poor woman. The story of her tragic exile became the story of Xi'er in the opera, which goes on to provide a "rational" explanation of her whiteness: having been living in the dark cave for several years, she "saw no sunlight and ate [food] without salt, so her whole body has turned white."[20] She stole food offerings from the Nainai temple, so the villagers took her as the manifestation of Nainai—the White-haired Goddess.

As favorite dwelling places for immortal maidens with extraordinary bodily features, mountain caves have been a familiar *topos* in popular and literati writing since ancient times. The mountains in the Shaanxi and Shanxi region have been home to some of the most well-known legends about female immortal maidens since at least medieval times.[21] In particular, the legend of a "haired maiden" (*maonü* 毛女) was recorded in various historical texts such as *Liexian zhuan* 列仙傳 and *Taiping guangji* 太平廣記. She was believed to be a palace maiden of the First Emperor of the Qin Dynasty (221–206 BCE), and she had lived on Mount Hua for more than 170 years by the time of the Former Han (202 BCE–9 CE). She "had hair grown all over her body," and "after a Daoist taught her to live on pine resin, she was no longer subject to hunger and the cold and she had gained a light body."[22] In late imperial times, various versions of the haired maiden story were recorded in literati writings. Up until today, the Cave of the Haired Maiden (*Maonü dong* 毛女洞) on top of the Peak of the Haired Maiden (*Maonü feng* 毛女峰) on the famous Mount Hua in southern Shaanxi still keeps the legendary stories of the haired maiden alive in local folklore.[23]

The early popularity of the story must have a great deal to do with the aforementioned folk-religious elements. Not surprisingly, upon hearing the story, some of He Jingzhi's comrades in Yan'an dismissed it as a "meaningless story of spirits and the strange." Others took it as a good piece of "anti-superstition" material.[24] The grassroots propaganda workers in Hebei were committed to the wartime Communist social reforms from the bottom up: drawing on real-life stories, they combined the theme of anti-superstition with that of women's liberation. The landlord's power was condemned, but, as the party's wartime policy of the United Front required, the landlord class was not the main target of attack.

It is significant then that in the Yan'an re-creation, the Luyi artists decided to abandon the obvious "anti-superstition" theme in the original materials and reframe them into a new opera about "the contrast between the old and the new society and the liberation (*fanshen* 翻身) of the people."[25] With their Western training and urban education, neither Zhou Yang nor most of the Luyi crew were much interested in the "old forms" before 1942. Mao's 1942 talks, which required that all writers and artists submit themselves to the party line and to the service of "the workers, peasants, and soldiers and their cadres in the Party, government, and army," changed the situation. Those who created the opera *White-haired Girl* were all members of the Luyi Propaganda Troupe, which was set up in 1943 particularly for carrying out Mao's ideas. Their experience with the new Yangge movement, which directly contributed to the making of *White-haired Girl*, marked the success of the CCP's central leadership in transforming the petit bourgeois art and literature workers into the party's propaganda tools at the grassroots level.[26]

Like their May Fourth predecessors, the Luyi crew continued to use the peasant as a metaphor for the nation. Yet they departed from the Enlightenment mission of social and cultural reforms. In choosing to express peasant liberation over anti-superstition, they highlighted one central theme: the Old Society forces people to become ghosts, and the New Society restores ghosts back to life (*jiu shehui ba ren biancheng gui, xin shehui ba gui biancheng ren* 舊社會把人變成鬼, 新社會把鬼變成人). Xi'er's ghostly body was identified with the oppressed peasant class and the whole Chinese nation. Xi'er's salvation would be the Chinese nation's salvation. In this myth-making endeavor, the complexity of conflicts and problems in Chinese peasant life were simplified into a clear-cut antagonism of two opposite forces: the old versus new social order, or the peasant versus the landlord class.[27] On stage, this antagonism would be conveniently transferred into the confrontation between good and evil, an eternal theme in popular literature and performing art that easily appealed to a wide range of audiences. Issues of anti-superstition, marriage reform, gender equality, and other social programs that would have more impact on peasants' real-life situations were left aside.

The opera's detachment from real peasant life did not go unnoticed among the Communist propaganda workers. As early as in 1945, Zhang Jichun 張季純—another playwright at Luyi who was not part of the *White-haired Girl* crew—already noted that on multiple accounts the opera's plot betrayed basic logic and common sense about peasant life in northern China. Girls from poor families, Zhang noted, were customarily expected either to be married out or sold to pay off family debts. It was implausible for a father to feel so guilty for selling his daughter that he had to commit suicide. Also, why did Huang Shiren insist on bringing Xi'er into his house on the day of Chinese New Year—was not a girl in mourning an extremely inauspicious presence for any household on such a festive occasion? In addition, Zhang pointed out, Huang's mother must have been a quite benign, if not benevolent, woman, because under her supervision Huang did not find an opportunity to rape Xi'er until several months after Xi'er entered the Huang household.[28] Zhang's questions, however, were quickly suppressed by the party. Upon the opera's immediate success in Yan'an, the CCP's central leadership instructed that the Question of the Peasant in the Chinese revolution was essentially about the peasants' struggle against exploitation by the landlord class. The opera was a timely propaganda piece because it "mobilize[s] the masses and enhance[s] peasants' self-awareness of class struggles."[29]

## From a Goddess to a Ghost

The change of theme resulted in eliminating folk-religious elements from the opera and changing the White-haired Girl from a goddess to a vengeful ghost. First of all, the order of narration is completely changed. The suspense built up over the mysterious "White-haired Goddess" in the beginning is now replaced by the opening scenes that highlight the tension between the landlord, Huang Shiren, and the poor tenants, represented by Yang Bailao, and between Huang's sexual interest in Xi'er and Xi'er's romantic commitment to Dachun. When Xi'er steals food offerings from the Nainai temple and is subsequently worshipped as the "White-haired Goddess," the audience would be fully aware of the fake identity of this goddess. Their attention is therefore more directed to Xi'er's misery rather than the mysterious white goddess. Xi'er's "whiteness" now becomes a matter-of-fact result of her victimization by the evil landlord and, by extension, the old social system.

Other adaptations either suppress religious elements or subvert the meanings of traditional motifs in the original story. The original story in its earlier part creates much curiosity about the unknown white goddess and exploits popular fascination with caves and immortal maidens. The cave is also an important motif in the opera, but it is presented as a cold, dark, and horrifying tomb hosting ghosts, and it symbolizes the old social order.

It is the cause of Xi'er's white, discolored body and it harbors Xi'er's grievances and hatred, which are also the peasant class's grievances and hatred:

> You want me to die and I won't die.
> I take shelter in the cave.
> For every day I have endured I mark a line on the cave's rock—
> But I cannot carve up my thousand layers of grievances and ten thousand layers of hatred!
> . . . The thousand layers of grievances and ten-thousand layers of hatred,
> They are carved into my bones and they are inscribed in my heart![30]

The story also features Xi'er's disembodied, shrieking voice, a common scene in folk stories and religion: the female deities spoke, often through mediums, to demand offerings and to threaten disasters if their requests failed to be answered. In the opera, Xi'er finds the temple shelter by chance, steals food from the altar, but never directly speaks out to the villagers, who, to the audience's eyes, understandably mistake her for a goddess. Here the opera as well as the 1950 film reenact the folk storytelling scene common in village life, in which a group of villagers sit around an old man who recounts:

> It was thundering and the road was slippery from the rain. There was no way to keep going, so I came to this Nainai Temple to stay the night. . . . I looked up and the curtain behind the altar was billowing. I looked more carefully and the curtain was moving back and forth more and more. I looked at the bottom of the curtain but I didn't see anything. I was really scared. So I knelt right down and kowtowed and prayed, kowtowed and prayed. I said, "White-haired Goddess, White-haired Goddess, please don't take offense, I had to come in here to get out of the rain. There was nothing I could do. Don't blame me." Nothing happened. So I relaxed and caught my breath. I slowly raised my head and, oh my, the White-haired Goddess was standing right above me. She was white all over. I felt a cold shiver run through me. I snuck a look, saw a flash of white, and then there was nothing.[31]

In this whole process, Xi'er was silent. She passively accepted the fake identity of the "White-haired Goddess" but never actively assumed this identity with the villagers.

It is by no means coincidental then that the opera and the film added a scene in which Huang and his underling Mu Renzhi take shelter in the same Nainai temple on a dark, rainy night. Xi'er quickly recognizes them, hurls objects at them, and chases them. Terrified by Xi'er's appearance, Huang and Mu run away screaming, "It is a ghost! It is a ghost!" It is from Huang and Mu's screams that Xi'er first realizes that she has lost her youthful beauty and has come to look like a ghost. She first protests: "I am the Xi'er that you persecuted! I am a human!" But soon she turns herself into a vengeful ghost: "You say I'm a ghost. Well then, I am a ghost! I am the ghost of a wrongful soul. I am a ghost of someone who died of injustice. I want to tear your flesh! I want to beat you! I want to bite you!"[32] Throughout the opera/film, this is the only time that Xi'er cries out, "I am a ghost!"; thus, she acknowledges herself as a victim of the two villains and launches a direct accusation against Huang and the old system he represents.

In Chinese folk religion, as mentioned previously, benevolent goddesses and vengeful ghosts are closely connected, and they are often the alter ego of each other. The most popular female deities housed in the Nainai temples in northern China, such as Bixia Yuanjun or Lady Taishan, usually embody the double features of female sexuality and motherhood. It is common for people to worship a ghostly figure and accord her with goddess status so that the menacing potential of a female ghost would be transformed into a benevolent power. The Yan'an artists here play on the ambiguity of folk beliefs in female divinities, rejecting female deities' protective power and emphasizing their ghostly features. Both the opera and the film eliminate Xi'er's shrieking voice and mute her from the altar. In denouncing Xi'er's divine associations, the opera and film deny Xi'er's agency to transform herself from a vengeful ghost to a goddess and save herself through religious power. The Yan'an artists' recreation of the story is therefore a rather ironic process: in order to redeem Xi'er's humanity from a ghostly life, they actually have to first bring her down from the altar of the goddess and underline her ghostly features. Note in the original story, the Communist cadres had to compete with the "White-haired Goddess" over peasant followers. Only in denouncing the divine power of folk gods and goddesses and identifying the peasants with an inhuman and ghostly life would a new belief in the power of the CCP and the new social order be fully established.

## Gender and Religion in Xi'er's Salvation

The Yan'an artists, however, did not completely leave aside the "anti-superstition" theme—they only subsumed it into the larger scheme to build a new faith. In the opera, Xi'er's ghostly features would invoke another side of the most enduring folk beliefs in rural China. Young women who have suffered and died often come back to their persecutors in the form of vengeful ghosts. These ghosts are both dangerous elements in folk beliefs and favorite topics in popular storytelling: the sense of horror, suspense, and, oftentimes, the romance that revolves around the female ghosts are the main attraction of popular stories. They offer not only a diverse range of intense emotional experience but also, as they are often told in gatherings of family, friends, and neighbors, great occasions for social bonding in rural communities.[33]

Yet unlike the familiar female heroines in traditional ghost stories, Xi'er is unable to exercise the power of retribution on her own in the opera/film: although Huang is chased away, his landlord status remains the same, as does Xi'er's miserable situation. In the eyes of the audience, she is an object of sympathy, to be pitied and rescued. In popular belief, the resurrection of female ghosts mainly relies on the power from the yang world and most notably the power of male sexuality. Female ghosts usually attempt to regain life through either possessing the body of the living or having sex with young men, and the stories featuring these female ghosts would lead to either the demise of the living or the exorcistic victory of traditional ritual specialists—Daoist priests, Buddhist monks, or spirit mediums.[34] In *White-haired Girl*, the traditional motif of male sexuality finds a new expression through Xi'er and Dachun's true love. With Xi'er having been deprived of her own vengeful power, her resurrection as well as retribution had to wait for the return of Dachun, or in the name's literary sense, the Great Spring.

Dachun does not exist in the oral story versions. The installation of this character in the opera is significant. Dachun had fled to join the Red Army after Xi'er's captivity by Huang. He later returns as a soldier from the Eighth Route Army to lead the village land reform. Meng Yue indicates that the character of Dachun adds a romantic touch with "the love of two people eventually becoming consummated" (*youqingren zhongcheng juanshu* 有情人終成眷屬), a traditional theme that suits popular entertainment tastes.[35] More than that, Dachun personifies the peasant class's self-identification with the Communist cause. In contrast to the Communist cadre from outside the village in the story version, Dachun is an insider of the village, sharing the same grievances and hatred with Xi'er and other villagers against Huang Shiren. His return and his leadership dissolve the barriers between the "enlightened" cadres and the superstitious "masses" and remove the obstacle of goddess worship from the Communist mobilization work. Consequently, Xi'er comes back to life upon the return of Dachun, a young and energetic male figure who is simultaneously her lover and a revolutionary leader and whose name, Great Spring, suggests cosmic regeneration. As Dachun leads Xi'er out of the dark cave and into the bright daylight, the stage lights up, accompanied by the chorus:

> "The sun has risen! The sun has risen!
> The sun—it shines ten thousand miles, ten thousand miles!
> . . . For thousands of years in the past, . . .
> We have been suffering all the hardships.
> Today we watch the sun rise,
> It expels ten thousand layers of darkness!"[36]

Living in the historical darkness, Xi'er and the peasant class are now to be resurrected though the life-regenerating Spring and the Sun—the cosmic yang force. As much as the Yan'an artists wanted to go beyond the "anti-superstition" theme, both the language and imageries they deployed here resonate with traditional cosmology, ritual exorcism, and some key features of what Barend ter Haar has termed as the "demonological messianic traditions."[37]

The opera not only silences Xi'er as a goddess but also casts the power of the goddess in a negative light. When the White-haired Goddess does speak out in the opera, she is separated from Xi'er's body and projected as the mouthpiece of Huang Shiren instead. This happens when Dachun's mobilization work has gained a larger number of peasant followers. Huang's underling, Mu Renzhi, uses the name of the White-haired Goddess to threaten the enthusiastic villagers: "The White-haired Goddess has efficacious power. People of all four directions should not make blunders."[38] In the film, Huang orders Mu to burn down the house of a village activist and post a demon-exorcising charm that warns: "The manifest White-haired Goddess is powerful. People of all directions should not make blunders. If they behave correctly and keep to their proper places, she will protect them. If they perpetrate outrages, Heaven will show no mercy."[39] The White-haired Goddess is no longer identified with Xi'er but is used as a weapon by Huang Shiren to suppress Xi'er and her saviors. The goddess' divine power is presented here to guard the old social order.

Other criticisms of folk religion and traditional moral values may be more symbolic but by no means less effective. It is by deliberate design that the villain's name is Shiren 世仁, which could mean "benevolence of a lifetime" or "benevolence from generation to generation." His underling bears the name of Renzhi 仁智, benevolence and wisdom, two of the five fundamental Confucian constants (*wuchang* 五常).[40] In the film, the cross-board hanging above the entrance of Huang's house reads: *Jishan tang* 積善堂 (House of Accumulating Goodness). These symbolic terms stand in stark contrast with the opera's representation of "reality": under the board, Huang's appetite for collecting debts is insatiable, forcing poor tenants into either exile or committing suicide. Xi'er is raped in Huang's study, where Confucian moral principles are supposed to be learned and cultivated. In the film, the rape scene happens in the Huang family's Buddhist Hall, under the watchful eyes of the various Buddha statues. In either case, the accusation is launched against the traditional moral system that Huang represents. Huang's wanton use of his power proves the uselessness of Buddhist gods and traditional morality in saving Xi'er and the peasant class from the landlord predators.

Perhaps the harshest criticism of traditional religion comes from the portrayal of another major female character, Huang's mother. The oral story has no such character, so what was the purpose of adding such a character in the opera? The answer seems to be in her age, her family status, and her Buddhist practices, which all help identify religion and the traditional moral system with the evil and hypocrisy of the landlord class and the old social order. The matriarchal image of Huang's mother is built first and foremost on her being a devout Buddhist. She debuts on the stage in the Huang family's Buddhist Hall, making incense offerings to the Buddhist statues and chanting, "Do as much goodness as possible in one's lifetime. Amitabha Buddha will send one to the Western Paradise." According to her prayers, the Huang family's prosperity has been brought about entirely by "the family's ancestral merits and the protection of Buddha." She offers her incense accordingly:

> I offer the first round of incense to the Buddha of the Western Paradise,
> You bless my family growing, my wealth growing, and my rent income growing;
> I offer the second round of incense to Bodhisattva Guanyin of the Southern Sea,
> You bless me with peace of four seasons and a happy family.
> I offer the third round of incense to Immortal Zhang who sends boys,
> You bless my family prosperity and more family members.[41]

Under the guise of a devout Buddhist, however, Huang's mother is a cruel monster. When Xi'er is taken by force into the Huang household on the very night of her father's death, Huang's mother laments how expensive it has become to purchase a maid like Xi'er. When Xi'er weeps over her father, Huang's mother renames Xi'er "Hongxi" 紅喜, meaning "red happiness," and says that "auspicious signs have arrived" (*xiqi linmen* 喜氣臨門). She then promises Xi'er good food and clothing, because Xi'er had been born to a poor family and "her father has maltreated her so much."[42] Huang's mother smokes opium and drinks lotus soup. On complaining that Xi'er has served the lotus soup either too bitter or too hot, she jabs Xi'er's mouth with sharp-pointed opium pipe sticks. In Xi'er's own words, "I have been in his household for several months. They scold me and beat me. I suffer day and night, and I can only swallow my tears."[43] Finally, Huang's mother orders the pregnant Xi'er to be sold again on Huang's wedding night. If Huang Shiren sexually defiles Xi'er's body, then Huang's mother imposes on her all other types of physical and emotional abuses. She echoes the image of the predatory old woman whose exhaustion of feminine fertility has always been perceived as a threat against young lives in folk culture.[44]

The music of the opera also connects popular Buddhism with old and evil women like Huang's mother. The opera has been widely hailed as a successful attempt at "creating a new type of opera that truly represents the Chinese nation."[45] This attempt is reflected in the Yan'an artists' innovative ways to combine Western performance art with various forms of the folk music of northern China that would strike familiar chords among the rural audience. "The Cabbage" (*Xiao baicai* 小白菜), for example, was a well-known children's song in northern China. It takes on the sad voice of a girl who cries over the loss of her mother and her miserable life with a malignant stepmother. In the opera, the musicians play the tune of "The Cabbage" during many scenes featuring Xi'er, and especially when Xi'er suffers abuses by Huang's mother.[46] Such tunes would efficiently connect Xi'er's tragedy with the audience's emotions and inspire sympathy and tears. In a similar vein, in representing Huang's mother, the opera uses (1) the tunes with which Buddhist women in Hebei chanted the "precious scrolls" (*baojuan* 寶卷)—popular Buddhist scriptures and tales, and (2) monastic Buddhist music pieces from Mount Wutai, the famous Buddhist pilgrimage center in Shanxi Province. The reason for using these music and tunes, the Yan'an musicians explained, was because they "all fit to the status of the landlords, and are related to Buddhism."[47] With the immense success of the opera, some kind of innate connection between popular Buddhist practices and the evil landlord class must have been planted in the audience's mind. Traditional religious practices, be they the worship of Buddha or of a popular goddess, are depicted in the opera as something just like Huang's mother, an old woman who is evil, cruel, and hypocritical.

Huang's mother is a contrast with Xi'er. As in many revolutionary works of literature and art, the young and beautiful woman is a common symbol of revolution itself: pure, innocent, and victimized, waiting to be saved.[48] The changes to the story's title testify to the making of Xi'er into such a symbol. One of the earlier versions was titled "White-haired Woman" (*Baimao nüren* 白毛女人), indicating that the story is about the survival of a mother and her baby.[49] The story recorded by He Jingzhi in Yan'an bears the title "White-haired Goddess," since the focus of the story is on the mysterious white body on the altar of the Nainai temple. It was the creators of the 1945 opera who finally came up with the title *White-haired Girl*. With each change, the original attention paid to the body of a mother and a popular goddess was erased and a new focus on the victimized body of a youthful maiden full of revolutionary potential was established.

The plot changed in the same direction. In the original stories, the poor woman survives in the wild with her baby girl. The opera initially kept this detail—that Xi'er comes out from the cave with her son (!) by Huang Shiren. Nevertheless, the change of the baby's sex from girl to boy reflects the Yan'an artists' shift of focus: the opera is not about gender equality. Huang Shiren abandons Xi'er not out of his traditional bias against girls but out of his exploitative nature as a member of the landlord class. In the 1950 film the baby dies right after he is born. No room is left for a mixed-blood product of the oppressor and oppressed, and Xi'er has to be a "pure" victim who cut herself off from any connections with the old social system.[50]

## Victimization and Collective Emotion in the Creation of Political Religiosity

David Johnson shows that in the ritual life of rural Shanxi, village festivals and opera performances could mobilize rich and complex emotions critical in constructing political power.[51] Elizabeth Perry argues that the CCP's political mobilization of collective emotions played an important role in their victory over their Nationalist rivals. In a recent article, Liu Yu demonstrates that the mobilization of emotion was a critical factor in building mass belief in the Communist system and Maoism during the PRC period. Political rituals held among the peasants and workers aimed at producing a sense of victimhood and therefore indignation and class hatred against landlords and the like. Through three specific techniques that Liu categorizes as "personalization, magnification, and moralization," the Communist mobilization generated emotive effects that made peasants and workers personalize the national discourse of revolution, politicize all aspects of life, and assume the moral high ground against their class enemies.[52]

Revolutionary art and literature like *White-haired Girl* were indispensable in inspiring collective emotions for political movements. Communist feminist writer Ding Ling (1904–1986) observed the opera's dramatic impact on the audience's emotion in Yan'an: "Every performance emptied villages and alleys. People came along with their elders and young kids. They were all over, on top of roofs, walls, trees, and hay piles. The sorrowful story and the melancholic music moved everyone in the audience. Some had tears streaming all over their faces, and some covered their faces weeping. The fire of anger was contained in everybody's heart."[53]

The victimization strategy worked efficiently to create anger and class hatred among the audience and to empower them, particularly young male peasants, to identify with the role of Dachun and to take the task of Xi'er's revenge upon themselves. Some recalled that after watching the show, an army cook who was chopping cabbage indignantly complained: "The play's all right, but not to shoot that evil bastard Huang Shiren, that's just too unjust."[54] In a widely publicized anecdote about a performance in 1946, a young soldier was so provoked with anger that he took out his gun and aimed at Huang Shiren on the stage. He was stopped while crying out, "I want to kill him!" From then on, as the legend has it, all troops had to have bullets unloaded from their guns before they watched the performance of *White-haired Girl*.[55] Nevertheless, the opera's final scene of the struggle meeting against Huang Shiren always evolved into a mass struggle meeting in the audience. In shouting "Down with Huang Shiren!" and "Revenge for Xi'er," the audience became part of the yang force that redeemed both Xi'er and themselves from the old society. Such a strong sense of self-identification and self-empowerment among the rural audience made *White-haired Girl* one of the most powerful propaganda weapons against the Nationalists in the late 1940s. It was a must-see for CCP soldiers everywhere during the Civil War, and reportedly it made numerous captured Nationalist soldiers turn around and join the Communist army.[56]

The audience's sense of self-empowerment rode on a voluntary identification with a higher power to redress their grievances and injustice. In the traditional moral order, as it appears in ritual operas and storytelling, gods, goddesses, and heaven are the default source of justice. In *White-haired Girl*, the contrast between the old and the new social order leads the audience to turn to the CCP as the higher moral authority. As He Jingzhi recalled in 1946, one man connected Xi'er with his own past of having to sell his daughter: "Now we have the Communist Party, and our poor people have been liberated!" Another man wrote, "The old society drives people to death, and the new society gives life to people. Now everybody in the Border Region has been liberated!"[57] It is only a natural course of development then that in the face of increasing popular demand the writers eventually received an order from the Central Committee of the CCP to have Huang sentenced to death in later editions. As the anti-Japanese war was coming to an end, and the Civil War against the Nationalists was underway, the execution of Huang marked a timely shift in the party's policy from the United Front to class struggles.[58] Huang's death seamlessly combined party policy shift with popular demand, making the party a de facto representative of the people's will. In switching from anti-superstition to national liberation, *White-haired Girl* contributed to establishing the power of the CCP as the new source of social justice and hope for better life for both the rural and urban populations.

An article published in early 1947 in *People's Daily*, the party's official voice, suggests how the opera inspired a gendered articulation of the CCP's and Mao's power over the Chinese people. The article assumes the voice of a traditional-style woman who has always stayed inside the home, followed the principles of "three obediences and four virtues" (*sancong side*), and believed in the simple karmic return of good deeds. The *White-haired Girl* awakens her, the article goes, making her cry and giving rise to her hatred of the exploiting class. She then announces: "The so-called bodhisattvas, living Buddhas . . . are nothing but the ruling class's tools to exploit people. . . . [The real saviors of human sufferings] are not some religion of vegetarian diet and chanting Buddha, but the Communist Party that works for people's interests. They are not Jesus, Śākyamuni, or the Living Buddha of Crazy Ji, but they are the Great Revolutionary Teacher—Mao Zedong!"[59]

## Conclusion: From Anti-Superstition to the Cult of Mao

Bringing the seemingly missing "religion" into the study of women and gender in Communist propaganda works like *White-haired Girl* may yield new perspectives on the construction of religion and nation-state building in twentieth-century China. It is a well-known fact that traditional Chinese religion suffered great destruction under Mao. The Communist attacks on Chinese religious traditions, often under the label of "feudal superstitions," and their relative success among the Chinese peasant followers in this time period, however, are only partially based on their proclaimed stand of science, atheism, and a secular nation-state. Instead, in both subtle and explicit ways, propaganda works such as the *White-haired Girl* treated religion as a vile competitor for popular piety. It aimed to replace the old religious elements with an omnipresent and omnipotent power ascribed only to the party and to Mao himself, and it achieved this goal through deploying gendered languages and imageries familiar in peasant life: Xi'er's white-haired body underwent transformations from a goddess to be worshipped to a ghost to be feared and saved. Xi'er's salvation is framed in the language of class struggle, symbolizing peasants' collective rejection of traditional religious-political authorities and their subsequent subjection to party leadership. Along the same lines, traditional religions and Confucian moral values are identified with the evils of the landlord class. They are particularly associated with the older elite woman as a devout Buddhist and cruel matriarch at the same time and thus reinforce a negative connection of traditional religion, the landlord class, and old women.

If, as Meng Yue has insightfully noticed, apolitical features, such as traditional ethics of everyday peasant life and popular entertainment themes, were just as important as the political messages of national myth in generating the opera's lasting popularity,[60] then it was the folk-religious elements, which were deeply embedded in the traditional ethical order and popular culture, that actually linked the apolitical features with the opera's larger political agenda. In denouncing the traditional religious power of the old order, the opera provided the peasants and Chinese masses a renewed ethical and cosmological rationale for Communist leadership in the land reform and in building a new nation-state. The continuing revisions of *White-haired Girl* since the 1950s witnessed the process of the party propaganda's switch to a more radical line of class struggle and the building of Mao's cult. In the changing ballet editions of *White-haired Girl* from the 1960s and 1970s, all traditional religious elements disappeared, but a language of devotion, salvation, and exorcism remained and radically developed to describe the fighting spirit of the peasant and the absolute leadership of Mao. Thus, the ballet opera ended, as the stage was lit up by the rising sun, with the final chorus: "Beloved Chairman Mao, People's Great Savior!" An authoritative literary critic of the time added his comments on these last two lines most passionately: "The sun has risen! The sun is Mao Zedong! The sun is the Communist Party!"[61] The increasingly simplified political messages in the newer editions of *White-haired Girl* in the 1960s and 1970s accompanied by the proliferation of similar propaganda works during the first ten years of the PRC further "purified" traditional religions from popular culture and thus paved the way for the popular fanaticism dedicated to the Cult of Mao in the forthcoming Cultural Revolution.

## Notes

*Earlier versions of this essay were presented at the Symposium on Body, Power and Identity at the Center for Body and Civilization Studies, National Chengchi University, Taibei, on December 11–12, 2010, at the conference from which this volume is derived, and at the Fairbank Center of Harvard University on April 20, 2012. I would like to thank the following people for inviting me to these occasions and/or providing valuable comments: Chen Jianhua, Susan C. Egan, Maria Jaschok, Jia Jinhua, Li Yu-chen, Liu Hsiang-kwang, Liu Xun, Rebecca Nedostup, Michael Puett, Robert Weller, and Yao Ping. All errors remain my own.

1. The talks were delivered in May 1942 and published in *Jiefang ribao* 解放日報, on October 19, 1943. See Bonnie S. McDougall, *Mao Zedong's "Talks at the Yan'an Conference on Literature and Art": A Translation of the 1943 Text with Commentary* (Ann Arbor: University of Michigan Press, 1980).

2. Meng Yue, "Female Images and National Myth," in Tani E. Barlow, ed., *Gender Politics in Modern China: Writing and Feminism* (Durham and London: Duke University Press, 1993), 118–136; Meng Yue 孟悅, "*Baimaonü* yanbian de qishi: jianlun Yan'an wenyi de lishi duozhixing" "白毛女" 演變的啟示: 兼論延安文藝的歷史多質性, in Tang Xiaobing, ed., *Zaijiedu: dazhong wenyi yu yishu xingtai* 再解讀: 大眾文藝與藝術形態 (Beijing: Beijing daxue chubanshe, 2007), 48–69; Li Yang 李揚, *50–70 niandai wenxue jingdian zaijiedu* 50–70 年代文學經典再解讀 (Jinan: Shandong jiaoyu chubanshe, 2003), 267–311. For research on *White-haired Girl* in the Chinese language, see Meng Yuan 孟遠, "Liushi nian lai geju *Baimaonü* de pingjia moshi de bianqian" 六十年來歌劇 "白毛女" 的評價模式的變遷, *Hebei xuekan* 河北學刊 25.2 (2005): 133–39.

3. On the turn-of-century reconstruction of Chinese religions and the newly invented categories of "religion" and "superstition," see, among others, Prasenjit Duara, "Knowledge and Power in the Discourse of Modernity: The Campaign against Popular Religion in Early Twentieth Century China," *Journal of Asian Studies* 50 (1990): 67–83; Duara, *Rescuing History from the Nation: Questioning Narratives of Modern China* (Chicago: University of Chicago Press, 1995); Mayfair Mei-Hui Yang, ed., *Chinese Religiosities: Afflictions of Modernity and State Formation* (Berkeley and Los Angeles: University of California Press, 2008); Rebecca Nedostup, *Superstitious Regimes: Religion and the Politics of Chinese Modernity* (Cambridge, MA, and London: Harvard University Asia Center, 2009); and Vincent Goossaert and David A. Palmer, *The Religious Question in Modern China* (Chicago: University of Chicago Press, 2011).

4. Patricia Stranahan, *Yan'an Women and the Communist Party* (Berkeley: Institute of East Asian Studies, University of California, 1983); Kay Ann Johnson, *Women, the Family and Peasant Revolution in China* (Chicago: University of Chicago Press, 1983); and Gail Hershatter, *Women in China's Long Twentieth Century* (Berkeley and Los Angeles: University of California Press, 2007), 90.

5. Tina Mai Chen, "Peasant and Woman in Maoist Revolutionary Theory, 1920s–1950s," in Catherine Lynch, Robert B. Marks, and Paul G. Pickowicz, eds., *Radicalism, Revolution, and Reform in Modern China* (Lanham, MD: Lexington Books, 2011), 55–78.

6. Yang, "Introduction," in Yang, ed., *Chinese Religiosities*, 19–29; Goossaert and Palmer, *The Religious Question*, 139–43.

7. David Holm, *Art and Ideology in Revolutionary China* (New York: Oxford University Press, 1991).

8. Ralph Thaxton, *China Turned Rightside Up: Revolutionary Legitimacy in the Peasant World* (New Haven: Yale University Press, 1983), 180, 192–93.

9. Barend ter Haar, "China's Inner Demons: The Political Impact of the Demonological Paradigm," in Woei Lien Chong, ed., *China's Great Proletarian Cultural Revolution: Master Narratives and Post-Mao Counternarratives* (New York and Oxford: Rowman & Littlefield, 2002), 27–68.

10. For a good summary of these studies, see Goossaert and Palmer, *The Religious Question*, 187–90.

11. He Huoren 何火任, "*Baimaonü* yu He Jingzhi" 白毛女與賀敬之, in *Wenyi lilun yu piping* 文藝理論與批評 2 (1998): 83–5; Meng Yuan, "Geju *Baimaonü* de xushi bianqian shi" 歌劇白毛女的敘事變遷史, in *Xueshu yanjiu* 學術研究 12 (2008): 152–56.

12. He Jingzhi mentioned in 1946 that the story was orally transmitted for years and was written down in various literary forms before it was made into an opera. See He, "*Baimaonü* de chuangzuo yu yanchu" "白毛女" 的創作與演出, in Yan'an Lu Xun yishu xueyuan (hereafter referred to as Luyi), *Baimaonü* (Beijing: Renmin wenxue chubanshe, 1953), 252. At least two early recreations of *White-haired Girl* existed, one by Shao Zinan 邵子南 (1916–1955) and the other by Lin Man 林漫 (1914–1991). Both works were lost, and both authors participated in the Yan'an recreation of the opera, but their versions were not accepted. See Zhang Tuo 張拓, Qu Wei 瞿維 (1917–2002), and Zhang Lu 張魯 (1917–2003), "Guanyu *Baomaonü* de tongxin" 關於 "白毛女" 的通信, *Dangdai wentan* 當代文壇 1 (1987): 59–60; Lu Hua 陸華, "Zhang Geng deng si tongzhi guanyu geju *Baomaonü* chuangzuo guocheng da Zhang Tuo tongzhi wen" 張庚等四同志關於歌劇 "白毛女" 創作過程答張拓同志問, *Wenyi lilun yu piping* 3 (2011): 76–82; Meng Yuan, "Geju *Baimaonü* de xushi bianqian shi," 152n.1.

13. The Luyi crew of *White-haired Girl* included the playwrights He Jingzhi and Ding Yi 丁毅 (1920–1998) and the composers Ma Ke 馬可 (1918–1976), Zhang Lu, Huanzhi 煥之 (1919–2000), Qu Wei, Xiang Yu 向隅 (1912–1968), Chen Zi 陳紫 (1919–), and Liu Zhi 劉熾 (1921–1998).

14. This plot is based on the opera script in Luyi, *Baimaonü.*

15. He, "*Baimaonü* de chuangzuo yu yanchu," 254; and Meng Yue, "*Baimaonü* yanbian de qishi," 53.

16. *White-haired Girl* still generates much public interest of all kinds today. A revised version of the opera has been performed on stage by the China National Opera House since November 2009. In the last few years there has been a heated online debate about whether Xi'er should marry Huang Shiren for his money. A surprising number of young people, who have grown up in the post-Mao market economy, seem to be oblivious to the Maoist discourse of class struggle in the story and thus support the marriage.

17. Here I translate the term *xiangu* as "goddess" according to the context in the opera, but I recognize that *xiangu* can refer to either spirit mediums, goddesses, or both at the same time in Chinese religious settings.

18. He, "*Baimaonü* de chuangzuo yu yanchu," 249–50.

19. See, for example, Kenneth Pomeranz, "Power, Gender and Pluralism in the Cult of the Goddess Taishan," in Theodore Huters, Robin Wong, and Pauline Yu, eds., *Culture and State in Chinese History: Conventions, Accommodations, and Critiques* (Stanford: Stanford University Press, 1997), 182–206; Xiaofei Kang, *The Cult of Fox: Power, Gender and Popular Religion in Late Imperial and Modern China* (New York: Columbia University Press, 2006), 133–47.

20. He, "*Baimaonü* de chuangzuo yu yanchu," 251.

21. See, for example, Li Fang 李昉 (925–996) et al., *Taiping guangji* 太平廣記 (Beijing: Zhonghua shuju, 1961), the section on "Nüxian" 女仙, 344–439.

22. *Taiping guangji*, 365, citing *Liexian zhuan*, "Maonü."

23. Many Chinese tourist websites today include the Cave of the Hairy Maiden as an attraction on Mount Hua; see for example, http://www.china-visit.com/xian/tours/5236.html and http://www.china-visit.com/xian/tours/5236.html, accessed January 9, 2014.

24. He, "*Baimaonü* de chuangzuo yu yanchu," 253.

25. He, "*Baimaonü* de chuangzuo yu yanchu," 253.

26. Holm, *Art and Ideology*, 91–108, 217–42.

27. Meng Yue, "Female Gender and National Myth," 119–22.

28. Zhang Jichun, "*Baimaonü* de shidaixing" "白毛女" 的時代性, *Jiefang ribao*, July 21, 1945.

29. Zhang Geng 張庚, "Geju *Baimaonü* zai Yan'an de chuangzuo yanchu" 歌劇 "白毛女" 在延安的創作演出, in *Xinwenhua shiliao* 新文化史料 2 (1995): 6–7; and Meng Yuan, "Liushi nian lai geju *Baimaonü* de pingjia moshi de bianqian."

30. Luyi, *Baimaonü*, 106–7.

31. This is from the film script of *White-haired Girl*, trans. Pete Nestor and Tom Moran, http://mclc.osu.edu/rc/pubs/moran2.htm (accessed October 28, 2010).

32. Nestor and Moran, trans., *White-haired Girl*, modified.

33. On literati writings about female ghosts in seventeenth-century China, see Judith Zeitlin, *The Phantom Heroine: Ghosts and Gender in Seventeenth-Century Chinese Literature* (Honolulu: University of Hawaii Press, 2007). Some of her arguments can be applied to cases beyond the seventeenth century.

34. See, for example, Arthur Wolf, "Gods, Ghosts and Ancestors," in Wolf, ed., *Religion and Ritual in Chinese Society* (Stanford: Stanford University Press, 1974), 131–82; and Kang, *Cult of Fox*, 73–77.

35. Meng Yue, "*Baimaonü* yanbian de qishi," 60–61.

36. Luyi, *Baomaonü*, 109.

37. Ter Haar, "China's Inner Demons."

38. Luyi, *Baomaonü*, 102.

39. Nestor and Moran, trans., *White-haired Girl*, modified.

40. The five constants are *ren* 仁 (benevolence or humaneness), *yi* 義 (righteousness), *li* 禮 (ritual propriety), *zhi* 智 (wisdom), and *xin* 信 (sincerity). Whether the names and characters in the opera are real is still open to debate. The first actress who played Xi'er recalls that Shao Zinan, who first wrote down the story, used homophones from his native Sichuan dialect to name the characters: Huang Shiren is a homophone of *wangshiren* 枉是人, not deserving to be a man, and Mu Renzhi, *meirenzhi* 沒人志, without human feelings. Wang Kun 王昆, "Tan geju *Baimaonü* de chuangzuo guocheng" 談歌劇"白毛女"的創作過程, *Wenyi lilun yu piping* 2 (2011): 81.

41. Luyi, *Baimaonü*, 42.

42. Luyi, *Baimaonü*, 43–44.

43. Luyi, *Baimaonü*, 55.

44. On the danger of old women in Chinese folk stories, see Barend ter Haar, *Telling Stories: Witchcraft and Scapegoating in Chinese History* (Leiden: Brill, 2006), 54–91, 282–321.

45. Ma Ke and Qu Wei, "*Baimaonü* yinyue de chuangzuo jingyan" "白毛女"音樂的創作經驗, in Luyi, *Baimaonü*, 267.

46. Luyi, *Baimaonü*, 270.

47. Luyi, *Baimaonü*, 271.

48. Zhang Hong, "Eros and Politics in Revolutionary Literature," in Tang Dongfeng, Yang Xiaobin, Rosemary Roberts, and Yang Ling, eds., *Chinese Revolution and Chinese Literature* (Newcastle upon Tyne, UK: Cambridge Scholars Publishing, 2009), 5.

49. This is one of the two works mentioned in note 12. The author, Lin Man, also under the name Li Mantian 李滿天, was a journalist for the *Jin Cha Ji ribao* 晉察冀日報.

50. In the 1964 and 1970s ballet versions, the rape never happens, let alone the baby's birth. Xi'er escapes after putting up a heroic fight against Huang's sexual assault. Thus she maintains her sexual purity to represent an equally pure peasant class.

51. David Johnson, *Spectacle and Sacrifice: The Ritual Foundations of Village Life in North China* (Cambridge: Harvard Asia Center, 2010), 326–29.

52. Elizabeth Perry, "Moving the Masses: Emotion Work in the Chinese Revolution," *Mobilization* 7.2 (2002): 111–28; Yu Liu, "Maoist Discourse and the Mobilization of Emotion in Revolutionary China," *Modern China* 36.3 (2010): 329–62.

53. Song Jianhua 宋劍華, "Cong minjian chuanqi dao hongse jingdian: *Baimaonü* gushi de lishi yanyi" 從民間傳奇到紅色經典:"白毛女"故事的歷

史演繹, *Nanjing shifan daxue wenxueyuan xuebao* 南京師範大學文學院學報 1 (2011): 134.

54. Zhang Geng, "Geju *Baimaonü* zai Yan'an de chuangzuo yanchu," 7.

55. This is a well-known and widely cited anecdote. See, for example, He Huoren, "*Baimaonü* yu He Jingzhi (xu)" "白毛女" 與賀敬之(續), *Wenyi lilun yu piping* 3 (1998): 42–43; Song Jianhua, "Cong minjian chuanqi dao hongse jingdian," 134–35.

56. Song, "Cong minjian chuanqi dao hongse jingdian," 135.

57. He, "*Baimaonü* de chuangzuo yu yanchu," 255.

58. Holm, *Art and Ideology*, 322.

59. *Renmin ribao* 人民日報, February 12, 1947.

60. Meng Yue, "*Baimaonü* yanbian de qishi," 48–69.

61. Li Xifan 李希凡, "Zai liangtiao luxian jianrui douzheng zhong dansheng de yishu mingzhu" 在兩條路線尖銳鬥爭中誕生的藝術明珠, *Guangming ribao* 光明日報, May 15, 1967.

6

# Negotiating between Two Patriarchies

## Chinese Christian Women in Postcolonial Hong Kong

*Wai Ching Angela Wong*

### Introduction

Shaoping,[1] born in 1933, was a physically abused child. Abandoned by her mother, she was once beaten nearly to death by her father when she was in her teens. "Everyone around me in my childhood years hated me," she said. She fled from her father's home eventually and joined the church some time later. Despite their maltreatment of her, in the years before they died, Shaoping showed proper filial piety toward her family as if they had never been the cause of her childhood nightmares. Until the day she was interviewed, she had never told anyone, including her husband and children, that she grew up a victim of domestic violence. All these years, she has set herself just one life goal—that is, to bring all her family members to Jesus. She succeeded. By the time she was seventy-eight, all eighteen members of her family, including her now deceased parents, elder sister, and an uncle who abused her, had been baptized. She was grateful for God's providence and insisted on bearing witness to her faith through forgiveness of others who wronged her.[2] Yet on the day she was telling of her abusive childhood for the first time, she burst into bitter tears. As I watched her recalling the tale of her abuse on different occasions since then, I saw her body shake repeatedly and heard her voice tremble. The fear and pain that were buried deep down in her mind and body flowed out only gradually as she began to revisit her past. The questions are: considering the shaken state of mind that characterizes her even today, has the Christian faith that has led her to forgive her abusers in fact allowed her to deny her pain and suffering for all these years? Has Christianity offered only a patriarchal replacement of the Chinese patriarchy from which Shaoping had barely escaped? What role has Christianity played in the life difficulties of a Chinese woman such as Shaoping in Hong Kong?

Hong Kong has been a unique venue for the meeting of Chinese and Christian cultures because of its colonial history. Missionary work began in Hong Kong after British takeover in 1841, at the time when China was in great political turmoil. Missionaries then saw the early Chinese settlers on the island as only "the refuse of the population of the neighboring mainland"[3] and the work in Hong Kong as a stepping stone to the *real* China.[4] Apparently, Hong Kong was not only regarded geographically as a small city situated at the margin of China's southern coast but also reluctantly placed at the margin of colonial interests. Nevertheless, it is precisely because of its double marginalities that Hong Kong was found a haven by the early Chinese settlers. Being a colony, Hong Kong served as a refuge for those fleeing all sorts of disturbances in China. The early population was constituted by people flowing to Hong Kong at different times of Chinese social and political upheavals, the least desirable elements of the Canton delta, so to speak. Over the years, Hong Kong has nurtured a Chinese community which had in the first place avoided or had problems identifying strongly with the Chinese nation. It has provided an ideal location for the expansion of Christianity as the settlers were, intentionally or not, cut off from the old customs and social networks in the mainland and were relatively free to take on new affiliations and to join the church.[5] Such location of double marginalities to both British and Chinese governance contributed to the ambiguity as well as opportunity embedded in the dual identities of the Chinese Christian women in Hong Kong.[6]

Women were taken as the contesting site between the Christian imperialists and the Chinese nationals at the turn of the twentieth century. Patriarchal control of women was considered by the missionaries as one of the essential vices of Chinese culture. The "heathen" women were described in missionary writings and correspondence as illiterate, secluded, idolatrous, and in dire need of the salvation of the Gospel. Footbinding, polygamy, concubinage, arranged marriages, and sales of child brides, maidservants, and girl prostitutes all presented the most pressing and urgent calls for Christian intervention.[7] In order to elevate women from their calamities, women's education had been identified as the most effective means to Christianize women for Chinese homes. Because of the active propagation of women's humanity in the missionary-led reform movements against the ill-treatment of girls and women in the Chinese family and the rigorous promotion of women's education in China, Chinese Christian women were trapped in a kind of perennial split: they were benefiters of the Christian (imperialistic) reform movement against Chinese (patriarchal) culture of which they were a part; their identities of being both Christian and Chinese were locked in irresolvable tension.

Worse still, the exit from Chinese patriarchy to Christianity is not a straightforward one. Christian patriarchy has itself become a target of critique since the late eighteenth century. Under the scrutiny of John Stuart Mill's *Subjection of Women* (1869), Christianity was criticized as the culprit of patriarchy in the society of the West; and the Bible and the church were seen as obstacles to the women's equal rights movement. Although Paul's conservative teachings on women were questioned by Chinese Christian women as soon as they began to acquire the ideas of equality and rights in the changing political environment of the time,[8] as a tiny minority in China then, women Christians were caught in the defense of the benefits of Christianity to China. The adoption of the models of the Christian home and therefore the building of strong families to be "a light unto the nation" seemed to sail as one of the most persuasive projects.[9] Unfortunately, what has been reinforced in this process of cultural translation of a Christian home is not only the role of the "good wife and virtuous mother" but also "women's submission to the male headship of the household"—a double legitimization of the confinement of women in the Chinese-Christian patriarchal family.

The ambivalence of women living between two cultures and the pressure of the double burden of patriarchal precepts from both are the focus of my study in this chapter. I argue that, despite the double patriarchies prescribed by the Christian and Chinese traditions together, the ambivalence lived by Christian women in the Chinese society of Hong Kong has provided them with a creative space of negotiation for the cause of women. There is also a space of creativity in the gap between theory and practice in religion. While religion has been documented to be oppressive in so many respects, negotiation between religions and cultures has always been exercised by women in their daily practices. As Pierre Bourdieu would argue, doctrines as theorization and institution as social regulations are only human attempts to seek objectification of lived experience. There is necessarily time deferral in practice that substitutes "strategy" for the rule and ensures irreversibility, and thus changes, of events and actions.[10] This study therefore is an examination of women's space of negotiation within Christianity in

Hong Kong in between two patriarchal cultures and their possibilities of agency and change in spite of those patriarchies.

In the following, I draw on the case of Chinese Christian women in Hong Kong for an analysis of the intricate relation between religion and gender and between women's lives and faith practice in the ambivalent history of Christianity in postcolonial Hong Kong. This research started as an oral history project for Christian women of sixty-five years old and above with selection done by snowball sampling. From there I have extended my study to Christian women of the younger generations from the ages of twenty-four to fifty-four. Over the period of 2008 to 2011, I have interviewed forty-two women from all different corners of society. While women in the elderly group are largely full-time housekeepers, the younger generations mostly work either full time or part time making a living while taking care of their families. While the Protestants in the elderly group are all married and the Catholics all single, the younger ones are living in a much wider range of familial states with some married, some divorced, some cohabitating, and a few sexually active singles. The interviews of the elderly women were nonstructured and left relatively open to their free narration from birth to the present, while the interviews of the younger generations were semi-structured with focus on their experiences and views toward family, marriage, and their Christian faith in Hong Kong. What I propose in this chapter is a study of women's agency as woven through their practices in Christianity in the midst of their marital crises and life changes over half a century. It is an act of weaving because, like doctrines and institutions, the understanding of women's subjectivity and agency cannot be a straightforward one. It is built in reaction to as well as in interaction with their surrounding structural demands and often with utilization of all resources available at the specific point in time of need.

## Out of Chinese Patriarchy

In my earlier study on the postcolonial identity of Chinese Christian women I have argued that in spite of the Victorian values of a submissive, domestic wife taught in the missionary schools till the twentieth century, women missionaries who were single and were able to travel alone to engage in teaching and medical vocations away from family had actually become the live models of the "New Woman" for Chinese students.[11] Indeed, many of the early Christian women who were educated in domestic science for "practical everyday use to the home mothers of China"[12] were inspired instead to be leaders of social reform movements and service to the community. As it turned out, the marginality of Christian women situated in a Chinese community away from the mainland under the "protection" of British colonialism allowed them the freedom to test out their idea of equality and champion the rights of girls and women in Hong Kong. The first of two most prominent examples was Mrs. Ma Huo Qingtang 馬霍慶棠 (1875–1957), an Anglican married into the Church of Christ in the China-Hong Kong Council (CCC), who founded the Young Women's Christian Association (YWCA) in 1920 and led the Abolition Movement of Meizai from 1923 to 1933.[13] The second example, a woman who was a little younger than Ma, was Ellen Li Cao Xiuqun 李曹秀群 (1908–2005), a member of the CCC and the first Chinese woman legislator, who contributed to the abolition of concubinage in Hong Kong in 1971.[14] During the last century of British rule, Christianity as a colonial religion has offered to some of these early generation Chinese women converts in Hong Kong a much widened social platform for new familial imaginings.

The transition from the Chinese patriarchy to new modern family structures in Hong Kong is deeply imprinted in the memories of the elderly group of women interviewees born in between the 1910s and 1940s. Life stories of their grandmothers and mothers were still very much alive in the interviewees' memories and were referred to as something belonging to the "ancient tradition." Among them were wives, the second, third or fourth concubines by arranged marriages. Their concubine-mothers were all women of lowly origins including *meizai* (sold girl servants), *pipazai* (under-aged singers who were still virgins), or Chinese opera actresses. They were remembered as timid and diffident and trying to avoid conflict where possible, except for a few who were vengeful and competed bitterly for power. While many of these women were not allowed to visit public venues including temples, one interviewee remembered how her mother took her along to work on a Japanese military vessel traveling to Vietnam and Cambodia during the war. What the mother did on the ship and in the Japanese-occupied cities was a mystery. It was highly probable that she might have served as a comfort woman for the Japanese army given the historical circumstances. That the details were highly evasive in the daughter's memory and that a strong sense of shame was often related in the daughter's personal account seemed to testify to a regional trauma that particularly affected women in wartime.

Changes came slowly in the generation of women born in the first four decades of the twentieth century. There were many more women like Shaoping who could vividly recall the experience of denials of their worth in their girlhood. Meimei was sent away to the care of her maternal grandmother because a fortune-teller warned her paternal grandmother of the destined crash between the fate of Meimei and that of her father. Zhen was deprived of a birth certificate because her father thought so lowly of girls that he did not even bother to register her birth with the government. Ying's situation was the most dramatic. Her mother adopted her because her birth father refused to marry her birth mother since Ying was not a boy. Her adoptive mother had no children of her own and was not allowed to adopt a boy, who would then have the right to family inheritance. "It was so ironic: one family abandoned me because I was a girl and another adopted me for this same reason." For women who were denied any value because of their sex, the Christian message of love came to them as something more than they could ever wish for. In contrast to the women's condition in Chinese families, girls born into Christian families recalled better treatment because of the relative liberal-mindedness of their parents. Those who were not born into Christian families quickly embraced Christianity as an alternative system of belief as well as an ideal for a loving Christian home and an exit out of "ancient" Chinese culture.

Many of their conversions had to do with the location of colonial Hong Kong, in which Christian schools flourished. They either studied with or taught in such schools and learned about the Christian characters of their teachers and colleagues and their faith. The Christian principals who were dedicated and compassionate to the evangelical mission, the missionary teachers who cared for them personally and intellectually, and the enthusiastic colleagues who shared with them their life witnesses, all contributed significant moments of enlightenment for them. After conversion, by some general understanding of the universal love of God for everyone regardless of their origins and nature, they were trying out new models of families privileging monogamy over polygamy, consensual marriages over arranged, and also a degree of mutual regard over the rule of one authoritative patriarch.

The more subtle Chinese cultural influence was still prevalent nevertheless. These elderly women were still highly respectful of the Chinese hierarchal familial orders such as the performance of filial piety toward paternal in-laws, particularly the family matriarchs—the husbands' mothers. They would even participate in Chinese traditional rites and religious rituals if their in-laws were not Christians. They would be under great pressure to bear sons for the progeny of the husbands' families and would submit themselves to their husbands' sexual desire and the latter's refusal of birth control even in times of economic difficulties. Not only were these practices not be regarded as contradicting Christian principles, these cultural compromises were hailed as excellent demonstrations of the Christian women's capacity for maintaining "good" Chinese family traditions. The most common rhetoric of these elderly women, regardless of their class and educational background, remained the practice of the ideal Christian wife and mother who would always put the welfare of the family first. In comparison to the distressful condition of their foremothers, it is not surprising to hear their positive opinions of the changes that had taken place in the transition from Chinese patriarchy to the modern family trusting in God.

Nevertheless, the transition to the Christian family has not always been promising. For example, Yimei, who was sold into the Christian Yang family for one hundred dollars as a child bride, was discouraged from running away by a Christian neighbor even though she was living a dreadful life. Most ironically, the church was just next door to the Yang family, witnessing her plight but not offering her any counsel or comfort. In another case, Shaoping, who was abandoned by her mother and physically abused by her grandmother, father, and uncle, was instructed to persevere and believe in the reward in heaven. Despite a highly oppressive mother-in-law and almost complete home confinement, another woman, Ying found her hope in the thought of God's care through the sight of a blooming branch instead of any real support for the deliverance of her difficulties in marriage. On the surface, these women seemed to have walked out of Chinese patriarchy only to step into another that similarly reinforced women's domesticity and submission. The offer of colonial religion to set the Chinese women free did not seem to be as assuring as it first appeared.

## Confronting Christian Patriarchy

As shown, despite the unintentional effect of packaging the conception of right into the modern, Christian education systems that gave rise to the early women's movement in Hong Kong, Christianity loosens up Chinese patriarchy at the same time as it reinforces it. Although there has never been a single interpretation of what the Christian tradition says regarding marriage and family, references to the Hebrew Bible and the New Testament have largely prescribed heterosexual marriage (not necessarily monogamous in the Hebrew Bible). Teachings of the reproductive Christian family have been developed on the theology of Martin Luther in Protestant churches and that of Thomas Aquinas in the Catholic Church. What has remained dominant in the official teachings of the church throughout seems to be the submissive and sacrificial role of the Christian wife and mother. In this conservative tradition, Christianity comes close to Chinese tradition and exercises together with it a double claim on women's conscience of duty and faithfulness.

Unfortunately, such rather static Christian approaches to defining family and marriage were adopted by the majority of evangelical churches in Hong Kong. Because of the historically cooperative relationship between the church and government under British colonial rule, Christianity has constituted a significant force of social and political influence in Hong Kong through 1997. By the time of the handover in the nineties, Christian operation in the three sectors—education, medicine, and social services—accounted for 40 percent, 30 percent, and 60 percent of the total number of service providers in each of the respective sectors, taking a share of the large pool of social resources and occupying a strategic position in the social and political networks of the community. In the survey conducted by the Hong Kong Church Renewal Movement in December 1999, Hong Kong churches were characterized as middle- and upper-middle class (58.9% of Protestants and 57% of Catholics), with a sizable portion of professionals (34%) and generally well educated (40.9% with postgraduate degrees). In the Special Administrative Region government of Donald Tsang, the second chief executive of Hong Kong, from 2005 to 2012 about 75 percent of the top administrative positions were Christians, an unusually high figure considering there were only about 9.6 percent Christians in the general population. In short, the churches of Hong Kong have successfully produced the most educated and professional population in Hong Kong, maximizing the protection and privileges afforded by British colonialism.[15]

Toward the late nineties, the revival of an evangelical sexual morality campaign aligned itself with the American pro-family movement and campaigned for the "protection" of the "traditional" family. This movement gained currency with the emergence of a strong Christian middle class that turned increasingly toward private values and family affections.[16] There is a recent survey indicating the dramatic increase of church members from 2004 to 2009, along with a significant drop of members' interests in social and political issues except for the issue of family.[17] Monogamous, heterosexual, lifelong reproductive marriage is upheld as the only divine family form guarding against any attempt to legislate for gay rights in Hong Kong. In 2011 a highly respected church leader of the pro-family movement hosted his golden wedding anniversary with an exclusive guest list inviting only married couples with children. Through a celebrative event, this prominent leader made a strong statement on how "God's family" should be defined—it should be productive and unified in marriage no matter what. In other words, divorcees, single parents, couples without children, singles, and any other forms of relationship are not welcomed into the Christian fellowship of his understanding. In this regard, the call to rescue the "endangered" family led by the pro-family movement in Hong Kong[18] has succeeded in the reinvention of tradition[19] in an idealized form of the modern nuclear family popularized in the Industrial Age, a form that is sustained through placing the care of the family once again in the hands of primarily women and the reinstatement of male headship and authority.

In the following, I draw on the cases of six Chinese Christian women whose marriage and families have been deeply affected by conservative Christian teachings. The six women are in their forties and fifties, two are married, two are divorced, one a lesbian and another transsexual. Career-wise, there is a freelance designer, part-time accountant, sales representative, social service worker, clerical worker, and full-time housewife. All except one of them belong to the middle class, and the one exception has income just barely enough for the regular expenses of a month. Despite the persistence of the androcentric ideology in Hong Kong churches, these women were able to exercise their perseverance and prudence in confronting Christian patriarchy. Built on their variant means of negotiation in their respective circumstances, there are two main strategies deployed by the six women: first, the manipulation of space and time and, second, the reinterpretation of tradition in order to make things work for them.

## Manipulating Space and Time

The history of Hong Kong is particularly marked by the changes over "time and place." Before the handover in 1997, Hong Kong was acclaimed the "borrowed time, borrowed place"—that is, a place in which no one would care about the long-term future because no one was in control of Hong Kong's destiny. The transition from colonial time and space to that of the postcolonial had been particularly anxious for the church because of its probable loss of all privilege to Communist-ruled China. Nonetheless, to women, as illustrated in the early period, Christianity offered not only a sacred space for the worship of God and spiritual nurturance but also concrete alternatives to the Chinese patriarchal family, and furthermore, for some, the extension of their world from the domestic to the public. Mircea Eliade argues that the arrangement of space and time is an extremely sacred moment in religion. The right time at the right place distinguishes the sacred from the profane.[20] While the geographical sense of the religious place is largely insufficient for the experience of the sacred, the physical makeup of the church as place has offered many Christian women a "second life" other than the one they were born into and seemingly destined for. Historically, the crossing from domestic space to religious space has been documented as a highly strategic move for women who did not want to simply submit to the destiny of being wife and mother.

Caroline Walker Bynum, a historian of religions, studies how medieval women manipulated time and space via food preparation in the family for religious rites. Through managing communal feasts and religious fasting, they were able to transgress the boundaries between the family and society and the personal and public. Some were successful in their demand to refrain from sexual activities, while others agreed to vacate the familial space for the religious space of the monasteries. For those medieval women, religious vocation in the monasteries had not only been an exit from the routine of marriage, childrearing, and housekeeping but also an entrance to the "world" in which women could occupy a place and space.[21] This was what happened to the early Chinese Christian women who studied under the tutorship of women missionaries and decided to pursue a religious career in preaching, teaching, and medical services as single women.[22] In a world where women were not encouraged to live independently away from marriage and the family, religious space served as an important "extraterritory" for shelter away from home, a training ground for independence, as well as a bridge to the world.

The three women who had maximized the use of space and time in the church and away from it are the older ones among the six. They grew up at a time when Chinese culture was still highly regarded and Christianity had begun to gain respect. Regardless of their class background, Manman, Linjie, and Willow were all prepared to live up to the demands of a Chinese-Christian family. To a different degree, all of them did—only with some skillful rearrangement of the world around them.

Manman was the youngest of the elderly group and was born into an elite Chinese-Christian family. She grew up acquiring Christian values at the same time that she internalized Chinese patriarchal family authority. She was born to her father's second wife, who had "an extremely weak" personality. Despite her faithful practice of filial piety to all of the members in the marital family, she could never satisfy the demands of her mother-in-law. Very soon she realized that she had to find her "extraterritorial" space outside of the family. It was a tactful management of time and space. Every day when her mother-in-law left for her mahjong games she would finish all the household chores as soon as possible, depart for church, and return before her mother-in-law was expected to be home. "I felt most relaxed whenever I was in church." She helped to build the new congregation near her married home, took all its biblical and discipleship training courses, joined all kinds of pastoral visitations to church members, led the Welfare and Women's departments of the church, became "spiritual" mother to innumerable young and old newly baptized members, and personally took care of the family of the pastor in charge by escorting his children to and from school—"I spent every minute afforded in the church." Half-jokingly, she said, "Attendance to church work is my full time, I do my household chores only part time." The church has been, in her own words, "my real life."

Linjie earned her second life in the church as well. She grew up as a rebellious young woman and decided to marry a cinema usher despite the disapproval of every member in her family. Her husband turned out to be a jerk, unemployed most of the time, and an addicted gambler. He had been imprisoned for three months for petty theft. Life after marriage for Linjie was simply plain hardship and poverty. Even today, the family is still paying his debts, the result of gambling losses over the years. Because of stress over the years, Linjie has developed problems with heart murmurs, a bone spur, periarthritis of the shoulders, and hypertension. Despite her seemingly unending troubles, Linjie felt like a different person after conversion into Christianity. In contrast to Manman's self-exile in the church, Linjie believed the church would be the only rescue for her husband. She persuaded him to join her at the church, made sure that he felt at home and fully respected there. "At church, he was seen as the master of the family. He is respected for what he says." At home she planned for her husband's cessation of gambling, managed his finances, and patted him on the back for his good performance. Returned from the edge of suicide, her husband now throws most of his time into serving the church. "He is a different person now." Through the full utilization of the sacred space of the church for the "taming" of her husband, Linjie regained control of her husband, her family, and her life.

Neither Manman nor Linjie considered divorce because they never thought it an option. Neither did Willow before she finally realized she could no longer hold onto her marriage. Both because of the Chinese notion of the integrity of the family (*qiqi zhengzheng* 齊齊整整) and the Christian precept of "till death do you part," many Chinese-Christian women would stick with their marriages even if they were miserable. For the divorcees, the first question they faced was the sin of breaking the marital covenant sanctified by God. Vivian is a young woman who was carrying a long family tradition of Christianity. In order to avoid being charged as one who sinned, she waited for her unfaithful husband to initiate the divorce even though she was resolute about it. There is also the question of guilt for failing to maintain the integrity of the family—an essential role defining a faithful Christian woman. So even when Ling was interviewed several years after her divorce, she had tears all over her face as she confessed her failure to be a faithful follower of Jesus. Whether it is divorce or separation, the involved parties have not many choices other than keeping quiet about their marital condition, refraining from regular church attendance, or withdrawing entirely from the church to which either party originally belonged. Almost all of the divorcees interviewed attempted suicide at some point in their most distressful period because of the deep sense of guilt and sinfulness and the isolation and rejection they faced. The Chinese appeal to women to be responsible for "holding the family together" and the Christian disapproval of divorce have doubled up the pressure for them.

Over the past two decades or so, there have been substantial changes in the marital status and family conditions of people in Hong Kong, underlying considerable changes in the roles of women in the sphere of family life. For instance, between 1986 and 2011, the number of those who had never married had increased by 60.8 percent for women, as compared to only 15.5 percent for men. The number of divorced has grown 9.5 times from 1981 to 2011. Single mothers grew by 110.6 percent from 1996 to 2011.[23] The divorce and separation rate for women was 0.7 percent in 1981 and 4.7 percent in 2006.[24] Considering the fact that Christians constituted about 10 percent of the total population, there would be about two thousand divorced couples estimated in 2011 alone.[25] Against the tide, however, the prevalent church teachings on marriage insist on the irrevocability of the marriage vow and reject divorce and separation as a Christian option. A biblical position is constructed on a few verses, including the preeminent one: "So they are no longer two, but one flesh. Therefore what God has joined together, let no one separate" (Matt. 19: 6). That is, marriage is regarded as sacred and should not be broken for any human reasons including spousal unfaithfulness. Strictly speaking, divorce is permitted only as the very last resort when the parties involved cannot be reconciled in any sense (Matt. 19: 9). In the case of separation, each party should remain single, and remarriage is permitted only in the case of the decease of a spouse (1 Cor. 7: 39). As is discussed later in this chapter, these instructions have not given rise to any solution to the problems faced by women and men in difficult marriages except for the perpetuation of the feeling of guilt.

Willow describes herself as a tough and strong-minded person from her youth. Both her natal and marital families were a mess, and she had to move from one place to another constantly. Then when all of the members of her marital family went to the same church, she had to move from one church to another to avoid complications of the problems. Although she met her husband in the church, he was a drug addict, had unceasing affairs before and after the marriage, and was a selfish wretch who would steal all that the family had for drugs. She first decided to leave the church she grew up in when she felt that she needed the time and space to deal with her own problems. There were more than a few times in the interview when Willow reiterated her desperation. "If not for the last ounce of control I would just go crazy." It was a long, lonely struggle for her during which she experienced, besides her own sense of guilt, her daughters' resentment, her in-laws' hostility, and the family's financial difficulties. Willow's temporal withdrawal from the religious space and return when ready served her well as she cleared her mind about her decision to divorce. "It was all because of my sense of pride—I have tried all my life to stay in control and I didn't want to admit that I failed."

The space and time in church meant different things for different families and individuals. Manman gave herself a second life when she decided to fully maximize her time in the church away from home; Linjie has utilized the church as a space of constraint for her husband so that she could regain control of her life; and in the case of Willow, she scheduled her time to step in and out of one space and another along with her needs to deal with her family members and herself. For all three, family and marriage turned out to be more burden than pleasure for them. Whereas Chinese culture played a part in the shaping of their "worthless" husbands and the difficulties they faced in their marital families, Christianity served to alleviate their problems only via a crooked path. While all parties concerned in these three cases were all Christian, there was no direct help coming from either the pastor or the Christian teachings in terms of addressing the problems. While the androcentric features of Chinese society and Christianity remain, the Chinese-Christian women made the best out of their state of existence and manipulated time and space "at their disposal" for the lightening of their burdens.

## Reinterpretation of Tradition

"Traditioning" is an ideological project. It has a highly constructivist and imaginary component, sometimes with the creation (recreation) of a myth, for the sustenance of a collective identity. In the introduction to *The Invention of Tradition* (1983), Eric Hobsbawm distinguishes three elements to the modern invention of tradition: it aims to establish social cohesion for members of a group or community, real or virtual, to legitimize institutional authority, and to inculcate beliefs, value systems, and conventions of behavior.[26] "Traditioning" is therefore core to many of the religious fundamentalist movements whose identities depend on the notion of an "origin," a call to return to the belief in the ideal state of a distanced past. Once the "origin" is claimed it becomes the founding narrative from which rules and regulations are derived and on which values and principles are fixed. The propagation of the divine form of family by the Christian pro-family movement is such an attempt. By mythologizing the ideal of family, the movement aims to mobilize Christians for a morality campaign against all deviant forms of sexual relationship.

The fact that women's role and status remain a debate is a testimony to the rich traditions of Christian understanding on the matter. Historically, there has always been a multiplicity of interpretations on marriage and family, or for that matter, sexuality. Although dominant biblical references seem to underscore heterosexual marriage, contradictory attitudes toward marriage and sexuality are also found throughout Christian Scripture. One of the reasons is simply the difference between the Hebrew and Greco-Roman contexts in which one demands fertility for an exilic community and the other chastity in anticipation of the Second Coming of Christ. There are also opposing commands in the Epistles and the Gospels. While the male head of household was affirmed in the Pauline Epistles, the "natural"[27] family was challenged (Mark 3: 20–35, 6: 1–6; John 7: 1–9), denounced (Luke 9: 57–62, 14: 25–33), and opened for collective imagination beyond (Luke 8: 15, 19–21; Mark 3: 34) in Jesus's teachings. The latter is particularly instructive as it projects a transformation of a household (*oikos*) into the *ekklesia*, a community built on the basis of faith rather than natural kinship ties (1 Cor. 1: 10, 4: 15; Rom. 16: 1). Not the least, Jesus's possible celibacy and Paul's declared celibacy over married life continue to undermine a stable view on the New Testament's perspective on sexuality and give rise to the continuous tension between whether sexuality is to be affirmed or suppressed.[28]

The first of three cases of answering back to the tradition is Chun. After many years of struggle, she was clear that divorce was inevitable. Yet the Chinese and Christian demands on women were still strong. Not only did she not love her husband any more, but she was also determined to give up the guardianship of her son. Her conscience was so heavily burdened that she was crying bitterly to the point of exhaustion when she revealed her decision to her pastor. In many ways, Chun was a nonconforming woman from her youth. She walked her blind mother to prostitution venues when she was a child, was sexually abused by her stepfather, and got married at twenty when she was already pregnant. She was completely changed when she became Christian. She never thought of abortion because, she remarked, "I have already been a Christian." Divorce was unthinkable for the same reason despite her far-from-ideal husband who had never been able to make ends meet. Therefore, when she was helplessly drawn sexually to a divorced brother in the church, she was totally lost. Her internal struggle and deep pain grew into insomnia and unceasing nightmare, including the generation of the idea of poisoning her husband's food. "It was in a way an idea pushed by my faith at that time because I believed that Christianity does not permit divorce," Chun remarked. Torn between her awakened sexuality and the pejorative self-indictment because of her faith, she pushed through her decision. It was an honesty with oneself that led her to a different understanding of the Christian faith. "I pray to God for a budding relationship with a man about twenty some years younger than me." She said with much resolution, "God must have given me these experiences with a purpose, even though I am still not clear about it."[29] She found a God who cares not only for her role as a wife and mother but also her sexual embodiment.

If divorce is a taboo in the church, transsexuals and same-sex unions are absolutely unacceptable offenses. Based on the evangelical faith proclamation, unless the sexual "pervert" confesses his or her sin and refrains from sexual activities, that individual can not be accepted into the church. In 2005 when the Hong Kong government began to conduct public consultation for the drafting of a bill for sexual orientation discrimination, Hong Kong evangelical Christians reacted strongly. Several Protestant alliances launched publicly a series of large signature campaigns in the name of preservation of sexual morality and family values against homosexuality and other sexual minorities.[30] They have, on the one hand, consolidated within the church a strong sentiment of homophobia and, on the other, built an antihomosexual atmosphere in society to pressurize the legislature. However, despite their violent protests, which obviously instigated further stress on Christian sexual minorities, they could not deny the existence of them. Some of the gay, lesbian, and transsexual Christians chose to stay with the church because of years of fellowship and interpersonal networking; some decided to leave and formed their own LGBT Church. In between, many cried desperately in their personal prayers to God and were immersed deeply in the sense of guilt for their failure to suppress their sexuality. Either faith or sexual orientation becomes for many LGBT Christians a choice both inevitable and yet impossible.

Both Ping, a lesbian, and Jewel, a transsexual, are in their early forties. Ping is a part-time accountant and Jewel a freelance designer. Ping's relationship with her family was so bad that she began to find shelter in the church every Sunday since she was fifteen. She had been going to that same church for more than ten years when she realized how much pressure she had been receiving from it regarding her sexuality. "My pastor always denounced homosexuality as sin. That statement really hurts me." "There was once when I was sitting in the pew, . . . it was filled with people, and yet a grave sense of loneliness just overwhelmed me. I felt as if there were none sitting beside me, even though there were lots of people. I was heartbroken. . . ." Fortunately, in the midst of frustration, Ping found a *Tongzhi*[31] church and experienced her faith entirely anew. "I was so moved, why would something I learned from the church for over a decade, that it was wrong and that people like us would go to hell, could become the reason for the strength and growth of another church?" "The new church made me think very hard on the question of God"; "I gradually began to understand that God is like the sky, there is no boundary to it. . . . I learned that this is what God has been . . . present everywhere, and never turns anyone away."[32] Rather than a judgmental faith, Ping has returned to a God who is truly omnipresent and all embracing.

Jewel was theologically articulate. She is a deeply dedicated Christian even through the time she[33] was struggling with her sex. She had always wanted to be a girl when she was still a boy. When she told her pastor she was about to undergo the sex reassignment surgery (SRS), he bluntly rebuked her. "People of your kind would not have any good ending, definitely no good ending at all."[34] The hurt that the church has inflicted on her has been so deep that she attempted suicide four times. "I felt dirty and could not accept myself." She finally began her life as a woman at the age of forty-six. Her testimony has been particularly persuasive for, despite rejection by the church, Jewel was sure that God was always on her side and accepts her as a transsexual. "I went from male to female, from sin to grace, from wrong to right, from a deadening entrapment to a much broader understanding of family. [I believe that] only through these processes could I obtain eternal life."[35] Rather than her pastor's accusation of her denial of the sex created by God, Jewel embraces her transsexuality as the creation of God. For her the surgery is just a means for living out the most appropriate identity intended by God for her. Today, Jewel has transformed her past experience of shame and guilt into her Christian call to lead the movement of sexual rights and equality for transgender people. She is now fully engaged in LGBTQ politics in Hong Kong and is a well-known spokesperson for sexual minorities.

Dealing with nonheterosexual, nonproductive, and nonmarital sexuality has always been taboo in the church in Hong Kong. The sexual morality movement of evangelical Christians is only a measure to pull the increasingly diverse forms of sexual engagement back under the umbrella of the natural family. Interestingly, an appeal to the tradition of the Chinese family was often utilized by these Hong Kong Christians as an attack on initiation in divorce and homosexuality. The emphases on the integrity of the family and promise of posterity are often cited as the core values of the Chinese family. Conversely, divorce, homosexuality, or any nonmarital form of sexual engagement are Western vices, problems arising from individualism and extreme liberalism. In real political terms, the China factor came in as an obstacle to open debate for legislation on equal rights for sexual minorities in postcolonial Hong Kong. In the face of Christian dissent, it is most unfortunate that the Special Administrative Region has lost its autonomy to push through any ordinance against discrimination against sexual orientation even though 60 percent support was reported in several public polls. As a matter of fact, homosexuality was decriminalized in 1991 under the British governance in Hong Kong. Unlike the defeat of the antihomosexuality campaign by the reasoning of the British rule of law in the Hong Kong legislature then, the priority of the present Hong Kong legislature is not to upset any political balance within Hong Kong or across the border in China.[36] It is therefore particularly important to have honest and faithful Christians such as Chun, Ping, and Jewel, who are bold enough to challenge the Christian conservatism and reinterpret their faith for a broader understanding of God and Christianity.

## Conclusion: Between Two Patriarchies

Christianity has a history of over a century in Hong Kong. For the first half of the century, it pretended to be a haven for women from the ills of the Chinese "heathen" land. While it succeeded in planting modern ideas in society through the Christian network of service and education, Christianity also brought with it a model of submissive women and reinforced a male-headed family. Because of British colonialism until 1997, Christianity has been deeply woven into the social and political fabric of Hong Kong structures and has more or less lost its tint as a foreign religion. Today, a Christian would not be charged with thinking or living the values of the West but would celebrate with the postwar generation of Hong Kong a unique identity embracing a mixture of the East and the West. Blessed with the dual identities of living between two cultures, Christians take pride in the emerging Hong Kong culture of a resistant hybridity that defies any one "pure" authority, be it colonial or national.[37] The only exception is when it comes to the issues of gender and sexuality. Ironically, until today, whenever the quest for gender equality in the workplace or equal respect for women's sexuality is made, Christian women who attempt to repudiate the submissive model would still be called "Western." Christian women remain "foreign" to the Chinese church when they press for equal opportunity to ordination and raise the questions of divorce, single parenthood, and singlehood, or join civil society for the movement for equal rights for sexual minorities. The dual identities of Christian women could be capitalized on either end for the purpose of a colonialist project or Chinese patriarchy in the Hong Kong church.

Returning to the theme of ambivalence of living between two cultures, despite the intention of missionaries and women's education in the twentieth century, Christian women found in Christianity a door to exit the Chinese patriarchal family. Because of the new social network brought forth, some women were able to pursue their careers and others enjoyed the first fruits of a modern family relatively consensual and free from the authoritative model. Women of the elite class in collaboration with the colonial government were encouraged to take part in the early social reforms of Hong Kong for the betterment of women's place and status in the family. The church serves as an alternative space for women's development, or more fundamentally as in the case of Manman, a second life, beyond familial captivity. Until today, some of the younger generations of Christian women have continued to benefit from the more liberal stream of Christian feminism and are able to challenge the dominant conservatism of the evangelical churches. Among them Chun, Ping, and Jewel are good examples.

Unfortunately, whereas early Chinese-Christian women with the backing of the church and British colonialism were able to take the lead in social reforms for the abolition of *meizai* in 1933 and the abolition of concubinage in 1971, campaigns for equal opportunities for women and sexual minorities lack the support of the motherland, China, after the handover. Rather than ambivalently enjoying the protection of the colonial elites in Hong Kong, Christianity has yet to find its place in the newly emergent politics of the Special Administrative Region situated in the tension inherent in the model of "one country two systems." Today the church is situated at the juncture of political contestation between the local democratic movement and the pro-establishment political forces with their pro-Beijing businessmen, political organizations, and personnel. They are confronted with an essential difference between two "colonial" masters: the former appeals to equality and rights as their national ethos despite its colonial setup; the latter is concerned with the reinstatement of legitimacy and control over Hong Kong in the context of the complexity of political battles internal to China. In order not to tip the balance, social reforms such as further legislation for affirmative gender policy or equal rights for sexual minorities are doomed to be forestalled. Until the democratic movement in Hong Kong succeeds in instituting thorough structures for the uplifting of minority rights, the voice of conservative Christians shall stay dominant.

Against the macro background of political changes over the century, Chinese-Christian women have been taking the best chances afforded them. Where there are heavily ideology-laden structures, Christian women exercise their prudence and creativity in their everyday practice of negotiation and resistance. In Bourdieu's theory of practice he proposes the conceptions of the "field" and "habitus." The fields are constituted by the habitus of many generations, that is, the ways people grow up and subscribe to the values inculcated in the different roles and places assigned to them.[38] In the case of Chinese-Christian women, the meeting of the two cultures—Chinese and Christian—serve as the "fields" in which they act the way they are expected to and speak the language they learn in the process in order to be "successful." The two cultures as fields and habitus provide the structure in which the meaning of an action is reproduced. In other words, there is no way one can understand an isolated action without placing it within the system in which the action is played out.[39] It is in the context of the merging of the two long-standing traditions in Hong Kong that Chinese-Christian women are constantly engaging in their negotiation, accommodation, and compromise.

As one might expect, internal contradictions are found in the account of each of the women's life experiences and their relation to the church and the Christian faith. The older generation of women were grateful for the opportunity provided by the colonial church to exit from Chinese patriarchy to the modern Christian family even though the process was not at all in their favor. Adopting the modern Western rhetoric of equality and rights, they remained "traditional Chinese" in terms of handling family relationships and holding onto the integrity of the family. In the case of Jewel, despite her subversive transgender identity, she still wishes for the stereotypical family and longs for a dependable lover. Despite their difficult marriages, most defend the complementary role of the two sexes, that men should be the master of the house whenever possible. They were living under double patriarchies as they tried their best to be faithful to the Chinese androcentric tradition and the conservative teachings on women and family in the church. Nevertheless, within the complex zone of ideology and action, Charlene Haddock Seigfried reminds us that no theoretical category can contain lived experience.[40] For practice is always pluralistic: it allows the meeting of different logics to advance the best result desired. Inconsistency is a source of creativity rather than a detriment for Chinese-Christian women in between two worlds.

Theorization as doctrine and institutional regulation is only an attempt to objectify lived experience "independent of individual consciousness and wills."[41] There is always a time lapse between theory and practice that makes every practice a unique event that cannot be repeated. Each woman reacts to her life happenings differently and singularly because no one event takes place twice in the same way. Chun's interpretation of God vis-à-vis her experience would not be the same as that of Willow even though they are both affected deeply by divorce. While the structure of a religious tradition (including its doctrines and institution) obliges the believer to act in accordance with its rules and regulation, the actor's everyday practice inevitably defies predictability and works instead in millions of ways toward improvement of one's situation.[42] If Chinese patriarchy and Christian conservatism are the theorized structures, the women's action of reinterpretation and manipulation are practices that necessarily refuse objectification. In the examination of women's practice in the micro level of everyday practice we find not only that women's submission is never totalistic but also where women's agency takes place.

## Notes

*Research for this chapter was supported by a grant from the Research Grants Council of HKSAR, China (Project no. CUHK#453309).

1. Pseudonyms will be used for all interviewees throughout the chapter, except for those whose oral histories were published with their real names in Wai Ching Angela Wong 黃慧貞 and Choi Po-king Dora 蔡寶瓊, eds., *Huaren funü yu Xianggang Jidujiao: Koushu lishi* 華人婦女與香港基督教: 口述歷史 (Hong Kong: Oxford University Press, 2010).

2. Wai Ching Angela Wong, Wu Keqing 吳克勤, and Xu Ermao 許二毛, "Ren ren suo buneng ren: Deng Li Shaoping" 忍人所不能忍: 鄧李少萍, in Wong and Choi, *Huaren funü yu Xianggang jidujiao*, 1–18.

3. George Smith, *A Narrative of an Exploratory Visit to Each of the Consular Cities of China and to the Islands of Hong Kong and Chusan, in behalf of the Church Missionary Society, in the Years of 1844, 1845, 1846* (London: Hatch & Son, 1847), 82.

4. Annie Sydenham, "Medical Work in Hong Kong," *The Chinese Recorder* 72.7 (July 1941): 350. Italics in original.

5. Carl T. Smith, *Chinese Christians: Elites, Middlemen, and the Church in Hong Kong* (Hong Kong: Oxford University Press, 1985), 182.

6. Wai-Ching Wong, "Negotiating Gender Identity: Postcolonialism and Christianity in Hong Kong," in Eliza Lee, ed., *Gender and Change in Hong Kong: Globalization, Postcolonialism and Chinese Patriarchy* (Vancouver: UBC Press, 2004), 151–76.

7. A. P. Happer, "Woman's Work for Woman," in *Records of the General Conference of the Protestant Missionaries of China Held at Shanghai, May 10–24, 1877*, 147.

8. Cf. Kwok Pui-Lan, *Chinese Women and Christianity 1860–1927* (Atlanta: Scholars Press, 1991), 83–93.

9. Jiang Hezhen, "Making the Home Christians," *The Chinese Recorder and Missionary Journal* 53 (1922): 472–73.

10. Pierre Bourdieu, *Outline of a Theory of Practice* (Cambridge: Cambridge University Press, 1977), 4.

11. See Wong, "Negotiating Gender Identity," 151–76.

12. The curriculum would include subjects in homemaking, childrearing, hygiene, first aid, social service, music, and so on. See Lida Scott Ashmore, *The South China Mission of the American Baptist Foreign Mission Society of Its First Cycle of Sixty Years* (Shanghai: Methodist Publishing House, 1920), 58–63.

13. The first ten Chinese converts, including Liang Fa (梁發), later also the first Chinese pastor, were inducted into the London Missionary Society in 1816. Mrs. Ma could be considered among the first-generation Christians who were born into Chinese-Christian families of the first crop of converts.

14. See Ellen Li, *My Way: Dr. Ellen Li: Her Life and Contribution* (Hong Kong: Ellen Li, 1998).

15. Cf. Wai Ching Angela Wong, "Postcolonialism and Hong Kong Christianity," in Peniel Jesudason Rufus Rajkumar, ed., *Asian Theology on the Way: Christianity, Culture and Context* (London: SPCK, 2012), 56–64.

16. Stephanie Coontz's study shows a close tie between the trend of inward-looking attitudes and the increase of middle-class Christians in her *The Way We Never Were: American Families and the Nostalgia Trap* (New York: HarperCollins, 1992), 94–98.

17. Zhen Minyi and Du Qi, "Results of Hong Kong Church Survey 2009 Announced: Rise by One-Third the Number of Sunday Churchgoers," *Christian Times* at http://christiantimes.org.hk/Common/Reader/News/ShowNews.jsp?Nid=59850&Pid=5&Version=0&Cid=220&Charset=big5_hkscs, accessed June 16, 2010.

18. Led by three Christian organizations, namely, the Society for Truth and Light (1997), Hong Kong Sex Culture Society (2001), and Hong Kong Alliance for Family (2003) and supported by the independent free evangelical churches of Hong Kong.

19. The phrase was first proposed by Eric Hobsbawm and Terence Ranger, *The Invention of Tradition* (Cambridge: Cambridge University Press, 1983). It has become an important concept today for the understanding of nations and traditions.

20. Mircea Eliade, *The Sacred and the Profane*, trans. Willard R. Trask (San Diego, CA: Harcourt Brace, 1987), 20–22.

21. See Caroline Walker Bynum, *Holy Feast and Holy Fast: The Religious Significance of Food to Medieval Women* (Berkeley: University of California Press, 1987), 189–219.

22. Jane Hunter, *The Gospel of Gentility: American Women Missionaries in Turn-of-the-Century China* (New Haven: Yale University Press, 1984), 249.

23. Census and Statistics Department, Hong Kong Special Administrative Region, *Women and Men in Hong Kong: Key Statistics* (2012 edition), at http://www.statistics.gov.hk/pub/B11303032012AN12B0100.pdf, accessed January 31, 2013.

24. Census and Statistics Department, Hong Kong Special Administrative Region, *Marriage and Divorce Trends in Hong Kong* (2007), at http://www.censtatd.gov.hk/hkstat/sub/sp160.jsp?productCode=FA100055, accessed January 31, 2013.

25. There are no official statistics about Christians who are divorced, separated, or engaged in any other forms of intimate relationship. It has been a government practice not to include religious affiliation as a census item since colonial times, and it is probably considered too sensitive for church surveys as well.

26. Hobsbawm, introduction to *The Invention of Tradition*, 9.

27. It is a term adopted by the pro-family movement designating the ideal of heterosexual, reproductive monogamy. It can be found on the website of World Congress of Families, a global alliance of the Religious Right movement based in the United States since 1997. See http://www.worldcongress.org/.

28. Luke Timothy Johnson and Mark D. Jordan, "Christianity," in Don S. Browning, M. Christian Green, and John Witte Jr., eds., *Sex, Marriage, and the Family in World Religions* (New York: Columbia University Press, 2006), 80–81.

29. Interview on August 6, 2010.

30. These public signatory campaigns include: May 14, 2003, a statement calling for the protection and respect of the marriage covenant for the benefit of the younger generation; May 29, 2004, the most elaborate coverage of four newspaper pages from A30-33 of *Mingpao Daily* with 374 group and 79,800 individual signatories, calling for the defense of heterosexual monogamy as against same-sex marriage; May 22 and July 26, 2005, two statements against legislation for a sexual orientation discrimination ordinance published in *Christian Weekly* claimed to have collected altogether over eighty-five thousand group and individual signatures; September 20, 2005, a statement made in the name of medical workers that denounced anal sex between men as behavior that would subject the community to high health risks; and October 18, 2006, a statement protesting against the court decision to "decriminalize" anal sex.

31. The Chinese slang for LGBT people that was first coined by the gay movement in Hong Kong, playing with its popular use in Communist China meaning "comradeship."

32. Interview on January 14, 2010.

33. Use of pronouns for Jewel is problematic before sexual reassignment surgery. Although she is a woman now, her past was lived in a male body with which she struggled.

34. Interview on April 19, 2011.

35. Interview on April 19, 2011.

36. A very mild proposal by a pro-human rights legislator, Cyd Ho, to seek public consultation on equal rights for sexual minorities was rejected in the Hong Kong Legislative Council on November 7, 2012.

37. Choi Po King, "1997 and De-Colonization," in Susan Romaniuk and Denise Tong Ka-wing, eds., *Uncertain Times: Hong Kong Women Facing 1997* (Hong Kong: Hong Kong Women Christian Council, 1995), 27–33.

38. Bourdieu, *Outline of a Theory of Practice*, 15.

39. Bourdieu, *Outline of a Theory of Practice*, 15.

40. Charlene Haddock Seigfried, *Pragmatism and Feminism: Reweaving the Social Fabric* (Chicago: University of Chicago Press, 1996), 9.

41. Bourdieu, *Outline of a Theory of Practice*, 4.

42. Bourdieu, *Outline of a Theory of Practice*, 9–10.

# Part III

# Recovering Bodily Differences

7

# Birthing the Self

## Metaphor and Transformation in Medieval Daoism

*Gil Raz*

### Introduction

Daoists in medieval China sought to transcend the limits of mundane time and space and attain long-lasting life among the celestial spirits. While various Daoist lineages and practitioners imagined the attainment of transcendence differently, they agreed that this ultimate attainment entailed a complete psycho-physical transformation. At the core of Daoist practice were meditation techniques that simultaneously led the mind to cognitively attain Dao and caused the physical body to become refined, light, and radiant as the primordial *qi*. Intriguingly, medieval Daoist texts that were aimed at male practitioners often describe the ultimate attainment as giving birth to a perfect self. Some texts describe the refinement of the body as producing a perfect embryo (*chizi* 赤子), which would emerge as the gross physical body fell away. In more complex meditative programs the practitioner was to meditate upon the process of gestation and return to an embryonic stage—and then give birth to himself while avoiding the "embryonic knots" that are produced during birth by a woman and are the cause of death. While these practices may be analyzed as metaphorical, they reveal important notions about the body and differences between male and female; also, they challenge accepted ideas about the attitudes of Daoists to women.

This chapter explores the following issues: (1) What were Daoist notions of embryology, and how did they relate to medieval medical notions?

(2) How did Daoists perceive differences between male and female bodies? (3) What do these practices reveal about Daoist perceptions of women and "femaleness"? I show that medieval Daoist meditative techniques were modeled on embryologies that differed radically from the commonly accepted embryologies presented in contemporary medical texts. According to Daoist embryology, mundane gestation and birth from female wombs were the inevitable cause of death. They therefore advocated meditative techniques by which adepts could give birth to their perfect selves. Intriguingly, while negating the function of mundane birth, and thence of women, in the quest for transcendence, these meditative techniques continued to be rooted in the notion of yin and yang as procreative forces. Thus, we need to realize a disjuncture between the aspect of yin as an abstract creative force and the physicality of the female body.

## Common Ideas of Embryology

Before examining medieval Daoist ideas of gestation and embryology, I briefly discuss more commonly held ideas about these processes. At least four similar, yet distinct, embryologies can be found in Han texts (see table 7.1 on page 186). Among the earliest available texts documenting these ideas is the Mawangdui manuscript titled *Taichan shu* 胎產書, which was translated by Donald Harper as *Book of the Generation of the Fetus*.[1] This text describes the gestation process of ten months, beginning with "entering and emerging from the dark and obscure" (*ruyu mingming chuyu mingming* 入于冥冥, 出于冥冥). As Harper notes, the phrase "dark and obscure" is an epithet or descriptor of Dao. The text goes on to list the developments of each month. The first three months are described in terms of physical transformation of the embryo. From the fourth month, the description is of receipt (*shou* 受) of the five phases in the sequence of the conquest cycle, beginning with water. Each phase is associated with the formation (*cheng* 成) of a particular physical aspect. Following the five phases, the text introduces "stone" (*shi* 石) as a sixth "element."

The seventh chapter of the *Huainanzi* 淮南子includes an embryology.[2] Most notably this embryology does not include a reference to the five-phase sequence. Moreover, the embryology here seems to focus on the physical development of the fetus, which seems to be complete by the seventh month. The verbs in the eighth and ninth months refer to movements of the fetus in utero, until the birth in the tenth month.

The tenth-century Japanese compilation *Ishinpō* 醫心方 includes two variant embryologies.[3] The first description, citing a *Scripture on Pregnancy* (*Chanjing* 產經), is quite different from both *Taichan shu* and *Huainanzi*, and includes both physical developments as well as fetal movements. The second description, which may also be from the *Scripture on Pregnancy*, is very close to *Taichan shu*, including the physical developments in the sequence of the five phases with the added phase of "stone."

The differences in these various descriptions of the process of gestation and of the development of the embryo are of course important, but they are beyond the scope of this chapter. Despite the obvious differences, it is clear that these various descriptions are working within the same basic theory of embryology. The medieval Daoist texts I turn to now do not concern themselves with this embryology. Rather, these Daoist texts view this mundane process of gestation as causing death, and they seek to reverse it or annul its harmful effects.

## Daoist Embryology of the Perfected

First, we should note that these texts focus on the psycho-physical transformation of male practitioners, whose attainment was perceived as giving birth to a perfected self. These texts present two basic types of practice for the production of a perfect embryo within the body of the male meditator. In the first type, the meditator activates internal corporeal deities, "the father and mother," and brings them together to produce the perfected self, often known as the Ruddy Infant (*chizi* 赤子). While we may interpret this meditative act as a hierogamy between male and female aspects that inhabit the body, this interpretation is insufficient to explain the full process, nor can it explain how this symbolic hierogamy actually leads to the experience of transcendence.

The second type of practice is far more complex. In this type the meditator contemplates the process of gestation in reverse in order to return to the moment of conception. The most important aspect of this practice, however, is that while the gestation process to some extent adheres to contemporary notions of embryology, this practice introduces the notion that regular gestation and birthing produces "knots and nodes" (*jiejie* 結節) in the body. It is these "knots and nodes" that are the cause of aging and death. The purpose of this meditation, which is named "undoing the knots" (*jiejie* 解結), is therefore not simply the return to the moment of conception but

Table 7.1. Han and Medieval Embryologies

| Month | *Taichan shu*(a) | *Huainanzi 7*(b) | *Ishinpō* 22(c)<br>"On Fetus" (citing *Chanjing*) | *Ishinpō* 22(d)<br>"On Pregnancy" *(huaishen* 懷身) |
|---|---|---|---|---|
| **1** | flowing into form<br>(*liuxing* 流形 [留刑]) | lard (*gao* 膏) | fertilization (*peibao* 胚胞) | first formation (*shixing* 始形) |
| **2** | lard | extension (*die* 胅) | fetus (*tai* 胎) | first lard (*shigao* 始膏) |
| **3** | suet (*zhi* 脂) | fetus | blood vessels (*xuemai* 血脉) | first fetal (form) (*shitai* 始胎) |
| **4** | Water (*shi* 水)<br>blood (*xue* 血) | muscle (*ji* 肌) | bone (*jugu* 具骨) | initial receipt of Water, formation of blood vessels (*shishou shuijing, cheng xuemai* 始受水精，成血) |
| **5** | Fire (*huo* 火)<br>qi (*qi* 氣) | tendon (*jin* 筋) | movement (*dong* 動) | initial receipt of Fire, formation of blood-*qi* (*shishou huojing, sheng xueqi* 始受火精，盛血氣) |
| **6** | Metal (*jin* 金)<br>muscle (*jin* 筋) | bone (*gu* 骨) | form completed (*xingcheng* 形成) | initial receipt of Metal, formation of tendons and bones *(shishou jingjin, cheng jin'gu* 始受金精，成筋骨) |

| | | | | |
|---|---|---|---|---|
| **7** | Wood (*mu* 木)<br>bone (*gu* 骨) | complete (*cheng* 成) | hair (*maofa* 毛髮) | initial receipt of Wood, formation of bone marrow (*shishou mujing, cheng gusui* 始受木精，成骨髓) |
| **8** | Earth (*tu* 土)<br>skin/flesh (*fuge* 肤革) | movement (*dong* 動) | bright eyes (*tongzi ming* 瞳子明) | initial receipt of Earth, formation of skin (*shishou tujing, cheng fucao* 始受土精，成膚草) |
| **9** | Stone (*shi* 石)<br>filament hair (*haomao*豪毛) | quickening (*zao*躁) | quickening (*gu ruwei* 鼓入胃) | initial receipt of Stone, formation of hair (*shishou shijing, cheng pimao* 始受石精，成皮毛) |
| **10** | | birth (*sheng* 生) | birth (*er chusheng* 兒出生) | |

(a) Harper, *Early Chinese Medical Literature*, 372–84; Zhou Yimou, *Mawangdui jianbo*, 19–26.
(b) *Huainanzi jishi*, 7.505–506.
(c) *Ishinpō*, 6 vols. (Taibei: Xinwenfeng, 1976), v. 4, 22.2a; v. 6, 220–21.
(d) *Ishinpō*, v. 4, 22.2b; v. 6, 220–21.

a reversal of the regular process of gestation, which is perceived as actually causing death. This is clearly stated in the *Shangqing Scripture of Nine-Fold Cinnabar for Transformation of Fetal Essence*:

> All persons who are born within a womb receive the *qi* of the nine heavens, which congeals into essence to form a person. Once born, there are congenital twelve knots and nodes that coagulate and solidify within the five viscera. The five viscera are thus blocked. These knots cannot be undone and these nodes cannot be removed. Therefore, men's illnesses are due to the blockages caused by these knots, and men's allotment is cut off due to the solidity of these nodes. If you are able to undo these twelve congenital knots and nodes, then death will not reach you forever.
>
> 凡人生在胞胎之中, 皆稟九天之氣, 凝精以自成人也. 既生, 而胞中有十二結節, 盤固五內, 內滯閡. 結不可解, 節不可滅. 故人之病由於節滯也, 人之命絕由於結固也. 兆能解於胞中十二結節, 則永死亦不得也.[4]

These two types of practice thus present two contrasting processes of meditative gestation. In the first type, the meditator replicates within his body the creative processes of the cosmos, to produce a perfect "embryonic" self. In the second, the meditator reverses the normal process of gestation in order to return to the incipient moment of conception prior to the emergence of the death-causing "knots and nodes." These two types clearly contrast, and I discuss these contrasts in more detail later. But, most importantly, both types agree that the gestation of a perfect embryo is an internal process within the body of the male meditator and does not require female participation. Women are thus excluded from the perfect gestation processes. Indeed, in practices within the scheme of "undoing the knots," the normal process of gestation is seen as the cause of illness, aging, and death. In the conclusion to this chapter, I return to examine this exclusion of women and this negative view of mundane gestation and consider what this may tell us about the gender views of medieval Daoists.

## Producing the Ruddy Infant

The first type of practice is exemplified by the *Central Scripture of Laozi* (*Laozi zhongjing* 老子中經).[5] This early text, possibly from the third century, provides a complex vision of the human body as a microcosm, or more precisely a vision of a cosmic body that incorporates a cosmic pantheon, beginning with the Primal One, the father of the Dao. The gods of the body include a variety of late Warring States and Han-era mythological figures, such as Laozi and Confucius, and cosmological aspects such as the series of temporal markers (six *jia* 甲, six *bing* 丙, six *gui* 癸, and six *xu* 戌). While clearly based on Han-era mythology and cosmology, this pantheon, however, expresses a unique vision of the cosmic body. Alongside the careful charting of the various deities in their corporeal locations, the text provides detailed instructions for visualizing, summoning, and activating these deities in the body. The central deity of the text is Taiyi 太一, Great One, which was established as the highest deity of the imperial pantheon by Emperor Wu of Han. In this text, however, the conceptualization of Taiyi is substantially different from the imperial imagination of this deity. On the other hand, the discussion of Dao in the *Central Scripture* also challenges what we expect of Daoist texts. Both points are apparent in the opening line of the text:

> The Supreme Taiyi is the father of the Dao, prior to heaven and earth. He dwells above the nine heavens, within the Great Clarity, beyond the eight obscurities, within the subtle and minute. I do not know his name. He is primordial *qi*. His spirit has a human head and bird's body, like a rooster-phoenix in form. His body is [lustrous like] pentachromatic pearls, and it is clothed in yellow and white. He is precisely nine feet above your head. He constantly dwells within the purple clouds, below the floriated canopy.
>
> 上上太一者, 道之父也, 天地之先也. 乃在九天之上, 太清之中, 八冥之外, 細微之內, 吾不知其名也, 元氣是耳. 其神人頭鳥身, 狀如雄奚鈁鳥, 鳳凰五色, 珠衣玄黃. 正在兆頭上, 去兆身九尺, 常在紫雲之中, 華蓋之下.[6]

We should first note here that Taiyi is declared as superior to the Dao. While this claim contradicts what we expect of Daoist texts, it may resonate with a variant tradition, represented perhaps by the Guodian 郭店 manuscript *Taiyi shengshui* 太一生水 (*The Great One Gives Birth to Water*).[7] We should also note, however, that Taiyi is defined as the father of Dao, explicitly undermining the fundamental mother and birthing metaphors of both *Daode jing* and *Taiyi shengshui*. The text proceeds to chart the cosmic and bodily locations of several deities and the correct method for visualizing and activating these deities. The culmination of these meditative exercises is the production of a perfected self, named Zidan 子丹, in the cinnabar field of the meditator. The most succinct description of this inner transformation is in passage 12. We should note the difficulty of this passage as the subject seems to shift from "I" (*wu* 吾) to "it" (*zhi* 之). This passage is structured in the same form as other passages of the text, and I try to maintain the rhetorical ambiguity in the translation:

> "I" is son of the Dao. Humans too possess it, but I am not the individual ego.[8] I sit upright facing south on a pearly jade dais with a yellow cloud floriated canopy in the great granary in the center of the stomach. I wear a pentachromatic pearled robe. The mother is to the right, embracing and nourishing it. The father is to the left, instructing and protecting it. Hence, the father is called *Lingyang*, and his byname is *Ziming*.[9] My mother is called *Taiyin*, and her byname is "Dark Radiance" Jade Maiden.[10] My body consists of Primal Yang and my name is Zidan. The Perfected Zhong Huang is the master of my perfect self. He constantly instructs me in the way of longevity. He is constantly at my side. His dwelling is the storehouse *taicang* at the spleen. Along with Master Yellow Skirt, he protects me.[11] They ensure the spirits receive their due, and they are in charge of summoning the Traveling Feast.[12] Hence, I constantly contemplate the Perfected Zidan sitting upright in the great granary in the center of the stomach, facing south and ingesting yellow essence and red *qi*, and imbibing of the liquor fountain. Zidan of Primal Yang is regularly a ninth of an inch tall. I contemplate him, and cause him to become equal to my body.
>
> 吾者, 道子之也. 人亦有之, 非獨吾也. 正在太倉胃管中, 正南面坐珠玉床上, 黃雲華蓋覆之, 衣五綵珠衣. 母在其右上, 抱而養之; 父在其左上, 教而護之. 故父曰陵陽字子明, 母曰太陰字玄光玉女, 己身為元陽字子丹. 真人字仲黃, 真吾之師也. 常教吾神仙長生之道, 常侍吾左右, 休舍太倉, 在脾中與黃裳子共宿衛吾, 給事神所當得, 主致行廚. 故常思真人子丹正在太倉胃管中, 正南面坐, 食黃精赤氣, 飲服醴泉. 元陽子丹長九分, 思之令與己身等也.[13]

The gestation of a perfected self is predicated on a hierogamy between male and female deities that inhabit the body. Now, who are the mysterious father and mother who nourish the perfected self?

The father, here named Lingyang 陵陽 and Ziming 子明, is a little hard to pin down. Without getting into the complex web of names and titles, it seems that the father is a manifestation of Taiyi or the Dao. The mother, here named Taiyin and Xuanguang yunü 玄光玉女, Dark Radiance Jade Maiden, is actually the Queen Mother of the West, who in passage 4 of the text is introduced in rich terms reflecting her antiquity and complex mythology. She is the Primal *qi* of Grand Yin (Taiyin 太陰). She is surnamed Spontaneity (Ziran 自然) and named Lordly Meditation (Junsi 君思). Below, her domain is Mt. Kunlun 昆侖, in a nine-layered gold citadel encompassed by multicolored clouds and myriad patterns atop cliffs one hundred thousand feet tall. Above, her domain is the Northern Dipper in the Floriated Canopy, below the Purple Chamber within Northern Asterism.

The Queen Mother is paired with King Father of the East (Dongwangfu 東王父), who is introduced in section 3. He is defined as the Primal Qi of Azure Yang (Qingyang 青陽), prior to the myriad spirits, and his domain is in the east, on Mt. Penglai 蓬萊. These two deities are also located within the human body, and in more than one location. They are first said to dwell in the eyes (King Father in the left eye, and Queen Mother in the right eye; 3.2a). They are also said to dwell in the breasts, as described in passage 4:

> A human has two breasts. They are the ford at which the essence and *qi* of yin and yang of the myriad spirits cross. Below the left breast is the sun; below the right breast is the moon. These are the residences of the King Father and Queen Mother. Their upper domain is the eyes; they cavort in the head. At rest they are below the breasts, sleeping in the Purple Chamber of the Scarlet Palace. They are the *qi* of yin and yang.
>
> 人兩乳者, 萬神之精氣, 陰陽之津汋也. 左乳下有日, 右乳下有月, 王父王母之宅也. 上治目中, 戲於頭上, 止於乳下, 宿於絳宮紫房, 此陰陽之氣也.[14]

Perhaps the most intriguing location of the Queen Mother, and arguably among the most fascinating aspects of this text, is in the complex topography of the lower abdomen. Here we find two key features that were to become central to the later *neidan* 内丹 (inner alchemy) tradition: the Cinnabar Field and the Ocean (later usually called Ocean of *qi*), which is introduced in passage 19:

> The [space] within the two kidneys is named Great Ocean, also known as Weak Waters.[15] In it there is a divine turtle that inhales and exhales primordial *qi*. As he travels he causes wind and rain, and his *qi* penetrates to the four limbs. There is no place it does not reach. On it are nine persons, arrayed in three ranks. [In the first row] on the left is Han Zhong, on the right Fan Li, and in the middle is Tai Chengzi. [In the second row] on the left is the Minister of Instruction, to the right is the Minster of Works, and in the center is Lord Taiyi. [In the third row] on the left is Blue-Waisted Jade Maiden, on the right is White-Water Plain Maiden, and in the center is Jade Maiden of Mystic Radiance, who is the mother of primordial *qi* of the Dao. On the left is the Minister of Emoluments, and to the right is the Minister of Fate. Wind Lord, Rain Master, Thunder, and Lightning serve as greeters, while transcendent lads and jade maidens guard the gateways. Hence, this is called the Palace of the Great Abyss. You must first correctly [envision] Taiyi of the Purple Palace, the Dark Maiden, and the Ruddy Infant. Hence, the Dark Maiden will constantly carry the bright asterism Venus and grasp the bright pearl. Their radiance will illuminate your body; your years will be extended and you will not die.
>
> 兩腎間名曰大海, 一名弱水. 中有神龜, 呼吸元氣, 流行作為風雨, 通氣四支, 無不至者. 上有九人, 三三為位. 左有韓眾, 右有范蠡, 中有太城子. 左為司徒公, 右為司空公, 中有太一君. 左有青腰玉女, 右有白水素女, 中有玄光玉女. 玄光玉女者, 道元氣之母也. 左有司錄, 右有司命, 風伯雨師雷電送迎, 仙人玉女宿衛門戶, 故名曰太淵之宮. 先正紫房宮太一, 玄女, 赤子. 故玄女常戴太白明星, 耳著太明之珠, 光照一身中, 即延年而不死也.[16]

We should note that like passage 12, this passage is also about a parental couple and infant, but the two passages clearly differ in nomenclature, terminology, and practice. I suggest this difference is due to the fact that the author-compiler of the *Central Scripture* borrowed from several different sources. The pantheon of the *Central Scripture* is thus a creative amalgam of different traditions, reformulated to fit the particular set of transformative meditative practices advocated in the text. Nevertheless, despite these discrepancies, the basic practice of the *Laozi zhongjing* may be summed up as the bringing together of the male and female aspects of the body in order to produce and gestate a perfected form of oneself. While this process is metaphorically modeled upon conception, gestation, and birth, it is in fact based on the basic yin-yang correlative system. In her discussion of what she labels the "androgynous body," Charlotte Furth has cogently shown that this cosmological scheme allows for the erasure of the most basic sex and gender differences by inscribing the physical dualities within a hierarchy of nested dualities. The physical differences are thus elided within the higher cosmological patterns.[17] I suggest that in the *Laozi zhongjing* we indeed find such an erasure of sex differences, which allows for the imagination of the male body as able to cycle within itself the productive energies of yin and yang.

## Reversing Gestation: Unknotting the Knots of Death

Turning now to the embryology of the *Shangqing Scripture of Nine-Fold Cinnabar for Transformation of Fetal Essence*, we find a detailed discussion of the formation of the fetus that frames the normal ten-month gestation within the familiar yin-yang cosmology but introduces a new esoteric cosmological explanation:

> The revolutions of heaven and earth and the matching of perfection of the two images [lead] yin and yang to send down their *qi*. Above, this corresponds to the nine dark realms.[18] Flowing (down) as nine-fold transformed cinnabar, causing *qi* to condense and become essence, and essence transforms to form spirit. Spirit changes to become man. Hence, man is the image of heaven and earth. *Qi* models upon the self-activating.[19] The *qi* of the self-activating are all the essences of the nine heavens, which transform to become the nourishment of the fetus within the body. After nine months, the *qi* [of the fetus] is replete as the *qi* of the nine heavens is complete. Then, in the tenth month there is the birth.
>
> 天地交運, 二象合真. 陰陽降氣, 上應九玄. 流丹九轉, 結氣為精, 精化成神, 神變成人. 故人象天地, 氣法自然. 自然之氣, 皆九天之精, 化為人身, 含胎育養. 九月氣盈, 九天氣普, 十月乃生.[20]

The transformation of the celestial *qi* during the ten months of gestation is further explained in a later passage:

> Yang *qi* is red and named Dark Cinnabar; yin *qi* is yellow and named Yellow Essence.[21] When yin and yang interact and the two *qi* descend, then essence is transformed and spirit coagulates, responding above to the nine heavens. The *qi* of the nine heavens then descends and fills the cinnabar field, merging and congealing with the essence, to coalesce at the Gate of Destiny. This [process] is to occur nine times, and is referred to as nine-cinnabar. Above [the *qi*] transform and below they congeal in order to form a human. In the first month, [the embryo] receives *qi*; in the second month, receives numinous spirit; in the third month, contains change; in the fourth month, congeals essence; in the fifth month, body and head appear; in the sixth month, transforms into shape; in the seventh month, the spirits array in their loci; in the eighth month, the nine orifices are clear; in the ninth month, the *qi* of the nine heavens pervades [the fetus] and sound appears; in the tenth month, the Minister of Destiny approves the register so the fetus receives an allotment and is born. Hence, man is bestowed with the *qi* of the nine heavens and the essences of yin and yang. This is called "the nine-cinnabar is merged and complete." If one already has a human body, he should follow this [practice]. Then he will revert to his original perfection, the [nine-cinnabar] will pervade his viscera, undo and release the womb-roots, and spontaneously one will attain transcendence.
>
> 陽氣赤, 名曰玄丹; 陰氣黃, 名月黃精. 陰陽交, 二氣降, 精化神結, 上應九天. 九天之氣則下布丹田, 與精合凝, 結會命門. 要須九過, 是為九丹. 上化下凝, 以成與人. 一月受氣, 二月受靈, 三月含變, 四月凝精, 五月體首, 六月化形, 七月神位布, 八月九孔明, 九月九天氣普乃有音聲, 十月司名勒籍受命而生. 故人稟九天之氣陰陽之精, 名曰九丹合成. 人身既得, 為人便應, 反其本真, 通理五藏, 解散胞根, 段滅死孔, 自然成仙也.[22]

The formation of the embryo is thus seen as the process of the descent of celestial *qi* into the womb, leading to a series of transformations that replicate the primordial and fundamental interaction of yin and yang. The normal process of gestation, however, causes twelve "knots and nodes" to appear in the body, with four knots located at each of the three realms of the body while still in the womb. In the upper part, the four knots are in the *niwan* 泥丸 (top of the head), the mouth, forehead, and between the eyes.[23] The knots in the center part of the body are located in the five viscera, in the stomach, in the great intestine, and in the small intestine.[24] The four knots of the lower part are located in the bladder, the genitals, the rectum, and between the legs.[25]

The text goes on to provide complex exercises by which these knots can be undone by the practitioner. At the core of these meditative visualization and incantatory exercises is the invocation of the Primordial Father and Dark Mother (Yuanfu Xuanmu 元父玄母), who are manifestations of the two primordial cosmic aspects. The Primordial Father and Dark Mother are thus the true parents of the perfected, rather than the physical parents who produced the practitioner. The purpose of these exercises is to undo the knots and nodes produced during the months of gestation and return the body of the practitioner to its incipient form as an embryo, and they are performed for each of the three realms. In each case the practitioner is to enter the meditation chamber at dawn on the day of his conception (*benming zhiri* 本命之日). After lighting incense, he should sit with his eyes closed and visualize:

> The Primordial Father is nine inches and nine *fen* tall, bearing a dark and yellow belt of the pristine numina, and on his head he wears a nine-ascendant kerchief of pearl and jade and a virtuous official cap of the Limitless. He resides in the Cavern-Primordial Village of the Cinnabar-Numinous District and serves at the Jade Treasure Bureau of the Grand Ultimate Gemmy Palace above the nine heavens. Riding a coral-green aurora-colored flying carriage drawn by twelve flying dragons and accompanied by twenty-four transcendents, he arrives from the northwest, descends, and enters my body. His domain is the *niwan*.
>
> 向本命平坐, 閉眼思元父. 身長九寸九分, 著玄黃素靈之綬, 頭戴九稱珠玉之幢無極進賢之冠. 居九天之上太極瓊宮, 玉寶之府丹靈鄉洞元里中. 乘碧霞飛輿, 從十二飛龍, 二十四仙人, 從西北来下. 入我身中, 治泥丸之境.
>
> Next, contemplate the Dark Mother, whose body is six inches and six *fen* tall. She wears an azure-treasure spirit-radiant silken robe, a frosty-gauze nine-colored belt, and on her head is a darned yellow cap of the purple primordial. She dwells above

> the limitless nine-*qi* in the Gemmy Forest of Seven Gems, at the Cinnabar Chamber, in the Jade-Treasure Cavern-Primordial Bureau, in Upper Clarity Village in Nine-Radiance District. She rides a feathered canopy chariot of purple clouds and flying essences, followed by twelve phoenixes and thirty-six jade maidens. Arriving from the southeast, she descends into my body. Her domain is within the Cavern Chamber. Contemplate the father and mother transforming into azure and yellow *qi* twisting, turning, and intermingling above your head.
>
> 次思玄母, 身長六寸六分, 著青寶神光錦繡霜羅九色之綬, 頭戴紫元玄黄寶冠, 居九氣无 極之上, 瓊林七暎丹房玉寶洞元之府 九光椰上清里中, 乘紫雲飛精羽蓋, 從十二鳳凰三十六玉女, 從東南來下. 入甲身中, 治面洞房之内. 思父母化為青黄二氣, 宛轉相沓, 兢於頭面之上.[26]

The visualization is followed by an incantation, which is very clear about the negative perception of mundane gestation:

> As for the transformations of the nine numina I have received, their knotted *qi* is not pure, the nodes clotted and solidified, and they secure and block the numinous gateways. I sincerely announce on this day of my conception to the High Dawn that the Primordial Father and Dark Mother send their brilliance to my body, to illuminate together with my eight effulgences so that my perfection equals the nine heavens. Together we will undo the four-knotted womb roots of the upper region, revert the numina and secure the doorways, and within my nine orifices will form transcendence. My inner embryo will be refined and transformed, and the nine cinnabar will congeal into spirits causing the dark to become red. The two *qi* will intermingle. My longevity will equal that of the three radiances, and my blessings will last a million years.
>
> 甲受九靈之化, 結氣不純, 節滯盤固, 鎮塞靈門. 謹以本命上告高晨, 元父玄母, 下映我身, 八景齊暉, 九天同真. 共解上部四結胞根, 廻靈鎮戶, 九孔結仙, 内胎鍊化, 九丹凝神, 變青為赤, 二氣纏綿, 壽同三光, 永享億年.[27]

Like the *Laozi zhongjing*, this text too instructs the meditator to produce and gestate a form of his self. However, unlike the *Laozi zhongjing*, which simply ignores mundane medical knowledge and contemporary embryology, and provides its own idiosyncratic vision of the body, the *Transformation of Fetal Essence* explicitly asserts that the regular birthing process from the womb is the inherent cause of death. The path to transcendence is by reversing and negating this process and producing within oneself a perfected form. This negation of mundane medical and common knowledge is eloquently expressed in yet another Shangqing scripture, the *Central Scripture of Nine Perfections* (*Jiuzhen zhongjing* 九真中經):

> The father and mother only know of the initial birthing and nurturing of the self. But, they are unaware that the Five Thearchical spirits descend within. The human body is populated by divine spirits who dwell in the nine [palaces] and who regularly enter and exit the upper, middle, and lower cinnabar fields.
>
> 父母唯知生育之始我也，而不覺帝君五神來適於其間也. 人體有尊神, 其局九, 常出入上中下三田.[28]

## Conclusion

Production of a perfected self, or more precisely "birthing the self," is a very common trope in medieval Daoist texts and perhaps also in the later *neidan* tradition. This chapter is a preliminary exploration of this intriguing theme. And I can only provide very brief sketches of two basic types of such practices. It is clear that these meditative exercises entail a vision of the body profoundly different, not just from our own modern biomedical vision, but more significantly, from contemporary medical and common knowledge. Indeed, the Shangqing scriptures seem to critique common knowledge and explicitly seek to undo the death-producing knots of regular birthing. Thus, while the basic metaphor of attaining transcendence is that of birthing, the actual process envisioned in these texts negates actual birthing. I suggest therefore that the metaphor in this case needs to be seen as transformative and creative. That is, metaphoric language is here meant to fully transform the cognitive experience of the meditator so that he is truly reborn into this world with a new vision.

But what does this tell us about the attitude of the authors of these texts to women?

It may be tempting to see these medieval Daoist texts as expressing gender reversal, as discussed by Elena Valussi in the following chapter, but we should note that the male adepts are not envisaged as transforming into females but as transforming their male bodies into unitive bodies that incorporate birthing abilities. These texts present these abilities as latent and inherent in all male bodies and that which can be activated through correct practice. This imagined unitive body is therefore superior to the gendered bodies of the mundane world.

The texts cited previously should remind us that the cosmological concepts of yin and yang and their common gender correlates of female and male, while correlated, are not in fact simultaneous. These texts alert us that the notions of yin and yang and the human sex correlates need to be kept distinct. The Daoist texts, especially of the Shangqing scriptural corpus, clearly advocate a rejection of female participation in the quest of transcendence pursued by male adherents. We find the same attitude in the rejection of physical sexual practice in Shangqing texts, as exemplified by the following passage from the *Purple Texts Inscribed by the Spirits* (*Lingshu ziwen* 靈書紫文): "Moreover, intercourse with a woman for the purpose of rising to the heavens and recycling *qi* in order to become a Celestial Transcendent are methods more treacherous than fire and water."[29]

I argue that there is sufficient evidence to show that despite the positive valuation of yin in Daoist texts, this valuation does not carry over to actual women. The idealized process of producing the perfected self is in fact a negation of the birth by a mother.

## Notes

1. Donald J. Harper, *Early Chinese Medical Literature: The Mawangdui Medical Manuscripts* (London and New York: Kegan Paul International, 1998), 372–84. See also Zhou Yimou 周貽謀, *Mawangdui jianbo yu gudai fangshi yangsheng* 馬王堆簡帛與古代房事養生 (Changsha: Yuelu shushe, 2006), 19–26.

2. He Ning 何寧, ed., *Huainanzi jishi* 淮南子集釋 (Beijing: Zhonghua shuju, 1998), 7.505–506.

3. Compiled in 982 by Tamba Yasuyori 丹波康賴 (912–995).

4. *Shangqing jiudan shanghua taijing zhongji jing* 上清九丹上化胎精中記經, *DZ* 1382: 3a. Much of this text also appears in *Shangqing Taiyi Dijun taidan yinshu jiebao shi'er jiejie tujue* 上清太一帝君太丹隱書解胞十二結節圖訣, *DZ* 1384. Studies of these materials include Chang Chaojan 張超然, "Liuchao Daojiao Shangqing jingpai cunsi fa yanjiu" 六朝道教上清經派存思法研究 (master's thesis, Cheng-chih University, 1999), 75–121; and Stephen R. Bokenkamp, "Simple Twists of Fate: The Daoist Body and Its *Ming*," in Christopher Lupke, ed., *The Magnitude of Ming: Command, Allotment, and Fate in Chinese Culture* (Honolulu: University of Hawaii Press, 2005), 151–68.

5. Studies of this text include: Liu Yongming 劉永明, "*Laozi zhongjing* xingcheng yu Handai kao" "老子中經" 形成於漢代考," *Lanzhou daxue xuebao* 蘭州大學學報 34 (2006): 60–66; John Lagerwey, "Deux Écrits Taoïstes Anciens," *Cahiers d'Extrême-Asie* 14 (2004): 139–71; Kristofer Schipper, "Le Calendrier de Jade—Note sur le Laozi zhongjing," *Nachrichten der Gessellschaft für Natur und Völkerkunde Ostasiens/Hamburg* 125 (1979): 75–80; Schipper, "The Inner World of the *Lao-tzu chung-ching*," in Chün-chieh Huang and Erik Zürcher, eds., *Time and Space in Chinese Culture* (Leiden: Brill, 1995), 114–31; Schipper (Shi Zhouren 施舟人), "*Laozi zhongjing* chutan" "老子中經" 初探, *Daojia wenhua yanjiu* 16 (1994): 204–16; Maeda Shigeki 前田繁樹, "*Roshi chukyō* ishō" "老子中經" 覺書, in Sakade Yoshinobu 阪出祥伸, ed., *Chūgoku kodai yōsei shisō sōgōteki kenkyū* 中國古代養生思想綜合的研究 (Tokyo: Hirakawa, 1988), 474–502; Kato Chie 加藤千恵, "*Roshi chukyō* to naitan shisō no kigen" "老子中經"と内丹思想の起源, *Tōhō shūkyō* 87 (1996): 22–38; and Alexandre Iliouchine, "A Study of the *Central Scripture of Laozi* (Laozi zhongjing)" (master's thesis, McGill University, 2011).

6. *DZ* 1032: 18.1a

7. Jingmenshi Bowuguan 荊門市博物館, *Guodian Chumu zhujian* 郭店楚墓竹簡 (Beijing: Wenwu chubanshe, 1998), 125. See Sarah Allan, "The Great One, Water, and the *Laozi*: New Light from Guodian," *T'oung Pao* 89 (2003): 237–85.

8. The Chinese has *feiduwu ye* 非獨吾也, which may also be read as "I am not the only one." I am here following Schipper's suggestion that this phrase accords with other similar statements in the texts, such as passage 2: "The Highest Limitless Primal Lord is the lord of the Dao. . . . He is the son of the Supreme Taiyi; he is not a [physical] son, but the spontaneous generation of primal *qi*" 無極太上元君者, 道君也 . . . 上上太一之子也. 非其子也, 元氣自然耳 (in Zhang Junfang 張君房 [*jinshi* 1005], comp., *Yunji qiqian* 雲笈七籤, *DZ* 1032: 18.12.1b). See Schipper, "Inner World," 124n21.

9. Intriguingly, Lingyang Ziming 陵陽子明 was a name of an early seeker of transcendence mentioned in *Liexian zhuan* 列仙傳, *DZ* 294: 2.14b. For variants and annotations, see Max Kaltenmark, *Le Liesien tchouan* (Paris: Collège de France, 1953; rpt. 1987), 183–87; and Wang Shumin 王叔民, ed., *Liexian zhuan jiaojian* 列仙傳校箋 (Taibei: Institute of Literature and Philosophy, Academia Sinica, 1995), 158. He is the purported author of the lost work *Lingyang Ziming jing* 陵陽子明經, which is cited in Wang Yi's 王逸 (ca. 89–158) commentary to the Chuci 楚辭 poem "Yuanyou" 遠遊, in Hong Xingzu 洪興祖 (1090–1155), comp., *Chuci buzhu* 楚辭補注 (Taibei: Da'an, 1995), 251. According to the *Zidu jing* 子都經 by Wu Yan 巫炎 (also named Zidu 子都), a *fangshi* active during the reign of Emperor Wudi of Han (r. 176–127 BCE), Lingyang Ziming was a master of sexual techniques. The *Zidu jing* is lost except for citations in chapter 28 of *Ishinpō*; collated in Li Ling 李零, *Zhongguo fangshu kao* 中國方術考 (Beijing: Dongfang, rev. ed. 2000), 512–14, translated in Robert H. van Gulik, *Sexual life in Ancient China: A Preliminary Survey of Chinese Sex and Society from ca. 1500 B.C. till 1644 A.D.* (Leiden: E. J. Brill, 1961), 137 ff., and republished with a

new introduction and bibliography by Paul R. Goldin (Leiden and Boston: Brill, 2003), 137 ff.

10. This is the Queen Mother of the West, see passage 4.

11. This line should be compared with section 45, which deals with the category of Primal Yang. The passage states: "Zidan of Primal Yang is my own self" (*yuanyang Zidan, wu shen ye* 元陽子丹, 吾身也). The passage further lists deities dwelling in the five viscera. Accordingly, within the spleen are three persons: in the center is Dark Radiance Jade Maiden, mother of the Dao, to the left is Yellow Skirt, and to the right is Central Yellow (Zhonghuang 中黃). The Perfected Zidan is within the stomach sitting on a pearl and jade dais covered with a net of golden colored clouds of *qi*.

12. For more on the intriguing notion of "traveling feast," see Terry Kleeman, "Feasting without the Victuals: The Evolution of the Daoist Communal Kitchen," in Roel Sterckx, ed., *Of Tripod and Palate: Food, Politics and Religion in Traditional China* (New York: Palgrave Macmillan, 2005), 140–62.

13. *Yunji qiqian*, 18.7b–8a.

14. *Yunji qiqian*, *DZ* 1032: 18.2b8–3a2.

15. This links the location to the Kunlun mythology.

16. *Yunji qiqian*, *DZ* 1032: 18.14a3–b2; also in section 23 (19a)

17. Charlotte Furth, *A Flourishing Yin*: *Gender in China's Medical History, 960–1665* (Berkeley: University of California Press, 1999), 306.

18. "Nine dark realms" is a translation of *jiuxuan* 九玄, which refer to the nine heavens of Shangqing cosmology. These are mentioned repeatedly throughout this text.

19. "*Qi* models upon the self-activating" (*qifa ziran* 氣法自然) is an allusion to *Daode jing* 25.

20. *DZ* 1382: 1b.

21. Note the possible links with the term Way of the Yellow and Red (*Huang chi zhi dao* 黃赤之道) used by critics of the sexual practice of the Celestial Masters.

22. *DZ* 1382: 3a.

23. *DZ* 1382: 3a.

24. *DZ* 1382: 7b.

25. *DZ* 1382: 11a.

26. *DZ* 1382: 4a.

27. *DZ* 1382: 4b

28. *Shangqing taishang dijun jiuzhen zhongjing* 上清太上帝君九真中經, *DZ* 1376: 1.2a. The lines seem somewhat fragmentary.

29. *DZ* 639: 13a; Stephen R. Bokenkamp, *Early Daoist Scriptures* (Berkeley: University of California Press, 1997), 330–31. For more on the rejection of physical sexual practice, see Gil Raz, *Emergence of Daoism, Creation of Tradition* (London: Routledge, 2012); and Raz, "The Way of the Yellow and the Red: Sexual Practice in Early Daoism," *Nan Nü: Men, Women and Gender in Early and Imperial China* 10 (2008): 86–120.

8

# Female Alchemy

## Transformation of a Gendered Body

*Elena Valussi*

What aspect of the body constitutes a woman's potential capacities, and what part articulates her oppression?

—Zillah Eisenstein, *The Female Body and the Law*

A mechanistic understanding of the body is harmful to feminist theory because it deprives women's bodies of agency by reducing the body to a passive object, seen as a tool or instrument of an intentional will rather than a locus of power and resistance.

—Elizabeth A. Grosz, *Volatile Bodies: Toward a Corporeal Feminism*

### Introduction

Female alchemy (*nüdan* 女丹) is a textual tradition of Daoist meditation and physiological exercises for women that emerged in China in the seventeenth century and developed throughout the nineteenth and twentieth centuries.[1] It is part and parcel of the much older inner alchemy (*neidan* 内丹) tradition, which advocates the possibility of achieving immortality through the progressive refinement of the body, aided by meditation, breathing, visualization, and massage exercises. Differently from *neidan*, though, *nüdan* adapts its theory and practice specifically to the female body. *Neidan* emerged in China in the Song dynasty (960–1279), and, until the emergence of *nüdan* much later on, it was considered a genderless practice, available to men and women alike, though there was, for social and historical reasons, much less participation by women. The first individual *nüdan* texts started appearing at the end of the Ming dynasty, and the first full-fledged collections appeared in the late eighteenth and early nineteenth centuries.

With the advent of *nüdan* in the seventeenth and eighteenth centuries, *neidan* was immediately given a gender valence and called, in *nüdan* manuals, *nandan* 男丹 (male alchemy). The introduction of *nüdan* as a category then marks a necessity to create a female sphere of activities in this field, where the woman is the central actor. The reasons for this new necessity, and the impetus for change behind it, are at the basis of this chapter.

Specifically, I entertain these questions: What can the *nüdan* tradition tell us about the interaction between power and subservience in gender relations? What does this tradition reveal about the level of agency Chinese women in the seventeenth and eighteenth centuries had over their bodies, in their world, and in society? Was *nüdan* tailored to women's bodies in order to satisfy the needs of a specific historical time, or was its emergence a response to women's desires and demands? I answer these questions by looking at the way this tradition is presented in the prefaces to the texts as well as by the way the female body is presented in the texts themselves. I argue that the appearance of *nüdan* reveals interesting aspects of the power relations between men and women, and that this relationship is displayed before us in the texts of the *nüdan* tradition through the description of female and male bodies, their differences and similarities. What we find is often parallel to what emerges in other contemporary writings about and by women, both religious and literary; however, with *nüdan* we are given a different perspective, because it combines in a unique way women's spirituality and their physical structure. I believe that the emergence of *nüdan* in this period denotes simultaneously the necessity of creating a female sphere of activities in this field, where the woman was the central actor, as well as a spiritual modality for women that would be safe and controllable. On a deeper level, however, *nüdan* texts and practices reflect Qing pervasive anxieties over women's public religious activities and their desire to contain them.

What defines a *nüdan* text? A *nüdan* text describes a woman's quest for achieving immortality through physical and mental transformation. This transformation is brought about by following a standard sequence of practices that include breathing exercises, internal visualizations, self-massage, mental concentration, and the suppression of emotions. This process is very similar in its structure to the non-gender-specific process of realization in *neidan* texts, which proceeds from *jing* 精 (essence/semen) to *qi* 氣, from *qi* to *shen* 神 (spirit), and from *shen* to *xuwu* 虛無 (vacuity). Female alchemy, though, uses a very specific technical language referring to body parts and processes inherent to the female body. The three main stages of the practice are transforming blood (*xue* 血) into *qi*, transforming *qi* into spirit, and transforming spirit into vacuity. While the second and third stages are very similar to the parallel ones in standard *neidan* practice, the first is very different, because the primary element to be transformed into energy is blood, not essence. This first stage is also called "refining the form of the Great Yin" (*taiyin lianxing* 太陰煉形), as opposed to what is referred to as the male practice of refining the *qi* of the great Yang (*taiyang lianqi* 太陽煉氣). The blood that the texts refer to, and the main element to be transformed, is menstrual blood; in *nüdan* texts, it is often referred to as the Red Dragon (*chilong* 赤龍).

The physical starting point for female practice is also different. Women start from the Sea of Blood (*xuehai* 血海), three and a half inches below the navel, which is not to be confused with the lower *dantian* 丹田, where the male practice begins. The Sea of Blood is the reservoir where the menstrual blood gathers before the transformation takes place. In *nüdan*, blood is considered to be the most fundamental element of the female body. It is an element that pervades a woman in different guises; it gathers in the Sea of Blood, ascends to the breasts as breast milk, and descends and flows out of the body as menstrual blood. It is through the loss of menstrual blood that female energies are depleted. This depletion is what is to be counteracted by alchemical practice, through the practice called Beheading the Red Dragon (*zhan chilong* 斬赤龍). The process of transformation involves breathing exercises and massaging the breasts (*rufang* 乳房). The breasts, and especially the point between the breasts (*ruxi* 乳溪), are an essential locus and passage of this transformation.[2]

Once a woman has transformed her bloody constitution, her breasts will shrink, her body will stop shedding menstrual blood, her structure will become more like a man's, and her practice will continue like that of a man. The male body and male practice are assumed to be the standard on which female practice models itself, in the same way that both males and females strive to produce a pure yang (and not, in the case of women, a pure yin) body. Issues including the necessity for women to transform blood, which is a polluting substance in many traditions including the Chinese; the necessity to gradually eliminate obvious female outer sexual attributes; and the fact the female body will resemble more and more a male body by the end of the practice all invite a discussion of gender identity, gender imbalance, and societal and cultural influence on religious practice in these texts.[3]

Different from *neidan*, then, which was practiced mainly by men but was never only directed at men, *nüdan*, from its inception, is thus eminently "female." It describes the female body as inherently different from the male body, and thus it proposes physiological exercises, inner visualizations, and self-massages that are closely tailored specifically to the female body, its processes, its loci, and its fluids. The process is also very much tuned into the specificity of "female" health issues (menstrual blockages, problems caused by menopause, stagnation). The goal of female practice, as in standard alchemical practice, is to refine one's constitution, reclaiming the energies with which one is endowed at birth and which get depleted as one grows old, in this way delaying or deleting the hour of death. In these texts, for the first time, we see a detailed description of men and women's inherently different structures. This gives a solid base to the claim for a gender-differentiated alchemical theory, which in turn allows for different practices.

## A Brief History of *nüdan* Texts

It is necessary here to include a very brief look at the historical emergence and development of *nüdan* into a full-fledged tradition parallel to *neidan* by the nineteenth century.[4] The beginning stage of *nüdan* text production is exemplified by texts written by the physicians Fu Shan 傅山 (1606–1684) and Cao Heng 曹珩 (fl. 1632). The general readership of such compendia might include other male physicians as well as readers interested in immortality techniques. These texts do not reflect a self-aware *nüdan* tradition, nor did they target a specifically female readership.[5]

The mid-eighteenth century to the mid-nineteenth century represents the second stage of the *nüdan* text tradition, when such texts surfaced in different parts of the country, mainly during spirit-writing séances. Within the context of spirit-writing cults, there emerges a more coherent portrayal of the tradition; together with the emergence of chastity and proper female behavior, these are central to the writings. Examples include short texts in Liu Yiming's 劉一明 (1734–1821) and Min Yide's 閔一得 (1758–1836) larger *neidan* collections as well as the first *nüdan* collection, titled *Nüjindan fayao* 女金丹法要 (Essential Methods for the Female Golden Elixir, 1813), received and edited by Fu Jinquan 傅金銓 (fl. 1820).[6]

In the 1906 collection *Nüdan hebian* 女丹合編 (Collection of Female Alchemy), edited by He Longxiang 賀龍驤 (fl. 1906) in Chengdu, we see the emergence of the authority of the editor and its preeminence over the authorities of the spirits who had transmitted the texts in the previous phase.[7] During this third stage of the *nüdan* tradition, preexisting texts were reorganized more "rationally" and "inconsistencies" were deleted; the original message behind the production of these texts and their divine origin was reshaped dramatically to serve different ideologies. This is even more evident in the 1936 collection *Nüzi daoxue xiaocongshu wuzhong* 女子道學小叢書五種 (Small Encyclopedia in Five Books on the Female Learning of the Dao), edited by Chen Yingning 陳櫻寧 (1880–1969), who uses *nüdan* as a tool for female self-strengthening in the face of foreign invasion.[8]

The fourth stage spans the 1980s and 1990s, and the texts have been republished and used as medical self-help tools in which religious origins are completely deleted. These publications are to be seen in the context of a general resurgence of publications on *qigong*, medicine, and self-help books. Examples are the *Nüdan jicui* 女丹集萃 (Selection of the Best Texts on Female Alchemy), published in 1989,[9] and the *Nüdan hebian xuanzhu* 女丹合編選注 (Annotated Selections from the *Nüdan hebian*), published in Chengdu in 1991.[10] The first publication includes an introduction by the main editor of the series, the well-known Daoist scholar Tao Bingfu. The book is a collection of excerpts from various *nüdan* texts and collections, and in the introduction Tao attempts to streamline the process for the target audience of *qigong* practitioners. The term used for the practice is, interestingly, not *nüdan* (female alchemy) but *nüzi liangong* (practice for women), a term less tied to religion and more to physical well-being. The second publication is a reprinting of selected passages from the *Nüdan hebian*, edited and annotated by two physicians. In the introduction to this publication, as in the previous one, the term *nüdan* is never mentioned. Instead, the authors prefer to present this practice as *nüzi qigong* (*qigong* for women), which also sidelines the religious elements.

The fifth stage has become apparent in the last decade, as temples and Daoist practitioners have rediscovered their religious and spiritual valence, which were eliminated in the 1930s, and have reappropriated this tradition as a spiritual one.

## The Rise of *nüdan* and Its Social Context

Before the mid-nineteenth century, even though most if not all of those who could afford alchemical practice had always been men, *neidan* texts had never clearly differentiated their practitioners. By stating this difference, and acknowledging that what had been written before that time was therefore mainly directed to men, writers of female alchemy texts formed and at the same time satisfied the need for a tradition of female alchemy. Why was there the need for such a tradition, after centuries of nongendered alchemical treatises?

From a purely social point of view, practice was always easier for men than for women. The Daoist alchemical practices required years of study and training; access to separate, quiet, and purified quarters set in a specific wooded landscape; the presence of helpers for the critical times of trance and of masters to follow and indicate the right way; freedom from familial and social ties to pursue these activities; and money or sponsors to set up this whole organization.[11] The sociohistorical reality often made it difficult for women to be active participants in such practices. Thus, even though nongendered in principle, in practice inner alchemy had been, since its full-fledged development in the Song, a mainly male domain, written and performed by males. By the late eighteenth century, women had begun to be mentioned in alchemical texts but mostly as tools to be used, as cauldrons in male practices, or as colleagues in "dual cultivation."[12]

The late imperial period, when *nüdan* flourished, has been described by many as a period of heightened awareness toward female proper behavior, of increased focus on female chastity, and generally a period delineated by much stricter rules about male-female relationships. Scholars have discussed several aspects of this changed attitude toward women. Janet Theiss has analyzed the emergence of a cult of female chastity, with a sharp increase in the construction of commemorative arches in honor of chaste widows and women.[13] Weijing Lu has rendered this inquiry into female chastity more complex by explaining the Faithful Maiden cult, in which young women whose fiancés had died either committed suicide or decided to live chastly ever after, as an active and engaged choice on the part of women who wanted to be remembered as moral heroes.[14] Susan Mann has discussed the greater degree of segregation of the inner quarters, which she interprets as an attempt to preserve a changing social order through the regulation of women's activities, bodies, and fertility. Maram Epstein has analyzed works of fiction and found examples of literati nostalgia for a cosmic order between the genders, in a period of great social and political disorder and instability.[15]

At the same time, though, this is also a period that saw a boom in the printing industry, especially in the area of books for and about women. These ranged from family handbooks to tales of women's exemplary lives, from orthodox writings on female proper behavior to sentimental romances and to books on female alchemy. There was also a flourishing of women writers, whose collected works started to appear in print[16] as well as an increased participation of women in cultic activities outside the home, which was strongly criticized by a part of the Confucian elite.[17] The stricter rules described previously and the harsh criticism are part of a normative stance, but as Dorothy Ko pointed out in her study of Chinese women in the seventeenth century, the reality on the ground might have been quite different. According to her study, traditional women were, in different and very creative ways, negotiating with a restrictive Confucian ideology, "crafting a space from within the prevailing gender system that gave them meaning, solace and dignity."[18]

With the increasing availability of written texts in most households, the spread of literacy to women of higher classes, and women's increasingly active involvement in religious activities, we could read the birth of this tradition as a welcome development that takes into account the differences of the female physiology from the male and the different social needs of women. We could read it as a development that followed what was happening in the Chinese medical field where women's medicine (*fuke* 婦科)—with its attention to problems of gestation, pregnancy, postpartum, and menstrual regularity—was already well established.[19] We could read it as a response to a request from women who, since they were very active in other cultural areas, had a desire to follow a spiritual path tailored for them. However, if we pay attention to the historical moment in which this tradition emerged, and to the discourse elaborated on in the prefaces, we could also read it as a way to forcibly divide men and women practitioners and to confine women and their practice to the safety of the home; this would eliminate the need for women to seek spiritual instruction outside the home and in the company of men, as this was perceived to be problematic.[20]

## The *nüdan* Discourse and the Patriarchal Tradition

Prefaces to female alchemy texts and collections are very important in understanding the reasons for the emergence of this tradition and the rationale behind it. In the prefaces, the male editors clearly articulate a need for this tradition. In the prefaces to two important collections published almost one hundred years apart by two influential male editors—the *Nüdan hebian*, collected by He Longxiang, and the *Nüjindan fayao*, collected by Fu Jinquan—this is how it is explained:

> There are heaven and earth and then there are men and women. Of men, many attain immortality; of women, few attain

immortality. Why? Because men can wander and look for the Dao, whereas for women it is difficult to leave home and find a master. Alchemical books for men are very numerous, but alchemical books for women are few and far between and are not transmitted. Seven or eight men out of ten can read and understand a written text, but only one or two out of a hundred women can.

有天地即有男女，男子成仙者多，女子成仙者少．何也？蓋男子可以遊方訪道，女子難以出門求師．男丹經汗牛充棟，隨地可購；女丹經零星散漫,無有專書．男能識字解義者十有七八，女能識字解義者百難一二.[21]

Finding a master is very difficult. Men can go and seek fortune [to meet a master] with affinity for ten thousand *li*, but for women, leaving the inner chamber by just half a step is very difficult.

然得師甚難．蓋男可尋緣萬里，女則跬步難離閨闥故也.[22]

There is a revealing insistence on the same set of themes in every preface: texts for women are lacking, and as a consequence very few women who want to practice inner alchemy are able to realize their desire. Being always confined in the inner quarters, they have no chance to meet teachers and have no discernment between good and bad teachers, or right and wrong practices. In this situation, the writers say, what could be better than a practice with which, without leaving home, the young girl can transform her *qi*, the old lady can ward off illnesses, and the widow can maintain her chastity?

These prefaces aim at presenting *nüdan* as a safe, controllable, and manageable female practice, one that would not take women away from home or expose them to improper influences. But are the editors of these books responding to a real need expressed by women who could not leave the home, who could read only simple books, and who were tired of having to apply non-gender-specific techniques to their bodies? And is the reality of the female condition in this period the one expressed in the prefaces? Is this a normative document, in fact a worried response to activities deemed dangerous in which women were already engaging?

Looking again, a little more information can be gleaned from the prefaces; we start to understand that there are different categories of women involved. Indeed, it is misleading to generalize about the category "Chinese women."[23] According to He's preface, this collection was created as a direct response to a request by female members of his family, first among them his mother, who wanted to know more about the female way to immortality but had no means to find out by herself because of her lack of experience and of access to the outside world. Here is how He himself describes the genesis of the collection:

> This (*nüdan*) is what my mother delighted in for almost thirty years without growing weary of it. After this, my elder brother's wife, my niece, my wife, my daughter, and many aunts and cousins of our clan continue to delight in it. If you talk about instructions and injunctions, they understand, but if you ask about the practice, then they are uncertain. My mother was sad about this. She ordered that I put my body and mind into [solving this problem].
>
> 此家慈所以樂此幾三十年不倦也. 厥後, 吾嫂, 吾姪女, 吾妾, 吾女, 吾族親諸姑伯姊相繼樂此者, 甚不乏人. 言戒言定, 亦有進境, 而叩其命工, 則茫然. 家慈憂之, 命吾放下身心.[24]

In the same introduction, though, we also find a list of behaviors, criticized by He, in which other (less responsible?) women engaged. The list offers us a glimpse into a diverse and lively world of spirituality for women. One part lists wrong behaviors caused by ignorance of the correct way to practice:

> There are those who do not discriminate between Qian 乾 and Kun 坤[25] and do not know that there are differences between female alchemy and male alchemy. There are those who know alchemical books for men but do not know that there are books for women. There are those who are converted to the Buddhist faith; they chant sutras and refine their inner nature but do not know that the crucial idea of the formulae for female alchemy is that you start from physiological practices. There are those who are converted to the mysterious way but still wrongly point at the male *qi* cavity, one *cun* and three *fen* below the navel, as the female mysterious pass. There are those who return and enter the "hall of goodness" but only know about fasting, revering the spirits, chanting the sutras, worshipping the Buddha, and

> releasing captive animals; they do meritorious acts in order to invite good fortune and to avoid problems, but they do not know that for women the most important and pressing need is to behead the red dragon.
>
> 有籠統乾坤, 不知與男丹有別者. 有知男丹經, 而不知有女丹經者. 有皈依佛門, 唸佛修性, 而不知點女丹訣竅以修命者. 有皈依玄門, 以男子臍下一寸三分中之炁穴誤指爲女玄關者. 有歸入善堂, 祇知吃齋敬神, 唸經拜佛, 放生行善, 邀福免禍, 而不知女子修行以斬赤龍爲急務者.[26]

Other women are hindered in their spiritual progress by social, economical, or family problems and cannot devote enough time and effort to the practice:

> There are those who desire to practice keeping their chastity, but they are obstructed by relatives of their natal family. There are those who wish to keep faithful to the rules in practicing, but they are not accepted by relatives of their husband's family.
>
> 有願守貞修行, 而爲娘家眷屬阻擾者. 有願守節修行, 而不見容於婆家眷屬者.[27]

Another part lists wrong behaviors that seem to be caused not by ignorance or strife but by sheer (and shrewd) will:

> There are those who secretly attract good girls to serve as human cauldrons (sexual tools), as they serve as the intermediary, the result being that they lose their name and integrity. There are those good women who are seduced by [male] sexual practitioners and willing to serve as cauldrons in order to attain immortality, but they soon lose their name and integrity. There are those (women) who go on pilgrimage, enter temples, and casually seek instructions from Buddhist and Daoist monks or male teachers of charitable families, ending up planting the seed of passion. There are those Buddhist and Daoist nuns and female teachers of charitable families, . . . they use the techniques of talismanic emblems, incantatory seals, spirit water, spirit swords, spirit blows, stepping on constellations, scorched cinnabar, ingesting

medicines, circulating them in the four directions, disclosing them to women, and using the Dao to collect riches.

有暗引良女作人爐鼎, 己作黃婆, 因而自敗名節者. 有良女爲御女家所惑, 甘作爐鼎, 以求成仙, 繼而敗名節者. 有朝山入廟, 亂投僧道或善門男師, 種下情根者. 有尼姑道姑及善門師 . . . 以符章, 咒印, 神水, 神劍, 神打, 步斗, 燒丹, 服餌之術, 周流四方, 開示女流, 借道歛財者.[28]

So there were women who were asking the lead male member of the family to provide useful information about the "correct" way to practice, like those in He Longxiang's family. But there were also "ignorant" women who were practicing whatever came their way and those who found themselves too tied to familial obligations and gave up the practice. There were women who cast aside doubts of impropriety, willfully participated in sexual unions with the aim of reaching immortality, and enjoyed it too. There were women, nuns or lay, who freely participated in pilgrimages and were thus chastised as promiscuous. There were even those women who made money on the ignorance of other women. Some of these behaviors might belong to women who were "crafting a space," in Ko's words, within the Confucian system, but some others were in clear defiance of it.

In the introduction to the *Nüdan hebian*, we also find a revealing discussion of the general age and family situation of the women targeted by the editors of these collections:

As for those wives whose personal affairs are still unfinished,[29] do not by any means transmit [the teaching to them] foolishly; you only ought to advise them to cultivate inner nature and cut desires, to be filial to their mother-in-law, and to respect their husbands.

婦人事未了, 切勿妄傳, 只宜勸伊養性, 寡慾, 孝姑, 敬夫.[30]

From this and other excerpts it is clear that women were encouraged to wait until they had performed their Confucian duties before taking up *nüdan*, to be faithful to their husband and fulfill their desire for offspring, and to respect and support their mother-in-law. This indicates that women were in general encouraged to take up the practice of *nüdan* (which would require chastity and eliminate their menstrual period) only after having fulfilled their duties to the patrilinear family—therefore, in their middle and old age. This is in part confirmed by the fact that menopause and its effects on the practice is discussed at length in these texts, thus suggesting that the problems of menopausal and post-menopausal women were preeminent.

## Female Physiology and Its Transformations

As mentioned previously, this tradition, more than *neidan*, focuses specifically on the physiology of the female body, its fluids, its organs, and its transformations. Paramount attention is given to blood, seen both as the main source of vitality in the body and as menstrual blood, which, because it is discarded every month, leads to depletion of that very vitality. The following is a detailed description of the essential elements of female physiology according to *nüdan* texts and how *nüdan* practice will transform these bodily differences.

### The Transformation of Blood

> When a female is still young, and the heavenly water fills the measure of one *jin*, the authentic original *qi* of the elixir field is sufficient[31] and ascends toward the origin of blood to produce blood. At this point, the yang reaches its apogee and transforms into yin and the turbid flux that flows outside the body.
>
> 當其少也, 天癸滿一斤之數, 丹田眞元之氣足, 上升血元生血. 陽極變陰, 化濁經而流形於外.[32]
>
> After beheading the red dragon, the woman's body will change into that of an adolescent, and the yin, turbid blood, will naturally cease to flow downward. She will then be able to escape death and enter life.
>
> 女子赤龍斬, 則變爲童體, 而陰濁之血自不下行, 可以出死, 可以入生.[33]

For Chinese medicine, concerns about the female body, female health, sickness, and treatment revolved around the idea that blood, as its energetic basis, flows around the body, is discharged through menstruation, feeds the unborn child, and transforms into breast milk. With this in mind, any cure was approached as an intervention on a woman's inherent depletion and coldness, as well as a way to promote blood flow and avert its congestion. For female alchemy this consideration of health was just the starting point of a radical transformation that still had blood as its main actor. In *nüdan* theory and practice, blood did not just need to be corrected and supported in its flow, but in addition to keeping its role as the energetic base of a woman, blood needed to be further transformed into a finer and more ethereal substance in order not to be dispersed anymore through menstruation, childbirth, or lactation. This ethereal substance would be the basis of the immortal embryo and not the basis for a healthy reproductive life. So a woman needs to treasure her blood and not allow it to flow outside the body. This, however, can be challenging, as is described in this quotation:

> When a girl is young, . . . she has a little bit of the "first menses" hidden inside the vagina; it is like a star or pearl; it is the great treasure from the before-heaven stage stored above the Kun abdomen. Its seat is within the Central Yellow region. If she knows to purify her nature, not to watch licentious plays, and not to hear licentious poems; . . . if in her actions she follows the rules of womanly behavior and is at ease in her tranquility, then this "thing" . . . will become the primal one and will not transform into the Red Pearl, will not become the heavenly water. This is unlike common women, who do not know this; they have a child-like nature and like to move about, to play and have fun, to jump and run. Invariably, this will cause their *qi* to move and their heart/mind to be agitated; their vitalities will become internally confused and their true *qi* will be unstable. Then, this star-like heavenly treasure will melt, will be hot like fire, and will forcefully open the door and descend, rushing through the vagina and coming out. The world calls this heavenly water.
>
> 蓋言女子 . . . 時當年少 . . . 於斯時也, 自有一點初經含於內牝, 如星如珠, 乃是先天至寶, 藏於坤腹之上, 位在中黄之中. 女子斯時, 若知潔性, 不看淫戲, 不聽淫詞, . . . 動循內則, 靜則釋如, 則此一物, . . . 便成元一, 不變赤珠, 不化天癸. 無如凡女無知, 童性喜動, 或隨嬉戲, 或逐跳奔, 不無氣動心搖, 精神內亂, 真氣不固. 則此星星天寶, 油然融化, 其熱如火, 奪門而下, 破扉而出, 舉世名曰天癸.[34]

Women are described as at the mercy of the powerful force of their own menstrual blood. This is related to the very nature of women, "child-like," full of energy and desire and thus, though not explicitly mentioned, unable to control themselves emotionally and, therefore, morally.

## The Transformation of Female Sexuality and Desire

As hinted at in the previous quotation, women need to conquer their emotions and sexuality in order to succeed in their spiritual transformation. As is well known, one of the concerns raised by allowing women to leave the home, participate in pilgrimages, and meet with (male) teachers is women's unbridled sexuality. Sexuality and desire are not only a problem when women attend outside gatherings but also during practice itself. Thus, women are not only aroused by their contact with male teachers, but sexuality seems to get in the way of their personal practice too. In fact, a serious obstacle against the successful completion of the practice, even when alone in the safely of the inner quarters, is sexual desire. The *Nüjindan* 女金丹 (Female Golden Elixir) reads:

> A woman's inner nature and feelings are easily unsettled; as soon as she covets sex, then the fire of her desire will burn her body, and the feelings will be hard to control. If she does not have a husband to follow her desire, she will inevitably engage in shameful conduct. Even if this does not cause her to lose her chastity, as soon as her heart/mind moves, the fire will take over her whole body, and her vitalities will no longer be preserved inside.
>
> 婦女之性情易蕩, 一貪淫事, 則慾火焚身, 情難自禁. 無夫以遂其欲, 必有喪廉之 行. 即使不至失身, 淫心一動, 火逼一身, 精氣已不存於中矣.[35]

The *Xiwangmu nüxiu zhengtu shize* by Min Yide also describes in detail the sexual feelings that might arise during practice, especially when it focuses on the area of the genitals:

> As for the infant's palace (uterus), the body feels a gust of warm *qi* encircling it; at this time, it is particularly important to lock the "gate of the spring" (vagina) and not allow it to relax. If you obtain a feeling of pleasure, you should mostly fear the arising of random thoughts; there might be a slight feeling of passion, which will lead to a sensation of numbness throughout the whole

> body. If you do not realize that you ought immediately to curb the emotions, this is where the immortal and mortal ways part.
>
> 若夫子宮體得一陣熱氣盤旋, 此時泉扉更宜緊閉, 莫教放鬆. 得有逸趣, 最忌念起, 稍有戀情, 便致遍體酥麻. 非惟急宜定情, 仙凡從此兩分.[36]

Min's notes on the text are even more specific:

> When we talk about the necessity to "lock," we cannot be vague about the meaning. If the gate is locked but relaxed ever so slightly, the true *qi* will leak out from it. . . . At this time, inside the gate there will be an extraordinary ticklish sensation, and after having gone through the "lifting and locking," then in the "feminine" (female genitals) you will have a feeling of great pleasure. If you do not curb this feeling, then this will definitely lead to a sensation of numbness throughout the body, and you will enter the "sea of feelings." Even though you desire to stop these feelings, you might not be able to.
>
> 言當緊閉, 不可大意. 扉閉稍鬆, 真氣扉洩. . . . 蓋以其時, 扉內必有非凡震癢, 再經提閉, 則此牝內必得非常逸趣. 不加定情, 必致遍體酥麻, 溜入情海, 雖欲定情, 恐不及矣.[37]

Since female practice does involve focusing on the genital area, the previous text warns women about letting feelings of sexual desire overcome the practice. The female body is not only ruled by blood but by its own desires.

## Body Transformation and Sex Change

Thus the aim of practice is to transform the female body and to go beyond the elements like blood, excessive desire, and bodily functions that keep it linked to the earth. Through *nüdan* practice the female body is transformed and loses its more visible sexual characteristics: the breasts shrink, the menstrual period is reabsorbed and does not flow anymore. There are more subtle changes too. Sexual desire is overcome, and the body feels lighter. This change is summed up in this way in the texts:

> When the female red channel has been cut, then her body will change and look like a male body; then the yin and turbid blood

will naturally not travel downward. She will be able to escape death and enter life.

女子赤脈斬, 則變為男體, 而陰濁之血自不下行, 可以出死, 可以入生.[38]

Intention is focused on the breasts, left and right revolving thirty-six times in each direction. The lips [are sealed] above and below, the teeth clench firmly, and the nostrils are closed tightly. Use internal breathing. On the breasts, with the palms of your hands, massage seventy-two times each side, first slowly and then more urgently, first lightly and then strongly. In a hundred days the work will be completed, and they will acquire the form of walnuts.

意注兩乳, 左右各旋三十六次. 唇門上下, 牙齒咬住, 鼻孔關閉, 用內呼吸. 在乳房內, 以兩手心, 各左右揉, 七十二次. 先緩後急, 先輕後重. 百日工全, 成核桃形.[39]

Tranquil and quiet, pure and peaceful, nurture inner nature and feelings.
The way of women indeed has complete virtue and is not light.
Concentrate often on the breasts and on the sea of blood,
in this way the form will shrink and unite with the *taiyin*.

幽閒貞靜養性情, 婦道克全德匪輕.
乳房血海常留意, 將形收斂合太陰.[40]

Menstrual blood and the breasts are the most outwardly visible signs of gender difference between male and female bodies, and through practice the woman is working to delete these signs of difference in order to come closer to an ideal body able to achieve transcendence. The language used to describe this transformation reveals underlying ideas about what constitutes a "realized" body. The female body becomes increasingly like that of a male, losing the menstrual period and some outer sexual attributes. However, in *neidan*, the male practitioner, too, considerably transforms his body:

If you transform the menses into *qi* then the breasts will shrink and be like those of a man, and the period will not leak any longer. Likewise, in a male who has refined his semen into *qi*, the yin root (penis) will shrink and be like that of a boy and the semen will not leak any longer.

返經成炁, 則乳縮如男子, 而經自不漏. 若男子則煉精化炁, 陰根縮如童子, 而精自不漏.[41]

Does the female body really change into a male body? This question is directly asked by a practitioner to the Longmen master Liu Yiming, who refers in this way to the changes that take place in the bodies of *nüdan* practitioners:

It was asked: Once the golden elixir has been achieved, if you swallow it and gulp it down, women will turn into men, and old people will turn into young. Is this so or not?

He answered: This is talking about its principle, not about its form. After women complete the Dao, they peel away all yin, and they transform themselves into a pure yang body; this is the same as men achieving the Dao. Therefore it is said: "Women change into men." [In the same way], the old, once they have achieved the Dao and returned to the before-Heaven stage, complete their yang pure body, which is the same as that of a youth in full bloom. Therefore it is said: "The old reverts to young." It is not talking about changing its illusory image (physical body).

問曰: 金丹成就, 吞而服之, 女轉成男, 老變為童. 此事有否? 答曰: 此言其 理, 不言其形. 女子成道以後, 剝盡群陰, 變為春陽之體, 與男子成道相同. 故曰女轉成男. 老者成道以後, 復還先天, 成其春陽之體, 與童子圓滿相同. 故曰: 老變為童. 非言其變幻像也.[42]

The previous passage seems to indicate that the issue is not so much that of sex change but more that of a shedding, on the part of a woman, of all her womanly characteristics, which are inherently yin, leaving her with a body that is pure yang. The man has to undergo a similar metamorphosis, resulting in a body of pure yang. But there is a difference. Since a man starts the practice with a body that is mostly yang, he does not need to change his outer image so dramatically as the woman. The woman is required to lose her femininity, all the characteristics that identify her as a woman and reach a yang bodily form, widely identified as an idealized male bodily form.

## Cosmological Transformations: Yin and Yang, Kun 坤 and Qian 乾, and Kan 坎 and Li 離

Thus, while the ultimate goal is the same for men and women, women still need to practice differently, due to the nature of their constitutions. While there is ample discussion of bodily functions, there is also a linking of these functions to a higher cosmological order that involves changes of yin and yang, Qian and Kun, and Kan and Li:

> Just as the man is yang, and yang is pure, the woman is yin, and yin is impure. Male nature is hard, while female nature is soft. . . . The man is associated with the trigram Li and, like the sun, he can complete a whole circuit of the Heavens in one year. The woman is associated with the trigram Kan and, like the moon, she can complete a whole circuit of the Heavens in one month.
>
> 如男屬陽, 陽則清; 女屬陰, 陰則濁. 男性剛, 女性柔. . . . 男爲離, 如日, 一年一週天. 女爲坎, 如月, 一月一週天.[43]

While Qian ☰ and Kun ☷ are the absolute male and female symbols before creation starts (*xiantian* 先天), one step further, after creation (*houtian* 後天), man and woman are associated with the *Yijing* trigrams Li ☲ and Kan ☵. The male structure is likened to that of the trigram Li, yang outside and yin inside, and the female structure to that of the trigram Kan, yin outside and yang inside. Kan and Li are closely related to Qian and Kun; they are the result of the very joining of those two principles. Once Qian and Kun join, their internal lines exchange, and pure yang and pure yin are mixed to produce Kan and Li. The aim of the practice, in *nüdan* as well as in *neidan*, is always to reconstruct the pure yang, to reposition the yang line within Kan into Li, thus re-forming Qian, reestablishing the original cosmic order of heaven, and producing the elixir. This aim is attained by transforming both Kan and Li into Qian.

## Role Reversal: Da Zhangfu 大丈夫

However, the gender distinctions do not seem to end here. Once the female body has been transformed and the blood refined, the woman, working harder than a man to achieve the same result, has completed an extremely hard process. If she concludes this difficult stage, she is often praised as "man-inside-the-woman":

> If it is a case of a man-in-the-woman (extraordinary woman) and she follows the masters' oral sayings to practice the [method of] "the great yin refines the form," in the course of three to five years she will be able to complete the Dao. Her method saves even more energy than the male [method]. But the man-inside-the-woman is the most difficult thing to obtain. Those most difficult to find are women who are strong and brilliant; they have to surpass men's strength by a hundred times, and only then can they resolve matters. For those women whose strength is equal to men's, it is not possible in thousands of millions.
>
> 果是女中丈夫, 得師口訣, 行大陰煉形法, 三五年間即可成道. 其法更男子省力. 但女中丈夫最不易得. 不易得者, 女子剛烈, 須過男子百倍之力者, 方能濟事. 若與男子等力者, 萬萬不能.[44]

The notion of exceptionality in women and its link to maleness is not new in religious writings involving women. Both Miriam Levering and Beata Grant, in their studies of Song and Qing dynasty female religious figures, discuss the rhetoric that grows around female religious figures who do indeed achieve a prominent place in society and have a fulfilling religious career.[45] Levering approaches the question of gender equality vis-à-vis enlightenment. The Song masters whose writings she analyzes all share the view that, in the perspective of enlightenment, gender is unimportant. Yet, if we look more closely, we are presented with a very subtle double rhetoric. On the one hand, the Chan tradition is clear on the overall doctrinal question of whether maleness or femaleness is relevant to the project of becoming enlightened; on the other, there is a use of gender-linked terms to refer to qualities needed for enlightenment that is revealing: the message is that only an exceptional woman can expect to attain enlightenment.[46]

The specific gender-linked term to which Levering alludes is the definition of "hero" or "great man" (*da zhangfu*). This term clearly conveys the idea of "manliness," as opposed to "womanliness,"[47] but it is used in the texts that Levering analyzes to refer to the women who attain enlightenment.[48] The need for a woman to have male psychological characteristics, to be a *da zhangfu*, a great hero, in her pursuit of enlightenment, is clear in most of the texts analyzed by Levering, by Grant, and by me. There is no possibility of being a great heroine, of being a woman and excelling in womanly characteristics and at the same time being considered enlightened;

"this tradition does not allow women's characteristics and language to have an equal influence on its expressive forms."[49]

As noted earlier, when a woman achieves her religious goal, she transcends all differences and is not a woman anymore. In a parallel way, men, too, transcend gender differences, once they have completed their training. But while male characteristics are the model for transcendence, the category "woman" is still used to indicate a being incapable of transcendence.

A woman wishing to pursue a religious path needs to show proof of her manliness before getting to the stage where sex and gender differentiations are no longer valid. Even when she has reached that level, she will still be praised in terms of "male" achievements or will be asked to change her form to a male form. Whoever cannot master realization will be called "a woman," since this category is inherently lacking.

## Conclusion

In traditional Chinese correlative thinking, the cosmos is divided into the complementary and interdependent forces of yin and yang. Many describe the vision of the cosmological body in Daoist texts as composed equally of yin and yang elements. Roger Ames has described the Daoist ideal as well as the Daoist person as truly androgynous, "a person in whom the masculine and feminine gender traits are integrated in some harmonious and balanced relationship."[50] Whether or not one agrees with this description of a Daoist "person" (Is he/she initially a man or a woman? What is their position in society?), the question is even more complicated when it comes to inner alchemy. It seems clear, especially when this process of continuous interaction is applied to internal alchemy, and even more so to female alchemy, that the goal to be reached, the meta-order, is yang in quality, and that the interactions of yin and yang are there to produce and support the final goal, the yang body.[51] In this sense men, who possess a naturally yang nature, are more equipped than women to access that meta-order. Thus there is an inherent deficiency in women and a difficulty in the practice that is made very explicit in *nüdan* texts, due to the physical, psychological, and emotional makeup of a woman. The model for that meta-order, as is quite evident in the discourse of sex change and of the great hero, is the male body and the male character. Thus how are we to interpret the language describing sex change, the praise of women who have achieved enlightenment as extraordinary men, the suggestion that, by refining the yin parts of their bodies, they have reached a yang meta-order equated with maleness, albeit a refined maleness? Surely the female body is a vessel for transformation. But is it also a locus of power and resistance? And what are we to make of the supposed "higher level" beyond sex and gender differentiation? In *nüdan*, the female body is indeed a vessel for transformation but cannot be seen as a locus of power and resistance, or even as a distinct alternative to male transformation. Female transformation is not ultimately seen as different from that of men; the achievements of men and women are equated. However, while at the same time eliminating the distinctiveness of women's transformation, true equality beyond sex and gender differentiation is never really achieved.

I find that texts of female alchemy reveal much about contemporary gender notions, the understanding of the female body, and the social tension between men and women in late imperial China. The tension between stricter rules and a growing demand for space for women's activities, the anxieties with respect to a changing order and the responses to these anxieties, as well as the varied and creative ways to adapt to it and find a space in which to operate, are at the basis of the emergence of *nüdan* as a textual tradition. By reducing the female to a body that has to be drained, the writers reveal their fears of pollution; by producing a literature that can be used in the inner chambers, they do the same thing on a different level, containing the dangers of women from spilling over into the male world. By expecting women to conform to the male practice once they are rid of their turbid constitutions, they invalidate their initial aim to create a truly "female" alchemy. And while claiming equality, the final achievement is always described in masculine terms.

## Notes

1. We know of *nüdan* because the texts that describe its practices have been resurfacing in China over the past twenty years. This resurfacing is not only true for *nüdan* but also for most religious and spiritual texts and practices that lay dormant during the period between the 1940s and the 1980s in China. For a thorough discussion of the emergence of *nüdan*, see Elena Valussi, "Female Alchemy: An Introduction," in Livia Kohn and Robin Wang, eds., *Internal Alchemy: Self, Society, and the Quest for Immortality* (Magdalena, NM: Three Pines Press, 2008), 141–62; and Valussi, "Female Alchemy and Paratext: How to Read *nüdan* in a Historical Context," *Asia Major* 21.2 (2008): 153–93.

2. This process of transformation is described in many *nüdan* texts. The most concise account is found in the preface to the *Nüdan hebian*, penned by He Longxiang and translated in its entirety in Valussi, "Female Alchemy," 152–55.

3. See, for example, Emily Ahern, "The Power and Pollution of Chinese Women," in M. Wolf and R. Witke, eds., *Women in Chinese Society* (Stanford: Stanford University Press, 1975), 193–214; Maurice Bloch, "Death, Women and Power," in Maurice Bloch and Jonathan Perry, eds., *Death and the Regeneration of Life* (New York: Cambridge University Press, 1982), 211–30; and Cordia Chu, "Menstrual Beliefs and Practices of Chinese Women," *Journal of the Folklore Institute* 17.1 (1980): 39–55.

4. I have described this process in more detail in "Female Alchemy and Paratext," 153–93.

5. Fu Shan, *Duan honglong* 斷紅龍 (received from Danting zhenren 丹亭真人), in *Shangcheng xiudao mishu sizhong* 上乘修道秘書四種, *Daozang jinghua* 道藏精華 ed. (Changsha: Yuelu shushe, 1993), 12.2; Cao Heng, *Nügong quebing* 女功卻病, in *Baosheng miyao* 保生祕要, in Tao Bingfu 陶秉福, ed., *Daoyuan yiqi* 道原一氣 (Beijing: Beijing shifan daxue chubanshe, 1990), 371–520.

6. Liu Yiming wrote about female alchemy in his *Xiuzhen biannan* 修真辯難, in *Daoshu shi'er zhong* 道書十二種, *ji* 7, in Hu Daojing 胡道靜 et al., comps., *Zangwai daoshu* 藏外道書 (Chengdu: Ba Shu shushe, 1992–1994), vol. 8, 467–92. Liu Yiming also wrote about female alchemy in the *Huixin waiji* 會心外集 (Collection of Meetings of Minds, 1801), in *Daoshushi'er zhong*, *ji* 9, *Zangwai daoshu*, vol. 8, 691–92. Min Yide collected two texts on female alchemy, the *Niwan Li zushi nüzong shuangxiu baofa* 泥丸李祖師女宗雙修寶筏 and *Xiwangmu nüxiu zhengtu shize* 西王母女修正途十則 (1799), in *Gushu yinlou cangshu* 古書隱樓藏書 (Wuxing: Jingai Chunyang gong cangban, 1834). Fu Jinquan, *Nüjindan fayao* (1813), in *Daoshu yiguan zhenji yijianlu*, reprint, *Zangwai daoshu*, vol. 11, 512–41.

7. *Nüdan hebian* (Chengdu: Erxian an 二仙庵, 1906). For a detailed history and analysis of the *Nüdan hebian*, see Elena Valussi, "Men and Women in He Longxiang's *Nüdan hebian* (Collection of Female Alchemy)," *Nan nü: Men, Women and Gender in Early and Imperial China* 10.2 (2008): 242–78.

8. *Nüzi daoxue xiaocongshu wuzhong* (Shanghai: Yihuatang, 1936).

9. Tao Bingfu, ed., *Nüdan jicui*, *Zhongguo qigong guji congshu* 中國氣功古籍叢書 (Beijing: Beijing shifan daxue chubanshe, 1989).

10. Qiu Xiaobo 邱小波 and Jiang Hong 蔣紅, eds., *Nüdan hebian xuanzhu* (Shanghai: Shanghai fanyi chubanshe, 1991).

11. Xun Liu has discussed in detail this side of the alchemical process in traditional China and up to the Republican period in *Daoist Modern: Innovation, Lay Practice, and the Community of Inner Alchemy in Republican Shanghai* (Cambridge, MA: Harvard University Press, 2009), 138–47.

12. For this topic, see Xun Liu, "Numinous Father and Holy Mother: Late Ming Duo-Cultivation Practice," in Livia Kohn, ed., *Internal Alchemy: Self, Society, and the Quest for Immortality* (Boston: Three Pine Press, 2009).

13. Janet Theiss, *Disgraceful Matters: The Politics of Chastity in Eighteenth-Century China* (Berkeley: University of California Press, 2004), 121–67.

14. Weijing Lu, *True to Her Word: The Faithful Maiden Cult in Late Imperial China* (Stanford: Stanford University Press, 2008), 1–48.

15. Susan Mann, "Grooming a Daughter for Marriage: Brides and Wives in Mid-Ch'ing Period," in Rubie Watson and Patricia B. Ebrey, eds., *Marriage and Inequality in Chinese Society* (Berkeley: University of California Press, 1991), 204–30; see also Mann's *The Talented Women of the Zhang Family* (Berkeley: University of California Press. 2007) and *Gender and Sexuality in Modern Chinese History* (New York: Cambridge University Press, 2011); and Maram Epstein, "Engendering Order: Structure, Gender and Meaning in the Qing Novel *Jinghua yuan*," in *Chinese Literature, Essays, Articles, Reviews* 18 (1996): 101–27. Francesca Bray also discusses the relationship between menstrual regularity, fertility, and ideal womanhood; see Bray, *Technology and Gender: Fabrics of Power in Late Imperial China* (Berkeley: University of California Press, 1997), 317–34.

16. See Wilt Idema and Beata Grant, *The Red Brush: Writing Women of Imperial China* (Cambridge: Harvard University Asia Center, 2004). On the issue of publications for and by women, see Dorothy Ko, "Pursuing Talent and Virtue: Education and Women's Culture in Seventeenth- and Eighteenth-Century China," *Late Imperial China* 13.1 (1992): 9–39; and *Teachers of the Inner Chambers: Women and Culture in Seventeenth-Century China* (Stanford: Stanford University Press, 1994), 29–68.

17. Glen Dudbridge, "Women Pilgrims to T'ai Shan: Some Pages from a Seventeenth-Century Novel," in Susan Naquin and Chün-fang Yu, eds., *Pilgrims and Sacred Sites in China* (Berkeley: University of California Press, 1992), 39–64.

18. Ko, *Teachers of the Inner Chambers*, introduction, 9.

19. Charlotte Furth, *A Flourishing Yin: Gender in China's Medical History, 960–1665* (Berkeley: University of California Press, 1999), 59–93, 134–54.

20. This need to keep women, and their bodies, safe in the home was felt in a very similar way in Europe: "Prominent male leaders in the French Revolution, for example, strenuously opposed increased female participation in public life on the grounds that women's physical nature, radically distinguished from that of men and represented most powerfully in the organs of reproduction, made them unfit for public life and better suited to the private sphere." See Thomas W. Laqueur, "Orgasm, Generation and the Politics of Reproductive Biology," *Representations* 14 (1986): 1–41.

21. *Nüdan hebian*, preface, 1a.

22. *Nüjindan fayao*, preface, 1a.

23. This has been already pointed out in the preface to the volume *Engendering China* by its editors Christina K. Gilmartin, Gail Hershatter, Lisa Rofel, and Tyrene Whyte (Cambridge: Harvard University Press, 1994), 1–26.

24. *Nüdan hebian*, introduction, 6a.

25. These two terms refer to two hexagrams of the *Yijing* 易經. Qian is formed by six unbroken lines, while Kun is formed by six broken lines; the two, respectively, also symbolize the masculine and the feminine.

26. *Nüdan hebian*, introduction, 1a.

27. *Nüdan hebian*, introduction, 1a.

28. *Nüdan hebian*, introduction, 1a.

29. Unfinished affairs refer to sexual, procreative matters.

30. Er'e shanren 二峨山人, *Nügong lianji huandan tushuo* 女功煉己還丹圖說 (*Nüdan hebian* ed.), 4b.

31. Here, elixir field means Sea of Blood, as explained in the (untranslated) previous lines.

32. *Nannü dangong yitong bian* 男女丹功異同辨, *Nüdan hebian*, 20b.

33. *Nannü dangong yitong bian*, 22a–b.

34. Min Yide, *Xiwangmu nüxiu zhengtu shize*, 4b–5a.

35. *Nüjindan* (*Nüdan hebian* ed.), 7a.

36. See *Xiwangmu nüxiu zhengtu shize*, 7a.

37. See *Xiwangmu nüxiu zhengtu shize*, 7a.

38. Liu Yiming, *Xiuzhen biannan*, 1.34b.

39. Lingyang daoren 靈陽道人, *Nügong zhengfa* 女功正法 (1880), in Chen Yingning, *Nüzi daoxue xiaocongshu wuzhong*, 10a–b.

40. *Nüdan shiji houbian* 女丹詩集後編 (*Nüdan hebian* ed.), 3a–b.

41. *Nüjindan*, 24a.

42. Li Yiming, *Xiuzhen biannan*, 1.35b–36a.

43. *Nüdan hebian*, introduction, 4a.

44. Liu Yiming, *Xiuzhen biannan*, 34b.

45. Levering, "The Dragon and the Abbess of Mo-shan: Gender and Status," *Journal of the International Association of Buddhist Studies* 5.1 (1982): 19–36; Levering, "Lin-chi (Rinzai) Ch'an and Gender: The Rhetoric of Equality and the Rhetoric of Heroism in the Ch'an Buddhist Tradition," in José Ignacio Cabezón, ed., *Buddhism, Sexuality, and Gender* (Albany: State University of New York Press, 1992), 137–58; Levering, "Stories of Enlightened Women in Ch'an and the Chinese Buddhist Female Bodhisattva/Goddess Tradition," in Karen L. King, ed., *Women and Goddess Traditions in Antiquity and Today* (Minneapolis: Fortress Press, 1997), 137–76; and Grant, "Da Zhangfu: The Gendered Rhetoric of Heroism and Equality in Seventeenth-Century Chan Buddhist Discourse Records," *Nan Nü: Men, Women and Gender in Early and Imperial China* 10.2 (2008): 177–211.

46. Levering, "Lin-chi (Rinzai) Ch'an and Gender," 140.

47. Levering discusses the origins and the *locus classicus* of this term in "Lin-chi (Rinzai) Ch'an and Gender," 143–45.

48. Interestingly, this term is also used in *nüdan* texts to refer to women who master the practice.

49. Levering, "Lin-chi (Rinzai) Ch'an and Gender," 140.

50. Roger Ames, "Taoism and the Androgynous Ideal," in Richard W. Guisso and Stanley Johannesen, eds., *Women in China* (Youngstown: Philo Press, 1981), 21–45.

51. On this meta-order, and its practical instantiations in Chinese rituals, see P. Steven Sangren, "Orthodoxy, Heterodoxy, and the Structure of Value in Chinese Rituals," *Modern China* 13.1, Symposium on Hegemony and Chinese Folk Ideologies, Part I (1987): 63–89.

9

# A Religious Menopausal Ritual

## Changing Body, Identity, and Values

*Neky Tak-ching Cheung*

### Introduction

It is a general view in feminist theorization that women have made it their mission to choose, modify, remake, or invent meaningful rituals self-consciously in order to create their own sacred space and time. This process is seen as a deliberate attempt by women to become liberated from the patriarchal hegemony that has not been adequately accommodating to women's needs and rights. There are apparently traceable backgrounds, patterns, narratives, and politics to the analysis of women's ritual in Western communities. Rita Gross has observed that the female cycle, including "menarche, menstruation, menopause, and even childbirth, is completely uncelebrated and unmarked in most traditional liturgies."[1] Barbara Walker laments, "Menopause rituals have altogether disappeared from our intensely patriarchal society."[2] Anne-Marie Korte quotes Rachel Adler, who pleads "for the incorporation of unacknowledged life-cycle events like first menstruation and menopause in Jewish religious ceremonies and religious language, as Jewish women have started practicing during the past two decades."[3] Korte further quotes Rosemary Radford Reuther, who in her work *Women-Church* urges the need for creating rituals that celebrate the life cycle of women; Reuther has designed liturgies for a puberty rite, menstruation, and menopause.[4]

Ritual designated for or performed by women in China is rarely documented or discussed. Among the very few records that detail rituals for women, Ann Waltner has focused on the notions of gender, life cycle, and royal ritual in her case study of the "coming-of-age ceremony" of a princess in the Northern Song dynasty (960–1126) in China.[5] The neglect of women's ritualization has been criticized by many feminists as reflective of an androcentric approach in academic research. Instead of being studied as an independent subject, rituals performed for or by women in China are mostly, if not randomly, put under the headings "ritual studies" or "popular religions," thus leaving an enormous hole in the study of religious practices and especially of rituals performed privately by women. The study of Jiezhu 接珠 (receiving Buddhist prayer beads) as a life-cycle ritual vital to the life of the women in the rural area of Ninghua xian 寧化縣, Western Fujian, may in part fill the gap. This chapter is an extended study of my previous work, *Women's Ritual in China: Jiezhu (Receiving Buddhist Prayer Beads) Performed by Menopausal Women in Ninghua, Western Fujian.*[6]

Ninghua is a Hakka county with a population of about 350,000.[7] I first went to Ninghua in early 2002 to start my field visits, which took place twice or thrice a year thereafter. Each visit lasted for two to three weeks, running over the course of almost five years. Based on historical, textual, and field studies, my previous work examines a women-oriented initiation rite called Jiezhu, which is a once-in-a-lifetime rite of passage that has been performed by menopausal women in Ninghua.[8] As it is believed in the villages of Ninghua that when a woman reaches her menopausal age, she has to do Jiezhu, without which her Amituofo recitation (*nianfo* 念佛) would not be efficacious. In other words, Jiezhu, as a prerequisite for Amituofo recitation, is at the same time a purification rite. Amituofo recitation is the chanting of the phrase *namo Amituofo* 南無阿彌陀佛, which is a rite commonly used among Buddhists for the attainment of merits. However, the attained merits would be nullified if the initiate gets pregnant after she has done Jiezhu. This has much to do with taboos related to female sexuality. In rural Ninghua, as well as in many places in China, women have had a marginalized status as the supposedly "weaker" gender, with a lower social position. The association of female bodily discharges with defilement further discredits their status. Jiezhu in effect reinforces the idea of "defilement" as attributed to the female body. The shame that the women feel with the male-defined negative female bodily image affirms patriarchal hegemony.

I have argued, however, that ritual acts provide therapeutic healing. The Jiezhu woman goes through a stage in which she has to handle the change of her role and identity as a life-giver (mother) with the end of her procreative cycle. The ritual provides both private and public meanings to the woman and helps her become relieved of the physical and mental difficulties that she faces in her menopausal stage. Ritual acts can bridge memory and imagination. The ritual program allows the woman to go back and forth between the past, the present, and the future. Jiezhu dramatically juxtaposes girlhood and mature womanhood, reenacts her wedding, and rehearses her future funeral. Death and rebirth symbols abound in Jiezhu. The woman "witnesses" her own funerary rites to ensure abundant personal possessions are burned for her to receive in the underworld after her death. She acquires spiritual strength to ease her menopausal stress and to allay fears of the approach of death. Jiezhu and Amituofo recitation make up a twin tool to ensure a more fortunate rebirth. Jiezhu also implies social meanings. The woman gains a new identity. She is now eligible for Amituofo recitation and becomes a member of the *nianfo* community. As social inferiority can be compensated for by a show of lavishness, Jiezhu as an expensive event creates symbolic capital of prestige and resources that in part enhances the status of the women. The woman's contributions as a wife and a mother are valued and celebrated in the Jiezhu ceremony. The youthful, bright, and colorful gift items given by the married daughter display a defiant tone against the association of Jiezhu with old age. Jiezhu celebrates an oft-neglected life crisis of women. I have concluded in my book that Jiezhu on the one hand "traditionalizes," and on the other hand, as a strategic mode of action, challenges traditions through religious and social empowerment. Jiezhu preserves the established order, but it also facilitates transformation in the initiate. The two dynamics of ritual are not antithetical; they produce and contend with each other.

As is well known, in traditional China a woman's role was defined by her attachment/submission to three men—her father, her husband, and her son—throughout her three stages of life: the period from birth to marriage (father), married life (husband), and old age (son). This Confucian moral code of "three attachments/obediences" (*sancong* 三從) has met fundamental challenges beginning in the early twentieth century, and it no longer holds absolute power over the lives of Chinese women today. Nevertheless, gender inequality persists in China, especially in rural communities, and marriage and having a male heir are still perceived as ideal ways of life and the ultimate realization of happiness for many women. Religious rituals in post-Mao times often embody a traditional social and moral order on the one hand and modern changes and the agency of the ritual participants on the other.[9] This chapter first examines how Jiezhu exemplifies the ritual significance for the rural elder women in Ninghua. The ritual inevitably espouses patriarchal family values with the husband as the transmitter of the Buddhist prayer beads and the male offspring as the lineage carrier. A woman is supposed to be "happy" if she has a husband and male offspring. As such, "single" women are disqualified to perform Jiezhu, and widows are not allowed to attend the first session (featuring the most important rite of "receiving the prayer beads") of the ritual. These exclusivities reiterate the need to have a "husband," and having one that is alive makes it all the better. It enacts and reinforces marriage as the "ideal" life for a woman with all the ritual symbols in its scriptures, texts, songs, accessories, and the like.

Within the patriarchal horizon, I argue, however, that certain twists and turns are at play, particularly through the involvement of two female agents: the "married-off" daughter (*waijia nü* 外嫁女) and the mother of the initiate. Jiezhu aligns three generations of mother-daughter bonding in a subtle manner—a very feminine one, if you will. These women express their power within the limits of their traditional roles. Through a ritual that announces their bodily change of menopause, they acquire new religious and social identities and reclaim the mother-daughter bonding of which they were inappropriately deprived. In addition, through Jiezhu, the women actively pursue a more fortunate rebirth in their next life and establish Jiezhu religious groups for mutual support and friendship.

## The Ritual of Jiezhu

Jiezhu may be understood to mean, literally, "receiving Buddhist prayer beads."[10] It is also called Nazhu 納珠 (accepting the beads),[11] or Guozhu 過珠 (passing on the beads).[12] *Jie* means to receive, *na* means to accept graciously, and *guo* means to pass on to. Incorporating all these terms, Jiezhu can be described as a rite in which a woman accepts or receives the *mālā* (prayer beads) which is passed on to her.[13] In Ninghua, there are two texts that describe what the 108 beads represent: *Fenzhu jing* 分珠經 (distributing the *mālā* scripture)[14] and *Guozhu jing* 過珠經 (passing on the *mālā* scripture).[15]

The ritual program of Jiezhu consists of two sessions.[16] The first session usually starts around midnight with a break between the two sessions, in which the ritual specialist(s), the *daifo mama* 帶佛媽媽, and fellow Buddhist friends (*foyou* 佛友) will go back home for a rest and return around six o'clock in the morning.[17] If the first session starts after 3:00 a.m., the second session follows through from the first session with breakfast in between.[18]

As a rite of passage that brings the participants into the next stage of life, Jiezhu also carries religious taboos. It is believed that if one has not done Jiezhu, in addition to the suffering that one would have to face in the underworld, one would become a cow or a horse in one's next life.[19] It is also said that when a woman dies but has not done Jiezhu, her coffin cover would have to be hit three times with an axe. Therefore, if a woman does not perform Jiezhu, her mind would not be at peace and she would feel guilty even while she is alive.[20] Jiezhu is an interesting ritual not merely because it allays these fears; more importantly, it is an initiation rite.[21] It initiates a woman to enter the Buddhist door[22] and become a *nianfo mama* 念佛媽媽 (literally, an Amituofo-recitation mother).

The Jiezhu communities believe that Amituofo recitation is effective only after performing Jiezhu. In other words, if a woman has not done Jiezhu, her Amituofo recitation would not be counted as merits. The formula used in Amitābha worship, *namo Amituofo*, has become the single phrase most representative of Buddhism as a whole. Not only is it commonly used among Buddhists, it is also a phrase popular with most of the East Asian population at large.[23]

## Glorification of a Married Life

As mentioned earlier, many women in Ninghua today still follow traditional prescriptions about marriage and a male heir. The Jiezhu ritual pretty much defines a "happy life" for a woman in Ninghua. She is supposed to be "happy" if she is married and has a son; hence her mission has been accomplished. Let us examine how Jiezhu endorses marriage as a woman's "ideal" destiny and how it reinforces the concept of "uterine family," a term made familiar to us by Margery Wolf.[24]

Traditions and rituals work hand in hand reinforcing each other. Rituals support a set of traditions that direct how people live and thereby confirm their values. Marriage as the "ideal" life for a woman is symbolized in the Jiezhu ritual: its ritual program, rites, and ritual objects highlight married life as being the "ideal" destiny for a woman. First, the husband of the initiate is seen as the master and host of the event. He takes up a prominent role in the ritual process. In the rite of passing on the *mālā*, the *mālā* is passed on from the ritual specialist to the *daifo mama*,[25] and from the *daifo mama* to the husband, who in turn puts the *mālā* into the palms of the initiate (see figure 9.1). The husband is also the host of the whole event. When the communal lunch is served, the husband goes from table to table with the initiate to make toasts to the guests. This is not only an act typical in Chinese wedding banquets but is also endorsing the husband as the host of the event.

Figure 9.1. Jiezhu: The Husband Passing the *Mālā* to the Initiate (Photo credit: Neky Tak-ching Cheung; taken during Sun Lanxiang's Jiezhu ritual on February 21, 2004)

Another obvious symbol of the concept of lineage is evident in the ritual arena, *xianghuo ting* 香火廳 (hall of *xianghuo*).[26] *Xianghuo* literally means the burning of incense sticks and candles. A temple that has a large number of worshippers or pilgrims is said to be flourishing with *xianghuo*. *Xianghuo* also means the family line. To continue with the family line is to have a son; therefore, having a son is said to *ji xianghuo* 繼香火 (continue the family line). Jiezhu may also take place at home, particularly so in the city gate (*chengguan* 城關) where there is no *xianghuo ting*.[27]

An altar is set up in the ritual arena. The general rule is that the more elaborate the ritual or the more days the ritual lasts, the more deities are to be called upon.[28] My observation of the four Jiezhu rituals shows a mixed variety of deities being worshipped. A so-called *shenxian pai* 神仙牌 (plate of the spirit), however, appeared on all four occasions. It stands on a stick in rice buckets (*dou* 斗) at the upper right corner of the central altar.[29] The *shenxian pai* is always written by the ritual specialist in black ink on a red sheet of paper and is stuck on cardboard to make it stand. It states that the light of the Buddha shines on the Jiezhu event and that the initiate is bringing all the members of her family to wish for blessings. The names of each member of the family are written in the order of seniority, with men's names being written before women's. The ritual space sets up a backdrop for Jiezhu to enact the woman's destiny.

The image of the uterine family tags along with the Jiezhu rites, the ritual texts/documents, and accessories. In the rite of *Dian xiang* 點香 (lighting the incense), the husband, the *daifo mama*, the initiate, and fellow Buddhist friends, led by the ritual specialist, place incense sticks in various areas of the ritual arena. When they are doing this, they chant *Namo Fofa dian xiang jing* 南無佛法點香經 (scripture of lighting the incense in paying homage to the Buddhist dharma). Ten wishes are mentioned in the scripture. Of the first five wishes, the first one asks for passing through the Buddhist door, and the second, third, fourth, and fifth wishes are built around the concept of a good family. These wishes are for the togetherness and longevity of the couple, the happiness of the sons, cooperation from the daughters-in-law, and the fulfillment of the sisters-in-law. The others are auspicious wishes for the initiate's rebirth in the Pureland.[30]

Another major rite is *shang dagong* 上大供 (grand offerings), in which ten bowls and ten dishes (*shiwan shidie* 十碗十碟)[31] are offered to the deities. A male member of the family has to be there to present the offerings to the deities. The ten bowls and ten dishes are first placed outside of the main ritual place, but at a reachable distance. The main ritual specialist picks up one bowl and one dish at a time and puts them in a tray while he walks up to the altar in step with the music. He chants and does ritualistic steps and turnings before passing the tray on to a male family member,[32] either the husband or the eldest son of the initiate, who also follows the ritual specialists to do turnings and then passes the tray to another ritual specialist. This ritual specialist also chants and makes ritualistic steps and turns before placing the bowl and the dish over the main altar table. This is done repeatedly ten times until all the bowls and dishes are transferred ritualistically from the outside into the ritual arena and are placed over the table. Of course, the message of male hierarchy is also seen in minor rites such as distributing the *jieyuan* 結緣 (friendship) snacks in the order of husband then sons before other female members and the Buddhist friends (who are obviously females).

In the rite of announcement (*fabiao* 發表), a ritual document (*wengao* 文誥) is read aloud by the ritual specialist. The rite is to announce to heaven that this woman is performing Jiezhu and asks that her wishes be granted. The document certifies that Jiezhu has been performed by the initiate and announces her wish for the forgiveness of sins: now (my) sins are gone, as such good fortune is bestowed (*yinzi miezui zuimie fusheng* 因茲滅罪, 罪滅福生).[33] There are two copies of *wengao*, one written on a piece of red paper and another one on yellow. The contents of them are the same. The yellow one, for filing with the bureau of the underworld, is burned at the end of Jiezhu. The red one, as a certificate (*bainian ya'nei zhizhao* 百年衙內執照) for the initiate to claim her merits in the underworld, is to be passed on to her by the ritual specialist at the end of Jiezhu. She keeps it in her *mālā* bag to be eventually burned at her funeral. The *wengao* states details known about the initiate and the family members, the reasons for the ritual, and their wishes. This is the only ritual document listing the names of all the Buddhist friends.[34]

Among the ritual objects and accessories required for performing Jiezhu, the most obvious conjugal symbols are found in a pair of silver thumb rings (*yinjiezhi* 銀戒指) and a pair of rectangular silver plates (*yinpian* 銀片) that have to be prepared for the event. One of the rings has the word Fo 佛 (Buddha) engraved on it, while the other has the word *fu* 福 (a fortunate life). The thumb ring with the word Fo is for the husband, while the one with the word *fu* is for the wife. One possible explanation of the use of Fo and *fu* for the husband and the initiate respectively is that the attainment of the Fo status is not believed to be possible at all by women, hence the Fo ring goes to the husband, while the women are better off staying with their wish for attaining *fu*. A fortunate life for a Ninghua woman is to be married and have male offspring. Other highly symbolic items are the silver plates (about 1.8 cm by 2.8 cm). The name of the husband and that of the wife are separately engraved on each piece. For the wife, her *foming* 佛名 (Buddhist name), which is given to her by the ritual specialist, is engraved. The plate is tied to the end of the *mālā*, which also helps identify it.

The initiate also needs to get a pair of lotus shoes made of cloth (*buxie* 布鞋) that are exquisitely embroidered with pink lotus floral patterns.[35] The number of lotus flowers varies from four to the more luxurious twenty-four. The greater the number of lotus flowers, the more expensive the shoes will be. The flowers can be big, or small, or a combination of big ones and small ones.[36]

I have visited a woman, Luo Shangxiu, who makes lotus shoes. She says that "shoe," pronounced as *xie* in Chinese, has the same pronunciation as "together." The idea is to be *tong xie dao lao* 同鞋[偕]到老 (the couple stays harmoniously together to old age). *Tong* 同 implies both "togetherness" and "money." It is phonetically the same as the *tong* in *tong qian* 銅錢, which means copper coins. The lotus flower is called *lianhua*, the fruit of a lotus plant has a head and a tail that makes it look like a fish. A fish carries many roe (*duozi* 多子); a fish is thus a common symbol of procreation in Chinese society. The concept of uterine family is all too clear.

How the *mālā* is passed on to the next generation reflects also the uterine family values. The *mālā* will not be carried to the grave; it has to be passed on, but to whom? The ideal is to pass it on to the eldest daughter-in-law. The emphasis on having a daughter-in-law is an extension of the need for male offspring. The daughter-in-law, upon receipt of the *mālā* from her mother-in-law, would ask her *daifo mama* to undo the string of *mālā* and have the beads strung up again with a new thread. A Jiezhu woman, Liao Huizhu, has told me that a woman is considered as having a fortunate life if the *mālā* can be passed on to her daughter-in-law; but for those who do not have a fortunate life, the *mālā* has to be disposed of in a river. However, in case the woman has passed away before being able to pass it on to her daughter-in-law, the *mālā*, as a sacred object, needs to be ritually disposed of.[37] In sum, the *mālā* is to be handed down from generation to generation as a family heirloom, but the heir is another woman who is to continue the family lineage. The *mālā* is yet another lineage-carrier symbol.

When we say Jiezhu is performed by the menopausal women in Ninghua, it does not mean that all women reaching menopause are eligible to perform the ritual. Women who have never married are not qualified to perform Jiezhu. Even those who are married but whose husbands are no longer living must also refrain from going to the first session of the Jiezhu ritual, which incorporates the most important rite of "receiving the *mālā*." A widowed Buddhist friend may go to the second session that begins at daybreak. While celibacy is not welcomed, neither is widowhood admired. What is being respected and celebrated is someone who has a living husband and male offspring, which are the "qualifications" required of the *daifo mama*. Her "qualifications" and duties are similar to those of a *qianjianiang* 牽嫁娘 in a wedding ceremony.[38] A *qianjianiang* accompanies the bride to the hall where the couple bow to one another in a wedding rite called *baiting* 拜堂. Both *qianjianiang* and *daifo mama* serve as respective chaperons of the bride/initiate. The *qianjianiang* has to be *ming hao* 命好 (having a fortunate life), and to be *ming hao* is to have son(s) and a living husband,[39] which is the "ideal" life for a Ninghua rural woman, if not for city dwellers.

## Changing Body, Changing Identity

In the Jiezhu ceremony of Zhou Weijin, her baby grandson carried a *baosan* 寶傘 (literally, precious umbrella, made of paper) for her; he followed (actually, he was carried by his mother) Zhou Weijin to *dia xiang* 點香 (light the incense).[40] Ritual specialist Zeng Yuanchuan told me that an umbrella is used by women in the Jiezhu rite much the same way that it is in a wedding when the bride is protected under an umbrella as she enters the bridegroom's place. The umbrella must be carried by a *zhiqin tongzi* 至親童子 (a lad who is the closest blood relation).[41] The umbrella used in a wedding and the paper ones used in Jiezhu are two similar symbols that signify protection for the woman who is passing over to the next stage of life. The wedding umbrella brings the bride from a state of virginity to a state of womanhood, whereas the Jiezhu umbrella brings the woman to a stage free of menstrual flow. Jiezhu marks the change of the woman's procreative female body to a state of nonprocreative being.

After examining the ideal life for a woman, we may as well ask, after all, if these women are happy with their "ideal" life. Most of the Jiezhu women I interviewed said they were not happy with their married life. They lamented, "Life as a woman is bitterly hard" (*shenghuo haoku* 生活好苦). Indeed, they have to bear children, suffer in childbirth, raise children, and work on the farm as well as do household chores; and worse still, they have to bear with their unsatisfactory husbands. With Jiezhu, they wish to have a better husband in their next life so that their life will be of better quality. Jiezhu and Amituofo recitation make up a twin tool to envisage a more fortunate rebirth. They chant, *Jin Fomen shi qiao sanxia zhong, xiashi jiage haolaogong* 進佛門時敲三下鐘，下世嫁個好老公 (When entering the Buddhist door, the bell is being rung thrice; wish us to marry a good husband in the next life).

For the Ninghua women, the most desirable future is to marry a good husband. Marriage remains their destiny, yet these women are taking the initiative to actively negotiate for a better husband, and thus a better life, through a ritual. I argue that not only does the Jiezhu ritual move the initiate further beyond the three traditional attachments by giving her new identities, it also enables the woman to reclaim bonds that have been broken. Her reconnection to her natal mother and to her married-off daughter reestablishes the socially neglected mother-daughter bond.

The newspaper *Sanming qiaobao* 三明僑報 had an article about Jiezhu, which says: "The Ninghua Hakka women perform Jiezhu when they are getting old. When a woman reaches the menopausal stage she should enjoy some leisurely days. Some couples would immediately opt for separate rooms."[42] In China, the term "separating rooms [between a couple]" is a euphemistic hint of abstention from sexual activities.[43] Let us gratefully take that hint as a departure from marriage, which, I would say, moves the woman's identity from wife to new roles.

The changing body is not only physiological, but also visible. When the initiate puts on the Jiezhu costume, which is also the apparel for her funeral, she is going through a process of ritual death and rebirth, a renouncement of her past and a transformation into a new person. This new body is made visible in the costume and the Jiezhu accessories. This is the liminal stage of a rite of passage. She forsakes her previous identity and enters, in Victor Turner's sense, into a liminal position.[44] As the transformation takes place, the initiate is not only given a ritualistic identity but also a name that she will go by publicly and socially. She is given a Buddhist name by the ritual specialist who performs Jiezhu for her. This makes her a *nianfo mama*, whereby she claims a new identity beyond the roles of wife and mother.

Not only does the initiate become a *nianfo mama,* she is also admitted to a community of Jiezhu women. A major theme common to most women's rituals is the bonding among women.[45] Lesley A. Northup notes that both Susan Starr Sered and Diane Stein have argued that their "post-menopausal, post–child rearing status allows them [the elderly women] the time and the autonomy to study ritual matters and exercise the detailed care they often require."[46] When a woman reaches menopause, her children have probably come of age, thus leaving her more free time on her own to pursue her own needs, such as doing Amituofo recitation and joining social groups. The Jiezhu community is called a *peng* 棚, literally, a group of people under the roof of a shack. One *peng* usually consists of about twenty women who live in the same neighborhood or those who come from the same village but have now settled in the county seat. When a woman is about to do Jiezhu, she invites members of the *peng* in her neighborhood or the *peng* made up of the women from her home village to come to her Jiezhu ceremony. These Buddhist friends become witnesses of the rites as well as supporters of the initiate's future annual Nianfo rites. Their presence indicates the acceptance of the initiate as a member of this *peng*. The idea of mutual support among members of the *peng* highlights the attribute of sisterhood.

The emphasis on sisterhood is accentuated also in two verses that the Jiezhu women sing: *Shou ban liangyou jinqiao guo, shizhi jianjian jie Mituo* 手伴良友金橋過，十指尖尖接彌陀 (Crossing the golden bridge hand in hand with my good friends; receiving [A]mituo with our refined fingers). The bridge they cross is over the Minghe 冥河 (river of the underworld). First, the verses highlight one of the properties of Jiezhu as a women's ritual with a strong overtone of sisterhood by saying that the woman is being accompanied by her good friends to go across the golden bridge. Second, the Chinese believe that the dead would have to cross the Minghe by going over a bridge to make a complete break from the past. The bridge is a significant ritual symbol in the Jiezhu process. The initiate makes this trip with the support of her sisters. Their fingers are described as "refined," indicating a new life because the refined fingers symbolize femininity, youthfulness, and a life free from chores. The word *jie Mituo* 接彌陀 (receiving [A]mituofo) means to accept and put their faith in Amituofo. They believe that Amituofo will give them wealth (gold) when they receive him and are devoted to him; as such, Amituofo dwells in them. These verses echo the themes of holding fast to the faith of Amituofo and devoting time to doing rituals in the hope for a more fortunate rebirth in their next life. The Jiezhu woman is making a break from the past when she crosses the bridge. It is her wish that the trip be made with her good friends [of the Amituofo group]. This metaphor of crossing the bridge to the underworld is enacted in the rites of ascending and descending the bridge, around which all the Buddhist friends circumambulate with the initiate.

Presenting golden flowers (*song jinhua* 送金花) is a rite highlighting friendship and the unity among the members of the Jiezhu community.[47] The flowers are cut out from red (or sometimes yellow) paper, and they represent the counts of Amituofo-recitation. One flower represents the recitation of Amituofo three thousand and three hundred times, which is called one *tang* 趟. The Buddhist friends usually give at least two flowers to the initiate, which means they transfer two *tang* to the initiate. The Buddhist friends who are not able to attend the ritual may also send their flowers through those who come.

The initiate receives these flowers in a highly modest and humble manner. On her knees, she holds a tray with both hands, eyes downcast, waiting for her Buddhist friends to put flowers onto the tray. The Buddhist friends line up one by one while they are presenting her their flowers by putting them on the tray she is holding (see figure 9.2). They are at the same time greeting the initiate with auspicious wishes and blessings. Instead of using a tray to collect the flowers, the initiate may hold up her robe to form a pouch for receiving the flowers from her Buddhist friends.[48] After collecting all the flowers, the initiate carefully places the flowers over the altar. These flowers are to be kept in one of the *mālā* bags to be burned eventually in the initiate's funeral. This presentation of the gift of flowers is performed in a devout manner, giving a deeply solemn character to the Jiezhu members' symbolic support and acknowledgment of the initiate as a new member of the group. The rite also highlights the bonding among the members of the Amituofo group. The gift of paper flowers symbolizes the

Figure 9.2. *Song jinhua*: The Initiate Receiving Flowers from a Buddhist Friend (Photo credit: Neky Tak-ching Cheung; taken during Zhou Weijin's Jiezhu ritual on December 31, 2003)

transfer of spiritual merits from the fellow Buddhist friends to the initiate. As the spiritual merits of Amituofo recitation are believed to be valid only after one has done Jiezhu, the flowers can only be transferred by women who have done Jiezhu. Moreover, not only do the flowers represent spiritual merits, they are also signs of acceptance, attention, and caring for the new member of the group. The bonding is not only on earth; it goes on to the next life as the names of all the Buddhist friends are listed on the *wengao*, one copy of which is to be burned at the initiate's funeral to be carried to her next life.

A vegetarian lunch is served in the afternoon. All the *nianfo mama* express thanks to the people who prepared the food for them by saying, "Paying Homage to Amituofo, we hold on to your name at this time. Thanks be given to those who prepare the food at the kitchen, collecting the firewood and carrying the water are toilsome. Like us, they are also cultivated and will obtain enlightenment."[49]

After lunch, the Buddhist friends may choose to leave, but most would stay to do what they call *nuanfo* 暖佛, in which they do more Amituofo recitation so that they may present more flowers to the initiate. The *nuanfo* time is very relaxing. No longer do they wear their Jiezhu costumes; they just pin the *nianfo* handkerchief onto their outfit. It is not a continuous recitation time; they laugh, chat, and share information. It is run like a social gathering. Indeed, friendship is much emphasized. Everyone who has attended the ritual is given a bag of *jieyuan* 結緣 snacks. *Jie* means "to tie"; *yuan* means "destiny." Distributing *jieyuan* snacks literally means to tie up in destiny. In other words, the act builds up friendship. This theme of sisterhood and friendship is further enhanced by the communal meal.[50]

## Mother-Daughter Bonding

Margery Wolf remarks that even "under the best of circumstances in late traditional China, women were given minimal protection by their father's lineages or domestic organizations, for once married, they belonged to someone else."[51] Yes and no: yes, because the male members of a woman's lineage play no prominent role in the woman's Jiezhu ritual, and yet two women—her natal mother and her married-off daughter—are significantly involved. If the married-off daughter has been marginalized in the androcentric community, she is now the gifted agent in the menopausal ritual.

### Reuniting with the Mother and the Matrikin

In traditional Chinese thinking, a daughter, once she gets married, stops being a member of the family.[52] However, Jiezhu puts a great emphasis on the tie between the mother and the married-off daughter. The rite of "repaying mother's kindness" (*bao niang'en* 報娘恩) reconnects the initiate to her premarital identity with her natural mother. She pays her respects and expresses her gratitude to her mother for the hardship she had gone through in bringing her up. They chant the text of "Homage to the Buddha for Repaying Mother's Kindness" (*Zanfo bao niang'en* 贊佛報娘恩) during this rite.[53] If the mother of the initiate is alive, the initiate has to kneel down before her mother on a straw kneeling mat (*putuan* 蒲團) and present her with ten red packets. It should also be noted that if her mother has given her a pair of *putuan*, she must not kneel on them. They are to be kept at home as a remembrance of her mother. Ten packets represent the ten months during which she was in her mother's womb. The mother would give her one red packet in return. Alternatively, the initiate may offer only one red packet to her mother, but she must make sure that the amount she gives to her mother is bigger than what is being given to her.

If her mother has passed away, a pair of candles and three lit incense sticks, together with one bowl of rice and several bowls of vegetarian food are to be put on a small bench placed at the main entrance of the hall or home. She would kneel down and bow to the sky (*bai dangtian* 拜當天) and eat the rice and vegetable as a remembrance of being fed by her mother.

The presence of the matrilateral relatives and the gifts they bring are vital to the ceremony. Except for the cash that has to be provided by the husband and sons, all other gift items are to be given by female relatives or by the matrikin. The initiate receives from her natal family red candles with floral patterns (*huazhu* 花燭), bed sheets, fabric (*yiliao* 衣料), and shoes. But a notable quantity of edible items is to be provided by the matrikin. Marla Powers notes that the Oglala women are given groceries from their female relatives during mourning rituals.[54] Turner notes that Isoma rites require that a white pullet and other edible gifts be supplied by the female patient's matrikin.[55] The edible items are usually cassava rhizomes and sweet potato tubers, which represent "the body" of the female patient.[56] In Jiezhu, the other food items include sugar cake (*tanggao* 糖糕) and vegetarian food (*sucai* 素菜) that may include fragrant mushrooms (*xianggu* 香菇), red mushrooms (*honggu* 紅菇), flat noodles made of sweet potatoes (*digua fenpi* 地瓜粉皮), bean curd skin, dried bean curd and noodle, and friendship snacks. These gift items come in big quantities. The vegetarian food is to be cooked for the several meals served during Jiezhu. The friendship snacks should be sufficient to give everyone attending the ceremony a full bag to take home.[57] These edible gifts have several implications. First, they reaffirm the woman's role in taking charge of the food supply for the family. Xiaofei Kang identifies meals as an expression of women's religious piety.[58] Caroline Bynum argues that women's food behavior manifests their efforts to gain power and give meaning.[59] Traditional interpretation has been that medieval women hated their bodies and their sexuality.[60] Their food practices were to control their sexuality.[61] A woman's body is associated with food because breast milk was the human being's first and essential nourishment, and men are being nursed while women are nursing.[62] As a major source over which women have the most control, food is also a means through which women control their world. With the supposedly "weaker" gender having a lower social status and the implicit asexual identity associated with menopause, women use food as a means of control over their daily life. The edible gifts from the matrikin and the married-off daughters are symbolic of women's role as food provider.

Second, matrilineal support provides a sense of reassurance and security for the woman who has been married off as an "outsider" of the family she married into. A supportive and—better still—a well-off natal family helps boost the woman's status and helps her gain respect from the family she married into. The big piece of rice cake, mushrooms, candies, snacks, and other edible items given by her natal family (*niangjia* 娘家) are used for the various meals during the Jiezhu ceremony. These edible gifts are not to be kept by the recipient. The huge piece of rice cake is publicly displayed in a prominent place, typically over the main altar, for everyone to see. Therefore, the size and weight of the cake are subject to scrutiny by all the guests. Moreover, the cake would be cut up into pieces to be served to the guests during the intermittent meal times. The candies and snacks are distributed and packed into red plastic bags for all the guests to take home to share with their family members. The woman would feel herself to be "having face" (*you mianzi* 有面子) for being well supplied with food by her *niangjia*. These gifts are strategic in demonstrating the strong tie and support of the woman's *niangjia*.

Third, the gifts from the matrikin symbolically reconnect the woman to her previous identity with the parental family. The ritual gifts remind her obliquely of the roots from which she draws support and care, and emphasizes her alliance with that family. Furthermore, the members of her parental family are thought to have great influence over the health and welfare of the woman. Proper gifts being offered to her by the appropriate people will enhance the welfare, status, and prestige of the initiate. Finally, it shows that a marriage joins not only two individuals but also two families together, and the maintenance of the cohesion is enforced in the gift-giving ethic in Jiezhu.[63] In this system, women play an important role in maintaining interlineage relations.

## Reuniting with the Married-Off Daughter

While the initiate is a married-off daughter to her natal family, she herself also has her own daughter who has been married off. Jiezhu brings her married-off daughter back. In the traditional Chinese concept, a woman who has married is supposed to have left her parental family and becomes a member of her husband's family. The *waijia nü* 外嫁女 (a daughter married off) is no longer considered as a member of her natal family because she has been married "out." This concept continues to a large extent in present-day Chinese society. Rubie S. Watson notes that a family from the New Territories in Hong Kong found it natural to say that daughters "are born looking out; they belong to others."[64] In China, a daughter is also seen as someone who "belongs to others." However, it is interesting to note how this tradition is played out in the gift ethics in Jiezhu. This *waijia nü* connects with her natal family through her mother. That is why the term that describes the natal family of a *waijia nü* is *niangjia* 娘家 (literally, the mother's family).[65] When a *waijia nü* visits her natal family, she is *hui niangjia* 回娘家 (returning to her mother's family) but not to her father's family. Keeping this concept in mind, I proceed to analyze the interplay of gift-giving and the married-off daughter.

As the initiate is reconnected to her natal family, her married-off daughter is likewise being reconnected to her through Jiezhu. At this point, it is necessary to list the ritual items that the initiate must receive from her married-off daughter. One of them is the *mālā* bag. The Jiezhu woman needs two *mālā* bags.[66] One is to be given by her married-off daughter, the other by her own mother or someone from her *niangjia*.

One of the bags is for keeping the *mālā* that accompanies her as she attends her Buddhist friends' annual *nianfo*. The other bag keeps the *wengao* and the golden flowers. The *wengao* is a ritual document certifying her performance of Jiezhu and annual *nianfo*. The golden flowers represent the counts of Amituofo recitation. This bag is kept at home and will be burned at the woman's funeral.

Another item that the married-off daughter has to give her mother is the lotus shoes the initiate wears at her Jiezhu ritual. As mentioned previously, the shoes are made of cloth (*buxie*) and are exquisitely embroidered with pink lotus floral patterns. The number of lotus flowers varies from four to the more luxurious twenty-four. The greater the number of lotus flowers, the more expensive the shoes will be. The flowers can be big or small or in a combination of big ones and small ones. The *mālā* and the *mālā* bags, and even the shoes, are easily available at shops and market stalls that sell Buddhist-related goods. Exquisite, nicely made shoes have to be tailor-made by special shoemakers.[67]

The Amituofo recitation handkerchief (*baijin* 拜巾)[68] is another item that must be given by her married-off daughter. Unlike the Jiezhu costume, which is in a plain solid color of blue or black, the *nianfo* handkerchiefs come in all sorts of floral patterns and colors. I have seen them in green, red, and light blue with multicolored patterns. There is a small triangular patch of colored cloth with a buttonhole-knot at one of the corners that can be buttoned up to the right shoulder (*jin* 襟) of the Buddhist top. This handkerchief is about twenty inches square and hangs down from the shoulder to reach one's thigh. When the woman is doing Amituofo recitation in a sitting position, the handkerchief is neatly spread over the woman's lap so that the *mālā* is kept "clean" because it rests on the handkerchief. Instead of wearing the Jiezhu costume, sometimes the women simply put on the *nianfo* handkerchief atop their regular clothes when they do Amituofo recitation.

The initiate also needs a pair of straw kneeling mats (*putuan*), to be woven by her married-off daughter. If the mother of the initiate is alive, she will also give the initiate an extra pair of straw kneeling mats. However, the kneeling mats from the mother are more symbolic than functional, as the initiate never actually kneels on this pair of mats. The personification of the kneeling mats is made apparent in the rite of "giving thanks to the kneeling mats" (*xie putan* 謝蒲團). Kneeling on the mats given by the mother would be seen as unfilial. The mats serve as a reminder of the heritage of religiosity and the blood connections with her mother.

It is different with the pair given by her married-off daughter, whose filial piety is symbolized by the straw mats she personally wove for her mother to kneel upon. Each mat has a handle that makes it easy for the women to carry it about to the annual *nianfo* of their Buddhist friends and to the Jiezhu ritual of new members. The initiate needs also a piece of white cotton cloth called *baidang* 拜襠 for putting over the kneeling mat when she does her worship.[69] The *baidang* must also be made and given by her married-off daughter. The *foming* 佛名 (Buddhist name) of the Jiezhu woman is written on the top edge of the *baidang* in the following words: *Geifu xiuyin xinnü [foming]* 給付修因信女[佛名] (presented to [the Buddhist name] woman follower by the ritual specialist). The dharma seal (*fayin* 法印) of the ritual specialist is also affixed on the *baidang*.

An important ritual food that must be given by the married-off daughter is a big Chinese-style sugar cake called *tanggao*,[70] which is made of glutinous rice and weighs at least 25 to 30 catties.[71] This cake is cut up into small slices to be eaten as a snack during the Jiezhu ceremony and is also distributed to relatives and friends as part of the *jieyuan* snacks for them to take home. The *jieyuan* snacks usually include fruits such as apples and mandarin oranges plus various kinds of candies, biscuits, peanuts, and the like. The snacks are to be distributed to relatives and friends who attend the ceremony. The married-off daughter typically also gives her mother a regular outfit of any style and shoes for daily wear. A *jinggai* 經蓋 (canon cover) is an optional luxurious gift that the married-off daughter may acquire for her mother. A *jinggai* is a piece of double-layered silk, mostly embroidered with colorful patterns, used to cover the canons or liturgical texts during ritual events when the texts are not being recited.[72]

## The Married-Off Daughter Comrade

To understand the significance of the gifts given by the *waijia nü*, it is necessary to know what items the woman has to buy for herself in order to make sense of the rationale of why the *waijia nü*'s gifts must never be bought by the woman herself. The items that the Jiezhu woman buys for herself are the Jiezhu costume, the silver rings, plates, and pins. It is important to bear in mind that these items are all for identification purposes. When the initiate puts on the Jiezhu costume, she is transformed into a new person. The silver plate has her newly given Buddhist name and is to be attached to her *mālā*. The ring and the pin make her status known as being a woman who has done Jiezhu. One thing common to these items is that they are all of a dull, solid color of black, white, or blue.

In contrast, all the bright and colorful gift items, including *mālā* bags, lotus-pattern shoes, Amituofo recitation handkerchief, and the canon cover, have to be given to her by her married-off daughter. The rule is that the initiate must not buy the *mālā* bags for herself. It is best to have her married-off daughter(s) give her the these gifts, but in case she does not have one, the preference goes in this order: an unmarried daughter or her (nominally) adopted daughter (*gannü'er* 乾女兒), her sister, or any female relative who is younger than herself.

This contrast of dull, solid-color items (brought by the initiate) versus the colorful, beautifully patterned items (given by the married-off daughters) indicates subversive references. This also has to do with "choice." The Jiezhu costume is the apparel that the woman will be dressed in for her funeral. In traditional Chinese society, the women admit their advancement in age by wearing dark, solid-colored dress. A woman has no choice but to abide by this tradition when accepting the Jiezhu costume. However, she does have a way to make her own choice when it comes to the gifts given by her married-off daughter; although the items are gifts, actually the women have the choice of color, pattern, and even style, because she may express her preference to her daughter. The *nianfo* handkerchiefs may come in all sorts of colors such as green or blue, with patterns and with a bright-colored triangular knot at one corner for tying up on the Jiezhu costume. Moreover, the size of the *nianfo* handkerchief is so large that once it is put on, it covers quite a big part of the dull-colored Jiezhu outfit.[73] And even if the woman chooses a *nianfo* handkerchief of a solid dull color, it is her own choice. The exercise of the woman's own choice works in like manner with respect to the new outfit and shoes as part of the gifts given by the married-off daughter. To be in a position to make her own choice, though indirectly in the case of Jiezhu, is also a form of power for these women.

The *mālā* bags are red with colorful floral patterns. The red or green lotus shoes and the canon cover are also exquisitely pretty and exotic. This also reflects the Hakka women's love of chromatic outfits. Besides allowing the woman a choice of beautiful items according to her preference, an element of subversion is at work in a subtle manner. It is also noteworthy that the *mālā* bags of men have a black or blue background color. Black and blue are seen as funerary colors and are seen as suitable for older people. In contrast, those of the women are red, which generally represents joy and happiness and is seen as suitable for younger women. It should also be noted that the Jiezhu men do not have lotus shoes or *nianfo* handkerchiefs, as the women do.

A corollary to this line of thinking is the symbolic character of the pair of *putuan*. The emphasis on having a pair of *putuan* woven by the married-off daughter and/or another pair by her mother suggests several meanings. *Putuan* are commonplace in temples, monasteries, and nunneries, and are functional, for they protect the knees of the worshippers. They have a lowly position and are always laid on the ground, seldom being noticed. Women, like *putuan*, are perceived as functional: they are needed but are placed in a secondary if not lowly status. Jiezhu turns the tables by giving the lowly object two rites. One rite is to worship them, and the other is to give thanks to them. There are no liturgical texts relating to *putuan*, but there are songs that the women sing during the two rites. They worship the *putuan* for a humble and an open heart, as well as a purified body, and they thank the *putuan* for bringing perfect friendship.[74] The initiate never kneels on the pair of *putuan* given by her mother because they represent the mother persona.

As mentioned earlier, the married-off daughter is considered an ex-member of the family. Her position of being an ex-member gives her room to provide the initiate with all the beautiful accessories to downplay the sense of agedness created by the Jiezhu costume. This subversive tone is subtly played out because it is after all not someone *in* the family who defies the tradition. Borrowing from Wolf, who once remarked, "A worthless girl is no longer quite as worthless as she once was,"[75] I would call her the married-off daughter comrade.

## Conclusion

Some women saw female birth as a misfortune; to give birth to a female child is another curse, to both herself and her daughter. Another Jiezhu woman, Feng Wanying, recounted that in her younger days she knew of a woman who had given birth to a baby girl. The woman put the baby girl on the roadside in the hope that someone would take it. Having waited for one day, she brought the baby home and tried again the next day.[76]

The rules prescribed in Jiezhu no doubt acknowledge female negativities. A woman is penalized if she gets pregnant after she has done Jiezhu.

The merits of Amituofo recitation would be nullified; she would also have to recompense her fellow Buddhist friends with towels/aprons, which has a symbolic cleansing implication. This requirement has a humiliating nature in its emphasis on the recurrence of impurities attached to women and women's bodily discharge.[77] The women are participating, probably unknowingly, in the social construction of gender definitions and relationships. Reflecting females' subordination to males, the women do not get the *mālā* directly from the ritual specialist. The *mālā* is passed from the ritual specialist to the husband and/or other members of the family before it goes to the *nianfo mama* and then to the woman. Moreover, the position of ritual specialist remains in the hands of men. Furthermore, the *mālā* would have to be passed on to the woman's eldest daughter-in-law by the time the daughter-in-law is about to perform her Jiezhu. The tradition of having the eldest daughter-in-law inherit the *mālā* emphasizes the role of women in continuing and upholding the uterine family. Finally, women never actually "retire" from their domestic work. The woman as the protagonist reinforces her centrality in the domestic realm—the family.

I argue, however, that the involvement of the initiate's natal mother and married-off daughter makes a witty twist on the apparent conformity to the traditional androcentric family values. Jiezhu brings the woman into a new phase of being. She is given a Buddhist name and establishes bonding with a community of Jiezhu women. Integral to these new identities, Jiezhu juxtaposes the initiate's attachments to her husband and her son with her reconnection to her mother and her married-off daughter. The only rite dedicated solely to a single person—the initiate's natal mother—*bao niang'en* (repaying mother's kindness) emphasizes her filial bonding to her mother and notably not her father. This is a ritualistic enactment of a woman's bonding to her mother instead of to her father. Parallel to this endorsement, the married-off daughter also comes to her mother's Jiezhu ceremony with colorful gifts that downplay the agedness that the menopausal rite proposes. In China, a married-off daughter's homecoming is called returning to her mother's family instead of returning to her father's family. Not only does the Jiezhu ritual, as a strategic mode of action, move the initiate further beyond the traditional attachments by giving her new identities, it also enables the woman to reclaim bonds that have been taken away. Her ritual reconnection to her natal mother and to her married-off daughter reinstates the mother-daughter bonds. The woman's contributions as a wife, a mother, and a daughter are valued and celebrated in the Jiezhu ceremony. I conclude that Jiezhu should be appreciated not only for its celebration of an oft-neglected life crisis of women but, more importantly, for its nonconfrontational politics. Beneath the apparent conformity to the androcentric supremacy, these women express their power within the limits of their traditional politics. Not only do they actively pursue a more fortunate rebirth and establish friendship and sisterhood among the Jiezhu women, they also celebrate motherhood and move further beyond the traditional three attachments to three generations of mother-daughter bonding through ritualistic endorsement.

## Notes

*I am grateful to Professors Jinhua Jia and Xiaofei Kang for their advice and suggestions that have been most helpful in improving the chapter.

1. Rita Gross, *Feminism and Religion: An Introduction* (Boston: Beacon Press, 1996), 205.

2. Barbara G. Walker, *Women's Rituals: A Source Book* (New York: Harper & Row, 1990), 193.

3. Anne-Marie Korte, "Female Blood Rituals: Cultural-Anthropological Findings and Feminist-Theological Reflections," in Kristin De Troyer et al., eds., *Wholly Woman, Holy Blood: A Feminist Critique of Purity and Impurity* (Harrisburg, PA: Trinity Press International, 2003), 183–84.

4. Korte, "Female Blood Rituals," 184–85. See also Rosemary Radford Reuther, *Women-Church: Theology and Practice of Feminist Liturgical Communities* (San Francisco: Harper & Row, 1986).

5. Ann Waltner, "A Princess Comes of Age: Gender, Life-Cycle and Royal Ritual in Song Dynasty China," in Joëlle Rollo-Koster, ed., *Medieval and Early Modern Ritual: Formalized Behavior in Europe, China and Japan* (Leiden: Koninklijke Brill NV, 2002), 35–56.

6. Neky Tak-ching Cheung, *Women's Ritual in China: Jiezhu (Receiving Buddhist Prayer Beads) Performed by Menopausal Women in Ninghua, Western Fujian* (New York: Edwin Mellen Press, 2008).

7. For a detailed description of the social and religious background of Ninghua, see Cheung, *Women's Ritual in China*, 15–64.

8. In my previous work, I proffered that Jiezhu might have begun sometime during the Ming (1368–1644) and Qing (1644–1911) periods. See Cheung, *Women's Ritual in China*, 107.

9. On how folk religious practices in the post-Mao revival help reinforce traditional gender inequalities in rural Guangdong, see Pui-lam Law, "The Revival of Folk Religion and Gender Relationships in Rural China: A Preliminary Observation," *Asian Folklore Studies* 64 (2005): 89–109.

10. John Lagerwey calls this ritual "Receive the Rosary" or the "Rosary Initiation," both of which are excellent translations that provide the ritual with an explicit and clear meaning to readers. See Lagerwey and Yang Yanjie, eds., *Lineages,*

*the Economy and Customs in Ninghua County (II)*, Traditional Hakka Society Series, vol. 24 (Hong Kong: International Hakka Studies Association, 2005), 28. However, this chapter uses the Chinese term Jiezhu on the following basis. First, the use of a rosary, which comes from the Latin for "crown roses," is specifically a Christian ritual. The rosary is closely identified with Mary, the mother of Jesus. Moreover, the number and arrangement of the Christian and the Buddhist beads, not to mention the meaning, are quite different. Finally, the use of Buddhist beads may have predated Christian use.

11. Jiezhu is also called Nazhu in Quanshang zhen 泉上鎮, Ninghua, as I was told in my interview with the ritual specialists and other informants during June 10–14, 2002.

12. Jiezhu is also called Guozhu in Hucun zhen 湖村鎮, Ninghua; see Deng Guangchang, Huang Ruiyi, and Zhang Guoyu, "The Worship of Dingguang in Hucun, Ninghua," in John Lagerwey and Yang Yanjie, eds., *Customary Religion and Society in West-Central Fujian*, Traditional Hakka Society Series, vol. 11 (Hong Kong: International Hakka Studies Association, 2000), 208.

13. A *mālā* (or *mālyā* in Sanskrit) is a string of beads generally used for keeping count of Amituofo recitation. A *mālā* is sometimes called *nianzhu* 念珠 (prayer beads), *fozhu* 佛珠 (Buddha's beads), or *puti(zi)* 菩提[子] (Bodhi seed) in scriptures.

14. For the full text of *Fenzhu jing*, see Cheung, *Women's Ritual in China*, 267–70.

15. For the full text of *Guozhu jing*, see Cheung, *Women's Ritual in China*, 270–73.

16. This is a one-day Jiezhu program. A Jiezhu ritual may also last for two or three days. I have not observed a three-day ritual myself. I was told by informants and ritual specialists that there will be multiple penitential litanies and reciting sutra sessions for a multiday Jiezhu. See Cheung, *Women's Ritual in China*, 119–63, for a full list and description of the ritual program.

17. The Jiezhu ritual of Zhou Weijin (December 30–31, 2003), Sun Lanxiang (February 20–21, 2004), and Zhang Jingyun (October 16–17, 2006) started at midnight; therefore there was a break between the first and the second sessions. For the privacy of the informants, Chinese characters are not given for their names throughout this study.

18. The Jiezhu ritual of Zhang Fengnü (May 16–17, 2004) started at about 3:45 a.m.; therefore the second session followed through the first session with breakfast in between.

19. Liu Shanqun 劉善群, *Kejia lisu* 客家禮俗 (Fuzhou: Fujian jiaoyu chubanshe, 1995), 146.

20. Liu, *Kejia lisu*, 146.

21. See also Lagerwey and Yang, eds., *Lineages*, 28.

22. Liu, *Kejia lisu*, 145.

23. See David W. Chappell, "The Formation of the Pure Land Movement in China: Tao-Ch'o and Shan-tao," in James Foard, ed., *The Pure Land Tradition: History and Development* (Berkeley: The Regents of the University of California, 1996), 159.

24. Margery Wolf, *Women and the Family in Rural Taiwan* (California: Stanford University Press, 1972).

25. A *daifo mama* is a veteran *nianfo mama* who serves as the leader of the *nianfo* community. See later in this chapter for more about the *daifo mama.*

26. It should be noted that a *xianghuo ting* is different from a *citang* 祠堂. A *citang* functions both as a place to worship the ancestors and as a court for family or domestic tribunals. A *xianghuo ting* keeps the dead body before it is delivered for cremation or burial, something that a *citang* never functions as. A *citang* keeps ancestral tablets, which are never found in a *xianghuo ting*. For the purpose of differentiating the two places, I call *xianghuo ting* the incense lineage hall and *citang* the ancestral hall. A *xianghuo ting* in Ninghua is a hall built by a number of families, usually five or six, that belong to the same clan (*jiazu* 家族). These families usually live close to one another. *Xianghuo ting* functions as a communal place for these families to hold both *hongshi* 紅事 (joyous and festive events, such as a wedding, a newborn's completion of its first month of life) and *baishi* 白事 (funerary events). A *xianghuo ting* is sometimes a *zuwu* 祖屋, that is, a house inherited from a forefather and kept by its successors to be used as a communal place that serves the same purposes of a *xianghuo ting*.

27. I observed the Jiezhu ritual of Sun Lanxiang on February 20, 2004, and that of Zhang Jingyun on October 17, 2006, both of which took place at home.

28. A remark made by ritual specialist Zeng Yuanchuan during an interview with him on August 24, 2006.

29. For the content of a *shenxian pai*, see Cheung, *Women's Ritual in China*, 276–77.

30. For the full text of the *Nama Fofa dian xiang jing*, see Cheung, *Women's Ritual in China*, 137.

31. The ten bowls (*shiwan*) are edible offerings. They are all vegetarian food items such as bean curd, rice-flour noodle, mushrooms, eggplant, cabbage, lotus fruit, gourd (*gua* 瓜), *jinzhencai* 金針菜 (a day lily), *yin'er* 銀耳 (an edible tree fungus considered a tonic), and *fuzhu* 腐竹 (tightly rolled dried skin of bean milk), each in one bowl. The ten dishes (*shidie*) are offered to the deities. They are *xiang* 香 (fragrance), *hua* 花 (flower), *deng* 燈 (lamp, usually a burning lamp wick in a small dish filled with lamp oil), *tu* 塗 (ointment), *guo* 果 (fruit), *cha* 茶 (tea), *shi* 食 (food), *bao* 寶 (treasure, for example, a gold/silver bracelet), *zhu* 珠 (typically a *mālā*), and *yi* 衣 (clothes, for example, a piece of handkerchief or towel).

32. It was the husband who did the transfer of offerings in the *shang dagong* rite in the Jiezhu ritual of Zhou Weijin.

33. The reference to sins here is a generic term that may include any kind of transgressions; female uncleanness can be understood to be one of them.

34. For a sample of *wengao* showing where the names of the Buddhist friends are listed, see Cheung, *Women's Ritual in China*, 278.

35. Lotus is one of the symbols that represent Buddha, and it is also an emblem of grace and purity. The Buddha and the Bodhisattva in Chinese sculptures and paintings always sit on a lotus seat.

36. The *mālā* and the *mālā* bags, and even the shoes, are quite easily available at shops and market stalls that sell Buddhist-related goods. I have also seen some women selling them in front of the Dongyue 東岳 Temple during its festival. However, exquisite, nicely made shoes have to be tailor-made by special shoemakers who make lotus shoes to order.

37. A ritual specialist, Wu Ruiyang, told to me how the *mālā* should be ritually handled in such cases: within three days of her death, a piece of black roof tile is to be placed over a brick and the *mālā* is to be put in the concave side of the tile. Some oil would be put over it; then it would be covered by another piece of black roof tile. The open ends of the two pieces of roof tiles have to be covered by dregs from soybean milk makings (*doufu zha* 豆腐渣). It is to be burned by her daughter or her daughter-in-law at the entrance of the main hall of their home. Then the ashes will be placed inside a Buddhist mansion made of paper, which will be set over a pile of straw to be burned at her funeral service. A Jiezhu woman from Chengnan 城南, Wu Qiugen, mentioned to me a similar rite of handling the *mālā*.

38. See also Li Genshui 李根水 and Luo Huarong 羅華榮, eds., *Ninghua Kejia minsu* 寧化客家民俗 (Beijing: Zhongguo huaqiao chubanshe, 2000), 24.

39. See Li and Luo, *Ninghua Kejia minsu*, 24.

40. The Jiezhu ceremony of Zhou Weijin took place on December 30–31, 2003.

41. See Li and Luo, *Ninghua Kejia minsu*, 18.

42. The article was published on page 11 of *Sanming qiaobao* on November 30, 2002.

43. Chen Fenggen, who did Jiezhu when she was fifty-three, told me that after Jiezhu, one should not have *ernü siqing* 兒女私情 (literally, romance between men and women but referred to as "sex" here). My interview with Chen took place on August 15, 2003.

44. Victor Turner, *Ritual Process* (Chicago: Aldine, 1995; 1969 rpt.), 95–96.

45. See Catherine Bell, *Ritual: Perspective and Dimensions* (New York: Oxford University Press, 1997), 238.

46. Lesley A. Northup, *Ritualizing Women* (Cleveland, OH: Pilgrim Press, 1997); see also Susan Starr Sered, *Women as Religious Experts: The Religious Lives of Elderly Jewish Women in Jerusalem* (New York: University Press, 1994),78; Diane Stein, *Casting the Circle* (Freedom, CA: Crossing, 1990), 86.

47. It is also called *song xianghua* 送香花 (presenting fragrant flowers), or *song lianhua* 送蓮花 (presenting lotus flowers). Brigitte Baptandier points out a possible comparison of *song xianghua* with the Daoist ritual of *zaihua* 栽花 (cultivating flowers) in her review on my book *Women's Ritual in China*, in *Journal of Chinese Studies* 51 (2010): 402.

48. Instead of using a tray, Zhang Jingyun held up his Buddhist robe with his hands for receiving the flowers. A man who has done Jiezhu would become a *nianfo gonggong* 念佛公公 (literally, an Amituofo recitation grandfather); see Cheung, *Women's Ritual in China*, 159–60, about men co-opting Jiezhu.

49. Xiaofei Kang also notes that working in the kitchen is seen as an effort to gain religious merits; see Kang, "Rural Women, Old Age, and Temple Work: A Case from Northwestern Sichuan," *China Perspectives* 4 (2009): 49.

50. For details of the communal meal, see Cheung, *Women's Ritual in China*, 218–19.

51. Margery Wolf, "Beyond the Patrilineal Self: Constructing Gender in China," in Roger T. Ames, ed., *Self as Person in Asian Theory and Practice* (Albany: State of University New York Press, 1994), 252.

52. Wolf, *Women and the Family*, 32–41.

53. See Cheung, *Women's Ritual in China*, 148–49, for the ritual text.

54. Marla N. Powers, *Oglala Women: Myth, Ritual, and Reality* (Chicago: University of Chicago Press, 1986), 196. See also Northup, *Ritualizing Women*, 20.

55. Turner, *Ritual Process*, 21.

56. Turner, *Ritual Process*, 21.

57. Zhang Enting 張恩庭 mentions that the friendship (*jieyuan*) snacks are distributed to the relatives and friends to thank them for their attendance and that *jieyuan* means *weicheng fodao, guangjie shanyuan* 未成佛道, 廣結善緣 (not yet being able to attain the way of the Buddha, just to make benevolent connections with people); see Zhang, *Ninghua siguan* 寧化寺觀 (Ninghua: Ninghua xian caise yinshuachang youxian gongxi, 2001), 17.

58. See Kang, "Rural Women, Old Age, and Temple Work," 49.

59. Caroline Walker Bynum, *Holy Feast and Holy Fast: The Religious Significance of Food to Medieval Women* (Berkeley: University of California Press, 1987), 227–37.

60. Bynum, *Holy Feast and Holy Fast*, 208.

61. Bynum, *Holy Feast and Holy Fast*, 216–18.

62. Bynum, *Holy Feast and Holy Fast*, 270.

63. For an easy reference to the gift items involved in Jiezhu, see Cheung, *Women's Ritual in China*, 264–66.

64. See also Rubie S. Watson, "Chinese Bridal Laments: The Claims of a Dutiful Daughter," in James L. Watson and Rubie S. Watson, eds., *Village Life in Hong Kong: Politics, Gender, and Ritual in the New Territories* (Hong Kong: Chinese University Press, 2004), 224.

65. See also Ellen R. Judd, "Niangjia: Chinese Women and Their Natal Families," *Journal of Asian Studies* 48.3 (1989): 525–44.

66. Also called *fodai* 佛袋 (Buddhist bag) or *zhudai* 珠袋 (bag for the prayer beads).

67. See previous discussion of ritual accessories for more details about lotus shoes.

68. *Baijin* is also called *nianfo shoujin* 念佛壽巾 (Amituofo recitation long-life hanky).

69. The length of a *baidang* is 3 *chi* 尺 and 8 *cun* 寸 (a little over 90 cm), and its width would be the width of the roll of cloth.

70. Also called *niangao* 年糕 (literally, New Year cake).

71. One catty equals approximately 0.5 kilograms.

72. It is not easy to get a tailor-made *jinggai* these days. I have interviewed a ninety-year-old woman who used to make beautiful and exquisite canon covers, but she is now too old to do that.

73. See figures 7 and 8 in Cheung, *Women's Ritual in China*, for photos illustrating the dramatic difference in appearance between a woman with and a woman without a *nianfo* handkerchief over her Buddhist robe.

74. See Cheung, *Women's Ritual in China*, 154, for the words of giving thanks to *putuan*, plate 35 for the photo showing the *nianfo mama* giving thanks to *putuan*.

75. Wolf, *Women and the Family*, 99.

76. The interview took place on August 15, 2003.

77. For more discussions on the concept of female pollution, see, for example, Mary Douglas, *Purity and Danger: An Analysis of Concepts of Pollution and Taboo* (New York: Routledge, 1966); and Emily M. Ahern, "The Power and Pollution of Chinese Women," in Margery Wolf and Roxane Witke, eds., *Women in Chinese Society* (Stanford: Stanford University Press, 1975), 193–214. For taboos associated with Jiezhu and negative beliefs concerning female sexuality and ritual, see Cheung, *Women's Ritual in China*, 167–80.

# Bibliography


Abe, Stanley. "Art and Practice in a Fifth-Century Chinese Buddhist Cave Temple." *Ars Orientalis* 20 (1990): 1–31.

Adamek, Wendi. "The Literary Lives of Nuns: Poems Inscribed on a Memorial Niche for the Tang Nun Benxing." *T'ang Studies* 27.1 (2009): 40–65.

Ahern, Emily M. "The Power and Pollution of Chinese Women." In Margery Wolf and Roxane Witke, eds., *Women in Chinese Society*, 193–214.

Ahmed, Leila. *Women and Gender in Islam*. New Haven and London: Yale University Press, 1992.

Allan, Sarah. "The Great One, Water, and the *Laozi*: New Light from Guodian." *T'oung Pao* 89 (2003): 237–85.

Allès, Elisabeth. "Une organisation de l'islam au féminin: le personnel des mosquées féminines en Chine." *Lettre d'information*, Programme de Recherches Interdisciplinaires sur le Monde Músulman Périphérique 14 (1994): 1–12.

———. *Músulmans de Chine: Une anthropologie des Hui du Henan*. Paris: EHESS, 2000.

Ames, Roger T. "Taoism and the Androgynous Ideal." In Richard W. Guisso and Stanley Johannesen, eds., *Women in China*, 21–45.

Asad, Talal. *Genealogies of Religion: Discipline and Reasons of Power in Christianity and Islam*. Baltimore and London: Johns Hopkins University Press, 1993.

Ashiwa, Yoshiko, and David Wank, eds. *Making Religion, Making the State: The Politics of Religion in Modern China*. Stanford: Stanford University Press, 2009.

Ashmore, Lida Scott. *The South China Mission of the American Baptist Foreign Mission Society of Its First Cycle of Sixty Years*. Shanghai: Methodist Publishing House, 1920.

*Bai Kong liutie* 白孔六帖. *Siku quanshu*.

Baptandier, Brigitte. *The Lady of Linshui: A Chinese Female Cult*. Trans. Kristin Fryklund. Stanford: Stanford University Press, 2008.

Barlow, Tani E., ed. *Gender Politics in Modern China: Writing and Feminism*. Durham: Duke University Press, 1993.

———. *The Question of Women in Chinese Feminism*. Durham: Duke University Press, 2004.

Barrett, T. H. *Taoism under the T'ang*. London: Wellsweep Press, 1996.

Bastid-Bruguiere, Marianne. "Liang Qichao yu zongjiao wenti" 梁啓超與宗教問題. In Hazama Naoki, ed., *Liang Qichao, Mingzhi Riben, Xifang* 梁啓超, 明治日本, 西方, 400–57.

Bays, Daniel, ed. *Christianity in China from the Eighteenth Century to the Present.* Stanford: Stanford University Press, 1996.

Becher, Jeanne, ed. *Women, Religion and Sexuality*. Philadelphia: Trinity Press International, 1991.

Beck, Lois, and Nikki Keddie, eds. *Women in the Muslim World*. Cambridge, MA: Harvard University Press, 1978.

Bell, Catherine. *Ritual: Perspective and Dimensions*. New York: Oxford University Press, 1997.

Benn, Charles D. *The Cavern-Mystery Transmission: A Taoist Ordination Rite of A.D. 711*. Honolulu: University of Hawaii Press, 1991.

———. "Daoist Ordination and Zhai Rituals." In Livia Kohn, ed., *Daoism Handbook,* 311–22.

Benn, James. *Burning for Buddha: Self-Immolations in Chinese Buddhism.* Studies in East Asian Buddhism 19, Koroda Institute. Honolulu: University of Hawaii Press, 2007.

Bergmann, Sigurd. *God in Context: A Survey of Contextual Theology*. Aldershot and Burlington: Ashgate, 2003.

Bernos, Marcel, ed. *Sexualité et religion*. Paris: Les Éditions du Cerf, 1988.

Birrell, Anne. *Chinese Mythology: An Introduction*. Baltimore: Johns Hopkins University Press, 1999.

Bloch, Maurice. "Death, Women and Power." In Maurice Bloch and Jonathan Perry, eds., *Death and the Regeneration of Life*, 211–30.

Bloch, Maurice, and Jonathan Perry, eds. *Death and the Regeneration of Life*. New York: Cambridge University Press, 1982.

Bokenkamp, Stephen R. "Time after Time: Taoist Apocalyptic History and the Founding of the T'ang Dynasty." *Asia Major* 3.7 (1994): 59–88.

———. *Early Daoist Scriptures*. Berkeley: University of California Press, 1997.

———. "Tianshidao hunyin yishi 'heqi' zai Shangqing Lingbao xuepai de yanbian" 天師道婚姻儀式"合氣"在上清靈寶學派的演變. *Daojia wenhua yanjiu* 道家文化研究 16 (1999): 241–48.

———. "Simple Twists of Fate: The Daoist Body and Its Ming." In Christopher Lupke, ed., *The Magnitude of Ming*, 151–68.

Boltz, Judith M. "In Homage to T'ien-fei." *Journal of the American Oriental Society* 106.1 (1986): 211–32.

Bourdieu, Pierre. *Outline of a Theory of Practice*. Cambridge: Cambridge University Press, 1977.

Bray, Francesca. *Technology and Gender: Fabrics of Power in Late Imperial China.* Berkeley: University of California Press, 1997.

Brière, Octave. "Sou Mei [Su Mei] ou Lou I [Lu Yi]: ses contes et sa critique." *Wanxiang* [Toutes choses] 4.4 (1943): 920–33.

Brink, Judy, and Joan Mencher, eds. *Mixed Blessings: Gender and Religious Fundamentalism Cross Culturally*. New York: Routledge, 1997.

Brough, John. "A Kharosthi Inscription from China." *Bulletin of the School of Oriental and African Studies* 24 (1961): 517–30.

Butler, Judith. *Gender Trouble*. New York: Routledge, 1990.

———. *Excitable Speech: A Politics of the Performative*. New York: Routledge, 1997.

Buswell, Robert E. "The 'Short-Cut' Approach of K'an-hua Meditation: The Evolution of a Practical Subitism in Chinese Zen Buddhism." In Peter N. Gregory, ed., *Sudden and Gradual*, 321–77.

Bynum, Caroline Walker. *Holy Feast and Holy Fast: The Religious Significance of Food to Medieval Women*. Berkeley: University of California Press, 1987.

Cabezón, José Ignacio, ed. *Buddhism, Sexuality, and Gender*. Albany: State University of New York Press, 1992.

Cahill, Suzanne. "Sex and the Supernatural in Medieval China: Cantos on the Transcendent Who Presides over the River." *Journal of the American Oriental Society* 105.2 (1985): 197–220.

———. *Transcendence and Divine Passion: The Queen Mother of the West in Medieval China*. Stanford: Stanford University Press, 1993.

———. *Divine Traces of the Daoist Sisterhood*. Magdalena, NM: Three Pines Press, 2006.

Calef, Susan. "Charting New Territory: Religion and the 'Gender-Critical Turn.' " *Journal of Religion and Society* 5 (2009): 1–5.

Campany, Robert Ford. "On the Very Idea of Religions in the Modern West and Early Medieval China." *History of Religions* 42.4 (2003): 287–319.

———. *Making Transcendents: Ascetics and Social Memory in Early Medieval China*. Honolulu: University of Hawaii Press, 2009.

Cao Heng 曹珩 (fl. 1632). "Nügong quebing" 女功卻病. In *Baosheng miyao* 保生祕要 (1632), collected in *Daoyuan yiqi* 道原一氣 (1634).

*Cao Ye* 草野. *Xiandai zhongguo nüzuojia* 現代中國女作家. *Shanghai: Renwen shudian, 1932.*

Carlitz, Katherine. "Shrines, Governing-Class Identity, and the Cult of Widow Fidelity in Mid-Ming Jiangnan." *Journal of Asian Studies* 56.3 (1997): 612–40.

Carr, Anne. *Transforming Grace: Christian Tradition and Women's Experience*. San Francisco: Harper & Row, 1988.

Carver, Terrell. *Gender Is Not a Synonym for Women*. Boulder, CO: Lynne Rienner Publishers, 1996.

Cass, Victoria B. "Female Healers in the Ming and the Lodge of Ritual and Ceremony." *Journal of the American Oriental Society* 106.1 (1986): 233–40.

———. *Dangerous Women: Warriors, Grannies, and Geishas of the Ming*. Lanham, MD: Rowman & Littlefield, 1999.

Chan, Alan K. L. "Goddesses in Chinese Religion." In Larry W. Hurtado, ed., *Goddesses in Religions and Modern Debate*, 9–25.

Chan, Alan K. L., and Sor Hoon Tan, eds. *Filial Piety in Chinese Thought and History.* New York: RoutledgeCurzon, 2004.

Chan, Alan K. L., and Yuet-Keung Lo, eds. *Philosophy and Religion in Early Medieval China.* Albany: State University of New York Press, 2010.

Chang Chaojan 張超然. "Liuchao daojiao shangqing jingpai cunsi fa yanjiu" 六朝道教上清經派存思法研究. Master's thesis, Cheng-chih University, Taibei, 1999.

Chang, Hsun, and Lin Mei-rong, eds. "Culture, Narrative, and Community of the Cult of Mazu." *Taiwan Journal of Anthropology*, special issue, 6 (2008): 103–31.

Chao, Shin-yi. "Good Career Moves: Life Stories of Daoist Nuns of the Twelfth and Thirteenth Centuries." *Nan Nü: Men, Women and Gender in Early and Imperial China* 10.1 (2008): 121–51.

Chao Xiang 超祥, ed. *Jizong Che Chanshi yulu* 季總徹禪師語錄. In *Jiaxing Dazangjing* 嘉興大藏經, vol. 28, no. B211; *Chinese Buddhist Tripitaka Electronic Text Collection, Taipei Edition.* http://taipei.ddbc.edu.tw/sutra/JB211_001.php.

Chappell, David W. "The Formation of the Pure Land Movement in China: Tao-Ch'o and Shan-tao." In James Foard, ed., *The Pure Land Tradition: History and Development.* Berkeley: The Regents of the University of California, 1996.

Charlotte, Furth. *A Flourishing Yin: Gender in China's Medical History, 960–1665.* Berkeley: University of California Press, 1999.

Chau, Adam. *Miraculous Response: Doing Popular Religion in Contemporary China.* Stanford: Stanford University Press, 2008.

Chen, Ellen M. "Nothingness and the Mother Principle in Early Chinese Taoism." *International Philosophical Quarterly* 9.3 (1969): 391–405.

———. "Tao as the Great Mother and the Influence of Motherly Love in the Shaping of Chinese Philosophy." *History of Religions* 14.1 (1974): 51–64.

Chen Guofu 陳國符. *Daozang yuanliu kao* 道藏源流考. Beijing: Zhonghua shuju, 1963.

Chen, Jinhua. "Family Ties and Buddhist Nuns in Tang China: Two Studies." *Asia Major* 15.2 (2002): 51–85.

Chen Shangjun 陳尚君, ed. *Quan Tangshi bubian* 全唐詩補編. 3 vols. Beijing: Zhonghua shuju, 1992.

Chen Siguang 陳思廣. "Zai shengcheng yu ronghui zhizhong: 1929–2009 nian *Jixin* de chuanbo yu jieshou yanjiu" 在生成與融匯之中: 1929–2009年"棘心"的傳播與接受研究. *Jianghan luntan* 江漢論壇 3 (2011): 127–31.

Chen, Tina Mai. "Peasant and Woman in Maoist Revolutionary Theory, 1920s–1950s." In Catherine Lynch, Robert B. Marks, and Paul G. Pickowicz, eds., *Radicalism, Revolution, and Reform in Modern China*, 55–78.

Chen Wenhua 陳文華. *Tang nüshiren ji sanzhong* 唐女詩人集三種. Shanghai: Shanghai guji chubanshe, 1984.

Chen Xiyuan 陳熙遠. "Zongjiao: yige Zhongguo jindai wenhuashi shang de guanjianci" 宗教: 一個中國近代文化史上的關鍵詞. *Xin shixue* 新史學 13.4 (2002): 37–54.

Chen Yingning 陳櫻寧, ed. *Nüzi daoxue xiaocongshu wuzhong* 女子道學小叢書五種. Shanghai: Yihuatang, 1936.

Cheung, Neky Tak-ching. *Women's Ritual in China: Jiezhu (Receiving Buddhist Prayer Beads) Performed by Menopausal Women in Ninghua, Western Fujian*. New York: Edwin Mellen Press, 2008.

Chen Yifeng 陳一風. "Wei Jin Nan Bei chao shiqi Ru Fo de xiaodao zhi zheng" 魏晉南北朝時期儒佛的孝道之爭. *Nandu xuetan* 南都學壇23.2 (2003): 23–27.

Ch'en, Kenneth K. S. "Filial Piety in Chinese Buddhism." *Harvard Journal of Asiatic Studies* 28 (1968): 81–97.

———. *Chinese Transformation of Buddhism*. Princeton: Princeton University Press, 1973.

Cheng Ya-ju 鄭雅如. "Wei Qiyi muzhiming shidu jianlun Tangren de xiaodao yishi" 韋契義墓誌銘釋讀: 兼論唐人的孝道意識. *Zaoqi Zhongguo shi yanjiu* 早期中國史研究1 (2009): 63–80.

Cherif, Leila. "Ningxia, l'école au féminine." *Etudes Orientales* 13–14 (1994): 156–62.

*Chinese Buddhist Tripitaka Electronic Text Collection, Taipei Edition* 臺北版電子佛典集成. http://taipei.ddbc.edu.tw/jiaxingzang.php.

Choi, Po King. "1997 and De-colonization." In Susan Romaniuk and Denise Tong Ka-wing, eds., *Uncertain Times: Hong Kong Women Facing 1997*. Hong Kong: Hong Kong Women Christian Council, 1995, 27–33.

Chow, Fong. "Chinese Buddhist Sculpture." *The Metropolitan Museum of Art Bulletin*. New Series 23.9 Part 1 (1965): 301–24.

Christ, Carol P. "Why Women Need the Goddess: Phenomenological, Psychological, and Political Reflections." In Charlene Spretnak, ed., *The Politics of Women's Spirituality*, 71–86.

Chu, Cordia. "Menstrual Beliefs and Practices of Chinese Women." *Journal of the Folklore Institute* 17.1 (1980): 39–55.

Cleary, J. C. *Meditation with Koans*. Berkeley: Asian Humanities Press, 1992.

Cleary, Thomas, and J. C. Cleary, trans. *The Blue Cliff Record*. Boston: Shambhala, 1992.

Cline, Ellen. "Female Spirit Mediums and Religious Authority in Contemporary Southeastern China." *Modern China* 36.5 (2010): 520–55.

Cole, Alan. *Mothers and Sons in Chinese Buddhism*. Stanford: Stanford University Press, 1998.

———. "Homestyle Vinaya and Docile Boys in Chinese Buddhism." *Positions: Asia Critique* 7.1 (1999): 5–50.

Conn, Joann Wolski. "Women's Spirituality: Restriction and Reconstruction." In Joann Wolski Conn, ed., *Women's Spirituality: Resources for Christian Development*, 9–30.

Conn, Joann Wolski, ed. *Women's Spirituality: Resources for Christian Development*. New York: Paulist, 1986.

Coontz, Stephanie. *The Way We Never Were: American Families and the Nostalgia Trap*. New York: HarperCollins, 1992.

Cooper, Mick, and John Rowan. "Introduction: Self-Plurality—the One, and the Many." In John Rowan and Mick Cooper, eds., *The Plural Self: Multiplicity in Everyday Life*, 1–9.

Curtis, Sarah Ann. *Civilizing Habits: Women Missionaries and the Revival of French Empire*. New York: Oxford University Press, 2010.

Dai Jianguo 戴建國. "Tang 'Kaiyuan ershiwu nian ling tianling' yanjiu" 唐 "開元二十五年令田令" 研究. *Lishi yanjiu* 歷史研究 2 (2000): 36–50.

Dao'an 道安 (312–385). *Erjiao lun* 二教論. In Sengyou 僧祐 (445–518), ed., *Hongming ji* 弘明集, 8.3a.

Daoxuan 道宣 (596–667). *Ji gujin fodao lunheng* 集古今佛道論衡. In *Taishō shinshū daizōkyō* 大正新修大藏經, vol. 52, no. 2014.

———. *Guang hongmingji* 廣弘明集. *Sibu congkan.*

*Daozang* 道藏. Beijing, Shanghai, and Tianjin: Beijing wenwu chubanshe, Shanghai guji chubanshe, and Tianjin guji chubanshe, 1988.

*Daozang jinghua* 道藏精華. Changsha: Yuelu shushe, 1993.

Davis, Edward L., ed. *Encyclopedia of Contemporary Chinese Culture*. London: RoutledgeCurzon, 2005.

Dazui 達最 et al., eds. *Yuechuang Liao chanshi yulu* 月幢了禪師語錄. In *Jiaxing Dazangjing* 嘉興大藏經, vol. 29, no. B237; *Chinese Buddhist Tripitaka Electronic Text Collection, Taipei Edition.* http://taipei.ddbc.edu.tw/sutra/JB237_001.php.

Dean, Kenneth. "Local Communal Religion in Contemporary China." In Daniel Overmyer, ed., *Religion in China Today*, 32–52.

———. "Daoist Ritual Today." In *Daoism Handbook,* 659–82.

Deng, Guangchang, Huang Ruiyi, and Zhang Guoyu. "The Worship of Dingguang in Hucun, Ninghua." In John Lagerwey and Yang Yanjie, eds., *Customary Religion and Society in West-Central Fujian*, Traditional Hakka Society Series, vol. 11.

des Rotours, Robert. *Courtisanes chinoises à la fin des T'ang, entre circa 789 et le 8 Janvier 881: Pei-Li Tche (Anecdotes du quartier du nord)*. Paris: Presses Universitaires de France, 1968.

Despeux, Catherine. "L'ordination des femmes taoïste sous les Tang." *Etudes chinoises* 5 (1986): 53–100.

———. *Prescriptions d'acuponcture valant mille onces d'or: traité d'acuponcture de Sun Simiao du VIIe siècle.* Paris: Trédaniel, 1987.

———. "Women in Daoism." In Livia Kohn, ed., *Daoism Handbook*, 404–5.

Despeux, Catherine, and Livia Kohn. *Women in Daoism*. Cambridge, MA: Three Pines Press, 2003.

DeVido, Elise A. *Taiwan's Buddhist Nuns*. Albany: State University of New York Press, 2010.

Dexter, Miriam R., and Victor H. Mair. *Sacred Display: Divine and Magical Female Figures of Eurasia*. Amherst, NY: Cambria Press, 2010.

Dissanayake, Wimal. *Narratives of Agency: Self-Making in China, India, and Japan.* Minneapolis: University of Minnesota Press, 1996.

Dong Gao 董誥 (1740–1818) et al., comp. *Quan Tangwen* 全唐文. Beijing: Zhonghua shuju, 1983.

*Dongshen badi miaojing jing* 洞神八帝妙精經. *DZ*, vol. 11, no. 640.

*Dongxuan Lingbao Sandong fengdao kejie yingshi* 洞玄靈寶三洞奉道科戒營始. *DZ*, vol. 24, no. 1125.

*Dongzhen huangshu* 洞真黃書. *DZ*, vol. 33, no. 1343.

Dooling, Amy D., and Kristina M. Torgeson. *Writing Women in Modern China, Vol. 1*. New York: Columbia University Press, 1998.

Douglas, Mary. *Purity and Danger: An Analysis of Concepts of Pollution and Taboo*. New York: Routledge, 1966.

Duan Qi 段綺. *Zhongguo jidujiao bensehua shigao* 中國基督教本色化史稿. Taibei: Yuzhouguang Press, 2005.

Duara, Prasenjit. "Knowledge and Power in the Discourse of Modernity: The Campaign against Popular Religion in Early Twentieth-Century China." *Journal of Asian Studies* 50 (1990): 67–83.

———. *Rescuing History from the Nation: Questioning Narratives of Modern China*. Chicago: University of Chicago Press, 1995.

DuBois, Thomas David. "Hegemony, Imperialism, and the Construction of Religion." *History and Theory* Theme Issue 44 (2005): 113–31.

Dudbridge, Glen. "Women Pilgrims to T'ai Shan: Some Pages from a Seventeenth-Century Novel." In Susan Naquin and Chün-fang Yu, eds., *Pilgrims and Sacred Sites in China*, 39–64.

———. *The Legend of Miaoshan*. Oxford: Oxford University Press, 2004.

Du Guangting 杜光庭 (850–933). *Yongcheng jixian lu* 墉城集仙錄. *DZ*, vol. 18, no. 783; and Zhang Junfang 張君房 (*jinshi* 1004–1007), comp., *Yunji qiqian* 雲笈七籤. Beijing: Zhonghua shuju, 2003.

Ebrey, Patricia B. *The Inner Quarters: Marriage and the Lives of Chinese Women in the Sung Period*. Stanford: Stanford University Press, 1993.

Eisenstein, Zillah. *The Female Body and the Law*. Berkeley: University of California Press, 1988.

Eliade, Mircea. *The Sacred and the Profane*. Trans. Willard R. Trask. San Diego, CA: Harcourt Brace, 1987.

Eller, Cynthia. "Relativizing the Patriarchy: The Sacred History of the Feminist Spirituality Movement." *History of Religions* (1991): 279–95.

Entenmann, Robert. "Christian Virgins in Eighteenth-Century Sichuan." In Daniel Bays, ed., *Christianity in China from the Eighteenth Century to the Present*, 180–93.

Epstein, Maram. "Engendering Order: Structure, Gender and Meaning in the Qing Novel *Jinghua yuan*." *Chinese Literature: Essays, Articles, Reviews* 18 (1996): 101–27.

Fitzgerald, Timothy. *The Ideology of Religious Studies*. New York: Oxford University Press, 2000.

———. *Discourse on Civility and Barbarity: A Critical History of Religion and Related Categories*. Oxford: Oxford University Press, 2007.

Foucault, Michel. "An Aesthetics of Existence." In Lawrence D. Kritzman, ed., *Politics, Philosophy, Culture: Interviews and Other Writings, 1977–1984*, 47–56.

———. "What Is Enlightenment?" In Paul Rabinow, ed., *The Foucault Reader*, 32–50.

———. "Technologies of the Self." In L. H. Martin et al., eds., *Technologies of the Self: A Seminar with Michel Foucault*, 16–49.

Fu, Charles Wei-hsin, and Sandra A. Wawrytko, eds. *Buddhist Ethics and Modern Society*. New York: Greenwood Press, 1991.

Fu Jinquan 傅金銓. *Nüjindan fayao* 女金丹法要 (1813). In *Daoshu yiguan zhenji yijianlu*, 11: 512–41.

Furth, Charlotte. "Rethinking Van Gulik: Sexuality and Reproduction in Traditional Chinese Medicine." In Christina K. Gilmartin, Gail Hershatter, Lisa Rofel, and Tyrene White, eds., *Engendering China: Women, Culture, and the State*, 125–46.

———. *A Flourishing Yin: Gender in China's Medical History, 960–1665*. Berkeley: University of California Press, 1999.

Fu Shan 傅山 (1606–1684). *Duan honglong* 斷紅龍. In *Shangcheng xiudao mishu sizhong* 上乘修道秘書四種, *Daozang jinghua* 道藏精華.

Fu Xuancong 傅璇琮, ed. *Tang caizizhuan jiaojian* 唐才子傳校箋. 5 vols. Beijing: Zhonghua, 1990.

———. *Tangren xuan Tangshi xinbian* 唐人選唐詩新編. Xi'an: Shaanxi renmin jiaoyu chubanshe, 1996.

Gao Shiyu 高世瑜. *Tangdai funü* 唐代婦女. Xi'an: Sanqin chubanshe, 1988.

Ge Zhaoguang 葛兆光. "Huangshu heqi yu qita: Daojiao guodu yi de sixiangshi yanjiu" 黃書合氣與其他: 道教過度儀的思想史研究. *Gujin lunheng* 古今論衡 2 (1999): 62–76.

Gilmartin, Christina K., Gail Hershatter, Lisa Rofel, and Tyrene White, eds. *Engendering China: Women, Culture, and the State*. Cambridge, MA: Harvard University Press, 1994.

Goldin, Paul R. "The Cultural and Religious Background of Sexual Vampirism in Ancient China." *Theology and Sexuality* 12.3 (2006): 285–308.

Goossaert, Vincent. "Le destin de la religion chinoise au 20e siècle." *Social Compass* 50–54 (2003): 429–40.

———. "Le concept de religion en Chine et l'Occident." *Diogène* 205(2004): 11–21.

———. "1898: The Beginning of the End for Chinese Religion?" *Journal of Asian Studies* 65.2 (2006): 307–36.

———. "L'invention des religions en Chine moderne." In Anne Cheng, ed., *La Pensée en Chine Aujourd'hui*, 185–213.

———. *The Taoist of Peking, 1800–1949: A Social History of Urban Clerics*. Cambridge, MA: Harvard Asia Center, 2007.

———. "Irrepressible Female Piety: Late Imperial Bans on Women Visiting Temples." *Nan Nü: Men, Women and Gender in Early and Imperial China* 10.2 (2008): 212–41.

Goossaert, Vincent, and David A. Palmer. *The Religious Question in Modern China*. Chicago and London: University of Chicago Press, 2011.

Graham, Elspeth, Hilary Hinds, Elaine Hobby, and Helen Wilcox, eds. *Her Own Life: Autobiographical Writings by Seventeenth-Century Englishwomen*. London and New York: Routledge, 1989.

Grant, Beata. "Female Holder of the Lineage: Linji Chan Master Zhiyuan Xinggang (1597–1654)." *Late Imperial China* 17.2 (1996): 51–76.

———. *Daughters of Emptiness: Poems of Chinese Buddhist Nuns*. Somerville, MA: Wisdom Publications, 2003.

———. *Eminent Nuns: Women Chan Masters of Seventeenth-Century China*. Honolulu: University of Hawaii Press, 2008.

———. "Da Zhangfu: The Gendered Rhetoric of Heroism and Equality in Seventeenth-Century Chan Buddhist Discourse Records." *Nan Nü: Men, Women and Gender in Early and Imperial China* 10.2 (2008): 177–211.

Gregory, Peter N., ed. *Sudden and Gradual: Approaches to Enlightenment in Chinese Thought*. Studies in East Asian Buddhism 5. Honolulu: University of Hawaii Press, 1987.

Gregory, Peter N., and Daniel A. Getz Jr., eds. *Buddhism in the Sung*. Honolulu: University of Hawaii Press, 1999.

Gross, Rita M. "Studying Women and Religion: Conclusions Twenty-Five Years Later." In Arvind Sharma, ed., *Today's Women in World Religions*, 327–62.

———. *Feminism and Religion: An Introduction*. Boston: Beacon Press, 1996.

Grosz, Elizabeth A. *Volatile Bodies: Toward a Corporeal Feminism*. Bloomington: Indiana University Press, 1994.

Guang Xing 廣興. "Filial Piety in Early Buddhism." *Journal of Buddhist Ethics* 12 (2005): 82–106.

———. "Ru Fo xiaodaoguan de bijiao yanjiu" 儒佛孝道觀的比較研究. In Liu Xiaogan 劉笑敢 and Kawada Yoichi 川田洋一, eds., *Ru Shi Dao zhi zhexue duihua* 儒釋道之哲學對話, 121–53.

Guisso, Richard, and Stanley Johannesen, eds. *Women in China: Current Directions in Historical Scholarship*. Youngstown, NY: Philo Press, 1981.

Guo Maoqian 郭茂倩 (fl. 1084). *Yuefu shiji* 樂府詩集. Beijing: Zhonghua shuju, 1979.

Guo Peng 郭鵬, et al., eds. *Foguo ji zhushi* 佛國記註釋. Changchun: Changchun chubanshe, 1995.

Haboush, Jahyun Kim. "Filial Emotions and Filial Values: Changing Patterns in the Discourse of Filiality in Late Choson Korea." *Harvard Journal of Asiatic Studies* 55.1 (1995): 129–77.

Halfon, Constance-Hélène. "Souvenirs de voyage dans la Chine islamique profonde: Être femme et musulmane à Lanzhou, au Gansu." *Etudes Orientales* 13/14 (1994): 151–55.

Halperin, Mark. "Domesticity and the Dharma: Portraits of Buddhist Laywomen in Sung China." *T'oung Pao* 92.1–3 (2006): 50–100.

Han Guopan 韓國磐. *Beichao Sui Tang de Juntian zhidu* 北朝隋唐的均田制度. Shanghai: Shanghai renmin chubanshe, 1984.

Harper, Donald J. *Early Chinese Medical Literature: The Mawangdui Medical Manuscripts*. London and New York: Kegan Paul International, 1998.

He Dunpei 何敦培. "Zongjiao funüguan dui funü xiandaihua de yingxiang" 宗教婦女觀對婦女現代化的影響. *Funü yanjiu luncong* 婦女研究論叢 4 (2005): 51–55.

He Guangyuan 何光遠 (fl. 938–964). *Jianjie lu* 鑒戒錄. *Siku quanshu*.

He, Huoren 何火任. "*Baimaonü* yu He Jingzhi" "白毛女" 與賀敬之. *Wenyi lilun yu piping* 文藝理論與批評 2 (1998): 83–93.

———. "*Baimaonü* yu He Jingzhi (xu)" "白毛女" 與賀敬之(續)" *Wenyi lilun yu piping* 文藝理論與批評 3 (1998): 38–47.

Heine, Steven, and Dale S. Wright, eds. *Zen Ritual: Studies of Zen Buddhist Theory in Practice*. Oxford and New York: Oxford University Press, 2008.

He, Jingzhi 賀敬之. "*Baimaonü* de chuangzuo yu yanchu"白毛女的創作與演出. In Yan'an Lu Xun wenyi xueyuan, comp., *Baimaonü*, 249–61.

He Longxiang 賀龍驤 (fl. 1906). *Nüdan hebian* 女丹合編. Chengdu: Erxian'an 二仙庵, 1906.

He Ning 何寧, ed. *Huainanzi jishi* 淮南子集釋. Beijing: Zhonghua shuju, 1998.

Henansheng gudai jianzhu baohu yanjiusuo 河南省古代建築保護研究所, ed. *Baoshan lingquansi* 寶山靈泉寺. Zhengzhou: Henan renmin chubanshe, 1991.

Hershatter, Gail. *Women in China's Long Twentieth Century*. Berkeley: University of California Press, 2007.

*He Yubo* 賀玉波. *Zhongguo xiandai nüzuojia* 中國現代女作家. *Shanghai: Xiandai chubanshe, 1932.*

Hinsch, Bret. "Confucian Filial Piety and the Construction of the Ideal Chinese Buddhist Woman." *Journal of Chinese Religions* 30 (2002): 49–76.

Hobsbawm, Eric, and Terence Ranger, eds. *The Invention of Tradition*. Cambridge: Cambridge University Press, 1983.

Hollywood, Amy. "Performativity, Citationality, Ritualization." *History of Religions* 42 (2002): 93–115.

———. "Practice, Belief, and Feminist Philosophy of Religion." In Kevin Schibrack, ed., *Thinking through Rituals: Philosophical Perspectives*, 52–71.

Holm, David. *Art and Ideology in Revolutionary China*. New York: Oxford University Press, 1991.

Hong Xingzu 洪興祖 (1090–1155), ed. *Chuci buzhu* 楚辭補注. Taibei: Da'an, 1995.

Hsieh, Ding-Hwa E. *Lives of the Nuns: Biographies of Chinese Buddhist Nuns from the Fourth to Sixth Centuries: A Translation of the Pi-Ch'iu-Ni Chuan*. Honolulu: University of Hawaii Press, 1994.

———. "Images of Women in Ch'an Buddhist Literature of the Sung Period." In Peter N. Gregory and Daniel A. Getz Jr., eds., *Buddhism in the Sung*, 148–87.

Hsu, Eileen Hsiang-Ling. "Visualization Meditation and the Siwei Icon in Chinese Buddhist Sculpture." *Artibus Asiae* 62.1 (2002): 5–32.

Hsu, Sung-peng. *A Buddhist Leader in Ming China: The Life and Thought of Han-shan Te-ch'ing, 1546–1623*. University Park: Pennsylvania State University Press, 1979.

Huang, Julia C. Y. *Charisma and Compassion: Cheng Yen and the Buddhist Tzu Chi Movement*. Cambridge, MA: Harvard University Press, 2009.

Huang, Nicole. *Women, War, Domesticity: Shanghai Literature and Popular Culture in the 1940s*. Leiden and Boston: Brill, 2005.

*Huangtian Shangqing Jinque Dijun lingshu ziwen* 皇天上清金闕帝君靈書紫文上經. *DZ* vol. 11, no. 639.

Huang Shizhong 黃世中. "Lun *Quan Tangshi* zhong suo fanying de nüguan 'ban-chang shi' lianqing" 論全唐詩中所反映的女冠 "半娼式" 戀情. *Xuchang shizhuan xuebao* 許昌師專學報 15.2 (1996): 39–43.

Hu Daojing 胡道靜 et al., comps. *Zangwai daoshu* 藏外道書. Chengdu: Ba Shu shushe, 1992–1994.

Hunter, Jane. *The Gospel of Gentility: American Women Missionaries in Turn-of-the-Century China*. New Haven: Yale University Press, 1984.

Hurtado, Larry W., ed. *Goddesses in Religions and Modern Debate*. Atlanta: Scholars Press, 1990.

Hutchinson, John. *The Dynamics of Cultural Nationalism*. London: Allen and Unwin, 1987.

Huters, Theodore, R. Wong, and Pauline Yu, eds. *Culture and State in Chinese History: Conventions, Accommodations, and Critiques*. Stanford: Stanford University Press, 1997.

Hu Zhenheng 胡震亨 (1569–1645). *Tangyin guiqian* 唐音癸籤. Shanghai: Shanghai guji chubanshe, 1981.

Hymes, Robert P. *Way and Byway: Taoism, Local Religion and Models of Divinity in Sung and Modern China*. Berkeley: University of California Press, 2002.

Idema, Wilt L. *Personal Salvation and Filial Piety: Two Precious Scroll Narratives of Guanyin and Her Acolytes*. Honolulu: University of Hawaii Press, 2008.

Idema, Wilt, and Beata Grant. *The Red Brush: Writing Women in Imperial China*. Cambridge: Harvard University Asia Center, 2004.

Ikeda On 池田溫. *Chūgoku kodai shahon shikigo shūroku* 中國古代寫本識語集錄. Tokyo: Tokyo daigaku Tōyō bunka kenkyūjo, 1990.

Iliouchine, Alexandre. "A Study of the *Central Scripture of Laozi* (*Laozi zhongjing*)." Master's thesis, McGill University, 2011.

Jaschok, Maria, and Jingjun Shui. *The History of Women's Mosques in Chinese Islam: A Mosque of Their Own*. Richmond, Surrey: Curzon, 2000.

———. *Women, Religion, and Space in China: Islamic Mosques and Daoist Temples, Catholic Convents and Chinese Virgins*. New York: Routledge, 2011.

Jensen, Tim, and Mikael Rothstein, eds. *Secular Theories on Religion: Current Perspectives*. Copenhagen: Museum Tusculanum Press, 2000.

Jiang Hezhen. "Making the Home Christians." *The Chinese Recorder and Missionary Journal* 53 (1922): 472–73.

Ji Xianlin 季羨林 et al., eds. *Da Tang xiyu ji jiaozhu* 大唐西域記校註. Beijing: Zhonghua shuju, 2000.

Jia Jinhua 賈晉華. "Tangshi zhong youguan nüdaoshi de lianqingshi kaobian" 唐詩中有關女道士的戀情詩考辨. *Daojia wenhua yanjiu* 道家文化研究 24 (2009): 126–14.

———. "Du Guangting and the Hagiographies of Tang Female Daoists." *Taiwan Journal of Religious Studies* 1 (2011): 81–121.

———. "The *Yaochi ji* and Three Daoist Priestess-Poets in Tang China." *Nan Nü: Men, Women and Gender in Early and Imperial China* 13.2 (2011): 205–43.

Jia Jinhua and Fu Xuancong. *Tang Wudai wenxue biannian shi: Wudai juan* 唐五代文學編年史: 五代卷. Shenyang: Liaohai chubanshe, 1999.

*Jiaxing Buddhist Canon* 嘉興大藏經; *Chinese Buddhist Tripitaka Electronic Text Collection, Taipei Edition.* http://taipei.ddbc.edu.tw/jiaxingzang.php.

Ji Xian 季嫻 (1614–1683). "Qianyin ji" 前因紀. Trans. Grace Fong. In Susan Mann and Yu-yin Cheng, eds., *Under Confucian Eyes: Writings on Gender in Chinese History*, 136.

Jingmenshi Bowuguan 荊門市博物館. *Guodian Chumu zhujian* 郭店楚墓竹簡. Beijing: Wenwu chubanshe, 1998.

Johnson, David, Andrew J. Nathan, and Evelyn S. Rawski, eds. *Popular Culture in Late Imperial China*. Berkeley: University of California Press, 1985.

Johnson, David. *Spectacle and Sacrifice: The Ritual Foundations of Village Life in North China*. Cambridge, MA: Harvard Asia Center, 2009.

Johnson, Kay Ann. *Women, the Family and Peasant Revolution in China*. Chicago: University of Chicago Press, 1983.

Johnson, Luke Timothy, and Mark D. Jordan. "Christianity." In Don S. Browning, M. Christian Green, and John Witte Jr., eds., *Sex, Marriage, and Family in World Religions*, 80–81. New York: Columbia University Press, 2006.

Jones, Stephen. *In Search of the Folk Daoists of North China*. New York: Ashgate, 2010.

Judd, Ellen R. "Niangjia: Chinese Women and Their Natal Families." *Journal of Asian Studies* 48.3 (1989): 525–44.

Judge, Joan. *The Precious Raft of History: The Past, the West, and the Woman Question in China*. Stanford: Stanford University Press, 2008.

Kaiben 開本 et al., eds. *Shishuang Mizhan chanshi yulu* 石霜爾瞻尊禪師語錄. In *Jiaxing Dazangjing*, vol. 27, no. B200; *Chinese Buddhist Tripitaka Electronic Text Collection, Taipei Edition.* http://taipei.ddbc.edu.tw/sutra/JB200_001.php.

Kalinowski, Marc. "La transmission du dispositive des Neuf Palais sous les Six dynasties." In Michel Strickmann, ed., *Tantric and Taoist Studies*, 773–811.

Kaltenmark, Max. *Le Liesien tchouan*. Paris: Collège de France, 1987 (originally published 1953).

Kang, Xiaofei. *The Cult of the Fox: Power, Gender, and Popular Religion in Late Imperial and Modern China*. New York: Columbia University Press, 2006.

———. "Rural Women, Old Age, and Temple Work: A Case from Northwestern Sichuan." *China Perspectives* 4 (2009): 42–52.

Kato Chie 加藤千恵. "*Roshi chukyō* to naitan shisō no kigen" "老子中經" と内丹思想の起源. *Tōhō shūkyō* 87 (1996): 22–38.

Katz, Paul. "Religion and the State in Postwar Taiwan." In Daniel Overmyer, ed., *Religion in China Today*, 89–106.

Kieshnick, John. *The Eminent Monk: Buddhist Ideals in Medieval Chinese Hagiography*. Honolulu: University of Hawaii Press, 1997.

Kim, Nami. "Women, the Ba-ram Bearers: Asian Feminist Spiritualities." In Maria Pilar Aquino and Elisabeth Schussler Fiorenza, eds., *In the Power of Wisdom: Feminist Spiritualities of Struggle (Concilium)*, 13–22.

King, Karen L., ed. *Women and Goddess Traditions in Antiquity and Today*. Minneapolis: Fortress Press, 1997.

King, Ursula, ed. *Religion and Gender*. Oxford: Blackwell, 1995.

———. "Introduction: Spirituality, Society, and the Millennium—Wasteland, Wilderness, or New Vision?" In Ursula King, ed., *Spirituality and Society in the New Millennium*, 1–18.

———. "General Introduction: Gender-Critical Turns in the Study of Religion." In Ursula King and Tina Beattie, eds., *Gender, Religion and Diversity: Cross-Cultural Perspective*, 1–12.

King, Ursula, and Tina Beattie, eds. *Gender, Religion and Diversity: Cross-Cultural Perspectives*. New York: Continuum, 2004.

Kirkland, Russell. "Taoists of the High T'ang." PhD diss. Indiana University, 1986.

———. "Huang Ling-wei: A Taoist Priestess in T'ang China." *Journal of Chinese Religions* 19 (1991): 47–73.

———. "Ssu-ma Ch'eng-chen and the Role of Taoism in the Medieval Chinese Policy." *Journal of Asian History* 31.2 (1997): 105–38.

Kleeman, Terry. "Feasting without the Victuals: The Evolution of the Daoist Communal Kitchen." In Roel Sterckx, ed., *Of Tripod and Palate: Food, Politics and Religion in Traditional China*, 140–62.

Kobayashi Masayoshi 小林正美. *Rikuchō Dōkyō shi kenkyū* 六朝道教史研究. Tōkyō: Sōbunsha, 1990.

Ko, Dorothy, JaHyun Kim Haboush, and Joan R. Piggott, eds. *Women and Confucian Cultures in Premodern China, Korea, and Japan*. Berkeley: University of California Press, 2003.

Ko, Dorothy. "Pursuing Talent and Virtue: Education and Women's Culture in Seventeenth- and Eighteenth-Century China." *Late Imperial China* 13.1 (1992): 9–39.

———. *Teachers of the Inner Chambers: Women and Culture in China, 1573–1722*. Stanford: Stanford University Press, 1994.

Kohn, Livia. *Laughing at the Dao*. Princeton: Princeton University Press, 1995.

———. *Seven Steps to the Tao: Siman Chengzhen's Zuowang lun*. St. Augustin: Steyler Verlag, 1987.

———. *The Daoist Monastic Manual: A Translation of the Fengdao Kejie*. Oxford: Oxford University Press, 2004.

Kohn, Livia, ed. *Daoism Handbook*. 2 vols. Leiden: Brill, 2004.

Kohn, Livia, and Robin Wang, eds. *Internal Alchemy: Self, Society, and the Quest for Immortality.* Boston: Three Pines Press, 2008.

Korte, Anne-Marie. "Female Blood Rituals: Cultural-Anthropological Findings and Feminist-Theological Reflections." In Kristin De Troyer et al., eds., *Wholly Woman, Holy Blood: A Feminist Critique of Purity and Impurity*, 165–88.

Kou Qianzhi 寇謙之 (365–448). *Laojun yinsong jiejing* 老君音誦戒經. *DZ*, vol. 18, no. 785.

Kritzman, Lawrence D. *Politics, Philosophy, Culture: Interviews and Other Writings, 1977–1984*. New York: Routledge, 1988.

Kroll, Paul W. "Notes on Three Taoist Figures of the T'ang Dynasty." *Society for the Study of Chinese Religions Bulletin* 9 (1981): 19–41.

———. "In the Halls of the Azure Lad." *Journal of the American Oriental Society* 105 (1986): 75–94.

Kwok, Pui-lan. *Chinese Women and Christianity, 1860–1927*. Atlanta: Scholars Press, 1992.

Lagerwey, John. "Deux Écrits Taoïstes Anciens." *Cahiers d'Extrême-Asie* 14 (2004): 139–71.

Lagerwey, John, and Yang Yanjie, eds. *Lineages: The Economy and Customs in Ninghua County* (I). Traditional Hakka Society Series, vol. 23. Hong Kong: International Hakka Studies Association, 2005.

Laqueur, Thomas W. "Orgasm, Generation and the Politics of Reproductive Biology." *Representations* 14 (1986): 1–41.

Larson, Wendy. *Women and Writing in Modern China*. Stanford: Stanford University Press, 1998.

Law, Pui-lam. "The Revival of Folk Religion and Gender Relationships in Rural China: A Preliminary Observation." *Asian Folklore Studies* 64.1 (2005): 89–109.

Lee, Haiyan. *Revolution of the Heart: A Genealogy of Love in China, 1900–1950*. Stanford, CA: Stanford University Press, 2007.

Leeb, Leopold 雷立柏. *Lun jidu zhi da yu xiao: 1900–1950 nian huaren zhishifenzi yanzhong de jidujiao* 論基督之大與小: 1900－1950 年華人知識份子眼中的基督教. Beijing: Shehui kexue wenxian chubanshe, 2000.

Leung, Angela Ki Che. "Women Practicing Medicine in Premodern China." In Harriet T. Zurndorfer, ed., *Chinese Women in the Imperial Past: New Perspectives*, 101–34.

Leung, Beatrice, and Patricia Wittberg. "Catholic Religious Orders of Women in China: Adaptation and Power." *Journal for the Scientific Study of Religion* 43.1 (2004): 67–83.

Levering, Miriam. "The Dragon and the Abbess of Mo-shan: Gender and Status." *Journal of the International Association of Buddhist Studies* 5.1 (1982): 19–36.

———. "Lin-chi (Rinzai) Ch'an and Gender: The Rhetoric of Equality and the Rhetoric of Heroism." In José I. Cabezón, ed., *Buddhism, Sexuality, and Gender*, 137–56.

———. "Women, the State, and Religion Today in the People's Republic of China." In Arvind Sharma, ed., *Today's Women in World Religions*, 171–224.

———. "Dōgen's Raihaitokuzui and Women Teaching in Sung Ch'an." *Journal of the International Association of Buddhist Studies* 21.1 (1997): 77–110.

———. "Stories of Enlightened Women in Ch'an and the Chinese Buddhist Female Bodhisattva/Goddess Tradition." In Karen L. King, ed., *Women and Goddess Traditions in Antiquity and Today*, 137–76.

———. "Miao-tao and Her Teacher Ta-hui." In Peter N. Gregory and Daniel A. Getz Jr., eds., *Buddhism in the Sung*, 188–219.

———. "Women Ch'an Masters: The Teacher Miao-tsung as Saint." In Arvind Sharma, ed., *Women Saints in World Religions*, 180–204.

———. "Was There Religious Autobiography in China before the Thirteenth Century? The Ch'an Master Ta-hui Tsung-kao (1089–1163) as Autobiographer." *Journal of Chinese Religions* 30 (2002): 97–122.

Levine, Marilyn A., and Chen San-Ching. "Communist-Leftist Control of the European Branch of the Guomindang, 1923–1927." *Modern China* 22.1 (1996): 62–92.

Liang Liling 梁麗玲. "Liuchao Dunhuang Fojiao xiejing de gongyang gongdeguan" 六朝敦煌佛教寫經的供養功德觀. *Dunhuangxue* 敦煌學 22 (1999): 119–38.

Liang Qichao 梁啓超. *Liang Qichao quanji* 梁啓超全集. Beijing: Beijing chubanshe, 1999.

Li Chuanjun 李傳軍 and Jin Xia 金霞. "*Fumu en zhong jing* yu Tangdai xiaowenhua jiantan Fojiao zhongguohua guocheng zhong de tongru yu jisu xianxiang" "父母恩重經" 與唐代孝文化: 兼談佛教中國化過程中的 "通儒" 與 "濟俗" 現象. *Kongzi yanjiu* 孔子研究 3 (2008): 90–96.

Li Dingguang 李定廣 and Xu Kechao 徐可超. "Lun Zhongguo wenren de Wushan shennü qingjie" 論中國文人的巫山神女情結. *Fudan xuebao* 復旦學報 5 (2002): 112–17.

Li, Ellen. *My Way: Dr. Ellen Li: Her Life and Contribution*. Hong Kong: Ellen Li, 1998.

Li Fang 李昉 (925–996) et al., eds. *Taiping guangji* 太平廣記. 10 vols. Beijing: Zhonghua shuju, 1961.

Li Fengmao 李豐楙. *Wuru yu zhejiang: Liuchao Sui Tang Daojiao wenxue lunji* 誤入與謫降：六朝隋唐道教文學論集. Taibei: Xuesheng shuju, 1996.

———. *You yu you: Liuchao Sui Tang xiandao wenxue* 憂與遊: 六朝隋唐仙道文學. Taibei: Xuesheng shuju, 1996; reprint, Beijing: Zhonghua shuju, 2010.

Li Genshui 李根水 and Luo Huarong 羅華榮, eds. *Ninghua Kejia minsu* 寧化客家民俗. Beijing: Zhongguo huaqiao chubanshe, 2000.

Li Linfu 李林甫 (683–752) et al., eds. *Tang liudian* 唐六典. Beijing: Zhonghua shuju, 1992.

Li Ling 李零. "Donghan Wei Jin Nanbeichao fangzhong jingdian liupai kao" 東漢魏晉南北朝房中經典流派考. *Zhongguo wenhua* 中國文化 15–16 (1997): 141–58.

———. *Zhongguo fangshu xukao* 中國方術續考. Beijing: Zhonghua shuju, 2006.

———. *Zhongguo fangshu zhengkao* 中國方術正考. Beijing: Zhonghua shuju, 2006.

Li Tao 李燾 (1115–1184). *Xu Zizhi tongjian changbian* 續資治通鑒長編. Beijing: Zhonghua shuju, 1979.

Li Xiaomin 李曉敏. “Zaoxiang ji: Sui Tang minzhong Fojiao xinyang chutan” 造像記：隋唐民眾佛教信仰初探. *Zhengzhou daxue xuebao* 鄭州大學學報 1 (2007): 91–95.

Li Xiaorong 李小榮. “Lüelun Dunhuang bianwen zhong de xiaoqin sixiang” 略論敦煌變文中的孝親思想. *Yancheng shifan xueyuan xuebao* 鹽城師範學院學報 2 (2000): 19–22.

Li Yang 李揚. *50–70 niandai wenxue jingdian zaijiedu* 50–70 年代文學經典再解讀. Jinan: Shandong jiaoyu chubanshe, 2003.

Li You 李攸 (fl. 1111–1134). *Songchao shishi* 宋朝事實. *Congshu jicheng chubian*, 7.107.

Lieberman, Sally Taylor. *The Mother and Narrative Politics in Modern China*. Charlottesville: University Press of Virginia, 1998.

*Liexian zhuan* 列仙傳. *DZ*, vol. 5, no. 294.

Lin Shushi 林富士. “Lüelun zaoqi Daojiao yu fangzhongshu de guanxi” 略論早期道教與房中術的關係. *Lishi yuyan yanjiusuo jikan* 歷史語言研究所集刊 72.2 (2001): 241–48.

*Liu, Jianmei. Revolution plus Love: Literary History, Women's Bodies, and Thematic Repetition in Twentieth-Century Chinese Fiction.* Honolulu: University of Hawaii Press, 2003.

Liu Lixia 劉麗霞. “Cong *Wenyi yuedan* (jiaji) kan tianzhujiao chuanjiaoshi de zhongguo xiandai wenxue guan” 從 “文藝月旦 (甲集)” 看天主教傳教士的中國現代文學觀. *Guangxi shehui kexue* 廣西社會科學 2 (2003): 111–12.

———. “Jindai laihua shengmushengxin huishi dui zhongguo xiandai wenxue de pingjie” 近代來華聖母聖心會士對中國現代文學的評介. *Zhongguo xiandai wenxue yanjiu congkan* 中國現代文學研究叢刊 2 (2011): 171–82.

Liu Ning 劉寧. “Shixi Tangdai changjishi yu nüguanshi de chayi” 試析唐代娼妓詩與女冠詩的差異. *Zhongguo dianji yu wenhua* 中國典籍與文化 4 (2003): 49–57.

*Liu Ruozhuo* 劉若拙. *Sandong xiudao yi* 三洞修道儀. *DZ*, vol. 32, no. 1237.

Liu Shanqun 劉善群. *Kejia lisu* 客家禮俗. Fuzhou: Fujian jiaoyu chubanshe, 1995.

Liu Shu-fen 劉淑芬. “Foding zunsheng tuoluonijing he Tangdai zun sheng jingchuang de jianli: jingchuang yanjiu zhiyi” 佛頂尊勝陀羅尼經和唐代尊勝經幢的建立: 經幢研究之一. *Zhongyang yanjiu lishi yuyuan yanjiusuo jikan* 67.1 (1996): 145–93.

———. “Jingchuang de xingzhi xingzhi he laiyuan jingchuang yanjiu zhi er” 經幢的形制, 性質和來源: 經幢研究之二. *Zhongyang yanjiu lishi yuyuan yanjiu suo jikan* 68.3 (1997): 643–786.

———. “Linzang: Zhongguo Fojiao lushizang yanjiu zhi yi” 林葬: 中古佛教露屍葬研究之一. *Dalu zazhi* 大陸雜誌 96.3 (1998): 22–136.

———. "Shishi cuoku: Zhongguo Fojiao lushizang yanjiu zhi er" 石室瘞窟: 中古佛教露屍葬研究之二. *Dalu zazhi* 98.4 (1999): 49–152.

———. "Death and the Degeneration of Life: Exposure of the Corpse in Medieval Chinese Buddhism." *Journal of Chinese Religions* 28 (2000): 1–30.

———. "Tang Song shiqi de gongdesi yi canhui yishi wei zhongxin de taolun" 唐宋時期的功德寺: 以懺悔儀式為中心的討論. *Zhongyang yanjiu lishi yuyuan yanjiusuo jikan* 中央研究院歷史語言研究所集刊 82.2 (2011): 261–323.

Liu Xiaogan 劉笑敢 and Kawada Yoichi 川田洋一, eds. *Ru Shi Dao zhi zhexue duihua* 儒釋道之哲學對話. Hong Kong: Shangwu yinshuguan, 2007.

Liu Xu 劉昫 (888–947) et al. *Jiu Tangshu* 舊唐書. Beijing: Zhonghua shuju, 1975.

Liu, Xun. *Daoist Modern: Innovation, Lay Practice, and the Community of Inner Alchemy in Republican Shanghai*. Cambridge, MA: Harvard University Asia Center, 2009.

Liu Yiming 劉一明. *Huixin waiji* 會心外集 (1801). In *Daoshu shi'er zhong* 道書十二種, vol. 9.

———. *Xiuzhen biannan* 修真辯難 (1798). In *Daoshu shi'er zhong*, vol. 7, in *Zangwai daoshu* vol. 8, 467–92.

———. *Daoshu shi'er zhong*, vol. 7. In *Zangwai daoshu* vol. 8, 467–92.

Liu Yiqing 劉義慶 (403–444). *Youming lu* 幽明錄. Beijing: Wenhua yishu chubanshe, 1988.

Liu Yongming 劉永明. "*Laozi zhongjing* xingcheng yu handai kao" "老子中經"形成於漢代考. *Lanzhou daxue xuebao* 蘭州大學學報 34 (2006): 60–66.

Liu, Yu. "Maoist Discourse and the Mobilization of Emotion in Revolutionary China." *Modern China* 36.3 (2010): 329–62.

Lo, Yuet-Keung. "Filial Devotion for Women: A Buddhist Testimony from Third-Century China." In Alan Chan and Sor Hoon Tan, eds., *Filial Piety in Chinese Thought and History*, 71–90.

———. "Recovering a Buddhist Voice on Daughters-in-law: The *Yuyenü jing*." *History of Religion* 44 (2005): 318–50.

Lu Hua 陸華. "Zhang Geng deng si tongzhi guanyu geju *Baomaonü* chuangzuo guocheng da Zhang Tuo tongzhi wen" 張庚等四同志關於歌劇 "白毛女" 創作過程答張拓同志問. *Wenyi lilun yu piping* 文藝理論與批評 3 (2011): 76–82.

*Lutz, Jessie G. Chinese Politics and Christian Missions: The Anti-Christian Movements of 1920–28.* Notre Dame: Cross Cultural Publications, Cross Roads Books, 1988.

———, ed. *Pioneer Chinese Christian Women: Gender, Christianity, and Social Mobility*. Bethlehem: Lehigh University Press, 2010.

Lu, Weijing. *True to Her Words: The Faithful Maiden Cult in Late Imperial China*. Stanford: Stanford University Press, 2008.

Lupke, Christopher, ed. *The Magnitude of Ming: Command, Allotment, and Fate in Chinese Culture*. Honolulu: University of Hawaii Press, 2005.

Lynch, Catherine, Robert B. Marks, and Paul G. Pickowicz, eds. *Radicalism, Revolution, and Reform in Modern China*. Lanham, MD: Lexington Books, 2011.

Ma, Ke 馬可, and Qu Wei 瞿維. "*Baimaonü* yinyue de chuangzuo jingyan" 白毛女音樂的創作經驗. In Yan'an Lu Xun wenyi xueyuan, comp., *Baimaonü*, 266–75.

Ma Xiangbo 馬相伯. "Ma Xiangbo zhi Xu Zongze xin" 馬相伯致徐宗澤信. In Zhu Weizheng 朱維錚, ed., *Ma Xiangbo ji* 馬相伯集. Shanghai: Fudan daxue chubanshe, 1996, 508.

Maeda Shigeki 前田繁樹. "*Roshi chukyō* ishō" "老子中經" 覺書. In Sakade Yoshinobu 阪出祥伸, ed., *Chūgoku kodai yōsei shisō sōgōteki kenkyū* 中國古代養生思想綜合的研究, 474–502.

Mair, Victor H. "What Is *Geyi*, After All?" In Alan K. L. Chan and Yuet-Keung Lo, eds., *Philosophy and Religion in Early Medieval China*, 227–64.

Mann, Susan. "Grooming a Daughter for Marriage: Brides and Wives in the Mid-Ch'ing Period." In Rubie Watson and Patricia B. Ebrey, eds., *Marriage and Inequality in Chinese Society*, 204–30.

———. *Precious Records: Women in China's Long Eighteenth Century*. Stanford: Stanford University Press, 1997.

———. *The Talented Women of the Zhang Family*. Berkeley: University of California Press, 2007.

———. *Gender and Sexuality in Modern Chinese History*. New York: Cambridge University Press, 2011.

Mann, Susan, and Yu-yin Cheng, eds. *Under Confucian Eyes: Writings on Gender in Chinese History*. Berkeley: University of California Press, 2001.

Martin, L. H., et al., eds. *Technologies of the Self: A Seminar with Michel Foucault*. London: Tavistock, 1988.

Maspero, Henri (1882–1945). *Taoism and Chinese Religion*. Trans. Frank Kierman. Amherst: University of Massachusetts Press, 1981.

McDougall, Bonnie S. *Mao Zedong's "Talks at the Yan'an Conference on Literature and Art": A Translation of the 1943 Text with Commentary*. Ann Arbor: University of Michigan Press, 1980.

McNamara, Jo Ann. *Sisters in Arms: Catholic Nuns through Two Millennia*. Cambridge, MA: Harvard University Press, 1996.

McNair, Amy. *Donors of Longmen: Faith, Politics, and Patronage in Medieval Chinese Buddhist Sculpture.* Honolulu: University of Hawaii Press, 2007.

McNay, Lois. *Gender and Agency: Reconfiguring the Subject in Feminist and Social Theory*. Cambridge: Polity Press, 2000.

Menegon, Eugenio. *Ancestors, Virgins, and Friars: Christianity as a Local Religion in Late Imperial China*. Cambridge: Harvard University Asia Center, 2010.

Meng, Yuan 孟遠. "Liushi nian lai geju *Baimaonü* de pingjia moshi de bianqian" 六十年來歌劇 "白毛女" 的評價模式的變遷. *Hebei xuekan* 河北學刊 25.2 (2005): 133–39.

———. "Geju *Baimaonü* de xushi bianqian shi" 歌劇 "白毛女" 的敘事變遷史. *Xueshu yanjiu* 學術研究 12 (2008): 152–56.

Meng, Yue 孟悅. "Female Images and National Myth." In Tani E. Barlow, ed., *Gender Politics in Modern China: Writing and Feminism*. Durham and London: Duke University Press, 1993, 118–36.

———. "*Baimaonü* yanbian de qishi: jianlun Yan'an wenyi de lishi duozhixing" "白毛女" 演變的啟示: 兼論延安文藝的歷史多質性. In Tang Xiaobing, ed., *Zaijiedu: dazhong wenyi yu yishu xingtai* 再解讀: 大眾文藝與藝術形態, 48–69.

Miller, Jean Baker. "A New Psychology of Women." In Joann Wolski Conn, ed., *Women's Spirituality: Resources for Christian Development*, 107–27.

Min Yide 閔一得. *Xiwangmu nüxiu zhengtu shize* 西王母女修正途十則. In *Gushu yinlou cangshu* 古書隱樓藏書.

———. *Niwan Li zushi nüzong shuangxiu baofa* 泥丸李祖師女宗雙修寶筏. N.d.

Mohanty, Chandra Talpade. "Under Western Eyes: Feminist Scholarship and Colonial Discourses." In Chandra Talpade Mohanty, Anne Russo, and Lourdes Torres, eds., *Third World Women and the Politics of Feminism*, 51–80.

Mohanty, Chandra Talpade, Anne Russo, and Lourdes Torres, eds. *Third World Women and the Politics of Feminism*. Bloomington: Indiana University Press, 1991.

Monsterleet, Jean. "De l'amour d'une mère à l'amour de Dieu: Sou Siue-Lin [Su Xuelin] (Sou Mei [Su Mei]) témoin de son temps." *China Missionary Bulletin* 1 (1952): 8–15.

———. *Sommets de la Littérature Chinoise Contemporaine*. Paris: Domat, 1953.

Morgan, Sue. "Rethinking Religion in Gender History: Historiographical and Methodological Reflections." In Ursula King and Tina Beattie, eds., *Gender, Religion and Diversity*, 113–24.

Moroto Tatsuo 諸戶立雄. *Chūgoku Bukkyō seidoshi no kenkyū* 中國佛教制度史の研究. Tokyo: Hirakawa, 1990.

Mou, Sherry J., ed. *Presence and Presentation: Women in the Chinese Literati Tradition*. New York: St. Martin's Press, 1999.

Naquin, Susan. *Peking: Temples and City Life, 1400–1900*. Berkeley: University of California Press, 2000.

Naquin, Susan, and Chün-fang Yu, eds. *Pilgrims and Sacred Sites in China*. Berkeley: University of California Press, 1992.

Narayan, Uma. *Dislocating Cultures: Identities, Traditions, and Third-World Feminism*. New York: Routledge, 1997.

Nedostup, Rebecca. *Superstitious Regimes: Religion and the Politics of Chinese Modernity*. Cambridge: Harvard University Press, 2009.

Nelson, Sioban. *Say Little, Do Much: Nurses, Nuns, and Hospitals in the Nineteenth Century*. Philadelphia: University of Pennsylvania Press, 2001.

Nestor, Pete, and Tom Moran. *White-Haired Girl*, English translation of the 1950 film script. http://mclc.osu.edu/rc/pubs/moran2.htm.

Niida Noboru 仁井田陞 and Ikeda On 池田溫. *Tōrei shūi ho: tsuketari Tō-Nichi ryōrei taishō ichiran* 唐令拾遺補: 附唐日兩令對照一覽. Tokyo: Tōkyō Daigaku Shuppankai, 1997.

Northup, Lesley A. *Ritualizing Women*. Cleveland, OH: Pilgrim Press, 1997.

*Nüdan shiji houbian* 女丹詩集後編. In *Nüdan hebian*.

*Nügong lianji huandan tushuo* 女功煉己還丹圖說. In *Nüdan hebian*.

*Nügong zhengfa* 女功正法 (1880). In Chen Yingning, ed., *Nüzi daoxue xiaocongshu wuzhong*.

*Nüjindan* 女金丹. In *Nüdan hebian*.

Ouchi Humio 大内文雄. "Hōzan Reisenji sekkutsu tomei no kenkyū: Zui-Tō jidai no Hōzan Reisenji" 寶山靈泉寺石窟塔銘の研究: 隋唐時代の寶山靈泉寺. *Tōhōgakuhō* 東方學報 69 (1997): 287–355.

Ouyang Xiu 歐陽修 (1007–1072). *Xin Tangshu* 新唐書. Beijing: Zhonghua shuju, 1975.

Overmyer, Daniel L. "Values in Chinese Sectarian Literature: Ming and Ch'ing Pao-chuan." In David Johnson, Andrew J. Nathan, and Evelyn S. Rawski, eds., *Popular Culture in Late Imperial China*, 219–53.

———. "Women in Chinese Religions: Submission, Struggle, Transcendence." In Koichi Shinohara and Gregory Schopen, eds., *From Benares to Beijing: Essays on Buddhism and Chinese Religions in Honour of Professor Jan Yün-hua*, 91–120.

———. *Local Religion in North China in the Twentieth Century: The Structure and Organization of Community Rituals and Beliefs*. Leiden: Brill, 2009.

Overmyer, Daniel L., ed. *Religion in China Today*. Cambridge: Cambridge University Press, 2003.

———, ed. *Huaren zongjiao zhong de nüxing* 華人宗教中的女性 (Special Issue on Women in Chinese Religions). *Minsu quyi* 民俗曲藝 168 (2010).

Pan Gaofeng 潘高鳳. *Tangdai taming yanjiu* 唐代塔銘研究. Master's thesis, Zhejiang University, 2010.

Pang, Keng-Fong. "Islamic 'Fundamentalism' and Female Empowerment among the Muslims of Hainan Island, People's Republic of China." In Judy Brink and Joan Mencher, eds., *Mixed Blessings: Gender and Religious Fundamentalism Cross-Culturally*, 41–57.

Pang, Shiying. "Familial Identity and Buddhist Nuns in Tang China: A Study of Tomb Inscriptions." Master's thesis, University of Santa Barbara, 1999.

Pan Zhonggui 潘重規. "Cong Dunhuang yishu kan Fojiao tichang xiaodao" 從敦煌遺書看佛教提倡孝道. *Huagang wenke xuebao*華崗文科學報12 (1980): 197–268.

Paul, Diana Y. *The Buddhist Feminine Ideal: Queen Srimala and the Tathagatagarbha*. Atlanta: Scholars Press, 1980.

———. *Women in Buddhism: Images of the Feminine in Mahayana Tradition*. Berkeley: University of California Press, 1985.

Peng Dingqiu 彭定求 (1645–1719) et al., eds. *Quan Tangshi* 全唐詩. Beijing: Zhonghua shuju, 1960.

Perry, Elizabeth. "Moving the Masses: Emotion Work in the Chinese Revolution." *Mobilization* 7.2 (2002): 111–28.

Pillsbury, Barbara. "Being Female in a Muslim Minority in China." In Lois Beck and Nikki Keddie, eds., *Women in the Muslim World*, 671–87.

Pino, Angel, and Isabelle Rabut. "Les Missionnaires Occidentaux Premiers Lecteurs de la littérature Chinoise Moderne." In Jean-Louis Bacqué-Grammont and Angel Pino under the direction of Samaha Khoury, *D'un Orient l'autre, Actes des Troisièmes journées de l'Orient, Bordeaux, 2–4 octobre 2002*. Paris: Peeters, 2005, 465–93.

Poceski, Mario. "Chan Rituals of the Abbot's Ascending the Dharma Hall to Preach." In Steven Heine and Dale S. Wright, eds., *Zen Ritual: Studies of Zen Buddhist Theory in Practice,* 83–112.

Pomeranz, Kenneth. "Power, Gender, and Pluralism in the Cult of the Goddess of Taishan." In Theodore Huters, R. Wong, and Pauline Yu, eds., *Culture and State in Chinese History: Conventions, Accommodations, and Critiques,* 182–204.

Powers, Marla N. *Oglala Women: Myth, Ritual, and Reality*. Chicago: University of Chicago Press, 1986.

Pregadio, Fabrizio. *Awakening to Reality: The "Regulated Verses" of the Wuzhen pian, a Taoist Classic of Internal Alchemy*. Mountain View, CA: Golden Elixir Press, 2009.

Qian Qianyi 錢謙益 (1582–1664). *Muzhai youxueji* 牧齋有學集. *Xuxiu siku quanshu* 續修四庫全書 ed.

———. "Zuotuo biqiuni Chaoyin taming" 坐脫比丘尼潮音塔銘. In *Muzhai youxueji* 牧齋有學集, "Bu" 補, 29b–30b.

———. "Chaoyin ni huaxiang can." In *Muzhai youxue ji fu. Sibu congkan.*

———. *Jiangyunlou shumu* 絳雲樓書目. *Congshu jicheng chubian.*

*Qian Xingcun* 錢杏邨. *Dangdai zhongguo nüzuojia lun* 當代中國女作家論. *Shanghai: Guanghua chubanshe, 1933.*

Qian Yi 錢易 (968–1026). *Nanbu xinshu* 南部新書. Shanghai: Zhonghua shuju, 1958.

Qin, Wenjie. "The Buddhist Revival in Post-Mao China: Women Reconstruct Buddhism on Mt. Emei." PhD diss., Harvard University, 2000.

Qing Xitai 卿希泰, ed. *Zhongguo daojiao shi* 中國道教史. Chengdu: Sichuan renmin chubanshe, 1992.

Qiu Gaoxing 邱高興. "Jie xiao guanxi lun: Fojiao dui Zhongguo chuantong lunli guannian tiaohexing jieshi" 孝戒關係論: 佛教對中國傳統倫理觀念調和性解釋. *Shehui kexue zhanxian* 社會科學戰線 5 (2005): 24–29.

Qiu Xiaobo 邱小波 and Jiang Hong 蔣紅, eds. *Nüdan hebian xuanzhu* 女丹合編選注. Shanghai: Shanghai fanyi chubanshe, 1991.

Rabinow, Paul, ed. *The Foucault Reader*. Harmondsworth: Penguin, 1984.

Ran Yunhua (Jan, Yün-hua 冉雲華*).* "The Role of Filial Piety in Chinese Buddhism: A Reassessment." In Charles Wei-hsin Fu and Sandra A. Wawrytko, eds., *Buddhist Ethics and Modern Society*, 27–39.

———. "Zhongguo Fojiao dui xiaodao de shuorong ji houguo" 中國佛教對孝道的受容及後果. In Ran Yunhua, *Cong Yindu Fojiao dao Zhongguo Fojiao*, 42–55.

———. *Cong Yindu Fojiao dao Zhongguo Fojiao* 從印度佛教到中國佛教. Taibei: Dongda tushu, 1995.

Rao, Vinay Kumar. "Women in Early Buddhist Inscriptions." *Buddhism and Nordland* (online publication of Estonian Nyingma), December 2010. http://budcon.com/index.php/2013-03-14-08-21-28/2013-03-15-11-40-47/articles/139-women-in-early-buddhist-inscriptions-by-vinay-kumar-rao.

Raphals, Lisa. "Fate, Fortune, Chance, and Luck in Chinese and Greek: A Comparative Semantic History." *Philosophy East and West* 53.4 (2003): 537–74.

Raz, Gil. "The Way of the Yellow and the Red: Re-Examining the Sexual Initiation Rite of Celestial Master Daoism." *Nan Nü: Men, Women and Gender in Early and Imperial China* 10.1 (2008): 86–120.

———. *Emergence of Daoism, Creation of Tradition*. London: Routledge, 2012.

Ren Jiyu 任繼愈, ed. *Zhongguo daojiao shi* 中國道教史. Beijing: Zhongguo shehui kexue chubanshe, 2001.

Reuther, Rosemary Radford. *Women-Church: Theology and Practice of Feminist Liturgical Communities*. San Francisco: Harper & Row, 1986.

Robinet, Isabelle. *La Révélation du Shangqing dans l'histoire du taoïsme*. Paris: Ecole française d'Extrême-Orient, 1984.

———. "Sexualité et taoïsme." In Marcel Bernos, ed., *Sexualité et religion*, 51–71.

Rowan, John, and Mick Cooper, eds. *The Plural Self: Multiplicity in Everyday Life*. London: Sage, 1999.

Sangren, P. Steven. "Female Gender in Chinese Religious Symbols: Kuan Yin, Ma Tsu, and the 'Eternal Mother.' " *Signs* 9.1 (1983): 4–25.

———. "Orthodoxy, Heterodoxy, and the Structure of Value in Chinese Rituals." *Modern China* 13.1, Symposium on Hegemony and Chinese Folk Ideologies 13.1, Part I (1987): 63–89.

Sarti, Odile. *The Ligue patriotique des Françaises, 1902–1933: A Feminine Response to the Secularization of French Society*. New York: Garland, 1992.

Schafer, Edward H. *The Divine Woman: Dragon Ladies and Rain Maidens in T'ang Literature*. Berkeley: University of California Press, 1973.

———. "The Jade Woman of Greatest Mystery." *History of Religions* 17 (1978): 387–97.

———. "The Capeline Cantos: Verses on the Divine Loves of Taoist Priestesses." *Asiatische Studien* 32 (1978): 5–65.

———. "Three Divine Women of South China." *Chinese Literature: Essays, Articles, Reviews* 1 (1979): 31–42.

———. "Wu Yün's 'Cantos on Pacing the Void.' " *Harvard Journal of Asiatic Studies* 41 (1981): 377–415.

———. "Wu Yün's Stanzas on 'Saunters in Sylphdom.' " *Monumenta Serica* 35 (1983): 1–37.

———. "Cantos on 'One Bit of Cloud at Shamanka Mountain.' " *Asiatische Studien* 36 (1983): 102–24.

Schibrack, Kevin, ed. *Thinking through Rituals: Philosophical Perspectives*. New York: Routledge, 2004.

Schipper, Kristofer M. "The Taoist Body." *History of Religions* 17 (1978): 355–86.

———. "Le Calendrier de Jade: Note sur le Laozi zhongjing." *Nachrichten der Gessellschaft für Natur und Võlkerkunde Ostasiens/Hamburg* 125 (1979): 75–80.

———. *The Taoist Body*. Trans. Karen C. Duval. Berkeley: University of California Press, 1993.

———. (Shi Zhouren 施舟人). "*Laozi zhongjing* chutan" "老子中經" 初探. *Daojia wenhua yanjiu* 16 (1994): 204–16.

———. "The Inner World of the *Lao-tzu chung-ching*." In Chün-chieh Huang, and Erik Zürcher, eds., *Time and Space in Chinese Culture*, 114–31.

Schipper, Kristofer M., and Franciscus Verellen. *The Taoist Canon: A Historical Companion to the Daozang*. Chicago and London: University of Chicago Press, 2004.

Schneiders, Sandra M. "The Effects of Women's Experience on Their Spirituality." In Joann Wolski Conn, ed., *Women's Spirituality: Resources for Christian Development*, 31–48.

———. "Theology and Spirituality: Strangers, Rivals, or Partners?" *Horizons* 13 (1986): 265–67.

Schopen, Gregory. "Filial Piety and the Monks in the Practices of Indian Buddhism: A Question of Sinicization Viewed from the Other Side." *T'ung Pao* 70 (1984): 110–26.

———. "Separate but Equal: Property Rights and the Legal Independence of Buddhist Nuns and Monks in Early North India." *Journal of the American Oriental Society* 128.4 (2008): 625–40.

Schyns, Joseph. *Romans a Lire et Romans a Proscrire Shuo pu chên p'ing*. Tientsin: Chihli Press, 1946.

Schyns, Joseph, et al., eds. *1500 Modern Chinese Novels and Plays*. Hong Kong: Lung Men Bookstore, 1966.

Scott, Joan. "Gender: A Useful Category of Historical Analysis." *American Historical Review* 91.5 (1986): 1053–75.

Seigfried, Charlene Haddock. *Pragmatism and Feminism: Reweaving the Social Fabric*. Chicago: University of Chicago Press, 1996.

Sengyou 僧祐 (445–518). *Erjiao lun* 二教論. *Sibu congkan.*

Sered, Susan Starr. *Women as Religious Experts: The Religious Lives of Elderly Jewish Women in Jerusalem*. New York: New York University Press, 1994.

*Shangqing huangshu guodu yi* 上清黃書過度儀. *DZ*, vol. 32, no. 1294.

*Shangqing jiudan shanghua taijing zhongji jing* 上清九丹上化胎精中記經. *DZ*, vol. 34, no. 1382.

*Shangqing mingtang xuanzhen jingjue* 上清明堂元真經訣. *DZ*, vol. 6, no. 424.

*Shangqing taishang dijun jiuzhen zhongjing* 上清太上帝君九真中經. *DZ*, vol. 34, no. 1376.

*Shangqing Taiyi Dijun taidan yinshu jiebao shi'er jiejie tujue* 上清太一帝君太丹隱書解胞十二結節圖訣. *DZ*, vol. 34, no. 1384.

Sharma, Arvind, ed. *Today's Women in World Religions*. Albany: State University of New York Press, 1994.

———, ed. *Women Saints in World Religions*. Albany: State University of New York Press, 2000.

Shi Xiaoying 石小英. "Ba zhi shi shiji Dunhuang ni seng yu shisu jiating de guanxi 八至十世紀敦煌尼僧與世俗家庭的關係." *Shijie zongjiao yanjiu* 世界宗教研究 1 (2009): 58–64.

Shinohara, Koichi, and Gregory Schopen, eds. *From Benares to Beijing: Essays on Buddhism and Chinese Religions in Honour of Professor Jan Yün-hua*. Ontario, Canada: Mosaic Press, 1991.

Shui Jingjun 水鏡君 and Maria Jaschok. *Zhongguo qingzhen nüsishi* 中國清真女寺史. Beijing: Sanlian hafo yanjing xueshu congshu, 2002.

Slater, Peter, et al., eds. *Traditions in Contact and Change: Selected Proceedings of the XIVth Congress of the International Association for the History of Religions.* Waterloo, Ontario: Canadian Corporation for Studies in Religion, Wilfred Laurier University Press, 1983.

Smith, Carl T. *Chinese Christians: Elites, Middlemen, and the Church in Hong Kong.* Hong Kong: Oxford University Press, 1985.

Smith, George. *A Narrative of an Exploratory Visit to Each of the Consular Cities of China and to the Islands of Hong Kong and Chusan, in Behalf of the Church Missionary Society, in the Years of 1844, 1845, 1846.* London: Hatch & Son, 1847.

Smith, Paul. *Discerning the Subject.* Minneapolis: University of Minnesota Press, 1988.

Smith, Sidonie. "Performativity, Autobiographical Practice, Resistance." In Sidonie Smith and Julia Watson, eds., *Women, Autobiography, Theory: A Reader*, 108–15.

———. *A Poetics of Women's Autobiography: Marginality and the Fictions of Self-Representation.* Bloomington: Indiana University Press, 1987.

Smith, Sidonie, and Julia Watson, eds. *Women, Autobiography, Theory: A Reader.* Madison: University of Wisconsin Press, 1998.

Smith, Wilfred Cantwell. *The Meaning and End of Religion.* New York: Macmillan, 1963.

Song Jianhua 宋劍華, "Cong minjian chuanqi dao hongse jingdian: *Baomaonü* gushi de lishi yanyi" 從民間傳奇到紅色經典: "白毛女" 故事的歷史演繹. *Nanjing shifan daxue wenxueyuan xuebao* 南京師範大學文學院學報 1 (2011): 132–42.

Song Ruoxian 宋若憲 (d. 835). "Tang Daminggong Yuchenguan gu Shangqing Taidong Sanjing dizi Dongyue qingdi zhenren Tian fashi xuanshiming bingxu" 唐大明宮玉晨觀故上清太洞三景弟子東嶽青帝真人田法師玄室銘並序. In Zhou Shaoliang 周紹良 and Zhao Chao 趙超, eds., *Tangdai muzhi huibian xuji*, 892–93.

Song Yu 宋玉 (fl. fourth century BCE). "Gaotang fu" 高唐賦. In Xiao Tong 蕭統, comp., *Wenxuan* 文選, 19.1b–6b.

———. "Dengtu zi haose fu" 登徒子好色賦. In Xiao Tong, comp., *Wenxuan*, 19.9b–11b.

Soper, Alexander C. "Imperial Cave-Chapels of the Northern Dynasties: Donors, Beneficiaries, Dates." *Artibus Asiae* 28.4 (1966): 241–70.

Spretnak, Charlene, ed. *The Politics of Women's Spirituality.* New York: Doubleday, 1982.

Stanton, Domna C. "Autogynography: Is the Subject Different?" In Sidonie Smith and Julia Watson, eds., *Women, Autobiography, Theory: A Reader*, 131–44.

Stein, Diane. *Casting the Circle.* Freedom, CA: Crossing, 1990.

Stein, Rolf A. (1911–1999). "Remarques sur les mouvements du taoïsme politico-religieux au IIe siècle ap. J.-C." *T'oung-pao* 50 (1963): 1–78.

Stranahan, Patricia. *Yan'an Women and the Communist Party*. Berkeley: Institute of East Asian Studies, University of California, 1983.

Strickmann, Michel. "A Taoist Confirmation of Liang Wu-ti's Suppression of Taoism." *Journal of the American Oriental Society* 98.4 (1978): 467–75.

———. *Le Taoïsme du Mao Chan: chronique d'une révélation*. Paris: Collège de France, Institut des hautes études chinoises, 1981.

———, ed. *Tantric and Taoist Studies*. Brussels: Institut Belge des Hauters Etudes Chinoises, 1985.

Strong, John. "Filial Piety and Buddhism: The Indian Antecedents to a 'Chincse' Problem." In Peter Slater et al. eds., *Traditions in Contact and Change: Selected Proceedings of the XIVth Congress of the International Association for the History of Religions*, 171–86.

Su Xuelin 蘇雪林. *Jixin* 棘心. First edition. Shanghai: Beixin, 1929.

———. "Qingmo zhishi jieji de zongjiao re" 清末智識階級的宗教熱. In *Tulong ji* 屠龍集. Beijing: Shangwu yinshuguan, 1941, 113–30.

———. *Jixin* 棘心. Second edition.Taizhong: Guangqi Press, 1957.

———. *Wo de shenghuo* 我的生活. Taibei: Wenxing shudian, 1967.

Sun Changwu 孫昌武. *Daojiao yu Tangdai wenxu* 道教與唐代文學. Beijing: Renmin wenxue chubanshe, 2001.

Sun Guangxian 孫光憲. *Beimeng suoyan* 北夢瑣言. Shanghai: Shanghai guji chubanshe, 1981.

Sun Qi 孫棨. *Beili zhi* 北里志. Shanghai: Gudian wenxue chubanshe, 1957.

Sun Simiao 孫思邈 (581–682). *Beiji qianjin yaofang*. *DZ*, vol. 26, no. 1163.

Swann, Nancy Lee. *Pan Chao: Foremost Woman Scholar of China*. Ann Arbor: Center for Chinese Studies, the University of Michigan, 2001.

*Taishang Laojun zhongjing* 太上老君中經. *DZ*, vol. 27, no. 1168.

Tamba Yasuyori 丹波康賴 (911–995). *Ishimpō* 醫心方. Taibei: Xinwenfeng chubangongsi, 1976, in Li Ling, *Zhongguo fangshu zhengkao*, 396–416.

Tang Yongtong 湯用彤. "Lun zhongguo fojiao wushizong" 論中國佛教無十宗. *Zhexue yanjiu* 哲學研究 3 (1962): 47–54.

———. "Zhongguo fojiao zongpai wenti bulun" 中國佛教宗派問題補論. *Beijing daxue xuebao* 北京大學學報 5 (1963): 1–18.

Tao Bingfu 陶秉福, ed. *Nüdan jicui* 女丹集萃. In *Zhongguo qigong guji congshu*. Beijing: Beijing shifan daxue chubanshe, 1989.

———. *Daoyuan yiqi yiqi* 道原一氣 (1634). Beijing: Beijing shifan daxue chubanshe, 1990.

Tao Feiya 陶飛亞, ed. *Xingbie yu lishi: jindai Zhongguo funü yu Jidujiao* 性別與歷史: 近代中國婦女與基督教. Shanghai: Shanghai renmin chubanshe, 2006.

Tao Hongjing 陶弘景 (456–536). *Zhengao* 真誥. *DZ*, vol. 20, no. 1016.

Teiser, Stephen F. *The Ghost Festival in Medieval China*. Princeton: Princeton University Press, 1988.

Teng, Jinhua Emma. "The Construction of the 'Traditional Chinese Woman' in the Western Academy: A Critical Review." *Signs* 22.1 (1996): 115–51.

ter Haar, Barend. "China's Inner Demons: The Political Impact of the Demonological Paradigm." In Woei Lien Chong, ed., *China's Great Proletarian Cultural Revolution: Master Narratives and Post-Mao Counternarratives*, 27–68.

———. *Telling Stories: Witchcraft and Scapegoating in Chinese History*. Leiden: Brill, 2006.

Thaxton, Ralph. *China Turned Rightside Up: Revolutionary Legitimacy in the Peasant World*. New Haven: Yale University Press, 1983.

Theiss, Janet. *Disgraceful Matters: The Politics of Chastity in Eighteenth-Century China*. Berkeley: University of California Press, 2005.

Tianyige bowuguan 天一閣博物館 and Zhongguo shehui kexueyuan lishi yanjiusuo Tianshengling zhengli ketizu 中國社會科學院歷史研究所天聖令整理課題組, eds. *Tianyige cang Ming chaoben Tianshengling jiaozheng, fu Tangling fuyuan yanjiu* 天一閣明鈔本天聖令校證, 附唐令復原研究. Beijing: Zhonghua shuju, 2006.

T'ien, Ju-k'ang. *Male Anxiety and Female Chastity: A Comparative Study of Chinese Ethical Values in Ming-Ch'ing Times*. Leiden: Brill, 1988.

Tomm, Winnie. *Bodied Mindfulness: Women's Spirits, Bodies, and Places*. Waterloo, Ontario: Wilfrid Laurier University Press, 1995.

Tranvouez, Yvon. "Mission et communisme: la question du progressisme chrétien (1943–1957)." *Le Mouvement social* "Utopie Missionnaire, Militantisme Catholique" 177 (1996): 49–69.

Tsai, Kathryn Ann. "The Chinese Buddhist Monastic Order for Women: The First Two Centuries." In Richard Guisso and Stanley Johannesen, eds., *Women in China*, 1–20.

Tung, Jowen R. *Fables for the Patriarchs: Gender Politics in Tang Discourse*. New York: Rowman & Littlefield, 2000.

Turner, Victor. *Ritual Process*. Chicago: Aldine, 1995 rpt. (originally published 1969).

Unschuld, Paul U. "Der chinesische 'Arzneikönig' Sun Simiao: Geschichte—Legende—Ikonographie." *Monumenta Serica* 42 (1994): 217–57.

Valussi, Elena. "Men and Women in He Longxiang's *Nüdan hebian* (Collection of female alchemy)." *Nannü: Men, Women and Gender in Early and Imperial China* 10.2 (2008): 242–78.

———. "Female Alchemy and Paratext: How to Read *nüdan* in a Historical Context." *Asia Major* 21.2 (2008): 153–93.

———. "Female Alchemy: An Introduction." In Livia Kohn and Robin Wang, eds., *Internal Alchemy: Self, Society, and the Quest for Immortality*, 141–62.

van Boven, Henri. *Histoire de la Littérature Chinoise Moderne*. Beiping: Chihli Press, 1946.

van Gulik, Robert H. (1910–1967). *Sexual Life in Ancient China: A Preliminary Survey of Chinese Sex and Society from ca. 1500 B.C. till 1644 A.D.* Leiden: E. J. Brill, 1961; republished with a new introduction and bibliography by Paul R. Goldin, Leiden and Boston: Brill, 2003.

von Glahn, Richard. "The Enchantment of Wealth: The God Wutong in the Social History of Jiangnan." *Harvard Journal of Asiatic Studies* 51.2 (1991): 651–714.

Walker, Barbara G. *Women's Rituals: A Source Book*. New York: Harper & Row, 1990.

Waltner, Ann. "T'an-yang-tsu and Wang Shih-chen: Visionary and Bureaucrat in the Late Ming." *Late Imperial China* 8.1 (1987): 105–33.

———. "A Princess Comes of Age: Gender, Life-Cycle and Royal Ritual in Song Dynasty China." In Joëlle Rollo-Koster, ed., *Medieval and Early Modern Ritual: Formalized Behavior in Europe, China and Japan*. Leiden: Koninklijke Brill NV, 2002, 35–56.

Wang, David Der-wei. *The Monster That Is History: History, Violence, and Fictional Writing in Twentieth-Century China*. Berkeley: University of California Press, 2004.

Wang Ka 王卡. "Huangshu kaoyuan" 黃書考源. *Shijie zongjiao yanjiu* 世界宗教研究 2 (1997): 65–73.

Wang, Kun 王昆. "Tan geju *Baomanü* de chuangzuo guocheng" 談歌劇 "白毛女" 的創作過程. *Wenyi lilun yu piping* 2 (2011): 80–82.

Wang, Lingzhen. "Modern and Contemporary Chinese Women's Autobiographical Writing." PhD diss., Cornell University, 1998.

Wang, Robin. "Kundao: A Lived Body in Female Daoism." *Journal of Chinese Philosophy* 36.2 (2009): 277–92.

Wang Shumin 王叔民, ed. *Liexian zhuan jiaojian* 列仙傳校箋. Taibei: Institute of Literature and Philosophy, Academia Sinica, 1995.

Wang Yongping 王永平. *Daojiao yu Tangdai shehui* 道教與唐代社會. Beijing: Shoudu shifan daxue chubanshe, 2002.

Wang Zhongxu 王中旭. "Henan Anyang Lingquansi huishenta yanjiu" 河南安陽靈泉寺灰身塔研究. Master's thesis, China Central Academy of Fine Arts, 2006.

Warne, Randi R. "Making the Gender-Critical Turn." In Tim Jensen and Mikael Rothstein, eds., *Secular Theories on Religion: Current Perspectives*, 249–60.

Watson, James. "Standardizing the Gods: The Promotion of T'ien Hou ('Empress of Heaven') along the South China Coast, 960–1960." In David Johnson et al., eds., *Popular Culture in Late Imperial China*, 292–324.

Watson, Rubie S. "Chinese Bridal Laments: The Claims of a Dutiful Daughter." In James L. Watson and Rubie S. Watson, eds., *Village Life in Hong Kong: Politics, Gender, and Ritual in the New Territories*. Hong Kong: Chinese University Press, 2004, 221–50.

Watson, Rubie S., and Patricia B. Ebrey, eds. *Marriage and Inequality in Chinese Society*. Berkeley: University of California Press, 1991.

Wei Shou 魏收 (506–572). *Weishu* 魏書. Beijing: Zhonghua shuju, 1974.

Weinstein, Stanley. "Schools of Buddhism: Chinese Buddhism." In Mircea Eliade, ed., *Encyclopedia of Religion*. New York: Macmillan, 1987, 2: 482–87.

Wen Yiduo 聞一多. *Shenhua yanjiu* 神話研究. Chengdu: Ba Shu shushe, 2002.

Whitney, Susan B. *Mobilizing Youth: Communists and Catholics in Interwar France*. Durham: Duke University Press, 2009.

Wiest, Jean-Paul. "The Legacy of Vincent Lebbe." *International Bulletin of Missionary Research* (January 1999): 33–37.

Wile, Douglas. *Art of the Bedchamber: The Chinese Sexual Yoga Classics Including Women's Solo Meditation Texts*. Albany: State University of New York Press, 1992.

Wing, Sherin. "Gendering Buddhism: The Miaoshan Legend Reconsidered." *Journal of Feminist Studies in Religion* 27.1 (2011): 5–31.

Wolf, Arthur. "Gods, Ghosts and Ancestors." In Arthur Wolf, ed., *Religion and Ritual in Chinese Society*. Stanford: Stanford University Press, 1974, 131–82.

Wolf, Margery. *Women and the Family in Rural Taiwan*. Stanford: Stanford University Press, 1972.

———. "Beyond the Patrilineal Self: Constructing Gender in China." In Roger T. Ames, ed., *Self as Person in Asian Theory and Practice*, 251–70.

Wolf, Margery, and Roxane Witke, eds. *Women in Chinese Society*. Stanford: Stanford University Press, 1975.

Wong, Wai Ching Angela. "Postcolonialism and Hong Kong Christianity." In Peniel Jesudason Rufus Rajkumar, ed., *Asian Theology on the Way: Christianity, Culture and Context*. London: SPCK, 2012, 56–64.

———. *"The Poor Woman": A Critical Analysis of Asian Theology and Contemporary Chinese Women's Stories*. London: Peter Lang, 2002.

Wong, Wai Ching Angela 黃慧貞, and Choi Po-king Dora 蔡寶瓊, eds. *Huaren funü yu Xianggang jidujiao: Koushu lishi* 華人婦女與香港基督教: 口述歷史. Hong Kong: Oxford University Press, 2010.

Wu Fuxiu 吳福秀. "Lun Fojing zhong de xiaoqinguan jiqi Zhongguohua" 論佛經中的孝親觀及其中國化. *Xiangfan xueyuan xuebao* 襄樊學院學報 29.4 (2008): 9–12.

Wu, Jiang. *Enlightenment in Dispute: The Reinvention of Chan Buddhism in Seventeenth-Century China*. Oxford and New York: Oxford University Press, 2008.

Wu, Pei-yi. *The Confucian's Progress: Autobiographical Writings in Traditional China*. Princeton: Princeton University Press, 1990.

Wu Qiming 吳企明. "Xue Tao" 薛濤. In Fu Xuancong 傅璇琮, ed., *Tang caizizhuan jiaojian* 唐才子傳校箋, vol. 3, 6.102–13.

Wu Renchen 吳任臣. *Shiguo chunqiu* 十國春秋. Beijing: Zhonghua shuju, 1983.

Wu Zhaoyi 吳兆宜 (fl. 1672), and Cheng Yan 程琰, eds. *Yutai xinyong jianzhu* 玉台新詠箋注. Beijing: Zhonghua shuju, 1985.

*Wushang biyao*無上秘要. *DZ*, vol. 25, no. 1138.

Xiao Tong 蕭統 (501–531), comp. *Wen xuan* 文選. Beijing: Zhonghua shuju, 1977.

Xie Shengbao 謝生保. "Cong *Shanzi jing bian* kan Fojiao yishu zhong de xiaodao sixiang" 從《睒子經變》看佛教藝術中的孝道思想. *Dunhuang yanjiu* 敦煌研究 68 (2001): 42–50.

Xie Wuliang 謝無量 (1884–1964). *Zhongguo funü wenxueshi* 中國婦女文學史. Shanghai: Shanghai shudian, 1990 rpt. (originally published 1926).

Xingjun 行浚 et al., eds. *Fushi chanshi yulu* 浮石禪師語錄. In *Jiaxing Dazangjing* 嘉興大藏經, vol. 26, no. B185; *Chinese Buddhist Tripitaka Electronic Text Collection, Taipei Edition*. http://taipei.ddbc.edu.tw/sutra/JB185_001.php.

Xiong, Victor Cunrui. "Ji-Entertainers in Tang Chang'an." In Sherry J. Mou, ed., *Presence and Presentation: Women in the Chinese Literati Tradition*, 149–69.

———. *Sui-Tang Chang'an: A Study in the Urban History of Medieval China*. Ann Arbor: University of Michigan, 2000.

*Xiuzhen biannan* 修真辯難 (1798). In *Daoshu shi'er zhong* 道書十二種.

*Xiwangmu nüxiu zhengtu shize* 西王母女修正途十則 (1799). In *Zangwai daoshu*.

Xu Qiao 徐嶠. "Jianxian zhanggongzhu shendao beiming bingxu" 金仙長公主神道碑銘並序. In Dong Gao et al., eds., *Quan Tangwen*, 267, 9b–11a.

———. "Datang gu Jianxian zhanggongzhu zhishiming bingxu 大唐故金仙長公主誌石銘並序. In Zhou Shaoliang 周紹良 and Zhao Chao 趙超, eds., *Tangdai muzhi huibian xuji* 唐代墓誌彙編續集, 552.

Xu Song 徐松 (1781–1848). *Tang liangjing chengfang kao* 唐兩京城坊考. Beijing: Zhonghua shuju, 1985.

Yan Shanzhao 嚴善炤. "Shoki dōkyō to kōaka konki bōchū jutsu" 初期道教と黃赤混氣房中術. *Tōhō shūkyō* 東方宗教 97 (2001): 1–10.

Yan Zehuan. *Nannü dangong yitong bian* 男女丹功異同辨. In *Nüdan hebian*.

Yan'an Lu Xun wenyi xueyuan (Luyi) 延安魯迅文藝學院 (魯藝), comp. *Baimaonü* 白毛女. Beijing: Renmin wenxue chubanshe, 1953.

Yang Liansheng (Yang Lien Sheng) 楊聯陞. "Laojun yinsong jiejing jiaoshi" 老君音誦誡經校釋. *Lishi yuyan yanjiusuo jikan* 歷史語言研究所集刊 28.1 (1956): 17–54.

Yang, Mayfair Mei-hui. "Goddess across Taiwan Strait: Matrifocal Ritual Space, Nation-State, and Satellite Television Footprints." *Public Culture* 16.2 (2004): 209–38.

———. "Introduction." In Yang, ed., *Chinese Religiosities*, 1–40.

Yang, Mayfair Mei-hui, ed. *Chinese Religiosities: Afflictions of Modernity and State Formation*. Berkeley: University of California Press, 2008.

Yang Tianhong 楊天宏. *Jidujiao yu minguo zhishifenzi: 1922–27 nian zhongguo feijidujiao yundong yanjiu* 基督教與民國知識份子: 1922－27年中國非基督教運動研究. Beijing: Renmin chubanshe, 2005.

Yao, Ping 姚平. "The Status of Pleasure: Courtesan and Literati Connections in T'ang China (618–907)." *Journal of Women's History* 14.2 (2002): 44–45.

———. "Contested Virtue: The Daoist Investiture of Princesses Jinxian and Yuzhen and the Journey of Tang Imperial Daughters." *T'ang Studies* 22 (2007): 1–41.

———. "Good Karmic Connections: Buddhist Mothers in Tang China." *Nan Nü: Men, Women and Gender in Early and Imperial China* 10.1 (2008): 57–85.

Yi Jolan 衣若蘭. *Sangu liupo: Mingdai funü yu shehui de tansuo* 三姑六婆: 明代婦女與社會的探索. Taibei: Daxiang chubanshe, 2002.

Ying, Hu. *Tales of Translation: Composing the New Woman in China, 1898–1918*. Stanford: Stanford University Press, 2000.

Yip, Ka-che. *Religion, Nationalism and Chinese Students: The Anti-Christian Movement of 1922–1927.* Bellingham: Center for East Asian Studies, Western Washington University, 1980.

Yu, Anthony. *State and Religion in China*. Chicago: Open Court, 2005.

Yü, Chün-fang. *Kuan-yin: The Chinese Transformation of Avalokitesvara*. New York: Columbia University Press, 2001.

———. "Humanistic Buddhism and Buddhist Nuns in Taiwan." *Minsu quyi* 168 (2010): 191–224.

Zeitlin, Judith T. *The Phantom Heroine: Ghosts and Gender in Seventeenth-Century Chinese Literature*. Honolulu: University of Hawaii Press, 2007.

Zhang Caitian 張采田 (1862–1945). *Yuxi sheng nianpu huijian* 玉谿生年譜會箋. Shanghai: Shanghai guji, 1983.

Zhang, Geng 張庚. "Geju *Baimaonü* zai Yan'an de chuangzuo yanchu" 歌劇"白毛女"在延安的創作演出. *Xinwenhua shiliao* 新文化史料 2 (1995): 6–7.

Zhang, Hong. "Eros and Politics in Revolutionary Literature." In Tang Dongfeng, Yang Xiaobin, Rosemary Roberts, and Yang Ling, eds., *Chinese Revolution and Chinese Literature*, 3–26.

Zhang Jichun 張季純. "*Baimaonü* de shidaixing" "白毛女" 的時代性. *Jiefangribao*, July 21, 1945.

Zhang Jiong 張冏. "Tang gu Jiuhua shu [one character missing] shi cangxing ji" 唐故九華書□師藏形記. In Zhou Shaoliang and Zhao Chao, eds., *Tangdai muzhi huibian xuji*, 795.

Zhang Naizhu 張乃翥. "Luoyang xin ji shike suo jian Tangdai Zhongyuan zhi Fojiao" 洛陽新輯石刻所見唐代中原之佛教. *Zhongyuan wenwu* 中原文化 5 (2008): 81–93.

Zhang Pengzhou 張蓬舟. *Xue Tao shijian* 薛濤詩箋. Beijing: Renmin wenxue chubanshe, 1983.

Zhang, Tuo 張拓, Qu Wei 瞿維, and Zhang Lu 張魯. "Guanyu *Baomaonü* de tongxin" 關於 "白毛女" 的通信. *Dangdai wentan* 當代文壇 1 (1987): 58–60.

Zhang Wanfu 張萬福. *Chuanshou Sandong jingjie falu lüeshuo* 傳授三洞經戒法籙略說. *DZ*, vol. 32, no. 1241.

———. *Sandong fafu kejie wen* 三洞法服科戒文. *DZ*, vol. 18, no. 788.

———. *Sandong zhongjie wen* 三洞眾戒文. *DZ*, vol. 3, no. 178.

Zhao Chengliang 趙承亮. "Tang gu nai Yuchenguan Shangqing Dadong Sanjing fashi cizi dade xianguanming bingxu" 唐故內玉晨觀上清大洞三景法師賜紫大德仙官銘並序. In Zhou Shaoliang and Zhao Chao, eds., *Tangdai muzhi huibian xuji*, 906.

Zhao Zhenhua 趙振華. "Luoyang xinchu biqiuni muzhi yu Tangdai Dongdu Shengshansi" 洛陽新出比丘尼墓誌與唐代東都聖善寺. *Luoyang shi zhi* 洛陽史誌3 (2005): 13–20.

Zhen Luan 甄鸞 (535–566). *Xiaodao lun* 笑道論. In Daoxuan, ed., *Guang hongmingji* 廣弘明集, 9.31a.

Zheng Xianwen 鄭顯文. "Tangdai *Dao Seng ge* yanjiu" 唐代道僧格研究. *Lishi yanjiu* 歷史研究 4 (2004): 38–54.

Zheng Zhimin 鄭志敏. *Xishuo Tangji* 戲說唐妓. Taibei: Wenjin chuban gongsi, 1997.

Zheng Zhiming 鄭志明. *Wusheng laomu xinyang shuoyuan* 無生老母信仰溯源. Taibei: Wenshizhe, 1985.

Zhiru (Ng). *The Making of a Savior Bodhisattva: Dizang in Medieval China.* Honolulu: University of Hawaii Press, 2007.

Zhong Laiyin 鐘來因. *Changsheng busi de zhuiqiu: Daojing Zhengao zhimi* 長生不死的探求: 道經真誥之謎. Shanghai: Wenhui chubanshe, 1992.

Zhou Shaoliang 周紹良 and Zhao Chao 趙超, eds. *Tangdai muzhi huibian* 唐代墓誌彙編. Shanghai: Shanghai guji chubanshe, 1992.

———, eds. *Tangdai muzhi huibian xuji* 唐代墓誌彙編續集. Shanghai: Shanghai guji chubanshe, 2001.

Zhou Yimou 周貽謀. *Mawangdui jianbo yu gudai fangshi yangsheng* 馬王堆簡帛與古代房事養生. Changsha: Yuelu shushe, 2006.

Zhou, Yiqun. "The Hearth and the Temple: Mapping Female Religiosity in Late Imperial China, 1550–1900." *Late Imperial China* 24. 2 (2003): 109–55.

Zhu Yueli 朱越利. "Huangshu kao" 黃書考. *Zhongguo zhexue* 中國哲學 19 (1998): 167–88.

———. "Liuchao Shangqing jing de yinshu zhidao" 六朝上清經的隱書之道. *Zongjiaoxue yanjiu* 宗教學研究 2 (2001): 1–12.

Zito, Angela. "Secularizing the Pain of Footbinding in China: Missionary and Medical Stagings of the Universal Body." *Journal of the American Academy of Religion* 75.1 (Spring 2007): 1–14.

Zito, Angela, and Tani E. Barlow, eds. *Body, Subject, and Power in China.* Chicago: University of Chicago Press, 1994.

*Zou Taofen* 鄒韜奮. *"Jieshao yiben haoshu Jixin"* 介紹一本好書 "棘心." *Shenghuo zhoukan* 生活週刊 June (1929): 304–5.

Zurndorfer, Harriet T., ed. *Chinese Women in the Imperial Past: New Perspectives.* Leiden: Brill, 1999.

# About the Contributors

**Neky Tak-ching Cheung** received her PhD from the Chinese University of Hong Kong. She is currently Visiting Assistant Professor at University of Macau, and Honorary Research Associate at the Centre for Studies of Daoist Culture, the Chinese University of Hong Kong. She is the author of *Women's Ritual in China: Jiezhu (Receiving Buddhist Prayer Beads) Performed by Menopausal Women in Ninghua, Western Fujian* (Edwin Mellen Press, 2008) and a number of articles.

**Beata Grant** received her PhD from Stanford University. She is Professor of Chinese and Religious Studies at Washington University in St. Louis. She is the author of a number of books and articles exploring the interface of gender, religion, and literature, most recently *Eminent Nuns: Woman Chan Masters of Seventeenth-Century China* (University of Hawaii Press, 2009) and, with Wilt L. Idema, *Escape from Blood Bowl Pond: The Tales of Mulian and Woman Huang* (University of Washington Press, 2011).

**Jinhua Jia** received her PhD from the University of Colorado at Boulder. She was Research Associate and Visiting Faculty at the Women's Studies in Religion Program, Harvard Divinity School, in 2005–2006 and is currently Professor of Philosophy and Religious Studies at the University of Macau. She is the author of a number of books and articles, such as *Gudian Chan yanjiu* or *Study on Classical Chan Buddhism* (Oxford University Press, 2010) and *The Hongzhou School of Chan Buddhism in Eighth- through Tenth-Century China* (State University of New York Press, 2006).

**Xiaofei Kang** received her PhD from Columbia University. She is Associate Professor at the George Washington University. She is the author of *The Cult of the Fox: Power, Gender, and Popular Religion in Late Imperial and Modern China* (Columbia University Press, 2006). She is finishing a collaborative book project on religion and tourism on China's ethnic frontier and is currently working on gender and religion in twentieth-century revolutionary propaganda.

**Zhange Ni** received her PhD from the University of Chicago Divinity School. She was Research Associate and Visiting Faculty at the Women's Studies in Religion Program, Harvard Divinity School, in 2010–2011 and is currently Assistant Professor at the Department of Religion and Culture, Virginia Tech. She is working on two book manuscripts, tentatively titled *The Pagan Writes Back: When World Religion Meets World Literature* and *Women, Literature, and the Subterraneous History of Religion in Modern China.*

**Gil Raz** received his PhD from Indiana University. He is Associate Professor at Dartmouth College. His publications include *The Emergence of Daoism: Creation of Tradition* (Routledge, 2012) and a number of articles on Daoist ritual, sacred geography, and bodily practices.

**Elena Valussi** received her PhD from SOAS, University of London. She teaches East Asian History, Chinese History, and Gender Studies in the History Department of Loyola University. She has published a number of articles on the history and transformation of the Daoist tradition of *nüdan* or female alchemy in late imperial China. She is interested in late imperial Daoist intellectual history and printing, and she is one of the editors of the *Daozang Jiyao* Project, based at the Centre for Studies in Daoist Culture of the Chinese University of Hong Kong.

**Wai Ching Angela Wong** received her PhD from the University of Chicago Divinity School. She is Associate Professor at the Department of Cultural and Religious Studies and Codirector of the Gender Research Centre, Hong Kong Institute for Asia-Pacific Studies, the Chinese University of Hong Kong. She is the author of a number of books and articles, including *Huaren Jidutu funü yu Xianggang jiaohui: koushu lishi* or *Chinese Christian Women and Hong Kong Christianity: An Oral History* (Oxford University Press, 2010); *Yazhou nüxing zhuyi shenxue* or *Asian Feminist Theology* (Jidujiao wenyi, 2008); and *"The Poor Woman": A Critical Analysis of Asian Theology and Contemporary Chinese Women's Stories* (Peter Lang, 2002).

**Ping Yao** received her PhD from the University of Illinois at Urbana-Champaign. She was Research Associate and Visiting Faculty at the Women's

Studies in Religion Program, Harvard Divinity School, in 2008–2009 and is Professor of History at California State University, Los Angeles. Her recent publications include a five-volume translation series, *Dangdai Xifang Hanxue yanjiu jicui* or *Western Scholarship on Chinese History* (coedited with Patricia Ebrey, Shanghai guji, 2010); *Sharing the World Stage: Biography and Gender in World History*, 2 vols. (coauthored with Melissa Bokovoy, Patricia Prisso, Patricia Romero, and Jane Slaughter; Houghton and Mifflin, 2007 and 2008); and *Tangdai funü de shengming lichen* or *Women's Lives in Tang China* (Shanghai guji, 2004 and 2006).

# Index